# Extraordinary Conditions

# Extraordinary Conditions

*Culture and Experience in Mental Illness*

Janis H. Jenkins

UNIVERSITY OF CALIFORNIA PRESS

University of California Press, one of the most
distinguished university presses in the United States,
enriches lives around the world by advancing scholarship
in the humanities, social sciences, and natural sciences. Its
activities are supported by the UC Press Foundation and
by philanthropic contributions from individuals and
institutions. For more information, visit www.ucpress.edu.

University of California Press
Oakland, California

Library of Congress Cataloging-in-Publication Data

Jenkins, Janis H., author.
   Extraordinary conditions : culture and experience in
mental illness / Janis H. Jenkins. — First edition.
      pages   cm
   Includes bibliographical references and index.
   ISBN 978-0-520-28709-9 (cloth : alk. paper)
   ISBN 978-0-520-28711-2 (pbk. : alk. paper)
   ISBN 978-0-520-96222-4 (ebook)
   1. Mental illness—Cross-cultural studies.
2. Mental illness—Social aspects.   3. Medical
anthropology.   4. Ethnopsychology.   I. Title.
   RC455.4.E8J46 2015
   362.196890089—dc23

                                            2015020400


Manufactured in the United States of America

24   23   22   21   20   19   18   17   16   15

10   9   8   7   6   5   4   3   2   1

In keeping with a commitment to support
environmentally responsible and sustainable printing
practices, UC Press has printed this book on Natures
Natural, a fiber that contains 30% post-consumer waste
and meets the minimum requirements of ANSI/NISO
Z39.48–1992 (R 1997) (*Permanence of Paper*).

*To TC*

# Contents

# Figures and Tables

# Prelude and Acknowledgments

Anthropology demands the open-mindedness with which one
must look and listen, record in astonishment and wonder that
which one would not have been able to guess.

—Margaret Mead

This book was born from a long-standing anthropological fascination
with the possibilities for being human. These possibilities entail fundamental human capacities and processes; what is fundamental is at the
theoretical outset premised on the inextricability of culture, biology,
and psyche. Attention to human life as rife with possibilities that are
contingent rather than invariant provides the foundation for social, personal, and political transformation. The panhuman possibilities for the
development of mental health problems are remarkably common across
countries, genders, and social classes. Yet there is substantial cultural
variation. Across the board, mental health problems are positioned by
social stigma and inequality of care. And because the majority of human
populations live under the press of socioeconomic adversity and gendered inequality that significantly affects mental health, the need for
social transformation is great.

Along with early anthropological thinkers such as Margaret Mead
and Ruth Benedict, my methodological approach involves the identification of patterns. Yet while anthropological analysis is predicated on the
identification of patterns, no less impressive are the divergent, the unusual, and the paradoxical. The relation of culture and mental health has
been my focal point for the study of fundamental human processes in a
series of anthropological studies carried out over two and a half decades.
The chapters in this book take up a range of mental conditions, cultural
orientations, and geographic locations. The mental health conditions

discussed were diagnosed as schizophrenia and schizo-affective disorders, depression, anxiety, and psychological trauma. The cultural orientations include Mexican-descent, Euro-American, African American, Salvadoran, Native American, and Hispano/Hispanic groups. Most of the persons and groups in this book are largely invisible to their fellow citizens. The geographic locations are wide-ranging, spanning the continental United States: the West Coast, the East Coast, the Midwest, and the Southwest. This geographic range reflects my own migratory pattern from the 1980s to the present. Given the scope of the studies incorporated and on the helpful urging of one of the peer reviewers of this book, I came to realize that it may be useful to provide a road map for how these studies came into being as a matter of academic migration and assembly. This led me further to the realization that I could not sketch a road map in the absence of an attempt to mark the indebted grounds for the very possibility of my work.

My early studies as an anthropology PhD student at UCLA in the 1980s in the Department of Psychiatry and Biobehavioral Sciences were conducted according to what I now recognize as a local cultural assumption: I imagined my research environment was representative of "simply the way things are." With my anthropology adviser, Robert B. Edgerton, I studied human conditions in a manner that incorporated biogenetic structuralism and cultural conceptions. Edgerton's 1966 publication in the *American Anthropologist,* "Cultural Conceptions of Psychosis in Four East African Societies," led me to think that comparative cultural study of psychosis was an obvious course of study. While this has certainly been the case for me, I have long since been disabused of the notion that this kind of work was, for most anthropologists or psychiatrists, anything but obvious or standard. With the passage of time came the inevitable observation that my early academic environment was located in a particular historical and cultural moment for the interface of anthropology and psychiatry. That moment and the training environment it generated shaped me as an interdisciplinary researcher among diverse social and health scientists and clinicians. The ethos at that time, one I still subscribe to, is that collaborative groups can get more done. And of course this ethos was made possible by the relatively large-scale research grants that were available. I thank the anthropologist John G. Kennedy for making cultural psychiatry a mainstream topic of sociocultural anthropology and for setting in motion dissertation research with my mentor, the eminent psychiatrist Marvin Karno. It is to Marv that I owe my greatest debt. From him I learned what mattered most: careful, empathic research to determine what makes a difference for improvement from mental illness (chapters 1–3). Together, Marv and I ran several collaborative projects with Spanish-speaking Mexican-descent families. Also at UCLA, I benefited greatly from the methodological training of Tom Weisner. Anthropological fieldwork with him on the Family Life Styles project fostered my abiding commitment to systematic empirical research of kin-based households large (e.g., a sprawling religious commune) and small (tipis, log cabins, huts) in naturalistic splendor (I once sat on a closed toilet seat while interviewing someone in a bathtub). I got the training message: whatever, wherever. It certainly stuck, and many of my own doctoral students who have continued this methodological tack under difficult field circumstances.

In 1986 I accepted an invitation from Byron Good, Arthur Kleinman, and Mary-Jo DelVecchio Good to join as a postdoctoral fellow the Program in Medical and Psychiatric Anthropology at Harvard Medical School, which was funded by the National Institute of Mental Health (NIMH). What was initially to be a one-year post, owing to the need to get back to UCLA to continue a new grant we had received and my reluctance to leave behind a rent-controlled apartment in Santa Monica and "beach culture" (conceptually foreign if not suspect in Boston), extended to four years. The appeal of the Harvard program proved irresistible given the caliber of the MD-PhD cohort that I trained with in these four years. The intellectual atmosphere fostered by then-peers (now luminaries) Paul Farmer, Jim Kim, Rob Barrett, Tom Csordas, Linda Garro, Pablo Farias, Anne Becker, Paul Brodwin, Lawrence Cohen, and Roberto Lewis-Fernandez was electric. Credit for creation of that exceptional program goes entirely to Byron, Arthur, and Mary-Jo, who together ran the NIMH-funded training grant for twenty-five consecutive years. It remains for me a transformative experience and an intellectual home. I thank Arthur Kleinman for rare gifts of intellectual honesty and depth and the courage of visionary leadership that revolutionized our field. As a deeply thoughtful anthropologist of mental illness, there is no one's scholarship I admire more than the works of Byron Good. His writings have powerfully influenced my thinking. My work has likewise been made far better than it otherwise would have been by virtue of key theoretical formulations advanced by Mary-Jo DelVecchio Good. Utmost thanks to Byron and Mary-Jo whose limitless energy and generosity of intellectual and social spirit across homes in Cambridge and Maine fostered what we long ago dubbed the "FQ" (Fun Quotient). Also in Boston, as a member of the Latino Team of the Cambridge Hospital, I was privileged to be part of a stellar team of sophisticated clinicians who welcomed an anthropologist into their midst and helped immensely with my research with Salvadoran refugees (chapters 4 and 5). I thank Mauricia Alvarez, Sylvia Halperin, Pablo Farias, Pedro Garrido, Roberto Lewis-Fernandez, and particularly Marta Valiente, a gifted and generous Salvadoran clinical psychologist.

In 1990 I joined the faculty of the Departments of Anthropology and Psychiatry at Case Western Reserve University in Cleveland. The research support at Case was terrific, and Case was an outstanding environment in which to accomplish a great deal of work (chapter 1), including two NIMH-funded studies on schizophrenia and depression for which I was Principal Investigator. I am particularly grateful to colleagues Milton Strauss, Woody Gaines, Jill Korbin, Jonathan Sadowsky, Jerry Floersch, Jeff Longhofer, and Martha Sajatovic. I thank the many superb graduate students I had the privilege of teaching in seminars and as research assistants. I dare not attempt to list all for fear of omissions. I do, however, wish to extend particular thanks to Elizabeth Carpenter-Song.

In late 2004 I moved back to California, where I am currently a member of the faculty of the Departments of Anthropology and Psychiatry at University of California, San Diego (UCSD). In 2005, along with Tom Csordas, I launched a new study of adolescent mental health in the American Southwest, headquartered in Gallup and Albuquerque, New Mexico. This collaborative effort involved a team of highly dedicated clinicians who generously supported our research. I am grateful in particular for the leadership of the interdisciplinary scholar and medical director David Mullen and the master therapist Sandra Hollingsworth who facilitated the research (chapter 6). This work could not have been accomplished without the research child psychiatrist Michael Stork and the research psychologist Mary Bancroft, along with Elisa Dimas. The UCSD research team included a talented group of PhD students who assisted with complicated fieldwork and data organization, including Heather Hallman, Allen Tran, Nofit Itzhak, Jessica Novak, and Celeste Padilla. My particular thanks go to Bridget Haas and Whitney Duncan for carrying out taxing fieldwork with great skill and dedication. At UCSD, I am fortunate to have as colleagues Steven Parish, Margaret Schoeninger, Katerina Semendeferi, Tom Levy, Guillermo Algaze, Geoff Braswell, Suzanne Brenner, Jonathan Friedman, Paul Goldstein, Joe Hankins, John Haviland, Nancy Postero, Kit Woolard, Shirley Strum, David Pedersen, Steffanie Strathdee, Thomas Patterson, Lew Judd, Igor

Grant, Sid Zisook, Dilip Jeste, Fonna Forman, Gerry Mackie, David Mares, Carol Franz, Bill Kremen, Vicky Ojeda, and Monica Ullibari. I appreciate lively interchange among my (former) students Ted Gideonse, Charlotte van den Hout, and Sonia Rackelmann. I have particularly enjoyed teaching with Paula Saravia and departmental organizing with Jorge Montesinos. Carolyn Baratz, Brad Waples, Ellen Kozelka, and Kaylan Agnew provided assistance with manuscript preparation for this book.

I extend thanks for support of my research through invitations to be in residence as a visiting scholar at the Russell Sage Foundation in New York City (1996–1997), a fellow of the American Philosophical Society (2004–5), and a member of the Institute for Advanced Studies in Princeton, New Jersey (2011–12). In addition to sabbatical support, the Russell Sage Foundation generously provided support to convene a conference in New York City organized by me and my dearly departed colleague the anthropologist-psychiatrist Robert Barrett. In addition to spending a year together at Harvard, a decade later Rob and I worked together across a fourteen-hour time difference to produce our coedited volume, *Schizophrenia, Culture, and Subjectivity: The Edge of Experience..* I express gratitude also to the School for Advanced Research in Santa Fe, New Mexico, for giving me the opportunity to convene an Advanced Seminar that resulted in the edited volume, *Pharmaceutical Self: The Global Shaping of Experience in an Age of Psychopharmacology.* Emily Martin kindly invited me to present work, represented in chapter 6, to her interdisciplinary and experimental seminar group Psyences at New York University in spring 2012. Thanks to Monash University and Renata Kokanovic for the invitation to be Distinguished Visiting Professor at Monash University in summer 2013 where pieces of this book were presented to audiences that provided useful feedback, as was also true for the kind invitation from Aaron Denham and Greg Downey at Maquarie University. Work presented in chapter 1 was made substantially better by those experiences. Warm thanks to Angela Woods for the invitation to attend and present work represented in chapter 2 at the annual Hearing Voices conference at Durham University, England, in September 2013.

I wish to acknowledge my gratitude also for comments that I received at invited lectures based on work in progress for chapters presented in this book: McGill University and Groupe Interuniversitaire de Recherche en Anthropologie Medical et en Ethnopsychiatrie (GIRAME) in Montreal; the Friday Morning Medical and Psychiatric Anthropology Seminar at

Harvard University; Fundación Granja Taller de Asistencia Colombiana, Fundación Santillana and Departamento de Psicología, Universidad de los Andes, Santafé de Bogota, Colombia; Department of Psychiatry, School of Medicine, Gadjah Mada University, Yogyakarta, Indonesia; International Society for the Psychological Treatment of the Schizophrenias and Other Psychoses at Hospital General Universitario Gregorio Maranón, Madrid, Spain; Ethnografeast conference at the University of Leiden, the Netherlands; Department of Anthropology, London School of Economics; Wissenschaftskolleg, Institute of Advanced Studies, Berlin, Germany; Van Leer Institute, Jerusalem, Israel; European Science Foundation–sponsored conference, Department of European Ethnology, Charité-Universitätsmedizin and Humboldt-University Berlin, Germany; Institute of Social and Cultural Anthropology, Freie Universität, Berlin, Germany; International Conference, "Theories of the Body and Anthropology in the Americas," Universidad de Buenos Aires, Argentina; Joint International Conference for the Society for Medical Anthropology (SMA) and Society for European Medical Anthropology (EASA), Fundació Universitat Rovira I Virgili, Tarragona, Spain; the UCLA Mind, Medicine, and Culture Seminar; presentations at the annual meetings of the American Anthropological Association and biennial meetings of the Society for Psychological Anthropology. In the run-up to the final version of the book (December 2014), I am grateful to Olga Odgers Ortiz and Olga Olivas for their gracious invitation to present the overall book project to faculty and graduate students at El Colegio de la Frontera Norte (COLEF), Tijuana, Mexico.

Among persons in the public eye with firsthand experience with extraordinary conditions that concern me in this book, I have been enormously enriched by conversations in London with Jaqui Dillon of the Hearing Voices Network;, with Eleanor Longden, clinical psychologist at the Institute of Psychological Sciences, University of Leeds, UK; jazz luminary Tom Harrell and his wife, Angela, of New York City; and Nobel laureate John Nash, who completed interviews with me in summer 2012 at the Institute of Advanced Study, Princeton. Funding for research reported on in this book was awarded me by the National Institute of Mental Health (NIMH R01 MH 33502, "Course of Schizophrenia among Mexican-Descent Families"; NIMH R01 MH 60232, "Southwest Youth & Experience of Psychiatric Treatment"; NIMH MH 60232, "Culture, Schizophrenia, and Atypical Antipsychotics") and a Young Investigator Award on culture and depression from the National Alliance for Research on Schizophrenia and Depression.

Over the time that I have collected materials represented in this volume, I have had the good fortune to receive lively input from many additional colleagues and friends I wish to note: Helene Basu, Julia Cassiniti, Gilles Bibeau, João Biehl, Nancy Chen, Ellen Corin, Greg Downey, Aurora de la Selva, Esperanza Diaz, Susan DiGiacomo, Joe Dumit, Stefan Ecks, Javier Escobar, Sue Estroff, Didier Fassin, Angela Garcia, Joe Gone, Peter Guarnaccia, Sushrut Jadhov, Ann Kring, Alex Hinton, Devon Hinton, Ladson Hinton, Douglas Hollan, Michael Hollifield, Kim Hopper, Renata Kokanovic, Donna Kwilosz, Steve Lopez, Anne Lovell, Judith Lusic, Catherine Lutz, Lenore Manderson, Emily Martin, Jonathan Metzl, Juli McGruder, Daniel Lende, Tanya Luhrmann, Hazel Markus, Sheila O'Malley, Angel Martínez-Hernáez, Emeline Otey, Douglas Price-Williams, Jamie Saris, Louis Sass, Nancy Scheper-Hughes, Rick Shweder, John Strauss, Milton Strauss, Charles Swagman, Kimberly Theidon, Jason Throop, Joe Westermeyer, Susan Reynolds Whyte, James Wilce, and Kristin Yarris. At the University of California Press, I thank my exceptional editor, Reed Malcolm, and Stacie Eisenstark.

Portions of chapter 3 appeared in "The 1990 Stirling Award Essay: Anthropology, Expressed Emotion, and Schizophrenia," *Ethos* 19 (1991): 387–431; "Conceptions of Schizophrenic Illness as a Problem of Nerves: A Comparative Analysis of Mexican- Americans and Anglo-Americans," *Social Science and Medicine* 26 (1988): 1233–43; and "Ethnopsychiatric Interpretations of Schizophrenic Illness: The Problem of *Nervios* within Mexican-American Families," *Culture, Medicine, and Psychiatry* 12 (1988): 303–31. Portions of chapter 4 appeared in "The State Construction of Affect: Political Ethos and Mental Health among Salvadoran Refugees," *Culture, Medicine, and Psychiatry* 15 (1991): 139–65; "The Impress of Extremity: Women's Experience of Trauma and Political Violence," in *Gender and Health: An International Perspective*, ed. Carolyn Fishel Sargent and Caroline Brettel (Upper Saddle River, NJ: Prentice Hall, 1996); and "Bodily Transactions of the Passions: El Calor (The Heat) among Salvadoran Women," in *Embodiment and Experience: The Existential Ground of Culture and Self*, ed. Thomas J. Csordas (Cambridge: Cambridge University Press, 1994). Chapter 6 is an expanded and revised version of an article that appeared as "Psychic and Social Sinew: Life Conditions of Trauma among Youths in New Mexico," *Medical Anthropology Quarterly* 29.1 (2015): 42–60.

To treasured friends of many decades with whom I share great love, humor, and the safe haven: Stacie Widdifield, Holly Hainley, and Teri Hart. Stacie, an art historian, helped with book design issues, but we have long been dedicated to each other for so much more. Without Holly, the richness of chapter 1 could not have come into being; she single-handedly organized the project (and even the clinic that was the site of the study) with her gifts of sheer braininess, brazen creativity, and love of life. Teri, my sister and touchstone for all things, I love you. I could not begin to imagine my life without you at every turn since being teenagers reading Ram Dass's *Be Here Now* and going to concerts in L.A. every chance we could.

To my daughter, whose fierce humor, intellect, and love never cease to astound: thanks for the care packages from New York with Agata & Valentina biscotti and teas to fuel the final writing. I thank my son for clever quips, musical innovations, and easy warmth that helps sustain life and work. To my husband and colleague, Tom Csordas, no words could begin to cut it. Approaching three decades together, our life is a fast train of love and creativity. Thanks for being amused by my daily quip, "Day in and day out, it's just one more damn day of anthropology." Despite the intense and near-constant work we are both bent on doing, there is a life and an anthropology that we share and love together, come what may.

Most of all I am profoundly grateful to the many people living with extraordinary conditions who allowed me and my research team entrée to their homes, clinic, and other settings to learn about their lives and what mattered. I am deeply honored to have had these engagements and to have learned from you. In the main, your desire to persist, prevail, and to be is nothing less than extraordinary.

# Introduction

*Culture, Mental Illness, and the*
*Extraordinary*

This book is an anthropological appraisal of life on the edge of experience, based in large part on studies that I carried out over the past three decades. I have come to think that a useful approach to such an undertaking is through the extraordinary conditions that define such life on the edge. My use of the term *extraordinary conditions* carries double meanings. In the first place, it refers to conditions—illnesses, disorders, syndromes—that are culturally defined as mental illness. However, I also mean conditions—warfare and political violence, domestic violence and abuse, or scarcity and neglect of basic human needs—constituted by social situations and forces of adversity.[1] My notion of the extraordinary emphasizes the nonordinary and spectacular qualities of mental illness in experience and representation. It also recognizes the compelling, impressive, and even heroic quality often evident in life at the edge of experience for both the afflicted individuals and their families. Central to my analysis of extraordinary conditions is the primacy of lived experience not only as possibility writ large but also as human capacity for struggle. I have observed this capacity across a range of conditions of extremity such as unrelenting depression, hearing voices, coming to terms with psychotropic medication, troubled emotional environments in families, flight from warfare and political violence, and children's lives marked by extreme instability, abuse, and inadequacy of care.

The subtitle of this book, *Culture and Experience in Mental Illness,* is intended to invoke the enduring relevance of A. Irving Hallowell's (1934,

1955) formulation of experience as culturally constituted. At the heart of this book is a continuation of my argument (Jenkins 2004) that conditions of mental illness must be understood as engaging fundamental human processes. A short list of these processes—which I take as invariably constituted by an intricate mélange of culture, biology, and psyche—includes self, emotion, cognition, gender, identity, attachment, and meaning. These processes are fluid rather than fixed. Indeed, they are hardly transparent among those *not* afflicted with mental illness; yet examining their modulations in the most extreme cases can help us understand how they work and why they are fundamental. Moreover, the chapters that follow cumulatively make the argument that perhaps paramount among fundamental human processes is the existential process of struggle. Recognition of struggle goes beyond the useful and increasingly prominent notion of individual resilience in the face of affliction. When we analytically elevate the study of struggle, we see beyond the usual conceptual categories of analysis and see instead a fundamental human process that comes to light as a product of an anthropological approach trained on lived experience.

As I hope to demonstrate, complex processes of struggle are remarkably salient across all the extraordinary conditions that I have had the privilege to engage through my research. Struggle is embedded in the often profound and even courageous social engagement with living, working, and caring for others *despite* an onslaught of subjective experiences diagnosed as schizophrenia and bipolar, depressive, and trauma-related conditions, along with the social stigma and discrimination that frequently accompany them. This is all too well known by those who live with or are familiar with such conditions. I invite those without such experience to imagine such conditions as the features of one's daily life. The struggles are formidable: to get out of bed, to confront voices that torment, or to live with memories of the mutilated bodies of loved ones. Superimposed on these are daily life experiences of socially applied stigma meted out by the public for being perceived as "different." There is the disdain exuded by a store clerk or fellow patrons when picking up one's medication at a pharmacy, the sense of exclusion conveyed because one can neither speak nor understand the dominant language, the constant fear that neighbors might call immigration authorities or undertake practices of witchcraft for which one must seek spiritual protection. What it takes to subsist, let alone to prevail, under these conditions cannot be understood without an understanding of struggle. In sum, the studies presented here provide an argument for understanding struggle as a fundamental human process in conditions extraordinary and ordinary alike.

Integral to my anthropological approach is a commitment to understanding and describing human phenomena as distributed along qualitatively defined continua rather than as defined by discrete and distinct categories (Jenkins 2004; Canguilhem 1989).[2] In adopting this approach, I have found theoretical value in an emphasis on what arguably can be considered "extreme" or uncommon experience that defines the further ends of such continua, in contrast to comparatively more ordinary or common experience. As I detail in the chapters that follow, taking this methodological tack leads to a variety of instructive observations. For example, in examining situations of mental illness, it has become clear to me that as a matter of lived experience there is no such thing as individual pathology. These situations are invariably constituted by intersubjectivity, social and economic conditions of possibility and constraint, and the shaping of cultural expectations of persons in relation to gender, mental, and political status. My analysis of the interlocking domains of extraordinary conditions can be summarized precisely by the well-known feminist recognition of the reciprocal relations of the personal and the political.

An emphasis on the extraordinary is deeply revealing for an understanding of fundamental human processes and the creation of cultural meaning. The infelicitous manner in which persons with mental illness have been regarded as somehow lacking culture, treated sometimes as footnotes but seldom the primary subjects for ethnographies, has generated a host of anthropological problems requiring attention. In fact, people living with conditions of mental illness (the afflicted; their kin, communities, and healers) regularly create an array of meanings attached to their experiences. A number of these are examined in this book. For example, the examination of extraordinary conditions can reveal cultural processes of anthropomorphosis and personification of illness and pharmaceutical treatment in an experiential mélange of self/medications/illness. Likewise, such analysis shows the inaccuracy of defining people with schizophrenia as somehow less gendered or sexual beings. The ironic and erroneous quarantine in clinical psychology and psychiatry of the "abnormal" there and the "normal" here is theoretically and empirically untenable. In short, this book calls out the implicit normative social and health science tendency to ignore the extraordinary. Sequestration of the extraordinary not only does damage to the integrity of nonordinary subjects but also leads to intellectual peril for scholarly fields that indulge in it.

## EXTRAORDINARY CONDITIONS IN AN ERA OF NEUROSCIENCE

In the United States, public representations of mental illness have become dominated by images produced by the pharmaceutical industry, on the one hand, and episodes of deranged gun violence, on the other. At once vexing and gripping, stories of mental illness are often accorded center stage in cultural attention. They proliferate in academic texts, newspapers, films, television, magazines, memoirs, pharmaceutical pamphlets, public health billboards, and innumerable Internet sites.[3] The *New York Times* regularly features mental illness as front-page news in relation to recovery, treatment facilities, incarceration, homelessness, or the denial of care for military veterans. Public health campaigns directed at mental health are increasingly common globally, with slogans such as "Defeat Depression, Spread Happiness" in India, "Chains Free" in Indonesia, "Una nueva comprensión, una nueva esperanza" (A New Understanding, a New Hope) in Spain, "El silencio no es salud" (Silence Is Not Health) in Argentina, and "Better Living through Chemistry" or "A Flaw in Chemistry, not Character" in the United States.

In the current biogenetic era defined by the completion of the human genome project, the 1990s "Decade of the Brain," and the Obama administration's 2013 National Institutes of Health (NIH) initiative to map every neuron in the human brain, biologically based neuroscience dominates the research agenda for mental health and illness. The zeal for neuroscience at the expense of social scientific and other approaches raises concern for a variety of reasons. First, despite decades of research and enormous financial investment, neuroscience has not yielded specific markers or diagnostic tests that can differentiate one condition from another. The quest to identify underlying mechanisms has not been, nor will it be, productive any time soon since current studies of neural circuitry, tissue sharing, and genetics hold "zero relevance for clinical care or epidemiology" (Insel 2014a). Second, neuroscience seeks to understand mental illness as a brain disorder instead of as behavioral disorder. In this view, behavior and symptoms are endpoints of neurodevelopment, and paying attention to these consequences can only lead one astray from the scientific task of identifying causes and mechanisms (Insel 2014b; Insel and Gogtay 2014). While the brain is indisputably a site and source of things gone awry in mental illness, exclusive emphasis on core pathology confined to the brain excludes core pathology that exists in sites and sources that are social, behavioral, and economic. And although there is talk of the "social brain," precious few neuroscientists have a basic grasp of concepts, theories, or methods for the examination of social realms. Since psychiatric neuroscience defines basic science largely in the absence of live human populations in real-world settings (Insel and Quirion 2005), the capacity to identify phenotypic or genomic expressions of illness is plainly impossible. Simply put, this is a question of balance, with prevailing scientific priorities gone awry.

Third, there is a lack of agreement on how to define psychiatric diagnostic categories. Prior to the publication of the American Psychiatric Association's fifth edition of the Diagnostic and Statistical Manual (DSM-V), the current director of the National Institute of Mental Health (NIMH) critiqued the official nosology's descriptive and classificatory approach as lacking in scientific validity (Insel 2014b). He further insisted that the DSM-V impedes research insofar as it defines disorders by their symptoms rather than by biological and genetic causes, asserting, "As long as the research community takes the DSM to be a bible, we'll never make progress. People think that everything has to match DSM criteria, but you know what? Biology never read that book" (Thomas Insel, quoted in Belluck and Carey 2013:A13). This rhetoric of scientific authority offers a rather startling personification of biology. Such rhetorical moves are hardly inconsequential given that a growing number of scientists are convinced that a new paradigm is needed yet have not even a rough idea of what it should be.

Steven Hyman, former director of NIMH, has critiqued what he sees as the underlying model employed in the writing of DSM-V. This model assumes that psychiatric illnesses are discontinuous from the "normal," with the result "an absolute scientific nightmare." "Many people who get one diagnosis get five diagnoses," he continued, "but they don't have five diseases—they have one underlying condition" (quoted in Belluck and Carey 2013:A13). The question remains whether this condition is itself radically discontinuous with nonpathological experience. In this respect I again concur with Canguilhem's (1989) identification of the ontological error in conceptualizing pathology in categorical versus continuous terms. Understanding disorders as entities not only objectifies and alienates them from individual experience but also creates an obstacle to understanding the modulations of experience across a continuum from normal to pathological, ordinary to extraordinary. Moreover, the logic that informs Hyman's attempt to debunk categorical thinking remains susceptible to reducing the locus of disorder to a bio-chemical "substrate" rather than understanding it in terms of the existential totality of an afflicted person's lived experience. In this situation more rather than less complexity is to the point, and to its credit DSM-V augments that categorical distinction between presence and absence of a disorder by recognizing multiple dimensions in diagnosis as well as degrees of severity (Markon and Krueger 2005; Regier et al. 2013).

It would be a mistake, following a strict interpretation of biological psychiatry, to view the successive iterations of DSM as progressively more accurate representations of an empirically stable domain of psychiatric disorders. Changing social conditions and cultural tendencies affect the manner in which and extent to which psychic distress is manifest in communities and populations. Scientific and clinical perspectives redefine normal as pathological and vice versa, recognize problems that previously existed but were ignored, and ignore problems that previously demanded attention. The field of psychiatry and mental health treatment is subject to a political economy of nosology under the powerful influence of pharmaceutical companies. Neurobiological and genetic factors invariably figure into this complex assembly (Gazzaniga 2011), not as determinants, but as factors that are themselves subject to cultural change and environmental modulation, as is increasingly evident in the recent development of epigenetics.

Likewise, the recent turn toward truly interdisciplinary social and cultural neuroscience provides a welcome challenge to one-sided biological accounts of mind and brain through movement toward theoretical integration of convergent factors (Hollan 2000; Lende and Downey 2012; Choudhury and Slaby 2012; Chiao et al. 2013). Interpersonal neurobiology has identified the process in which attention and social interaction entail neural firing across synapses, which forges new connections and changes in the internal biochemistry of the cell and ultimately cell structure; this neuroplasticity is especially evident in studies of mindfulness and attachment, and it has been invoked to argue for the biological effects of psychotherapy (Siegel 2006; Cozolino 2006; Fosha, Siegel, and Solomon 2009). Finally, there is intriguing speculation that the species-specific creation of the "soul" can be understood in part as a possibly unique evolutionary adaptation across a range of ecological environments, what Humphrey (2011) has termed a "soul niche." Used appropriately, these developments can become part of the anthropological tool kit in the quest for a science of things divine, magical, mysterious, and maddening.

## ANTHROPOLOGY AND PSYCHIATRY

Anthropology has a crucial role to play in making sense of mental illness as a feature of contemporary life for a variety of audiences with an interest or stake in psychopathology, as well as in sorting out biochemical, political, economic, spiritual, and cultural dimensions of the phenomenon. The basis for this role is that the study of mental illness is indispensable to anthropological understanding of culture and experience, and reciprocally an understanding of culture and experience is critical to the study of mental illness. As evident in the early writings of Franz Boas, Margaret Mead, Ruth Benedict, and A. Irving Hallowell, cultural anthropology as an approach to the study of humans was developed in full cognizance of mental illness as an existential and social problem, an internal threat to the coherence not only of individual but also collective experience. Similarly, in the field of psychiatry, early observations of mental illness by writers such as Emil Kraepelin and Sigmund Freud exhibited an appreciation of the importance of culture and differences among cultures. In the mid-twentieth century there were highly productive collaborations between anthropologists and psychiatrists like those of Edward Sapir and Harry Stack Sullivan and Clyde Kluckhohn, Alexander Leighton, and Jane M. Hughes. Unfortunately, subsequent attention to the study of mental illness and culture at the intersection of anthropology and psychiatry declined. In cultural anthropology, the primacy and particularity of mental illness as a key domain for theorizing culture goes largely unrecognized. In biomedical psychiatry, the central import of culture to the experience and manifestation of mental illness is similarly underappreciated. Ironically, cultural anthropologists became disappointed with the concept of culture, yet enamored of Foucault's biopolitics and technologies of the self; and psychiatrists came to think that culture and experience had little or nothing to do with mental illness and became captivated with the neuroscience of biogenetics.

In light of this situation, I want to reassert the importance of research at the juncture of anthropology and psychiatry. Indeed, the extraordinary conditions of mental illness provide limiting cases for anthropological understandings of culturally fundamental and ordinary processes and capacities of subjectivity. The extraordinary sheds light on the ordinary from which it diverges, and the edge of experience (Jenkins 2004) helps define the spectrum of human behavior. By the same token, studies of mental illness shed light on psychopolitical problems of alterity and "otherizing" in the social rendering of persons diagnosed with mental illness as nonhuman or less than fully human; this is a problem that has never gone away and pertains to the larger group of dangerous others composed of madmen, children, women, savages, and foreigners. Ironically, the social stigma attached to mental illness in communities worldwide is only reproduced when cultural anthropologists relegate such persons and conditions to the status of footnotes, at best of little relevance to theorizing the structure, function, political economic, religious, cultural ecological, symbolic-interpretive, neoliberal, or ethical aspects of indigenous societies, nation-states, or global systems. My point is parallel to Virginia Woolf's ([1930] 2002: 3–4) sense of wonderment that "illness has not taken its place with love and battle and jealousy among the prime themes of literature." After all, illness experience is consuming and enigmatic (Gadamer 1996) and can bring about great "spiritual change" (Woolf [1930] 2002). While in literature there has since been extensive treatment of illness and the body, the same cannot be said in cultural anthropology or biomedical psychiatry.

This is hardly to say that the stage has gone dark since the mid-twentieth century. The publication in 1980 of *Patients and Healers in the Context of Culture* by Arthur Kleinman was as a gale force for cultural psychiatry and psychiatric anthropology. There now is a wealth of ethnographic studies on health and mental health showing both the importance of culture and the need to formulate careful accounts of subjectivity.[4] There are also first-person memoirs of illness that owe much to Woolf's (2002) concept that the ill actually live in a different world from the well (e.g., Saks 2007).[5] Hybrid accounts are available, such as Kay Jamison's *An Unquiet Mind* (1997), which combines autobiographical and psychiatric scientific accounts of manic-depressive illness, particularly in relation to creativity. Likewise, Emily Martin's *Bipolar Expeditions* (2007) presents an in-depth ethnographic study of cultural models of productivity that systematically draws on cultural, historical, and first-person interpretations of bipolar illness experience. Recent accounts from the growing social movement of self-identified "voice hearers" often eschew the term *pathology* while also insisting on attention to violations of human rights and social justice (Deegan 1988; Greek 2012; Rudnick 2012; Longden 2012, 2013; Fisher 2014). Literature in phenomenological and existential anthropology offers a valuable platform for close consideration of lived experience and bodily being-in-the-world (Hallowell 1955; Becker 1995; Csordas 1994; Jackson 2005, 2012; Throop 2010; Duranti 2010; Hollan and Throop 2011; Desjarlais and

Throop 2011). The analysis of narrative is a methodological locus for understanding subjective experience and transformation of self in a cultural context through stories or descriptions of conditions and events (Bruner 1990; B. Good 1994; Kleinman1988b; Orr 2006; Peacock and Holland 1993; Sacks 1990; Mattingly 1998, 2010). Finally, important work is appearing in the fast-expanding field of global mental health in the twenty-first century (Sorel 2013; Becker and Kleinman 2013; Opakpu 2014; Kohurt and Mendenhall 2015) for which the declaration "no health without mental health" has been increasingly recognized as compelling (Prince et al. 2007). This recognition is strikingly clear, since overall neuropsychiatric disorders rank number one among noncommunicable diseases and depression is the leading cause of disability worldwide (WHO 2008, 2009).

Against the background of these bodies of work, the concept of culture (and there are many definitions of culture, both inside and outside anthropology) is a critical element in a philosophical and ethnographic approach to an understanding of experience (Hallowell 1955). Culture is not a place or a people, not a fixed and coherent set of values, beliefs, or behaviors, but an orientation to being-in-the-world that is dynamically created and re-created in the process of social interaction and historical context. Culture has more to do with human processes of attention, perception, and meaning that shape personal and public spheres in a taken for granted manner. What do we pay attention to and how? What matters, and what does not? What is remarkable about *Homo sapiens* is that while the cultures we create can be characterized by a remarkable degree of patterning, they can virtually never be described as uniform within a society. They are often rife with idiosyncrasy and individual variation (Garro 1986, 2002), along with a complexity and diversity and even hyperdiversity (M. Good 2011) of perspectives within institutional settings.

For my purposes, a cultural approach to the extraordinary conditions of mental illness as experience is deeply implicated in the nature of "the real" or reality. To be precise: (1) reality is culturally constituted; (2) reality is inherently in question in the experience of mental illness on the part of those afflicted and their families; and (3) what is recognized as mental illness or affliction is influenced by culture. In this view, "experience" is the encounter with the real phenomena of self, others, and the world as this encounter is lived out in the actions and events of everyday life. "Subjectivity" is the relatively durable structure of experience that is yet subject to transformation based on changing circumstances and modes of engaging the world. A cultural perspective allows identification of the conditions (social, symbolic, material, subjective) under which, for example, a hammer and an ancestral spirit are equally real. In the case of contemporary medicine, symptom complaints are considered meaningful only if they can be identified as "real" pathology by means of objective evidence of disordered physiology. Moreover, reality and rationality are inextricably intertwined and linked to culturally and historically specific notions of belief, which apply in both religious and secular contexts. Indeed, there is a "close relationship between science, including medicine, and religious fundamentalism that turns, in part, on our concept of 'belief.' For fundamentalist Christians, salvation follows from belief . . . and a-religious scientists and policy makers see a similar benefit from correct belief" (B. Good 1994: 64).[6] The social response to persons with mental illness is often undergirded by a robust belief about its nature and causes: weak will or lazy disposition, karmic punishment, witchcraft, chemical imbalance, psychic trauma, vulnerability due to gender. There is a wide array of cultural assumptions and interpretations about the repertoire of possibilities for what is real and what is not.

What, then, is reality as created, experienced, and represented by humans? At the deepest level, it is that which is taken for granted, and what is denied or goes unrecognized is entirely a matter of social, cultural, and psychological perspective. An understanding of the moral struggle and not infrequently social clash over assumptions about what can be taken as real lies at the root of the scholarly enterprise and is both the starting point and the holy grail of intellectual, scientific, and religious quests. Perhaps no set of human realities generates greater cultural, social, and personal heat as do instances of mental illness. As is the case in physics and chemistry, this heat is not a property of a single system or endothermic body but invariably a process produced from complex neural, cultural, social, psychological, and ecological interaction. People neither experience personally nor respond socially to persons with mental illness with indifference. The ontological charge surrounding realities of mental illness often runs high.

Cultural reality in this respect certainly encompasses the powerful influence of political, biological, and economic forces. This is inevitable in light of the reciprocal shaping of subjective experience and social institutional practices. Reductive accounts of a Hobbesian Leviathan or Foucauldian discursive apparatus, on the one hand, or rational man notions of free-willing individuals who choose their feelings and destiny, on the other, are unsatisfactory frameworks for overarching theories of mind and human organization. It is unacceptable to be complacent with a comfortable footing on one or the other side of the divide, and historically there appears to be no shortage of fear and loathing when it comes to border crossing between what are glossed as psychological, phenomenological, and individual experience, on the one hand, and social, cultural, and political institutions and processes, on the other. Globally, in fact, the divide is frequently bridged by "structural violence" (Farmer 2004a) that occurs systematically, directly and indirectly, through structural arrangements embedded in political and economic systems that do not provide for basic needs. Often the result is inadequate and harmful conditions that are of great political and existential immediacy for embodied selves and can severely compromise mental health.

For example, the dysphoric effects of exposure to combat have been increasingly recognized since the trench warfare of World War I. War has proven a bloody tableau of human brutality and fragility. War experiences exert an influence that is event-specific at the same time that they are context-dependent and subject to complex psychological processes of judgment, attention, emotion, identification, alterity, and defense. Yet the power of raw existence to at times transcend context and contingency must also be recognized. Recent research has found that pilots of drone aircraft experience mental health problems that include depression, anxiety and posttraumatic stress at the same rate as pilots of manned aircraft deployed in Iraq or Afghanistan (Dao 2013). Neither physical proximity nor presence in a cockpit mattered much for those controlling drones at bases thousands of miles from the battlefield. Changing technologies of warfare do not erase the psychological damage for pilots fully aware of their role in the destruction of vulnerable populations and infrastructure. Even the distance of thousands of miles does not consolidate warfare's "otherizing" of the enemy as "not fully human." Further study of the practices and psychology of cyber warfare should certainly be undertaken for analysis of the mental health effects of contemporary warfare in the twenty-first century and its consequences for the experiential constitution of reality.

. . .

Given the stakes in the nearly unfathomable suffering among persons and their kin who live with serious mental illnesses, the methodological starting place for this work must be the phenomenological immediacy of lives and the first-person narratives of those afflicted. Arthur Kleinman has directed attention to the primacy of the experiencing subject and a clear recognition of "suffering [as] one of the existential grounds of human experience; it is a defining quality, a limiting experience in human conditions," at the same time cautioning against "essentializing, naturalizing, or sentimentalizing suffering in its many forms," both extreme and ordinary (Kleinman and Kleinman 1997: 1–2). He observes the manner in which invocation of "suffering" contributes to the objectification of persons both through popular appropriations (e.g., commercialization of images in the mass media) and through professional transformation (e.g., the generation of diagnostic categories such as PTSD). In this respect, suffering is a social phenomenon constituted by patterned, collective modes of experience and characterized by the inevitability of its occurrence as an interpersonal affair that afflicts kin and community (Jenkins 1991a, 2010a, 2010b, 2015; B. Good 2004, 2012a, 2012b; M. Good et al. 2008; Kleinman, Das, and Lock 1997; Farmer 1997, 2004a; Das et al. 2001; Kleinman 1988b, 2012; Biehl, Good, and Kleinman 2007).[7] From this standpoint, theorizing mental illness in the absence of subjective experience does little to apprehend the subject matter because it fails to attend to what matters most in peoples' lives. Anthropologically, this constitutes the heart of the matter (B. Good 2012a).[8]

In making a methodological turn toward extraordinary conditions and the experience to which they give rise, and away from what has been traditionally been taken to be normative (Korsgaard 1996), we create an opening for the task of deciphering the possibilities for being human. In other words, rather than being dismissed as marginal or abnormal, the extraordinary can be recognized as vital and integral. The types of experience I examine accordingly include extremity in the forms of psychosis, anxiety, trauma, depression, and rage. Analysis at the edge of experience aims to promote a critique of categorical versus continuous conceptualizations that refashions the boundaries between the ordinary and extraordinary, the routine and extreme, the healthy and pathological. Thus throughout the book I examine these issues in relation to what I think of as concurrent potentials and capacities for being human: (1) culturally diverse modes of sensory experience and meaning-making; (2) social, economic, and political conditions of adversity that pose threats to social and psychic integration, mental health, and well-being; and (3) the pervasiveness of stark suffering fashioned by arcs of creative struggle, survival, and healing.

People existing under extraordinary conditions of adversity or affliction are usually described as vulnerable individuals or vulnerable populations. For my purposes it is of value to replace the notion of vulnerability with that of precariousness, or precarity.[9] Indeed, I prefer the term *precarity* to vulnerability because it is more precise from the standpoint of the person's immediate experience: the phenomenology of mental illness, it seems, is less that of vulnerability than of precarity. More than arguing that the mentally ill are not victims, this is an assertion that the afflicted live precariously on the edge of experience. More to the point, from the standpoint of subjective experience, persons are less likely to express themselves or act in terms of vulnerability than to live in anticipation of trouble or the possibility that things may fall apart. This includes recognition of their own volatility as well as the volatility of their immediate surroundings. In line with the replacement of vulnerability with precarity, it is more productive to think less in terms of the symptoms manifested by the afflicted and more in terms of the struggle in which they engage as a matter of everyday life and survival. In other words, ours is not a methodology predicated on vulnerability to symptoms but one predicated on struggle in the face of precarity.

For theoretical clarity, it is worth engaging Judith Butler's (2004, 2009) argument about precarity, despite the fact that she juxtaposes precarity to performativity rather than to vulnerability and refers primarily to populations without either explicitly invoking the term *vulnerable populations* common in the health sciences or addressing the phenomenology of individual members of such populations. In the context that the persistence of anything living is "in no sense guaranteed" and that social institutions exist in part to ensure the means "by which life can be secured" her definition is as follows:

> "Precarity" designates that politically induced condition in which certain populations suffer from failing social and economic networks of support and become differentially exposed to injury, violence, and death. Such populations are at heightened risk of disease, poverty, starvation, displacement, and of exposure to violence without protection. Precarity also characterizes that politically induced condition of maximized vulnerability and exposure for populations exposed to arbitrary state violence and to other forms of aggression that are not enacted by states and against which states do not offer adequate protection. (2009: ii)

Butler concludes that precarious lives are "lives who do not qualify as recognizable, readable, or grievable. And in this way, precarity is a rubric that brings together women, queers, transgender people, the poor, and

TABLE I    FUNDAMENTAL ASPECTS OF MENTAL ILLNESS THAT ARE CULTURALLY
SHAPED

- Risk/vulnerability factors (precarity)
- Type of onset (sudden or gradual)
- Symptom content, form, constellation
- Clinical diagnostic process
- Subjective experience and meaning of problem/illness
- Kin identification and conception of and social-emotional response to problem/illness
- Community social response (support, stigma)
- Healing modalities and health care utilization
- Experience, meaning, and utilization of health care/healing modalities (including psychotropic drugs)
- Resources for resilience and recovery
- Course and outcome

the stateless" (2009: xii–xiii). One would not accuse Butler of intentionally excluding the mentally ill but would have to conclude that their lives qualify as even less recognizable than the categories of precarity she mentions. In any case, in order to resist being beholden to a Foucauldian biopolitics, we must observe that it is inaccurate to think of the mentally ill as a population. As this book demonstrates, there are many settings across diverse populations in which psychopathology appears, and as a form or subjectivity it is precisely the themes of precarity and struggle that are common across them all.

In sum, the studies presented in this book are broadly directed toward three interrelated goals. First and most broadly, they aim to provide empirical data to systemically examine the cultural constitution and representation of human reality across ordinary and extraordinary modes of experience. Second and more specifically, they aim to address the pressing need to recognize and understand the lived experience and everyday struggle of persons living mental illness. Third, and bridging the first two goals, the studies are intended to further the ongoing task of psychological and psychiatric anthropology to specify the interplay of culture and mental illness, insofar as I have found the role of culture to be pervasive and profound (table 1). The recognition that, from onset to recovery, culture matters vitally in understanding the experience of mental illness has oriented the argument of this book at the most fundamental level.

The range and depth of cultural factors and processes listed in table 1 are compelling, but here I want to address one factor that I regard as paramount in the cross-cultural and transnational scholarly literature on schizophrenia: variation in course and outcome. There are three strong bodies of data to support this striking finding. First is the study by the World Health Organization's nine-country International Pilot Study of Schizophrenia that unexpectedly found a better course and outcome for persons diagnosed with schizophrenia outside of Europe and North America: persons from India and Nigeria fared far better than their counterparts in Denmark or the United States. As detailed in chapter 3, these transnational data have been examined and reexamined over decades, with the conclusion that this finding is robust and not reducible to methodological error (Hopper 2004). Second, longitudinal studies have found that when followed for long periods, many persons with schizophrenia tend to improve rather than deteriorate (Harrison et al. 2001). And third, detailed accounts by persons with schizophrenia and studies of such persons (such as our research) demonstrate that as a matter of subjectivity, improvement (if not full recovery) is definitively discernible among those who are afflicted (Deegan 1988). Taken together, these studies provide powerful evidence for both cultural and individual variation and a resounding rebuke to Kraepelinian presumptions (and assertions) of inevitable deterioration and chronicity.

Addressing the goals set forth for this book has been analogous to braiding several cords, each of which is in turn composed of interwoven threads. The core idea of the book is that human experience is culturally constituted, and this central cord is woven from intertwined understandings of experience as ordinary or extraordinary, healthy or pathological, normal or abnormal. Moreover, to address fundamental questions of reality from the direction of culture is to engage in problems of interpretation and of experience. I and other scholars working with a cultural approach to schizophrenia insist on the meaningfulness and primacy of lived experience, so that "symptoms" such as hearing voices are not meaningless random neurosynaptic misfires (Corin 1990; Good and Subandi 2004; Estroff 2004; Jenkins and Barrett 2004; Hopper 2004; Lovell 1997; McGruder 2004; Myers 2015; Rahimi 2015). The meaning of lived experience is accessed in this book by deploying a cord comprising meanings created through intersubjective communication (Gadamer 1996) and the empirical domains of talk, action, and embodiment (Holland and Skinner [1996] 2008). Particular attention is paid to the conceptual domains of magic, science, and religion. A social cord is constituted from the strands of individual, family, and institutions; a clinical cord is wound from the relation between diagnostic and indigenous conceptions of the problem and the relation between the course of illness and illness experience; and a self cord is constituted by the threads of suffering, struggle, resilience, and healing.

To take adequately into account contextual and cultural variation is to embrace the approach of comparison, and this methodological cord is constituted by the diversity represented in the pages that follow among Euro-American, Native American, African American, and Hispanic/Latino groups, the latter including both Mexican immigrants and Salvadoran refugees. My concern with mental illness is not based on a single disorder but is itself a cord woven from examination of schizophrenia, depression, and posttraumatic stress disorder (PTSD). The series of interrelated studies that form the basis of this book, funded by the National Institute of Mental Health over the past three decades, constitute another cord. Finally, each of the studies is the result of the interdisciplinary collaboration of anthropologists, psychiatrists, psychologists, and historians.

To circumnavigate the extraordinary conditions that are my concern here, I have chosen to divide the book into two parts, the first concerned explicitly with psychosis and the second with trauma. This is not to say that the two are unrelated, since those afflicted with psychosis are not unfamiliar with trauma, and those subject to trauma may also experience psychosis. However, the protagonists in the first part of the book are persons from a variety of backgrounds who have been treated for psychosis in the particular form of schizophrenia. Those encountered in the second part have also been in treatment but include women who are refugees from the trauma of political violence and adolescents many of whom have experienced the traumas of domestic abuse and gang violence; from a medical standpoint they exhibit a range of problems and diagnoses such as PTSD and depressive disorders, and only a minority have manifested forms of psychosis.

Part 1, "Psychosis, Psychopharmacology, and Families," is devoted to the problem of psychosis as extraordinary experience among individuals and their families. The opening chapter, "Cultural Chemistry in the Clozapine Clinic," is a self-contained ethnography that touches on virtually all of the themes and levels of analysis I have outlined so far, and in a way constitutes a book within the book. It defines a particular cultural-historical moment of mental illness and psychiatric treatment in which a new kind of drug sends cultural reverberations through subjectivity, institutions, and the cultural imaginary. The ethnography examines the experience of persons diagnosed with schizophrenia in the first clinic in the United States to emphasize treatment with second-generation, or "atypical," antipsychotic medications. Through the actual experience of persons who have taken them, I examine the cultural rhetoric touting these as miracle drugs that produce dramatic "awakenings." Following the core Euro-American metaphor of "chemical imbalance" through descriptions of how the medication affects them leads to an appreciation of how magic, science, and religion are intertwined in the cultural imaginary surrounding psychopharmaceuticals. From the standpoint of those who take the drugs, medication experience constitutes an existential totality, and through a narrative analysis I show how this totality encompasses sensory experience, toxicity, clarity and velocity of thought, balance, control, discipline, identity, normality, and daily life activities. A complex conjunction of self, medication, and illness leads to paradoxes of lived experience such as recovery without cure and stigma despite recovery. The chapter points beyond the study of schizophrenia with a reflection on whether we are all becoming pharmaceutical selves in global context.

Chapter 2 complements this discussion by switching frames from a clinical ethnography of schizophrenia to provide a close-up portrait of a young Mexican immigrant afflicted with psychosis. The case study presented in "This Is How God Wants It? The Struggle of Sebastián" is a vivid instance of how sociocultural and psychodynamic milieu affects the formation of extraordinary experience, how the core of that experience is better characterized in terms of struggle than of symptoms, and the ultimate unfathomability of schizophrenia as a form of human subjectivity. Afflicted at a time when atypical antipsychotic drugs were unavailable and his reactions to the drugs prescribed were starkly negative, Sebastián confronted and attempted to make sense of voices that claimed their identity as divine. The magnitude of Sebastián's struggle is compounded by his relationships to God, his family, his girlfriend, work, and school. Particularly compelling is the emotional tone of his life stemming from the devotion of his mother and rejection by his father. I conclude with recognition of how my emphasis on struggle emerges directly from the nature of the ethnographic encounter and the value and limitations of listening and understanding in the face of intense suffering.

Again with the intent of complementing the preceding chapter, the final chapter in part 1 shifts frames from the case study to a broader consideration of one of the critical factors evident in Sebastián's situation, namely, the interactive emotional tone that characterized his relation with his parents and others with whom he was close. Chapter 3,

"Expressed Emotion and Conceptions of Mental Illness: Social Ecology of Families Living with Schizophrenia," thus pursues the study of schizophrenia in family settings and in so doing offers a cross-cultural analysis comparing Mexican Americans and Euro-Americans. As will be clear throughout this book, I am convinced that as a mode of subjectivity, deployment of cultural conceptions of mental illness plays a role in shaping how it is experienced and how it is treated, as well as its course and outcome (Edgerton 1966, 1980; Fabrega and Silver 1973; White 1982; Jenkins 1988a, 1988b, 2004, 2010b). Chapter 3 is therefore a systematic examination of two closely related factors: how differing cultural conceptions of schizophrenia affect family response to the illness and how the culturally constituted emotional milieu of the family affects the course of illness. Mexican Americans are more likely to define their family member's problem as *nervios* (nerves), whereas Euro-Americans tend to think in terms of personality deficits. This difference is directly connected to the emotional milieu of the family, which I define using the paradigm of expressed emotion in the form of criticism, hostility, emotional overinvolvement, warmth, and positive comments. High levels of negative emotion in intimate interactional settings have been shown to predict relapse of psychosis, and I pursue this finding to cultural settings in other parts of the world, including India, China, Japan, Malaysia, Spain, Poland, and Iran. In the chapter's conclusion I summarize cultural issues essential to an understanding of variation in emotional milieu and the course of illness.

Part 2 examines the mental health consequences of extraordinary conditions defined by trauma, violence, and precarity among groups of refugees and youth. The chapters in this part reveal the importance of resilience. Chapter 4, "The Impress of Extremity among Salvadoran Refugees," introduces a group of women who fled the Salvadoran civil war in the 1980s and were in treatment in a clinic specializing in helping Latino patients. I elaborate what was for them a *political ethos*—the culturally standardized organization of sentiment pertaining to social domains of power and interest. This ethos was generated by the dangerous political conditions in their home country, to which they referred almost surreptitiously as *la situación*, and its effects were exacerbated by their often indeterminate immigration status in the United States, the continued presence of loved ones in El Salvador, and their own subjection to domestic violence by their male partners. I examine the existential considerations that issue from the interaction of suffering and resilience as the women move back and forth from the clinic to their everyday lives. Of particular interest with respect to their immediate experience and embodied subjectivity is the phenomenon of *el calor*, or spontaneous uncomfortable heat in one's body, a culturally specific somatic form in which *nervios* were frequently manifest among these women. Finally, I address the clinical considerations associated with depression and PTSD in the context of their daily construction of meaning, sense, and representation in the face of terror, torture, disease, and distress.

Chapter 5 complements the preceding discussion by broadening the consideration of the cultural constitution of reality among these same Salvadoran women refugees by addressing the relation between religion and mental health in their daily lives. "Blood and Magic: *No Hay que Creer ni Dejar de Creer*" (You Can't Believe nor Stop Believing) takes its key from the immediate and indisputable reality of religion and magic; paradoxically, for these women it makes no difference whether you believe or don't believe. The polyvalent symbolic meanings of this common saying are open-ended. On the one hand, in experiential realms (e.g., witchcraft) there's no way you can believe; on the other, hand, how can you not believe? These cultural interpretations of reality cannot be specified, nor can they be ignored without risk. Catholicism and indigenous practices are both in evidence, and they are relevant not only with respect to dealing with the traumatic effects of *la situación* but also with respect to managing relations with parents, spouses, children, or romantic rivals. Magical practice and religious involvement span the distance from El Salvador to the United States and extend to other Salvadoran immigrant communities. Careful attention to life history makes it clear that the salience of spiritual issues for these women varies along a continuum from casual and even secondhand familiarity to immersion in practices of protection and aggression in the most immediate activities of daily life. Above all, what becomes clear, as a matter of lived experience, is the way magic and religion help the women achieve their straightforward but essential goal, *salir adelante*, to go on. In this regard, the chapter elaborates the leitmotiv of human struggle that is central to this book. This ethnographic study of struggle serves further to broaden our understanding of extraordinary conditions by following a group from clinic to community, articulating not only with mental health services but also with religious and cultural resources to address their distress, thereby problematizing the relation between medicine and culture, mental health and religion, diagnosis and distress, illness episodes and everyday life. The chapter is intended to bring magic and religion to the forefront of our thinking about mental illness cross-culturally.

Chapter 6, "Trauma and Trouble in the Land of Enchantment," examines the extraordinary conditions and experience of adolescent psychiatric inpatients and their families in New Mexico. It continues in a different register the analysis of psychic trauma and psychopathology at the juncture of domestic and structural violence in one of the poorest states in the United States. Working from the most important children's psychiatric hospital in the state in the face of a severely constrained public mental health care system, I focus on the relevance of PTSD for answering the anthropological question of how to define the "problem" faced by each of these young people. I examine the palpable insecurity of their precarious lives, many characterized by having committed violent or suicidal acts, by experiencing the recent deaths of loved ones, by heavy use of drugs and alcohol, by legal troubles, by physical and/or sexual abuse (an alarming number of girls were raped multiple times), or by routine self-cutting. Drawing particularly on the experience of one young girl and one young boy who had experienced significant social neglect and abandonment, I suggest that a more broadly defined concept of trauma is better suited to ethnographic understanding than is the narrower (if more precise) psychiatric diagnostic category of PTSD.

The concluding chapter draws together the common factors and distinctive features of the extraordinary conditions addressed in the book and what can be learned from a focus on extraordinary conditions and the experience to which they give rise. Human scenarios viewed from this vantage point—from the edge of experience—are productive sites for illuminating the possibilities and conditions of being human. As an anthropologist I have been struck by the irrepressibility of human bodies and minds under the impress of extremity in a variety of forms. While the intricacy of humans and the precarity of their situations teach us humility with respect to what we can truly know of others and ourselves, I aim to convey what I consider knowable about human experience under conditions that are arguably among the most difficult or extreme. While it is important neither to romanticize nor to overstate the possibilities for human action and agency, one must recognize that the magnitude of the suffering is matched by no less mighty a struggle to live and to be well.

# PART ONE

# Psychosis, Psychopharmacology, and Families

## CHAPTER I

# Cultural Chemistry in the Clozapine Clinic

We see that recovery is an important and fundamental phenomenon. Although the phenomenon will not fit neatly into natural scientific paradigms, those of us who have been disabled know that recovery is real because we have lived it.

—Patricia E. Deegan, "Recovery: The Lived Experience of Rehabilitation"

The clinic in which I was conducting research from 1998 to 2004 was the focus of great media fanfare as the first American site to use a new "miracle drug" for the treatment of schizophrenia. The clinic was featured in the cover story of the July 1992 issue of *Time,* "New Drug Brings Patients Back to Life," in which clozapine was touted as a "magic bullet." A related article in the same issue was titled "Pills for the Mind."[1] The *New York Times* published an article that advocated greater access to the new miracle drug, saying, "Many who treat schizophrenia believe clozapine is the most important medication to come along in 30 years. The press is so excited, it keeps using '*Awakenings'* in headlines, conjuring images of film star Robert De Niro taking a new medicine suddenly going from comatose to superstar."[2] The *Harvard Review of Psychiatry* drew attention to the phenomenon of "awakenings" as an unprecedented therapeutic challenge: "often involv[ing] a fundamental reassessment of one's identity, relationships, and purpose in being[,] . . . [t]he psychological reaction to dramatic pharmacological response is largely uncharted territory" (Duckworth et al. 1997: 55).

Charting this territory required research involving persons ingesting psychotropic drugs to ascertain their myriad cultural, social, psychological, and biological effects. From an anthropological point of view, this required looking beyond the "main effects" of symptom control. What was needed was a detailed account of the lived experience of those who take these drugs, specifying the social and cultural contexts of claims of drug efficacy. There are several immediate questions from the perspective of persons taking them: How do they work? What are their effects? Do they really help? Are they transformative? What is their meaning? Can drugs really "mean" anything to people? How, anthropologically, could they not? Whyte and colleagues (2003) have intriguingly written of the "social lives of medicines," but what could *that* mean in the case of psychotropics? Are they like the late-night cavorting yams of the Dobu in Papua, New Guinea, that are magically enticed into a neighbor's garden (Fortune [1932] 1963)?

In this chapter I present ethnographic evidence to address these questions, but first I must outline my general approach to the understanding of psychopharmacology in contemporary global societies,[3] which is predicated on recognizing the interrelation of several levels of analysis, including (1) the *subjectivity* associated with medication use, where subjectivity is understood as the relatively stable yet transformable structure of experience; (2) the potential of psychotropic drugs to affect the *self,* where self is understood not as a discrete entity but as a configuration of processes by which people orient themselves to their own being, to others, and to the surrounding world; (3) the context of *culture,* in which the power of cultural meaning involves nothing less than the ability to shape the experience of agony and monotony, relief and recovery, identity and lifeworld among those who take these drugs; and (4) the *institutions* in which drugs and illness are embedded, including biomedicine, government, nongovernmental organizations (NGOs), insurance companies, the pharmaceutical industry, and the policies and practices of employers.

In this analysis, what sense can there really be to an assertion of a critical interrelation among subjectivity, self, culture, and institutions for an understanding of psychopharmacology? *What* are psychiatric medications really for? Unbearable suffering? Supplemental nutrient? Demonic affliction? Neuronal misfires? Personality deficits? Bad behavior? Violent behavior? *Who* are they for? The afflicted who find medications a relief in quieting unrelenting voices? Exposed populations of the elderly, children, indigent recipients of health care, and the mentally ill who are incarcerated?[4] In such cases, subjectivity is constrained by institutional structures of global capitalism in tandem with historically deep societal assemblages for social-political control and also in the service of establishing "the normal" (Foucault 1965, 1977; Deleuze and Guattari 1988; Rhodes 2004). This latter question of course concerns not only the use but also the misuse of psychotropic drugs.[5]

None of my cultural analysis is intended to deny or ignore that there are myriad biological processes critical to drug response. Neuroscientific research on correlates, mechanisms, substrates, and biological contexts of psychopharmacologicals has become voluminous (Ng et al. 2013; Stahl 2013). The field of pharmacogenomics, or the way genes influence response to drugs, may shed light on differential individual and group effects, as may the emergent fields of interpersonal and cultural neuroscience (Schore 2003; Lende and Downey 2012; Narváez et al. 2012; Chiao et al. 2013). There are a host of individually variable features of cognition, personality, and the unconscious that are likely to mediate drug response. A significant part of this variation might be explained through emergent theories of epigenetics as the chemical and environmental "turning on/triggering" or "turning off/inhibiting" of genetic codes. Further, in clinical trials, there is the problem for pharmaceutical companies of the statistical "noise" that is the well-known yet little understood "placebo" effect. In line with my approach here, a compelling interpretation conceptualizes the placebo effect as a kind of "meaning response" (Moerman 2002). Ultimately, to theorize the effects of psychoactive drugs, we need a model of the effects of psychopharmaceuticals that is grounded also in the "tuning" of biochemical response inseparable from the "tuning" of socioemotional response, cultural meaning, and ecological constraint. A wide-ranging model is required since surely all are at once integral to experience, to disease and illness processes, and to outcomes.

Within this framework, while we are compelled to attend to the magnitude of what can be an excruciating experience, no less critical are the lengths to which people go to seek relief and to alleviate this suffering, since healing and transformation are no less characteristic of the human condition than are intractability and misery. In the case of mental illness, for better *and* for worse, the practice of taking psychotropic drugs has increasingly become a central part of the process of seeking relief. Moreover, recovery or at least improvement over time—with and without psychotropic drugs and characterized by great endurance and struggle—is a reality for many people, though the subjective experience and cultural interpretation of the bodily and social effects of medication is anything but simple and straightforward. Finally, taking psychotropic drugs is not merely a routine and pragmatic process of the self. There is marked existential struggle and sociocultural contestation surrounding identity, power, and medication. The decidedly social-relational experience and meaning of medications requires elaboration. As a step in this direction, let us look again at the media attention to the introduction of atypical drugs highlighted at the outset of this chapter.[6]

## CULTURAL REPRESENTATIONS OF ATYPICAL ANTIPSYCHOTICS

The heralding of clozapine for use in the treatment of schizophrenia in the United States in *Time* magazine offers a glimpse of the two-edged popular appeal of the story. On the one hand, reference in the article to the medication as a "magic bullet" conjured the notion of dramatic and much desired improvement that had not occurred through prior use of other medications. The article was quite specific in portraying this drug as a new weapon in the scientific-medical armamentarium, invoking a militaristic metaphor of "a fight" against disease (see Martin 2001) through the highly valued medical competence of physician-scientists (M. Good 1995) while at the same time invoking the idea of magical technique. On the other hand, the christening of this particular medication as a "miracle drug" conjured the notion of a substance imbued with the power to bring patients back to life, invoking not only the power of pharmaceuticals but also the religious metaphor of miraculous healing. The anthropologist will likely see these symbolic connotations in light of Malinowski's (1954) classic discussion of the blurred conjunction of magic, science, and religion in the production of cultural meaning. The historian will most likely be reminded of the intimate connection between alchemy and chemistry in the history of pharmacological treatment. Contemporary discourse on psychopharmacology is steeped in a robust historical link between magic and chemistry.[7]

The other side of this cultural representation, however, is far from celebratory insofar as *Time*'s depiction taps into cultural imagery associated with an all too familiar social stigmatization of the mentally ill. The reproduction of social stigma is evident in two ways. First, in invoking a Christian allusion to resurrection (Wallis and Willwerth 1992), the apparently promising image of healing is embedded in the brutal presumption that persons with schizophrenia had somehow previously been "dead." It is difficult to imagine any social designation more offensive than reference to persons with schizophrenia as not among the living. Second, there is the notion that persons with schizophrenia are not really human but somehow alien. All too often this appears to mean that "they" must lack fundamental human capacities for subjective experience of the self, emotion, and social attachment; such assumptions are not only empirically false but also constitute a punishing cultural conception of persons with mental illness (Jenkins 2004; Kring and Germans 2004).

Another point of emphasis in the *Time* article was the sense of newly found possibilities to reach developmental milestones missed because of illness, such as participating in a cultural rite of passage like one's high school senior prom. In this bionarrative (see Carpenter-Song 2009a, 2009b), not having done so because the ravages of schizophrenia represents a biographical gap, which the promise of clozapine offered to fill. The article featured a staged event of a "better late than never" prom held for clozapine patients. One young man is shown dancing, presumably enjoying himself enormously, though his dance partner was a hired dance instructor and not a personally arranged date of the sort one imagines for oneself at a high school senior prom.

The *New York Times* article on clozapine (Winerip 1992), drawing on celebrity images of Robin Williams and Robert De Niro in Penny Marshall's 1990 film, *Awakenings,* reported that media and medical excitement was momentous because former patients could go from "comatose to superstar." The film had been advertised as a "true story" based on the book of the same title by the neurologist Oliver Sacks (1973) that invoked the image of Washington Irving's (1882) Rip Van Winkle to tell a story of institutionalized patients who became catatonic after having encephalitis. They experienced a dramatic but sadly temporary improvement through another "miracle drug," L-Dopa. The film ends with the protagonist physician standing over the protagonist patient behind a magical Ouija board, directing the patient's hands with the invocation, "Let's begin." The posters and trailers for the film, like the media coverage of clozapine, had tapped into the appeal of miracles and featured the theme of triumph with the opening of new, blue horizons. Reliance on religious language and symbols, along with magical practices, to convey scientific developments in medicine suggest the relevance of the association between these domains as critical to psychiatric discourse and practice.

Posing challenges to the scientific community, the *Harvard Review* article by Duckworth and colleagues (1997) urged the exploration of "awakenings" as a clinical phenomenon for understanding the dramatic change and subsequent developmental challenges that could occur.[8] Could "awakenings" be understood solely through resort to psychiatric science, or did realms of the unknown somehow come into play? Was the term *awakenings* merely a literary device to refer to psychological and social processes that could be accounted for biologically when induced by drugs? While in the 1992 *Times* story the clozapine proponent Herbert Meltzer was careful as a research psychiatrist to point out that recovery is not an overnight phenomenon, in speeches to advocacy groups and conferences he too deployed the term *awakenings*. Malinowski's intuition about the relation between magic, science, and religion is hardly restricted to small-scale societies. Indeed, a Zenith Goldline Pharmaceuticals advertisement for clozapine in the *American Journal of Psychiatry* promoted the drug by juxtaposing primitive "myth" of early hominids to modern "fact" in the form of scientific gold.[9]

## TOWARD THE STUDY OF CULTURAL CHEMISTRY

Clozapine (brand-name Clozaril), the first atypical, or second-generation, antipsychotic developed, was intended for patients who had little or unsatisfactory response to typical, or first-generation, antipsychotics (primarily phenothiazines such as Thorazine, Mellaril, Stelazine, and Prolixin). Clozaril was also used to replace another drug commonly prescribed during the 1970s, Haldol (haloperidol), a butyrophene derivative with pharmacological effects similar to the phenothiazines. In addition to the claim that it modifies positive symptoms of psychosis better than previous drugs, clozapine was said to have lesser extrapyramidal effects such as tardive dyskinesia and akathesia. Clozapine had already been introduced in Europe in 1971 but was withdrawn from the market in 1975 in the wake of cases of agranulocytosis, some fatal, involving dangerously depleted white blood cells. In the subsequent decade, most clinicians did not look upon clozapine favorably. Following trials that claimed both clinical efficacy and procedures for monitoring blood levels, along with approval by the U.S. Federal Drug Administration (FDA) in 1989, Sandoz Pharmaceutical Corporation brought the drug to the U.S. market in 1990. The drug was promoted as particularly efficacious for conditions of schizophrenia that were considered "treatment-resistant" or "last resort" (Alvir et al. 1993) and prescribed despite the additional risks of seizures, myocarditis, and weight gain. Heady hope accompanied the steady desperation of patients, families, and clinicians dissatisfied with typical antipsychotic drugs. The possibility of improvement appeared to eclipse the substantial risks involved. Clozapine was soon joined on the market and in the clinics in which we were conducting ethnographic research by other atypical antipsychotics such as Risperdal (risperidone), Zyprexa (olanzapine), and Seroquel (quetiapine), along with other drugs such as Geodon (ziparsidone) and Abilify (aripiprazole). Currently, these atypical antipsychotics are prescribed far more commonly than clozapine. Overall, the number of people using atypical antipsychotics increased from 0.3 million in 1996 to 1.6 million in 2001 (Zuvekas 2005). A recent report indicates that Abilify ranked number 1 in sales for *all* pharmaceuticals sold in the United States (IMS 2014).

The introduction of clozapine marked an important moment in the history of psychiatry and psychopharmaceutical medication. The 1960s had seen conventional antipsychotic drugs alter institutional methods of treatment, followed by mass deinstitutionalization of patients. Total available hospital beds declined from 550,000 in 1956 to less than one quarter of that number by 1998 (Eisenberg and Guttmacher 2010).[10] The introduction of the atypical antipsychotics in the 1990s—along with a patently neoliberal turn with respect to what constitutes treatment—served as the grounds for dramatically raised expectations for improvement, and indeed "recovery."[11] In early twentieth-century psychiatry, Emil Kraepelin set forth claims that until recently have held clinical authority as applied to schizophrenia (or dementia praecox). He conceived the condition as an inherently chronic and degenerative disease for which improvement, let alone recovery, was all but impossible. Kraepelin wrote that in the great majority of cases, periods of improvement did not last longer than three years and that over time the proportion of cases constituting recovery consisted of a mere 2.6 percent; deterioration and degeneration were nearly inevitable (Kraepelin 1919) By the early twenty-first century, a stark reversal of this clinical outlook was evident in the vision statement of the New Freedom Commission on Mental Health in which recognition of recovery appeared not only as a possibility but also virtually as a mandate:

> We envision a future when everyone with a mental illness will recover, a future when mental illnesses can be prevented or cured, a future when mental illnesses are detected early, and a future when everyone with a mental illness at any stage of life has access to effective treatment and supports—essentials for living, working, learning, and participating fully in the community. (2003: 9)

Whereas the introduction of first-generation antipsychotics was accompanied by the social process of deinstitutionalization (Rhodes 1995), the introduction of second-generation antipsychotics was accompanied by the cultural concept of recovery (Jenkins and Carpenter-Song 2005; Myers 2015).

Unsurprisingly, the long-standing Kraepelinian doctrine of progressive deterioration has hardly disappeared. Schizophrenia is often represented as an inescapable inferno akin to what Hector Berlioz portrayed in *La damnation de Faust*. Clinical delivery of prognosis can likewise be tormenting, as for example when the British psychologist Eleanor Longden was given a diagnosis of schizophrenia and told that it would have been better if she had cancer.[12] Needless to say, such crass pessimism can be crushing to vulnerable persons in states of severe psychic distress. And while the introduction of notions of recovery has opened a potentially significant alteration of clinical-cultural thinking, its coexistence alongside presumptive chronicity and defect has led to what I have identified as paradoxes of lived experience. Persons struggle with competing messages of recovery and incurability that create confusion and intolerable "double binds," as I argue further below. As a researcher, I have been taken aback more than once by clinical assumptions regarding not only prognosis but also presumptions regarding the subjectivity and fundamental human capacities of persons diagnosed with schizophrenia.[13]

With processes of subjectivity in mind, I see the need for attention to what I am calling *cultural chemistry,* whereby culture is understood as a petri dish for the cultivation of biology, desire, meaning, social practices, and institutions that together constitute what Deleuze and Guattari (1988) call an "assemblage" that shapes response to drugs and illness. Within this cultural chemistry, psychotropic drugs are variously represented—as "mind food for gastrointestinal nutrition" in India (Ecks 2013) or as "medication for chemical imbalance" in the United States (Jenkins 2010). In the United States especially, the cultural chemistry of treatment for mental illness is complicated by deep divides across social, economic, and political interest groups of patients, doctors, advocacy groups, governmental agencies, insurance companies, and pharmaceutical corporations. Everyone has differing goals and information, and those with the most at stake—people who actually take the medications—are the most neglected. The most vital information is not to be found in the package inserts provided by drug companies, publications in health science journals, or even recent black box warnings mandated by the Food and Drug Administration but must be obtained and revealed from the perspective of the lived experience of those taking the drugs. As we shall see, determination of the social and existential facts surrounding atypical antipsychotics is culturally complicated, calling to mind Oscar Wilde's quip that "the truth is rarely pure and never simple."

## THE SUBJECTIVE EXPERIENCE OF ATYPICAL ANTIPSYCHOTICS

My ethnographic study, "Subjective Experience and the Culture of Recovery with Atypical Antipsychotics" (SEACORA), addressed the use of atypical antipsychotic medications in the United States for conditions diagnosed as schizophrenia and schizoaffective illness.[14] My primary study site was the first clinic in the United States to be organized and promoted as a Clozapine Clinic. Nevertheless, over the course of our research project, the clinical prescribing patterns expanded beyond clozapine to include other atypical antipsychotics. This chapter therefore presents the experience of persons taking a variety of these "second-generation" drugs.

Large by ethnographic and qualitative standards, SEACORA was a six-year study (1998–2004) with ninety research participants. It was conducted in northeastern Ohio in close proximity to a major research university located in an urban district consolidated in the late nineteenth century as a center for a variety of educational, medical, musical, and cultural-historical institutions, with a surrounding park and lagoon. Within this locale, many participants in our study frequented one site in particular, the Clubhouse, an architecturally elegant three-story building in operation since 1961 as a psychosocial rehabilitation center for persons who live with mental illness. One of the first such centers in the United States, it is a member of the International Network of Clubhouses, part of the social justice movement founded by Fountain House in New York City in 1948.[15] In contrast, the two clinical settings in which participants received their outpatient care were located ten minutes away in a nondescript two-story commercial building in a suburban residential area of the city. On a warm day the distance was not significant when using public transportation; however, on a blustery or snowy day during typically long winters, travel was less comfortable.

We did not rely on clinical records but rather research diagnostic criteria to identify persons with schizophrenia or schizoaffective disorders, using the Structured Clinical Interview for DSM-IV (SCID). Subjects recruited to participate did not have a recent history of substance abuse (minimally the past two years) and were in regular outpatient psychiatric treatment. The study was carried out by an interdisciplinary research team whose goal was to go wherever the study participants went on a daily basis. This meant spending days in outpatient clinical settings, the community Clubhouse, homes, fast-food restaurants, drugstores, and parks, as well as walking the streets and riding the bus. In addition to recording detailed ethnographic observations of routine activities, we took systematic notes on interactions with peers and treating clinicians, group therapy sessions, and social activities organized by the clinics and the Clubhouse. Through the ethnographic observations we learned that many of the participants had regular social contact with others who were in the study. This frequently occurred in the form of routine visits to the Clozapine Clinic, where there were daily group therapy activities and customary hanging out by participants. The group therapy sessions were facilitated by one of two nurses who worked at the clinic, and the character and content of these sessions tended to vary in relation to which nurse facilitated and who happened to be present. At the request of the female participants, there was a women's group that was organized as a forum to discuss what they agreed was better not taken up in the presence of men. During these sessions, for both men and women and women only, we recorded detailed observations and verbatim comments that are rich, poignant, and filled with instances of outright resistance and hilarity (see Jenkins 2010b). From our daily presence in the clinic we became part of the scene and got to know who was friends with whom, who was going out with whom, who were desirable (and undesirable) sexual partners, and how clinical staff were regarded.

While the Clozapine Clinic was on the second floor of a commercial office building that was nondescript, the interior social atmosphere was anything but. Exceptional paintings by clinic clients covered the walls, and bulletin boards were covered with announcements of extracurricular events and photographs from field trips and holiday parties. The social composition was a mix of clinic patients, nurses, the psychiatry director, family member volunteers, and the SEACORA team of researchers. Of course, not all the various social members were present at all times, but a usual scene might consist of perhaps thirty. Appointment times were loosely scheduled. There was a good deal of hanging around, when social interactions were informal. If not in a therapy group or individual meeting with a nurse or psychiatrist, client hanging out often had no specific activity and might not have included much in the way of conversation. Even so, people made friends and had conversations both inside and outside the clinic. In the hallways and waiting areas, some people were well-known "talkers" who tended to dominate social encounters. Abby, an imposing thirty-nine-year old Euro-American woman (diagnosed with schizoaffective disorder) was one such talker. Some of her talk was spontaneous, but much of it was canned. In the women's group, others routinely told her they were annoyed that she kept repeating the same stories. This was true of some of her jokes too. When I first met her (in 1999) she saw the opportunity to add to her audience (if not her repertoire) and greeted me with one of her standards: "Hey, when you talk to God it's called prayer, but when he talks back it's schizophrenia!" Humor was common, and the comedic aspects of clinic social interaction are discussed elsewhere (Jenkins and Carpenter-Song 2008; Jenkins 2010b). Like many clinic participants, Abby had an active relationship with her voices. While some of them bothered her and were "not nice," she was quite fond of others, particularly someone she called "Mr. Steve Stallion." The relationship she had with Steve was remarkably similar to her relationships with people in the clinic, to whom she frequently and repetitiously communicated her appreciation of how attractive they looked on any given day: "You look *so* pretty today. Did you know?" With Steve, she appreciated the way he talked to her, describing what he said to her and how she felt:

> Well, every time I put makeup on in the morning, he says, "Boy, you look pretty today. Why don't you put a little bit more here? Put a little bit more there." I go to bed at night and he always says goodnight to me. And he likes Patsy [Abby's cat]. *And* he's really cute.

That sort of talk was often a prelude to her next stock sets of comments that could get downright bawdy.

Gossip was a common social currency, for example, in comments routinely relayed to members of the research team: "I don't like her. She accused me of being a bisexual." Or, "She can't keep her pants on. Maybe it's [related to] the medication." Some comments evinced social competition and comparison, including self-references by thirty-two-year-old Brady, a semibald Euro-American man with a diagnosis of schizophrenia, who pointed out, "You'll notice I'm much higher functioning than the others around here. There's no one here that I want to even go out with." That may well have been the case, but he had already been through more than a few sexual partners at the clinic. He wasn't bitter about it, he insisted, but it hardly seemed like he had resigned from the dating scene entirely. The whole thing was confusing to him, why and how things just don't work out. He mused, "Um, I just know that I,

I just have holes in my brain [laughs]!" Leticia, a thirty-seven-year-old African American woman with a diagnosis of paranoid schizophrenia, made a habit of whizzing by what she viewed as the usual nonsense of people hanging around. She had a reputation for being "together": she was well spoken, and she dressed neatly and smartly, with carefully applied red lipstick. She wasted no time getting to the women's group to discuss what was on her mind. Not a casual "talker," she still had plenty to say when problems arose. She was also known for giving good advice and indicated she felt she got a lot of support for family or logistical problems. She had had to move because her sister was bringing too many boyfriends around, when she herself was actively dealing with her own Catholic guilt about having had premarital sex (with a man she married and later divorced). She considered that as a source of the trouble she had keeping her mind "stable." She simultaneously dismissed and entertained the possibility suggested to her by her family that the problem might have involved someone putting a spell on her. She was aware that following her divorce there had been jealousy on the part of the daughter of the man she was dating. But who knew? It could just as easily have been her ex-husband. She couldn't spend much time thinking about it. She had a brother to see every day, along with her boyfriend. She needed to get to group and get out. Unlike a lot of the people at the clinic, she was busy.

We conducted in-depth semistructured interviews with every participant during which we asked about a range of topics, including medications. On the basis of previous studies, I designed the ethnographic interview, the Subjective Experience of Medication Interview (SEMI), to be conversational and to collect narrative data about daily routines and activities, current living situation, social life to include friends and dating, work or volunteer activities, and, later in the interview, the experience, practice, and effects of taking antipsychotic medications.[16] Tables 2 and 3 summarize the clinical and sociodemographic data collected for the ninety research participants.

Taken together, the ethnic composition of the study roughly reflected the adjacent suburban areas where the two community clinics were located, with a population composed of about three-fourths Euro-American and one-fourth African American. Both ethnic groups were from lower-middle-, middle-, and upper-middle-class families and on average were forty years of age and had been ill for over twenty years, usually with multiple hospitalizations. The vast majority were clinically considered "drug treatment refractory" insofar as first-generation anti-

TABLE 2   SOCIODEMOGRAPHIC CHARACTERISTICS OF RESEARCH PARTICIPANTS
($n = 90$)

|  | Number | Percent (%) |
|---|---|---|
| Gender |  |  |
| Male | 49 | 54.4 |
| Female | 41 | 45.6 |
| Mean Years Education (SD) | 13.0 (1.9) |  |
| Mean Age (SD) | 40.7 (7.9) |  |
| Ethnicity |  |  |
| European American | 70 | 77.8 |
| African American | 20 | 22.2 |
| Marital Status |  |  |
| Single | 76 | 84.4 |
| Married/partner | 5 | 5.6 |
| Divorced/widowed/separated | 9 | 10.0 |
| Living Situation* |  |  |
| Alone | 23 | 25.6 |
| Partner/spouse | 9 | 10.0 |
| Relative/parent | 38 | 42.2 |
| Roommate | 5 | 5.6 |
| Group home | 15 | 16.7 |
| Have Children |  |  |
| Yes | 16 | 17.8 |
| No | 74 | 82.2 |
| Working Situation* |  |  |
| Not working | 54 | 60.0 |
| Half-time or less (< 20 hours) | 20 | 22.2 |
| Half- to full-time (20+ hours) | 16 | 17.8 |

*Due to rounding, percent may not equal 100.

psychotic medications had not yielded satisfactory effects. For the study overall, about 60 percent (54 participants) frequented the university-affiliated outpatient site that had been initially organized as the Clozapine Clinic.[17] In an effort to obtain more participants than could be included in the first phase of the study, we recruited subjects from an additional community clinic across town. As shown in table 3, various kinds of atypical antipsychotics were taken by the research participants. Clozapine accounted for over half (57 percent), but other drugs (Risperdal, Zyprexa, and Seroquel) were also often prescribed. I reiterate that while the present research began by specializing in treatment using clozapine, that clinic and the second community clinic utilized by our research participants prescribed many kinds of second-generation drugs.

TABLE 3   CLINICAL CHARACTERISTICS OF RESEARCH PARTICIPANTS
(n = 90)

|  | Number | Percent (%) |
|---|---|---|
| Diagnosis (SCID) | | |
| Schizophrenia | 73 | 81.1 |
| Schizoaffective | 17 | 18.9 |
| Mean age at onset (SD) | 20.6 (7.3) | |
| Mean years ill (SD) | 20.1 (8.4) | |
| Mean admissions (SD) | 7.0 (7.0) | |
| 0 | 3 (3.3) | |
| 1–5 | 46 (51.1) | |
| 6–10 | 27 (30.0) | |
| 11–15 | 5 (5.5) | |
| 16–20 | 6 (6.6) | |
| 21+ | 3 (3.3) | |
| Outpatient treatment* | | |
| ≤ 5 years | 32 | 35.6 |
| 6–10 years | 33 | 36.7 |
| 11–15 years | 22 | 24.4 |
| ≥ 16 years | 3 | 3.3 |
| Current atypical antipsychotic** | | |
| Clozaril/clozapine | 51 | 56.7 |
| Risperdal/risperidone | 16 | 17.8 |
| Zyprexa/olanzapine | 15 | 16.7 |
| Seroquel/quetiapine | 6 | 6.7 |
| Melperone | 2 | 2.2 |

* For length of treatment at current clinical site.

** Due to rounding, percent may not equal 100.

## CHEMICAL IMBALANCE: THE MASTER TROPE

The principal ethnographic concern of the study was to understand the actual experience of the research participants. Given the fundamental importance of how people conceive of mental illness to define their experience and influence the course of their illness, it is important to have a sense of what kind of problem participants thought was involved and how it affected them. Of the ninety participants, fifty (55.5 percent) used the language of "chemical imbalance" to describe the problem. A smaller number, twelve (13.3 percent), said their problem was one of "stability." Yet another third (31.1 percent) endorsed neither idea, citing a wide array of illness concepts. Speculation regarding likely causes of the problem revealed a high proportion of distinctly nonbiological ones (society, supernatural or occult forces, traumatic events), but the ultimate effect of these causes was often a "chemical imbalance." When it came to offering an explanation for how the illness works, once again and by far the most common articulation was metaphoric reference to "chemical imbalance." A commonplace for over three decades now, this metaphor is invoked to refer to virtually any psychiatric diagnosis. Mental health professionals typically spoke to participants about their problem through reference to "chemical imbalance" as a presumptive brain-based disease. Given its fluidity of application, the cultural-clinical category of chemical imbalance serves as an odd-job category in a manner parallel to that of *nervios* (see chapter 3) as deployed by Mexican-descent families. These two broad cultural categories are, however, distinctively different in cultural meaning and consequence.

Comparing the Euro-American and African American narratives about their subjective sense and use of atypical antipsychotic medications revealed differences in ideas about the problem. Euro-Americans were more likely to speak in the language of chemical imbalances, while African Americans were relatively more concerned with bodily "stability" and "balance," which has less to do with chemicals and more to do with social problems—often familial—that may or may not entail spiritual struggle or a magical spell. Ethnographic work with African American children diagnosed with pediatric bipolar or ADHD conditions by Carpenter-Song (2009a, 2009b) found that compared to Euro-Americans, African Americans were less likely to have a biomedicalized perspective on the problem. In the present study, comparing African American and Euro-American responses, the former tended not to elaborate on illness-related questions. Responses were often brief relative to other narrative data they freely offered. Analysis of the data suggests three possible interpretations of this. First, in this study African Americans eschewed commentaries on medical knowledge. In this respect, such a tendency is not dissimilar for many Euro-Americans; however, African Americans have a culturally distinct set of ideas emphasizing a different order of importance. Disavowing medical expertise, one individual was reluctant to speculate on his illness and medications, saying, "I'm not a doctor, by chance, so I couldn't really say." Second, the reluctance of many African Americans to elaborate on illness-related questions can be summarized in the notion of family or personal "business" (see also Carpenter-Song 2009b). Because illness is often deeply embedded in familial and interpersonal relationships, talking about illness may be viewed as revealing things that are, in the words of one individual, "none of their business." It may be viewed as inappropriate to air the "dirty laundry" of illness, especially to Euro-American interviewers, physicians, and others outside of the individual's family or community. This hypothesis is substantiated in the narratives of several African Americans in the study. Third, in addition to either choosing not to discuss personal business or being encouraged not to do so, it is possible that African Americans do not elaborate illness narratives because illness is just one aspect of their lives among many with which they are currently dealing. As such, illness may not hold a privileged position in the way individuals thematize themselves. One African American woman, Mattie, put it like this:

> I think I'm doing okay. I mean, I mean, it's, I have to be, I gotta be. I mean, I gotta see that I have this mental illness, but still. I'm able to go on. Like I said, believe it or not, I do a lot of things. I mean, as far as help with my mother, help with my kids, or whatever . . . a good day for me . . . to function well, to take it, business is very important to me, you know. To take care of business. Business is, being able to, I don't know the word, just taking care of business, you know. Make sure the bills are paid, all the time. Make sure this and that, everything's been placed, that's all.

Although chemical processes are a dominant theme overall, the category becomes less objective and more evidently an abstract cultural artifact when teased out. Of the fifty persons who used the language of chemical imbalance to describe the problem, forty elaborated on the meaning of chemical imbalance, invariably as a problem located within the brain. Often this involved some kind of chemical deficit (37.5 percent), abnormal levels of chemicals (37.5 percent), excess chemicals (15 percent), abnormal brain structure (12.5 percent), or "firing neurons" (5 percent). One person mentioned "juices in the brain," and another mentioned "electro-physical" problems. Frequently embedded in these responses are intricate ethnopsychological models of the body, bodily and chemical processes, medication as a useful tool in the management of symptoms, chemistry as a form of magic, chemistry as it relates to subjective, lived experience, chemistry as a domain of specialized and authoritative knowledge, and bewilderment regarding how medications work and interact with the body.

The cultural conception of schizophrenia as a chemical imbalance serves as a master clinical trope in the United States to define and organize "a complex and unwieldy bit of reality into a simple and handy form" (Malinowski 1954: 35). This is significant given that there is evidence that cultural conceptions of mental illness play a role in shaping how illness is experienced and how it is treated, as well as its course and outcome (WHO 1979; Jenkins 1988a, 1988b; Jenkins and Karno 1992; Hopper 2004). With respect to psychiatry as a culturally constituted therapeutic enterprise, the conception of mental illness as a problem of chemical imbalance operates as a key symbol that is "crucial to its distinctive organization" (Ortner 1973: 1338). As a key symbol, it performs an essential "work of culture" (Obeyesekere 1990) to signal the neurobiological mechanism of illness and to suggest the psychopharmacological strategy for its treatment. It is precisely its imprecision and openness to polyvalent interpretations that allows the cultural notion to accomplish this work and thus that appeals to patients, kin, and physicians as a symbolic interpretation of what the problem could be.

Since so much rests on the notion of balance and claims by pharmaceutical companies that taking their drug is the quickest route to regain it and since the metaphor has penetrated into the lived experience of those who take the drugs, it is worth emphasizing the sense in which the idea is cultural and metaphoric rather than empirically descriptive pathophysiological objectivity.[18] Indeed, what comes to mind is the relevance of Malinowski's (1954) famous juxtaposition of magic, science, and religion as characteristic of contemporary society with respect to the place of psychopharmaceuticals, especially when we take into account the immediacy of lived experience. This is the case because the global prominence of biomedicine has neither banished nor rendered arcane the appeal of magic and religion as refracted through scientific knowledge in what I am here calling cultural chemistry. Along with analysis of cultural processes of the subjective experience of medications, the blurred conjunction of magic-science-religion can be applied to the analysis of pharmaceutical markets and global capitalism (Jenkins 2010a: 3). Pharmaceutical corporations deploy the lure of science, magic, and religion for economic gain by incorporating these cultural elements into advertising directed at customers (clinicians and clients/users/survivors), as well as public health campaigns.[19] This marketing is disseminated across economic strata and targeted at specific subgroups for ailments both serious and minor. It constitutes a complicated social field for the study of cultural chemistry that is usefully considered in relation to notions that I have formulated elsewhere as the pharmaceutical self and pharmaceutical imaginary (Jenkins 2010a, 2010b).[20]

Indeed, while chemicals and neurons might be involved, just how this could be was mysterious. Although the trope of chemical imbalance might initially seem an untroubled description and explanation of mental illness, it is not only empty on existential grounds, but also as a matter of subjectivity. I have observed a profound struggle for interpretation as people try to understand a chemical imbalance of the brain and what psychotropic drugs are, what they do, and how they work. In sum, beyond the notion of chemical imbalance there is a remarkably imprecise and elusive quality of language and interpretation. As a matter of subjectivity, the pervasive ascription to patients of a chemical imbalance is so generalized and vague that the phrase is virtually a throwaway. It explains everything and nothing. More important, it does not take us to the actual experience of participants on medication, to the bodily feeling of chemical imbalance.

## INCREMENTAL IMPROVEMENT AS SUBJECTIVE SELF-PROCESS

Against the background of these conceptions about the mechanisms of their illness, the vast majority (77.4 percent) of participants reported that they did experience a marked subjective sense of improvement. This was perceived precisely as a comparative and relative matter in light of biographical histories of symptomatic severity and suffering, on the one hand, and previous medications they had taken, on the other. It is significant that the majority of participants are quite clear if not emphatic that their conditions had improved. As significant as that observation is, so too is attention to the temporal dimension of the process as incremental and nonlinear but no less subjectively discernible. This central finding of the study must be borne in mind as we interrogate clinical and media claims of immediate and dramatic results. The appeal of instant and clear-cut results as opposed to those that are gradual and complex has more to do with the cultural orientation of American science and medicine than the trajectories of lived experience (see M. Good 1995, 2011). Americans are not typically fond of incremental results and far prefer—in this case certainly—the appeal of the "big and bold." In fact, however, when medication led to gradual improvement over time, participants saw the need to take it regularly. This was the rationale one man gave for taking his medication "religiously." Definitive reports of improvement were given by most people in the study and were not significantly related to variations in clinical or sociodemographic characteristics. However, while the majority of participants insisted on the importance of regularly taking their medications, the African Americans exhibited a numerically greater tendency to attribute their improvement explicitly to medications.

Although their effect may be incremental, the new generation of drugs has clearly been transformative for some study participants. They described definite and striking phenomenological differences as a result of taking or switching to atypical antipsychotics. Individuals commonly framed such differences in a before-and-after narrative structure. "Before," according to this scenario, refers either to before the onset of illness or to a period of time on previous medications. "After," in all cases, refers to after taking or switching to atypicals. In the case of thirty-two-year-old Brad, who received treatment at the Clozapine Clinic, it was transformative. During an interview, I asked him how things had been for him prior to taking Clozaril.

*Brad:* It's unmitigated suffering.

*JJ:* Unmitigated suffering?

*Brad:* Yes.

*JJ:* In what respect? Could you say a little bit more about that?

*Brad:* Well, I often allude to what the soldiers had to go through in the trenches, uh, during World War I. They're, they're, when dealing with this illness, there's almost an aspect of horror to it. It's very merciless. It's very cruel. I hope that doesn't sound like hyperbole or anything. Well, I think that, I think that it's because, in some respects, it's incommunicable. It's, um, something that, *if you haven't lived through it, you can't quite completely fathom it.* That's the way it was for the soldiers back in World War I. They could never quite really convey, for those who were on the home front, really, just, the horrors of the day-to-day sensations that they had in the trenches. Um, uh, in the moonscape, where everything is turned upside down, and where perception is, um, very, um, what's the word that could I, I could use, perception is all topsy-turvy and, um, and mercy is elusive.

This young Euro-American man called the effects of clozapine "liberating" and was pleased that he had more energy to invest in "things other than the illness." He further described the effect of the medication as "serenity" and noted that in terms of social relations his "bitterness, anger, and intolerance" were gone overnight. He described other effects as gradual, occurring over a period of six months.

Brad was convinced that clozapine had done nothing less than saved his life. At the same time he reported with some hesitance problems associated with this salvation: the medication made him feel depressed, isolated, and prone to overeating. Yet he qualified these comments by noting that he didn't really know if these were medication-related effects since he was "not a doctor." Another participant, David, recalled,

"I wrote this one poem saying that when I'd gone psychotic, the agony and the suffering would make Christ look like a teenage girl in bobby socks and saddle shoes and the Catholic girl skirt with white blouse sitting at the drugstore fountain."

While the NIMH Clinical Antipsychotic Trials of Intervention Effectiveness (CATIE) study found little difference in symptom improvement when comparing older and newer antipsychotics (Lieberman and Stroup 2011), the SEACORA data do not support this conclusion. This may be accounted for in part by the fact that as a group the participants in our study regularly took their medication while the CATIE participants had typically discontinued theirs. Moreover, as a group our research participants had been "treatment refractory" for typical antipsychotics, and the CATIE researcher noted that clozapine was most effective for those whose symptoms did not improve with first-line treatment. Another factor that must be taken into account is that whereas the CATIE study did not investigate the subjective experience of medications, this is the central concern of SEACORA. Based on our data for persons living with persistent psychosis for nearly two decades, the majority reported the definitive perception that the atypical antipsychotic drugs contributed to significant improvement. They were clear that, relatively speaking, things were better. At the same time, however, numerous inadequacies were apparent. I examine these further below.

MIRACLE DRUG OR AN "AWAKENING"?

It is possible to describe more precisely the extent of the participants' perceived changes and whether they endorsed the idea that specific terms like "miracle drug" applied to their situation. Over half (54.5 percent) of the participants endorsed the idea that the antipsychotic they were taking was a "miracle drug," either spontaneously or in response to a specific question. Surprisingly, given the saturation of a clinical ideology of and discourse about the drug's efficacy that characterized the ethos of the Clozapine Clinic, this endorsement did not vary between the two clinics in which we were working.[21] Nor did gender or ethnic differences matter. However, there were slight differences in relation to the type of antipsychotic drug used. Clozapine users were most likely to think of the drug as a miracle (56.9 percent), followed by those who took Risperdal (53.3 percent), Zyprexa/olanzapine (46.7 percent), and Seroquel/quetiapine (42.9 percent).

Several examples give a sense of those who affirmed, were equivocal about, or disavowed their medication as a miracle drug. One woman was emphatic: "Clozapine is a miracle drug." And another said:

> Seroquel is a miracle drug. To stop the voices. That's a miracle to me . . . that started with me with the Zoloft. It was just like, um, one day I just got up and it's like the first thing I noticed was the birds chirping. And I was, like, it just hit me like a ton of bricks. It was the most beautiful sound I ever heard. And I just sat there and started crying, going, thank you, God. You know, I, I just appreciated the birds chirping. And it was another day, a brand new day. It just felt like a cloud had lifted. That's the only way I can explain it. It's just like a, it was like a total change, like *zvoot* [makes noise] you know. Like from night to day, it was just like a cloud lifted over me . . . then I knew I was starting on the right road.

An example of a more measured response to their medication as "possibly" a miracle drug is as follows:

> Well, I think they're on the right track. I think they're making progress in getting a medication that will help a lot, you know. I think it's gonna be a while before they get a couple medications that work for everybody. I think they'll improve in the future. I'm looking forward to seeing what they come up with. 'Cause they might find something that will improve my life quite a bit, and that's the way I feel about it. I think they did the research . . . nobody wanted to give them any money for research or anything, and they stuck to it, and now they've made history. You know, they got on TV and the news and that. So I'm very encouraged by these medications.

Finally, I provide an example of the many (45.5 percent) who disavowed or were disaffected with the notion of their medication as a miracle drug.

> Um, um, well, I don't know. Um, I don't know. I mean, you don't feel like a miracle has happened and you're cured and everything's hunkydory . . . It's not like, not like a miracle happened, you know, I still, I still have things to deal with, you know? . . . It's not a miracle . . . I used to think that . . . Clozaril wasn't doing any good, and the other medicine was the one that was doing the good. But somehow I want to believe what they're saying, that the Clozaril remains an important drug, you know.

What about awakenings? We categorized participants as having experienced an "awakening" when, either in response to a direct interview question or spontaneously, they made a narrative statement during the primary research interview indicating that they had experienced a subjective sense of substantial and global transformation from a previous illness state. Only a quarter of participants (22, or 24.7 percent) reported that they had experienced an "awakening" under this defini-tion. There were no ethnic differences in response pattern, although there was variation in diagnostic subgroups, with persons diagnosed with schizoaffective illness significantly more likely than persons with schizophrenia to have experienced an awakening (Fisher's exact, p < 0.03). The phenomenological quality of awakenings differed as well, with eighteen of the twenty-two participants describing the experience as a profound transformation of reality. There were no gender differ-ences. Below is a description of what we called a phenomenological type of awakening, though the sense of profound transformation of reality for the better was not long lasting.

> It's kind of hard. It's like trying to describe the color blue to someone who has never had sight. You know what blue is, but you don't know how to say it to make them understand. .1 just know that I'm benefiting from the way I am now versus the way I was before . . . now I know what reality is.

Finally, less common was a "social" awakening that we defined as hav-ing experienced highly significant positive transformation of social rela-tions. Only four of twenty-two participants reported an awakening of this social sort, and, interestingly, all four were female. This is too small a number to conclude that women were more oriented to sociality to begin with, but the data are suggestive in this respect.

## ARTICULATING MEDICATION EXPERIENCE

Most studies would stop at this point rather than penetrate to an under-standing of medication experience as an existential totality in the expe-riential immediacy and intimacy of everyday life. Our data allow us to enter precisely this remarkable and sometimes surprising domain, recon-structing it across the experience of our ninety participants with the sense of mapping uncharted territory. I attend to the manner in which medication is reported by persons to transform the way they are ori-ented in the world, to themselves, and to others, which I refer to as ori-entation self-processes. As evidence for these processes I focus on narra-tive elements in the ethnographic interviews, following the line in the social sciences according to which narrative is a methodological locus for understanding subjective experience and transformation of self in a cultural context (Bruner 1990; B. Good 1994; Kleinman 1988a; Pea-cock and Holland 1993; Sacks 1990; Mattingly 1998, 2010). I give par-ticular attention to three salient narrative elements that emerge from these data: (1) a series of experiential loci ranging from immediate bodily sensation to intersubjective settings of everyday life; (2) a series of frequently recurring and usually transitive verbs used to describe the action of medications and that can be organized into several groups; and (3) a description of medication experience along an expressive continuum between literal and metaphoric where the boundary between the two is often indistinct.

We have seen that in general participant explanations of how their illness works emphasize notions of balance and stability, with a locus in brain function and chemicals. With respect to how they talk about the medication's effects on them, responses tend to address both what it does and how it feels. Both explanatory and descriptive statements tend to have recourse to metaphor, though often the boundary between literal and metaphoric statements is not clearly defined. Although occasionally persons talk in terms of the "happy pills" that keep them out of the "looney bin," close examination of their language use discloses a far richer existential engagement with the medication and its effects. Some unconventional but revealing expressions occur as well, such as that mental side effects may be good while physical side effects may not be, with the meaning that from the mental side the drugs can ameliorate symptoms while from the physical side the drugs can cause unwanted and substantial weight gain.[22]

### Bodily Sensation

One of the first and most striking results of the study's inquiry into medication experience is the immediate bodily experience of the drugs, a feature often ignored in accounts of patient experience but a phenomenological bedrock of the self-processes initiated by atypical antipsychotics. The following excerpts provide a sense of the somatic feel of antipsychotics and how participants talk about the bodily experience of the perceived effects of medications.

> *Vaughn:* Like a tingling feeling. Like my body starts to go to sleep before my head . . . I know when it's about to work . . . I can feel it working through my blood system . . . I think I told you before it was like THC so my tongue gets numb and feels like it's working through the legs. It's a tingling feeling.

> *Alice:* Well, like I said, it clears up my head better. I think even emotionally, as much as I dislike it, I have to admit it does make me feel better mentally . . . It's like a freight train in your head [i.e., running powerfully along the tracks], like your head's screwed on right.

*Joyce:* Well, it makes you feel numb in your brain. Your brain goes numb but that could be from the chemical imbalance. It gives your body a kind of numbing feeling . . . It numbs my brain so I can think. It numbs your body.

*Louise:* [It's hard to] get used to—my mind being normal sometimes. Like night and day. It's a relief that I have a mind released when it was all tied up in knots. Um, it's like an orgasm. It really is. It's a release. Except it's up here [points to head].

*Sally:* I feel like I have a different body for every drug I've been on.

Unelaborated as it may be, the experience of having different bodies for different drugs cannot be regarded as peripheral to the medication experience if our goal is to understand it as an existential totality. Likewise, vivid and explicit analogies of the somatic experience as akin to an orgasm in the head or like a freight train in the head must be taken seriously. Both describe a sensation of surging within the head, in one instance experienced as a powerful release and in the other as a powerful sense of moving forward "on track" rather than in a scattered, confused, distracted manner. The sensations of tingling and numbing both in the brain and elsewhere in one's body such as the legs or bloodstream concretely indicate that the medication is working. Perhaps most striking is the apparently contradictory statement that the medication "numbs my brain so I can think," where rather than numbness being associated with diminished thought processes, it neutralizes an alienated and uncontrolled brain, thereby allowing one's rational self room to assert its capacity for thought.

## Toxicity

In another kind of medication experience, the corporal and the cognitive are in close association under the sign of toxicity in the verbs *to poison, to be doped up, to be tranquilized* or *knocked out,* or *taking "gasoline."* Also evident is the fear of being addicted, in the sense of a narcotic, or of being dependent, in the sense of needing to take it indefinitely—not unrelated concerns from the standpoint of daily life.

*Jake:* I may skip the morning or afternoon once or twice or three times a week. To kind of clear my system out. Or to clear some of the toxicity out or something, with the drugs and my biochemistry and stuff.

*Ruby:* I'm afraid my brain might be poisoned or something. . . . Sometimes I'm afraid of chemicals and all that stuff about poisoning people . . . but I take the medicine anyway. . . . my friend thinks it's real bad for us and that we become poisoned or whatever . . . sometimes I worry about the chemicals and stuff like that in your brain, and I just pray about the neurotransmitters and all that.

*Ronald:* What it basically does, it allows me to flush my inner system and allows me to wake up for the next day . . . but I'm able to flush my system and wake up and things, so it also flushes my inner system. . . . And always being tranquilized and knocked out with medicines and having people around me trying to figure me out, you know. And they can pump their drugs or drill me . . . I reverse the effects when they think like they're going to use their technologies, like you know X-ray juices through the wall, or drugs coming in and agitating. . . . Even though they want to drug me and make me witness, that's not in my life, because that's all hallucination.

*Kirsten:* Well, if I miss a dose maybe I'll start to feel a little bit, you know, that I need the medicine, but I don't want to be addicted to it either. . . . Well, sometimes I feel like I have to have it. But I don't feel like it's, you know, like you know people who are taking crack and drugs so they feel they have to have their, you know. . . . Sometimes I worry about the side effects, but I was just wondering [whether] the chemicals in the medicine, can that really affect your system or your immune system or anything?

*Mattie:* I'm glad I don't have to take anything that got me drugged. I don't want to be on drugs. . . . One day I hope that medicine is improving over the years, like I said, medicine years ago, they drugged you. They literally drugged you. This medicine now, they come where you can get alert and you're not—you know, you're real alert.

*Derek:* Worries or fears about medication? I'm afraid I might become addicted and I might need it for the rest of my life.

*Felix:* Oh, I'm kind of dumb on clozapine. If you try to figure out what time it will be five hours from now it will take me a minute or two and I might even have to use a pencil and paper because it's more difficult to put things together. But it's okay because I'm not in any trouble where I need to put things together anyway.

*Valerie:* I think I'm taking enough meds as it is. But absolutely, I don't know how I would be without it. They tried me on Depakote before the Seroquel. That stuff almost killed me. It was like I was OD-ing on it. And I couldn't get out of bed. My voice got totally slurred. My speech was totally slurred. I felt like I was slowing down. It was a terrible feeling. So I stopped, because this one day I went, "This is not right. My body is limp like a ragdoll. Something is not right." So I stopped taking it . . . the best part is, the medication they have me on now, none of it is addictive. It's short acting in your system, like if I need to be taken off it, I really like that . . . I don't like the thought of being on something that I can be addicted to.

*Enoch:* You might want to try some other medications, because it [Clozaril] does attack you when you first start using it. It makes you feel strange . . . not altogether there, kinda.

Skipping doses or stopping the medication altogether is sometimes done explicitly to clear or flush the drug out of one's system and implicitly to maintain some control over what one puts into one's body. A sometimes palpable ambivalence about one's need for the drug stands out in many of these remarks, and this will become even more evident when I discuss the social lives of medications below. Yet for the most part the atypical antipsychotics come across better in this respect than typical ones, including Loxitane, Thorazine, Haldol, or the antidepressant Prozac.

## Thought Processes

The intimate connection between bodily experience and mental presence implied in comments such as that medication "numbs my brain so I can think" and concerns about poisoning and addiction bring to the fore the narrative deployment of verbs that describe the effect of medication on orientation to one's own thought process. The next group of verbs to which I will call attention refers to how the medication "straightens," or "clears." The following statements are typical.

> *Amelia:* I get psychotic is what they call it. I call it just a clear head. I see things clearer, I see myself as Christ figures. They say, you're crazy, man.
>
> *Daria:* It [medication] straightens up, it's supposed to straighten up the thoughts.
>
> *Mattie:* I feel, uh, clear headed. . . . What I go through, it's confusing. I have, uh, confusion and different things, but what I'm saying is clear headed. . . . It's just the best way I can explain it is clear headed, I'm alert, I'm alert.
>
> *Valerie:* You know, I'm just clearer. Back in the real world, so to speak. Which I'm very grateful for . . . when I basically wasn't really functioning well, I was just kind of like there. Not really listening to the conversation, nothing was sinking in. I was kind of in a fog so to speak.
>
> *Bertha:* It keeps me together and helps my thinking, my bad thoughts. It seems like it works on my mind. Like it holds it together.
>
> *Paul:* It really helps me have clear thinking. They told me this will help me have clear thinking. And I thought, how can a pill make your thoughts clearer? But now I understand.

Associating the psychotic state itself with clarity of mind is not common in this group, among whom symptoms were more or less successfully controlled. Thoughts that are straight, clear, and alert or that allow one to be in "the real world" stand out in these passages, in contrast to confusion and fog. The one outlier in this group of comments invokes coherence in the sense of holding the mind together and suppressing bad thoughts, but it is not much of a stretch to connect this kind of coherence with mental clarity.

In another category of effect related to thought and mental activity, the relevant verbs are that medication "mellows" or "slows" like a "mental anesthetic."

*Amelia:* I used to go in spinning states. I don't have those as often . . . you just kind of spin in your head and your brain, and your brain races, but it can't do anything.

*Alice:* It slows my head down. The medicine slows you down. Like I can't concentrate for anything, but the clozapine numbs you mentally, it's like a mental anesthetic. But the doctor told me the reason I gained weight is because it doesn't only slow your head down, it slows you physically down too. It slows your entire body down. It slows your metabolism down. I ate more food then [before medication] than I do now, and I'm heavier now than I was then. . . . It slows my head down. It stops the bad voices from taking effect as much as they would. As much as they were.

*Joline:* In the sense that it slows everything down, so there's not as much pressure. I was at the store, and I started hearing all this noise around me, and I thought, "Oh no. Oh, thank God, I've got my medication."

*James:* It kind of deadens me.

*Daria:* It helps the racing thoughts and helps me sleep and helps me to relax . . . I used to have racing thoughts and it helps that, I don't have those racing thoughts.

*Geoffrey:* I think they kind of keep my mind from racing. A lot of times it helps just to slow down and not try to do too much at once.

*Paul:* It will slow things down, so you're not racing, so you're not anxious that you're having thoughts come too quick and overlapping and everything.

The emphasis in these excerpts on clarity and velocity of thought does not imply that symptoms such as visual and auditory hallucinations are negligible by comparison. Nor does it suggest that the medication does not address the latter. I hypothesize instead that hallucinations are by definition ego-alien experiences and on some level less frightening and disturbing than confusion and the racing of what are unmistakably one's own thoughts. It is also possible that for these persons the current medication addresses their thought processes more observably or dramatically than was the case with their previous medications. While they mention concerns that the medication may poison their brain, have toxic side effects, or be addictive, by comparison effects of the older generation of antipsychotics are far more often described as making one feel doped up or dopey, tranquilized, knocked for a loop, knocked out, in the ozone, or drugged.

## Stability and Balance

Beyond the effects of medication on immediate thought processes, we can identify a domain of utterances that is a degree more reflective, existential, and metaphoric. Among the relevant verbs are *regulates, smooths,* or *stabilizes.* These expressions are often related to the dominant metaphor of the illness as chemical imbalance, so that the effect of the drug is to establish or reestablish the balance. For example:

> *Jerome:* I have a dead part in a part of my brain, so because of that dead part, I don't think normally . . . they [drugs] provide chemicals in your brain that will change your thinking . . . I think they are reacting with other chemicals in my brain to produce more of certain types or less of certain types.

> *Katherine:* Well, I think I was born with it. They say you're really born with it, but the chemical imbalance doesn't show up till you're older. . . . Well, it [the drug] replaces the chemicals in the brain.

> *Candace:* It's just like a chemical imbalance. I mean it's just like diabetes. You have to take your insulin and that's that . . . my brain doesn't make that chemical . . . I think it keeps some kind of chemical in my brain and it gets the chemicals working. . . . It's just they give me some kind of chemical that I need.

> *Geoffrey:* I guess it works or affects the dopamine in the brain. And if the dopamine is at the wrong level, you can start having symptoms. So I guess it kind of regulates the dopamine in your brain.

> *Thomas:* Well, I guess it changes your brain chemistry. I guess your brain chemistry is out of bounds, and it roughly, uh, reconfigurates it somehow.

> *Delbert:* I don't know. I guess it, um, I guess it works with the juices that are in the brain, you know, the chemicals that are in the brain . . . maybe it, um, regulates it. Regulates those juices or maybe I might be lacking something. . . . Maybe lacking something that you're supposed to have, like, um, maybe like them endorphins in the brain or something like that.

> *Karl:* I think what it does is, I think it interreacts with the chemistry of my brain, and there's like a balancing act going on.

However, in some instances the metaphor of balance is used not in reference to chemicals but in reference to experience, as in the following examples.

*Jordan:* It keeps me balanced. Like a scale, you know.

*Jane:* It smooths my mood.

*Katherine:* My moods have been pretty stable.

*Laszlo:* The more they put me on meds, the worse the seizures got, but I balanced it out with the new medication, Clozaril. . . . It's smoothed and controlled my microprocess . . . I get bewildered at times and the medication just does its function of keeping me back to the "s" word—stable.

*Mattie:* I know I'm mentally stable enough to get through life right now.

*Felix:* Sometimes it's almost like it can balance out, you know, as bad as the illness is, sometimes I feel pretty good.

*Ellen:* It ain't doin' nothing right now. I can't get level. Shit, I can't get level for NOTHIN'. 'Cause I'm not a level person right now. I'm too many peoples right now. I'm not level.

*Bertha:* It helps me to be stable. And when I don't take it, I can't function. I notice I need it. It keeps me stable.

*Nate:* Uh, stable—not better, but stable.

Closely related to the ideas of stability and balance insofar as these are states that need to be maintained are utterances defined by how medication "keeps" one in a steady state. Interesting in this respect is the verb *to keep,* which is multivalent in its referents. Most common is a variant of the articulation that it keeps the person stable, together, balanced like a scale, at the same level all day, busy or active, out of the hospital, from being depressed and anxious, from getting confused, from hearing voices, from being crazy. Others say that the medication keeps some kind of chemical in their brain, that it keeps their mind from racing or keeps everybody happy. Some participants described the effect as keeping their "head screwed on right" or "the mental disease indoors." Yet another person said, "[It] keeps me on top of my parents' kingdoms." When the primary verb employed to describe positive medication effects is *helps,* a common articulation was that it helps keep the person busy or active, that it helps keep up appearances, the apartment clean, or the person clean. Participants also stated that it helps with the hallucinations, helps have clear thinking, helps not to obsess (though it screws up the memory), or helps to function.

## Control

Given clozapine's association with control, it is unsurprising that participants often said that the medication keeps symptoms under control, keeps the body controlled, or keeps one from lack of control. The verb *to control* itself may refer to one's life, one's thoughts, one's symptoms, or oneself. One participant said that medication "controls red blood cells in my mind." We also heard "God is in control" and "Illness has control of me." However, the notion of control was most often heard with reference to trying to identify the locus of agency.

*Jake:* I try to control my thinking and my emotions and my problems and stuff like that by acting and behaving and thinking as normally as possible, in normal society as most people do, you know what I mean, a large percentage of people do . . . I think maybe it is biochemical and maybe the medicine itself, the biochemical makeup of the medicine actually affects my body chemistry and helps me to control and discipline myself, so whether or not its changing behavior is due to medicine, or if it's due to some psychological effect, or it's due to both, I don't know. Might be the medicine acts as a placebo.

*Amelia:* I'm real, real scared to be without them [the medications]. I feel handicapped by the fact that I'm going to be miserable without them . . . I feel handicapped by the thought that I have to take them. And I'm trapped if I don't take them.

*Alice:* I was hurting everybody, and I couldn't control it. I couldn't control my feelings. Or my emotions. I couldn't control myself [before the clozapine]. If I didn't take my medicine I would be totally out of control. . . . Oh, yeah, you can control mental illness. You just got to take care of yourself. Good hygiene. You can't let yourself go. If you let yourself go, your mental illness won.

*Sarah:* Just control the illness, control the chemicals. It [medicine] controls the dopamine and the serotonin, chemicals in the brain. I'm not sure how they do it, but they just do that . . . I think the medication can control it. I think there are things you can do to help yourself, but I mean everything else is beyond your control. But I think it was something, that no matter what I would have done, it would have happened. Especially if it's genetic, 'cause that's something you have no control over. . . . It's made [my emotions] under control. I'm not hostile anymore.

*Thomas:* Well, like I said, I have coping strategies. Other than that, I don't have any control. I take my medication. See a doctor, things like that. Those affect the intensity of the experience at the particular time, that's all. To think well, maybe—I hope I don't lose control of myself, you know. So I just—usually it goes away after a while. I get up and say I got to go. I say excuse me. I try to be polite and all, while I'm sitting there going . . . yeah.

*Valerie:* If I could have, I would not have let it happen. I never even saw it coming. But it's not like I'm just lying around either. At a point, I was. I had no control over it. But now I'm doing everything I can to stay limber and active [to avoid weight gain] . . . I don't want a medicine to make you feel like you're in the ozone layer. Like, I once went to the dentist and had to take this for the pain. I took it once, and I went, "Uh-uh." Because I know that I was not in control. That's what I don't like. And I guess that's what I'm kind of afraid of, you know. Some people take all sorts of drugs, and I don't know how they can maintain control.

*Karl:* I think it's under control now because of the medication. I think part of the Clozaril—I wasn't able to control it, even if I wanted to, I couldn't . . . and schizophrenia can control you. It gets you to do things a normal person wouldn't do. And I don't know how it is for you, but I know how it is for me with schizophrenia. I think it is beyond a person's control. I mean, if they could control it, then a lot of people that come down with it would not be coming down with it simply because they could control it, but you can't.

In these instances people struggled to situate themselves existentially within the complex constellation constituted by whether one can control and discipline oneself, whether the illness has control of one's life and behavior, whether the medication is controlling the illness, or whether the medication is helping one to control the symptoms and their consequences in everyday life.

## Discipline and Accountability

The discourse of control is closely associated with that of discipline and accountability. Participants say both that getting well requires self-discipline and that taking the medication is a way of disciplining oneself. The degree to which one can rely on medication in relation to one's own efforts and will to be well is more complex than this, however, including the possibility of relinquishing oneself to mental illness as if it were a form of temptation.

*Felicia:* I think maybe if I just decided not to mix myself up, by making a choice, I could either live a normal life or mess it up. I decided to mess it up, turn against the skies, you know, like Adam and Eve with the apple and stuff. They weren't supposed to, and they ate the apple, kind of what's happened to me, you know. . . . Sometimes I blame myself for my illness—I blame myself for confusing myself when I was little.

*Candace:* When I'm sick, no one can help me. I have to help myself. Well, there are people there to talk to you, but you got to be strong.

*Mattie:* And I gotta be able to maintain, so this medication gonna help me, I gotta help myself.

*Steven:* Well, a regular man, he's got stress, too. Working all day or whatever, but if you don't keep yourself busy on medication, it's just gonna slow you down. Because the medication's working with you, but you help yourself by working a couple nights a week. It'll get the energy. This way you won't feel like you're a couch potato. But if you move yourself, your body fast enough, the medication will help you. I'm not telling you it's gonna make you high or anything like that, but your strength and your working, you know.

*Paul:* Clozaril makes it possible, but you do the work, you know, with the mental illness struggle.

*Karl:* And the one who blows it is yourself. Who blows that opportunity to be out? You can't blame anybody else. You can only blame yourself, and maybe attribute it to your disease a little bit. 'Cause that's what it is, you know, it's a disease. But you can't die from it.

## Identity and "Normality"

It is a short step from concerns with discipline, accountability, and responsibility to overt concern with self and identity (Whyte 2009). We encountered statements such as the following: "I feel like a new person" (Candace); "The whole thing is I am a different person from then" (Paul); "I'm all in one piece" (Enoch); "I'm still me" (Nate). Problems with identity can be associated with the illness, as in "I feel uncomfortable about myself and, you know, having mental problems" (Kirsten), or with medication effects, as in "I'm not quite myself—if I talk to Dr. R maybe he can cut my medication and I start doing like I used to, on the get-go" (Alyssa). Statements of identity can be quite generic and more or less directly confounded with effect of the illness.

*Jake:* I like being myself, okay. I like being the kind of person I am. That might be part of the illness . . . I consider myself an individual, but I think I have some unique qualities. I believe other people have unique qualities, but on the other hand, I think we also all have things in common as human beings.

Other identity statements are more explicitly connected with the effects of illness and/or medication.

*Clark:* I used to think I was other people beside myself, and now I don't have that problem.

*Geoffrey:* I felt like I was outside myself or something, looking at myself from the outside. Like I was outside, out of my mind—like myself but I was outside of myself. Like I was hearing voices and stuff. I didn't really know what to make about that one, just because there was something wrong with me or I was just bad, like I was possessed or something.

*Karl:* When I was on Navane, I felt like I had a different body for every drug
I'd been on, and now I feel like I have my own body and my own mind. . . .
Sometimes I feel like my old self. The self I lost years ago to schizophrenia.

The thematization of identity links up with a discourse of normality
versus abnormality that while not exactly a preoccupation of most participants is often not far from the surface. Certainly the group therapy
sessions we observed were dominated by discourse on psychopharmacology and primarily oriented to the elusive "normal." This is true for
psychotropics ranging from antipsychotics to sleep drugs, as Martin
(2010) traces in the culturally peculiar search for "normal" sleep cycles.
In our study, the majority (64, or 71.1 percent) invoked the notion of
normality at some point in their interviews. Exceedingly rare was the
sentiment, "Sometimes I think I don't know what's wrong with being
psychotic. . . . Sometimes I think I don't know why people think psychotic is so wrong" (Amelia). Indeed, underlying the romanticization of
schizophrenia in popular culture is the presumption that the normal is
fundamentally boring. From the standpoint of the suffering inherent in
the illness experience, normality is by contrast a value and an aspiration
for everyday life, or at least a taken for granted baseline of the way
things are, have been, or could be.

*Jake:* I just try to act normal behavior, think normal, feel normal. Not just
go through the motions of being normal but live normal, as much as I can
. . . so it's not just a matter of going through the motion, or just acting—
that could be a beginning—but it's actually being as normal as possible.

*Thomas:* Well, I'm interested in what normal people think about—how they
view things, you know. I'm very reluctant to get involved with a bipolar
since I had that bipolar girlfriend. They can bring a lot of trouble, and I
guess I'm more comfortable around normal people than other mentally ill
people, except for ones I've known a while. But in general, I think I'm just
as bigoted as anyone else about mentally ill people.

There is a recognition of not being normal, sometimes with the sense
that the person was not aware of being abnormal prior to entering
treatment (isn't it normal to talk to oneself, or to hear voices?), as well
as of having to act normal in certain situations and this being more or
less of a strain. It is in this context that we must understand the following statements about medication and normality.

*Kirsten:* I'm not envious, I just wish I had a normal kind of background . . .
I wish I wouldn't have to take it. I wish I could just have a normal life. . . .
You know, I get depressed, I feel that if my life was different, if I had a
normal life like everyone else, I would not focus so much on the illness.

*Shirley:* I think I'm pretty normal. Luckily, you know, doing the medication, going to work, and going to school, and functioning like a normal person and everything. I feel pretty normal. I really do.

*Reginald:* Like, I feel normal taking it . . . I just can't think normally, like you want to feel normal but you can't really help yourself.

*Jerome:* Well, I know I have to take it to feel normal now . . . I [also] smoke cigarettes and drink coffee to feel normal. Well, because I need the nicotine and caffeine to feel normal.

*Katherine:* It's by far the best medicine I've ever been on. It makes you the most realistic. Even when I was on the Trilafon I would look in the past and say, "How could I have a mental illness because I was always so normal?," but on the clozapine I can look back and see how sick I used to be . . . I just feel more normal on the clozapine.

*Candace:* Keeps me not crazy, actually. Not weird, I mean, it makes me healthy. . . . It also made me gain a lot of weight, but be *crazy or fat. I choose fat.*

*Mattie:* I mean, in other words, I know I have a mental illness, but it's [medication] making me feel somewhat sane. Because normally what's in me stays in me because I can't talk to nobody about what goes on with me, because they would judge me.

*Bertha:* And then he said that I was doing good for me to be on my medication. I didn't seem like I was a mental patient or nothing like that, he said I have plenty of sense and that made me feel good, because people want me to think that I'm crazy but I'm not crazy. I know what I be seeing because I have mental illness, that don't mean that I'm crazy . . . [I want the medication to] make me stay stable and feel normal . . . make me back to normal.

*Nate:* It returns to feeling normal. Without the medication there's like, for a better word I'd choose "darkness," like a darkness of the mind and the medicine drives it off, gets rid of it—I might not be describing this real well, but that's my best.

## Everyday Life

Finally, one step beyond the overt concern with normality, we encountered articulations that described medication effects in everyday life in vivid and often poignant terms.

*Felix:* The clozapine has changed my mind many times. I'll be having a bad day and I'll come home and I'll have everything else completely fine. And I like that, you know—that it's not 5:30 and I'm still complaining about something that happened at 11:00. Or I wake up the next day still thinking that I had an awful day yesterday. The clozapine helps a lot. I just take it every day and I'm not having nearly as many problems with noises as I used to. It used to be one horrible symphony of annoying sounds.

And It's broken up now into little bits. You can deal with it a little bit at a time. And it's quieter.

*Ellen:* I got to find myself again, 'cause right now, I'm lost. Okay? But see, I know something goin' to happen, but right now, I'm lost. Like I say, them ambitions and things that I expect to want to do, right now, see, I lost that. No, I don't have that mood right now. I'm just goin' with the flow and whatever. I'm lost right now, but somethin' is gonna happen. I don't know when, I don't know how. But right now, just standin' nowhere, just lettin' these days go.

*Enoch:* Well, see, when I ran out of pills to take, I didn't sleep at *all*. I was up all around the clock for a couple of days. Then I tried to walk over the footprints in the sand, I barely made it back [to normality].

*Karl:* I like to say that the Clozaril is a mental dam that stops the flow of schizophrenia. The hallucinations are very seldom now. The paranoia is weakening considerably. I'm not really delusional in my thinking. I think my thoughts are more in line with reality. I am not raging out at people, accusing them of things. I'm not that loner anymore, walking the city streets, living on the streets . . . I couldn't forget on my own. By an act of my own law, I couldn't forget. But Clozaril has helped me forget the misery of the past. The craziness of it. Honestly, I don't think about it. And even if I tried to think about it, I couldn't remember how it was back then. . . . Some of the major things I can remember, but you know ten years ago I might have still been living in my mind. Now, ten years later, it's not living in my mind anymore. It's kind of like it died. It's like the memory died. It's not there anymore.

Two points are critical to understanding the domain of medication experiences defined by the kinds of responses considered here. In 1984 the anthropologist Lorna Rhodes published an article about the medication experience of psychiatric patients. Her exposition was framed in terms of the metaphors people used to describe their psychotic experience. She organized these metaphors into categories: blockage/release, clearance/fogging, distortion/straightening, poison/nurturance, breakage/remediation, and immobility/immobility. Our data include similar metaphorical expressions, with the difference that neither breakage/remediation nor immobility/mobility were prominent domains for us, whereas balance/imbalance and slowing/racing were relatively clearly elaborated. Given the twenty-year gap between these studies, it would interesting to know if these differences corresponded to a difference between the first-generation antipsychotics in use at the time of Rhodes's work and the second-generation drugs taken by our study participants. Unfortunately, to determine that would require analysis of both sets of data, as well as some means of taking into account differences in social characteristics and regional background among participants, the effect of the clinical ideology of biopsychiatry[23] that became consolidated in the interim and is likely to have effects on the discourse of medication experience in subtler ways than the obvious trope of chemical imbalance, and changes in expressive conventions among research participants and in the cultural milieu during the twenty years between studies. As for the metaphors themselves, what is evident from the research data is that often they are what might be called closely held metaphors in the sense that the usage is close to literal. Thus "it clears my head" or "it stops my mind from racing" is more readily understood as literal, as opposed to "it clears the fog from my head" or "it stops the runaway stagecoach in my mind." Likewise, occasional metaphors such as clozapine as a dam holding back the flow of schizophrenia or a freight train running through the brain are phenomenologically vivid but not deeply constitutive of a discourse of medication experience.

Further, I have chosen to understand the material on medication experience in terms of a discourse that integrates the use of metaphors with the deployment of verbs describing the action of drugs and to highlight the elaboration of substantive themes at several levels of analysis. To summarize, these themes are bodily sensation, toxicity, clarity and velocity of thought, balance, control, discipline, identity, normality, and daily life. My point is that these are not to be understood as a series of discrete themes or topics but as an existential totality weaving together interrelated levels of meaning and experience. At each of these levels medication experience is intertwined with orientational processes that taken together define the self and one's transformed place in the world. Bodily sensation produced by the medication and apprehension about poisoning and addiction are palpable and indeed inside one's skin. Concerns with clarity and velocity of thought are subjectively immediate, perhaps invoking descriptive metaphors but without need for interpretation. Balance is both an interpretive concept and a feeling, a metaphor in which the notion of physical vertigo extends to both an effort to understand the cause of illness and a disrupted subjectivity. Control encompasses the self insofar as it is one's self that is out of control and struggles for control, on one's own behalf and/or with the assistance of medication. Discipline is a means of control that can be embraced or abandoned. It can be expressed as the discipline of thoughts, emotions, actions, and symptoms but also as the discipline of adhering to a medication regimen. Identity is in part contingent on control and discipline, because it is not only being/becoming someone or remembering who one is, but more particularly being a person with mental illness and faced by its stigma. Identity is also a fully social and intersubjective issue and hence raises the concern with normality as simultaneously a problem, a standard, and a value specifically having to do with living among and in relation to other people. Finally, normality faces its tests and challenges in the kind of instances recounted in the final set of excerpts that open on moments of everyday life where possibilities are realized or foreclosed in ways unforeseeable by those who are not afflicted. Thought process, self, and social life are all represented in the discourse of medication experience, each element in relation to all the others and with profound consequences for existential coherence and the possibility for a meaningful life where the suffering of psychosis is held in check.

## SOCIAL RELATIONSHIP TO MEDICATION: SELF-PROCESSES OF ATTACHMENT AND ANIMATION

While our data on the ways in which people experience their medication were surprising insofar as they constituted emergent evidence of an existential totality of self-processes, it should perhaps come as no surprise that persons also develop what can properly be conceived as a social relationship with their medication. The "odd couple" social relationships created by regularly taking medication provide yet another frame for the specification of distinctly cultural dimensions of psychopharmacology. Whyte, Van der Geest, and Hardon (2003) have formulated the materiality of medicine (*materia medica*) in terms of the "social lives" of medicines with respect to their uses and consequences. In their view, the materia medica that should be currently of greatest anthropological concern are commercially manufactured drugs produced by pharmaceutical companies and disseminated to every part of the globe. Besides the intended bodily effects, they note that pharmaceutical medicines have effects that entail nothing less than changing "minds and situations and modes of understanding" (3–4). The strong version of this argument is that medicines, as material things, have "social lives" in the sense that things and people mutually constitute one another (Appadurai 1988).

### Anthropomorphosis and Personification of Medications

The anthropomorphosis of both psychotropic drugs and psychiatric disease is widely promoted in psychopharmacological advertising. The well-known Zoloft blob has been reproduced as an utterly bland yet rhetorically powerful embodied representation. How can a disease or a pill "be" (or be like) a (nondescript) person? But these generics have a face, changeable emotions, and capacity for movement. The antidepressant Zoloft blob is well-known as a nondescript entity with "eyes" that morphs from unhappy to happy, advertised to combat a "chemical imbalance": "When you know more about what's wrong, you can help make it right."[24] The television and magazine advertisements for the antipsychotic Abilify (ariprazole) by Bristol-Myers Squibb (marketed by Otsuka Pharmaceuticals America) have taken the anthropomorphizing of psychotropics a step further by marketing the product to capture the market for depression as an "adjunctive therapy" when an antidepressant alone is "not enough." Having tracked pharmaceutical marketing campaigns for some time, I was struck by the ubiquity of these ads as a particularly disturbing development. Depression is anthropomorphized as a dark blue blob-being following (virtually stalking) a woman as she makes her domestic rounds to care for her house and family.[25] She has an ever-present relationship with this personified being that is configured primarily as a power struggle over "who" is in charge: the woman or "her depression." The narrative accompanying the ad repetitively speaks in the possessive case, "my depression." The boundary between person and illness is murky, but it is clear they live together in uneasy tension in which the drug (which in other Abilify ads is also personified as a powerful being) intervenes to draw the line for "who's in charge."

## Self, Medication, and Illness

Narrative analysis of data from the SEACORA project suggests a complex conjunction of subjectivity among the self, the medication, and the illness, with overlap and indeterminacy such that sites are fluid and ineffable. This mélange is illustrated in figure 1. Figure 2 is an illustration of factors that participants perceived as critical in processes of improvement.

The "power" and "agency" of the medication not only "lies in person's perceptions of these qualities as resident within a given medication," as Whyte and colleagues empirically identify; it also is a quality of intimacy between persons and medications. Here another set of key verbs becomes relevant, including *reassure, show, like, give,* and *quiet.* For example, a thirty-two-year-old Euro-American man, Ronald, speaks of his medication as a knowing presence and refers to the medication as the arbiter of reality.

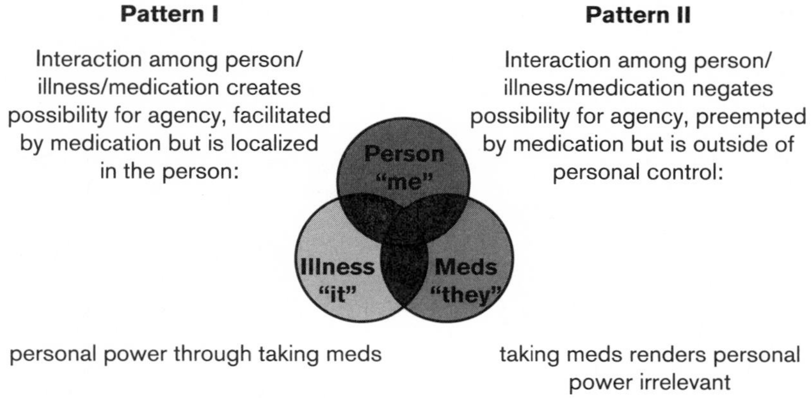

**Pattern I**

Interaction among person/
illness/medication creates
possibility for agency, facilitated
by medication but is localized
in the person:

**Pattern II**

Interaction among person/
illness/medication negates
possibility for agency, preempted
by medication but is outside of
personal control:

personal power through taking meds

taking meds renders personal
power irrelevant

FIGURE 1. Experiential mélange of person-illness-meds.

It [medication] reassures me. . . . It shows me that reality is indoors. When you go outdoors that's even a more burst of reality. But like if I'm laying down thinking I'm fighting this and that and I've got the front lines for the civil war and I'm loading cannons and I'm doing crazy things in Korea or Nam. And it . . . this is dead, hallucinations. It's not real [laughs] . . . Indoors means it's a happier place. Because outdoors can be very unbearable, to the death, you know.

In another instance, a forty-year-old woman, Alice, taking Clozaril feared "bad effects" such as agranulocytosis. She imagined that an "attack" could occur if "it [medication] doesn't like you anymore." People taking antipsychotics also described the effects as enabling them to interact socially, particularly with their families, in ways they otherwise could not. One person described this as the medication calibrating "spells" he would have in which he would "think negatively, like I'm dying or I'm going to. You'll have spells like that . . . and this medicine and stuff leads to one thing: family business" (Delbert). For him the critical feature of the medication was that it helped to differentiate "the ones you really should be with" from the ones (hallucinatory or not) who mean no good. Medication was an arbiter of the social and moral status of persons, pointing to who one should attend to or disregard.

### Supernatural and Magical

In some cases the social dimensions may be embedded in supernatural or magical forms of transformation. A forty-one-year-old African

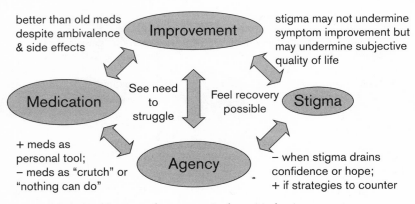

FIGURE 2. Relationship among factors perceived as critical to improvement.

American woman, Ruby, was as tenacious in taking her medication as she was unmovable in her stance that her trouble was not really "schizophrenia," as her doctor indicated, but a satanic "hex" placed on her by her stepfather, in collaboration with her mother, when she was a small child.

> They say they got the power to do that from my mother. She's with Satan. She, um, had me by her boyfriend, and from what I understand, my stepfather or her husband got real upset because she had gotten pregnant by another man. So he told her that he was gonna put "triple six" on her. And she said, "If I were you, I'd put it on that baby I'm carryin'." Said, "'Cause you don't want to go through what I'm gonna put you through." So she got on his side and together they ostracized me and put me, you know, they put me in a—a—foster home when I was born. An orphanage home. And he went out and got two other girls pregnant. And he told her—he said, "now, we even." He called me a bastard and dummy and stuff like that . . . there's different ways people say about doing black magic. Different kinds. White magic. Black magic. Different types. Yourself or to cause harm to somebody. They all [involve] Satan.

During the course of this interview, two sessions of an hour and a half each, Ruby let me know that she had "discovered" that the medication "got the power" to quiet the demons stirred up by the "666s." So, she said, "I never forget about [taking] it." For her, it was the way to make things "even." She was aware that her psychiatrist did not put much stock in her theory and told me she had decided it was best not to spend much time talking to him because he didn't "get it, he don't know better." For his part, the psychiatrist remarked to me once in the clinic hallway that this woman was a "good candidate" for atypical antipsychotic medication because she "takes it even though she doesn't have good insight. Normally that wouldn't happen. You don't see it. But in this case I think she'll stay [on the treatment regimen]." This physician statement implies that if he were to equate "lack of insight" to "lack of compliance," then the clinical logic would be to use a different medication (possibly a depot injectable antipsychotic) or to hold different clinical expectations regarding the likely course of treatment.

Other participants integrated the social qualities of taking medication into their relation with a monotheistic god or demon. Ruby, for example, added during her interview, "I just pray about the neurotransmitters and all that. I know it seems kind of stupid, but . . . " Mattie reported that she prayed to God daily that she "can keep medication." She understood the fact that she was able to maintain a regular supply as an affirmative response to her prayers, saying, "God looking out for me." Valerie was convinced that medication was a miracle directly attributable to God for which she also gave daily thanks. A male participant, Samuel, prayed for the "spell" placed on him to be broken and felt that his prayers succeeded both because of the medication and because of his active involvement in prayer: "I pray and when I wake up, it's gone . . . the spell is gone." Ketherine noted a change of heart; first, she said, "I thought I was demonically possessed," but she eventually came to the realization that the combination of good friends and her medication had "broken" the possession, reasons she cited for staying closely aligned with both. In such cases, God becomes a fourth element folded into the intimate self-medication-illness relationship.

## Interiorization of the Clinic

A final relational quality of medication is "interiorization of the clinic"—a kind of societal embodiment that involves not only the ingestion of medication but also the incorporation of the clinical ideology as transmitted by doctors, other service providers, and the myriad social actors who claim moral and working knowledge of mental illness and its treatment. In this context the medication is a kind of benefactor in the sense that, as Kirsten put it, "They say that it [medication/Clozaril] gives your life back to you. . . . [And] I feel like that." This effect is possible in part because, though unimaginable a few decades ago, the primary referent in psychiatric and psychological language for therapy has moved from "psychotherapy" to "pharmacotherapy" as the latter has become preeminent in terms of sheer frequency of "treatments" actually offered. Previously, no matter what the modality (psychoanalytic, psychodynamic, cognitive-behavioral, etc.), psychotherapy has always been practiced and understood as interpersonal. Now the term *pharmacotherapy* is widely employed *as if* prescribing psychotropic medication were on a par with psychotherapy. While clearly symptoms must be elicited and monitored and prescriptions must be called in to pharmacies, what happens as a social matter of engagement when you have a "therapy" and there's no one to interact with? Not much, if the pharmaceutical imaginary has been transduced by the social/relational quality of psychotropic medications evident in the data we obtained.

Given the inherently social nature of humans, it is anthropologically unsurprising, then, that people anthropomorphize their medications and develop a social and psychological relationship with "it" or "them." This relationship is intricately complicated by the unknowable and mysterious conjunction of the self, the illness, and the medication (see figure 1 above). What is the "it"? Medication? Disease? Myself? How as a matter of experience can these three (four, if we include God) be separable? How, as an entangled process of the self, do "we" all get along? Is this self-process cooperative or embattled, foreign or familiar, fixed or in flux? The narratives of research participants show that the process of taking medication is one in which the proper social relations must be actively managed.

## PARADOXES OF LIVED EXPERIENCE WITH PSYCHOTROPIC DRUGS

Ultimately, the management of proper social relations must take place in the context defined by several paradoxes of lived experience generated by psychopharmaceutical treatment that create significant ambivalence in the process of recovery from psychosis (table 4). Perhaps the most wrenching dimension of subjectivity in relation to taking antipsychotic medications is the despair and alienation created by the paradox of "recovery without cure." When prescribed these medications in the United States, patients are nearly always told that they must take them for the rest of their lives to alleviate symptoms and avoid relapse (see Dumit 2012 for elucidation of pharmaceutical regimes as "drugs for life"). They are explicitly given the grim news that there can be no "cure"—only management—of their condition. We can hold in abeyance the questions of whether interminable treatment is empirically justified longitudinally given the right personal strategies and peer support, or

TABLE 4 PARADOXES OF LIVED EXPERIENCE FOR PERSONS TAKING ATYPICAL
ANTI-PSYCHOTICS

- Recovery *without* cure
- Stigma *despite* recovery
- "Crazy" *or* "fat"
- Fault-free biochemical disease *yet* characterological "defect"
- Sexless and genderless *yet* desire and gendered conflicts
- Social developmental problems *yet* pharmaceutical "management" without psychotherapy
- Felt need for medication *in face of* fears of addiction, toxicity, and chronicity

how it contributes to sustained profit flow for pharmaceutical companies. Persons invariably process this clinical information with great ambivalence and conflict. One woman drew a picture of herself without eyes: "[I had] blinded myself to the fact that the medication could not 'cure' me." In an example of poignant confusion about the possibility of cure, a Euro-American man said:

> I'd like to be healthy, and I'd like my illness to be in remission. And I'd like to be cured of my illness if it's possible, and, uh, if, to the best of my knowledge, is that there's not a cure for schizophrenia. But, like I said, it depends on the doctor's philosophy too. Some say there are cures for all illnesses, some say there aren't. And some say you can put illnesses in remission, and cure them, so I don't know.

The deep desire for cure is no different in Ghana, where the anthropologist Ursula Read finds that Ghanaians regularly seek "hospital medicine" for mental illness—often *before* going to the local shrine. The paradox of "recovery without cure" thus poses a problem for global mental health in low- and high-income countries alike. As Read (2012: 438) observed, "Campaigns to scale up mental health services in low-income countries emphasise the need to improve access to psychotropic medication as part of effective treatment yet there is little acknowledgement of the limitations of psychotropic drugs as perceived by those who use them" (2012: 438).

Among the people she worked with, Read finds that

> whilst medication undeniably brings benefits for many with severe mental illness, such campaigns seem to have glossed over the limitations of psychotropic drugs, particularly antipsychotics, and the ambivalent attitudes they provoke in those who take them. In many cases antipsychotic treatment had been discontinued, even where it had been recognised to have beneficial

effects. The failure of antipsychotics to achieve a permanent cure also cast doubt on their efficacy. (438–39)

On the one hand, having been through terrible experiences of psychosis, the afflicted and their kin often wish to do nearly anything to avoid the recurrence of such an experience ever again. On the other hand, news that there is no cure and will be no cure cannot be unwaveringly accepted since the existential condition of humans afflicted with disease is to harbor hope that somehow, some way, the nightmare they have lived has simply got to come to an end. Bargaining for sanity and life, they have done their fair share by enduring hospitalizations and taking medications.

Another irreconcilable paradox is the forced choice between psychosis and side effects, or in the words of one participant, to be "crazy or fat." This paradox is fraught by the perverse practices of pharmaceutical companies that shaped clinical practice prior to the remarkably overdue "black box" warnings that were at long last issued by the FDA (2003, 2005, 2008) for atypicals as well as earlier antipsychotics. For example, Janssen Pharmaceuticals ran deceptive ads for Risperadal published in the *American Journal of Psychiatry* (156.9 [1999]: A41–43), the main copyrighted message of which was, "Efficacy uncompromised by excessive weight gain." This apparently purposefully unclear ad played on a double meaning of *uncompromised*. Did the ad mean that there was no excessive weight gain that might compromise efficacy in the form of psychotic symptom control or that there would be excessive weight gain but it would not compromise efficacy? Ultimately, like persons prescribed these medications, clinicians are encouraged to "choose fat, not crazy." Government-mandated black box warnings finally let the "consumer" know that weight gain is substantial (in the SEACORA study, we estimated that this was not infrequently 40 to 80 pounds) and constitutes not only a serious health problem in the form of obesity but also diminished social status through harsh societal stigma. The black box warnings also informed patients that atypical antipsychotics could lead to premature mortality ("increased risk of death compared to placebo") when used by elderly dementia patients. The warnings also finally acknowledge the extensive and serious metabolic syndrome problems of hyperglycemia, diabetes mellitus (for which elevated risk occurs also in earlier antipsychotics such as haloperidol and thioridazine), along with cerebrovascular adverse events (stroke, death).

A paradox of lived experience can also be traced to the familiar but unwelcome dehumanization of persons with schizophrenia that leads to the broad cultural assumption and not infrequently the clinical advice that they should not date or be active sexually—and certainly not reproduce. This was deeply troubling to participants and a matter of shame. Many have, or would like to have, active sexual or romantic relationships and resent the subtle insinuation across a variety of social settings they encounter that, unlike their healthy counterparts, they should not be involved in romantic entanglements, parental duties, or gendered identities.[26]

Meanwhile, patients are recognized to have social and developmental problems but are expected to rely primarily on pharmaceutical treatment, with little psychotherapeutic support. While accepting the need for medication, they fear they may be poisoned or become addicted. Though the disease model that has generated the root metaphor of the disease as a biochemical imbalance absolves patients from guilt, a lingering sense that the disease is also associated with some kind of character defect haunts them. The specter of stigma remains ever present both as a social fact and as a lived experience and is rendered paradoxical insofar as stigma persists despite recovery.

Another kind of paradox embedded in the ideology of contemporary biological psychiatry itself is the simultaneous denial of the relevance of the will and preoccupation with whether it is present, absent, or in a process of degeneration. In an analysis of Kraepelin's conception of dementia praecox as a pathology of the will, Byron J. Good (2010b) has underscored this problem by observing that "the absence of a robust conception of the will or volition in psychiatric nosology and theorizing" has created a "conceptual vacuum" in the realm of the voluntary (173). This is of considerable significance given the pervasive problem faced by participants that they will become the objects of social stigma despite their subjectively experienced improvement. Nearly all (96 percent) reported their experience of stigma daily across a variety of social settings such that, like the disease of schizophrenia itself, stigma is a potent force against which they must struggle vigorously. This is true even though many participants appear to endorse the notion that they have a biochemical imbalance that is theoretically "fault-free"; they still worried that having such an "imbalance" rendered them deficient or flawed, in effect generating a form of self-stigmatization. Against this obstacle, recognizing that the subjective experience of recovery is not limited in scope to symptom alleviation or medication compliance creates a space for agency and will in recovery from schizophrenia. Individuals actively participate in the work of recovery (Deegan 2005). The dimension of personal agency also extends the process of recovery away from the ill individual and into complex relationships with others. These social relations tend to deemphasize illness, highlighting the fact that their problems, success, sadness, and joy are not bounded by the illness but are instead informed by normatively imagined cultural orientations. Yet, as Myers (2010, 2015) demonstrates, the recent emphasis on recovery not only as possibility but also as neoliberal requirement places heightened and potentially stressful expectations on patients. This completes the vicious circle back to recovery without cure.

## CONCLUSION

Across many locales and for many decades, the familiar biomedical narrative of psychotropic drugs as chemical compounds with biological effects has become a matter of cultural common sense. Availability and use of psychopharmaceuticals can hardly be taken for granted, though, since global socioeconomic inequity can limit or preclude access. Indeed, discriminatory policies on mental health care have often created unequal and in some cases grossly inadequate access even to relatively inexpensive WHO-dubbed "essential medicines," let alone the "gold standard" of available treatments for serious mental illness. This is often the case even in high-income countries, where fewer than half of persons with serious mental illness actually receive any treatment at all,[27] but it is worse still in middle- and low-income countries where nearly three quarters of the affected population go without care (WHO 2013: 8).[28] Thus while psychiatrists in Indonesia, for example, are keenly aware of the most recent psychopharmacological compounds through pharmaceutical company–sponsored conferences, such knowledge is functionally irrelevant in light of the prohibitive cost involved (B. Good 2010a). So while the cultural presumption of efficacious biochemical effects is widespread, so too is the expectation of inevitable (if lamentable) "scarcity" of their distribution. Farmer and colleagues (2013) have critiqued the validity of the presumption and acceptance of "scarcity" regarding urgent health care. Anthropological studies of the global circulation of biomedicine and psychopharmacology have made significant advances in understanding social structural and market forces (Lakoff 2005; Petryna, Lakoff, and Kleinman 2007; Dumit 2012), as well as with respect to cultural influences on seeking, prescribing, taking, and responding to psychotropic drugs (Jenkins and Carpenter-Song 2005; Carpenter-Song 2009a, 2009b; Floersch et al. 2009).

In the United States, intensifying economic inequality can render any kind of treatment out of reach since large proportions of the population can neither fill a prescription nor see a doctor. Indeed, the United States exists as an "outlier" among industrialized countries with competitive health insurance markets (How et al. 2011). Considering health overall, there is a pervasive pattern of shorter lives and poorer health over the course of the life span compared to other high-income countries (Institute of Medicine 2013). Access to government-provided coverage of treatment for persistent mental illness is contingent on having income at the poverty level, a situation that encourages a kind of structural poverty among those who avoid obtaining employment to remain eligible to obtain medication. Yet structural economic conditions have not diminished awareness or efforts to seek out drugs that family and individuals think might be useful (Duncan 2012, 2015; B. Good 2010a; M. Good 2007; Basu 2014; Ecks 2013). Pharmaceutical companies, health care organizations, governmental agencies, media, schools, and family advocacy groups circulate discourse on psychotropic drugs as potent biological agents globally.

Lively controversy over the benefits and hazards of psychopharmacology occupies a prominent place in contemporary discourse on mental health. Proponents of psychotropics and critics whose judgments are grim hold their positions with equal fervor. In this chapter, I have drawn on ethnographic research to argue that any advance in this debate is contingent on close attention to the complexities of daily experience and the often substantial suffering among those who regularly take these medications. To be precise, experience-near perspectives must inform critical analyses of the economic and political dimensions of psychotropic use in order to demonstrate the numerous quandaries involved in understanding the remarkably indeterminate cultural, social, and biological effects of psychotropic drugs (Jenkins 2010a). The complexity of these effects is particularly marked in situations of serious and persistent mental illness treated with the most powerful of these agents.

The study of medication experience must recognize not only main effects and side effects but also a great many other "effects" that alter subjective experience in myriad ways and entail sacrifices in the context of self-presentation and social interaction across a variety of settings. Effects of the medication, in this sense, must be understood more broadly to include the influence of medications on one's way of interacting with and inhabiting the world. For research participants as well as others afflicted with mental illness around the globe, medications alone simply cannot be expected to produce a cure. One part of a solution would be to address the shortage of psychotherapy for such persons created by restrictive managed care and insurance coverage, along with addressing the long-standing but inadequate clinical perspective that psychotherapy is in any event of highly limited value for this population. Patients are grateful for their treatment, though it comes at the cost of facing multiple paradoxes of lived experience. They have the right to ask for more.

## CHAPTER 2

# This Is How God Wants It?

*The Struggle of Sebastián*

But I don't want comfort. I want God, I want poetry, I want
real danger, I want freedom, I want goodness. I want sin.

—Aldous Huxley, *Brave New World*

You must go on, I can't go on, I'll go on.

—Samuel Beckett, *The Unnamable*

If our research efforts are focused on learning about the perspectives of
persons actively dealing with serious mental illness, we must above all
attend to the immediacy and intimacy of their experiences, and psychosis is in this respect the most extraordinary of illnesses. As Karl Jaspers
wrote in 1923, "That they [psychoses] are there and that the world and
human life is such as to make them possible and inevitable not only
gives us pause but makes us shudder" ([1963] 1997: 778). Jaspers, who
began his career as a psychiatrist, had by the early 1920s moved toward
phenomenology and political theory with an emphasis on anthropological questions of lived experience. Connections between the phenomenological and the political have long seemed logical to me precisely as
the convergence of social domains of conflict and power that reciprocally structure psychic life through particular psychopolitical mechanisms such as repression, dissociation, and displacement.

In this chapter I examine the social and cultural experience of the
self under the press of psychosis by means of a case study. Taking an
ethnographic approach to the description of one person's extraordinary
experience highlights the complicated tangle of subjectivity as the everyday lived experience of thought, emotion, perception, attachment,

and identity. The case study also raises existential questions of being and belonging whereby individuality and dependency may be culturally played up or played down and a person's fate may be conceived as controlled by an individual or by forces beyond one's comprehension (Jackson 2005: xii; Kaufman 1994). In presenting this case study of mental illness, I argue that there is no such thing as individual pathology insofar as the sociocultural milieu profoundly affects the formation of subjective experience and that the core of extraordinary experience is better indexed by struggle than by symptoms.

The case study in psychosis adds not only to the description of pathology but also more broadly to the specification of possibilities for human subjectivity. First, conceived on a continuum of human possibility (Kleinman and Kleinman 1997; Parish 2008), the immense suffering of severe and sustained psychosis reveals an extraordinary human capacity for endurance as well as an extremity of human fragility (Jenkins 2004). Second, phenomenological realities of psychosis extend to the furthest reaches of the senses through which we perceive and differentiate the experience of "outside" and "inside" worlds. Through the experience of psychosis, spectacular modulations of human perception—olfactory, tactile, visual, and auditory—can occur. Third, whether from the vantage point of psychoanalysis or interpersonal neuroscience, the intricacies of the interpenetration of conscious and unconscious mental processes can be identified by attention to how psychosis is played out in everyday lifeworlds. This requires attention to the ways in which experience is interwoven with cultural interpretation and meaning, psychological dynamics of the family, and existential struggles of life-defining significance.

Defining this cultural, social, and psychological significance of psychotic experience requires attention to questions of content and temporality. In terms of content, the case study can convey a quality of experience that is difficult to fathom for those who have not been so afflicted and that is noncommunicable without adequate contextualization. My doctoral students asked questions such as the following: As a kind of human experience, what are hallucinations really like? How can such experience be described and understood? Is it "real"? What do people who have such experience think is happening? What is a delusion? How are delusions formed, and what is their content? How can they come to have such tenacious meaning? In terms of temporality, the range of variation in the duration of psychotic experience is vast. There can be brief episodes of minutes or hours that are neither personally distressing nor socially troublesome. There can be periods of weeks or months during which symptoms intensify or disappear entirely. There can be periods of recurrent and/or sustained psychosis that last for months, years, or even decades. Some people recover from these episodes; some simply cannot.

## ENCOUNTERING SEBASTIÁN

The day before I met Sebastián at the UCLA Neuropsychiatric Institute, the feel of the Santa Ana winds was unmistakable. As I descended the back staircase of my apartment in Santa Monica, I had the familiar native sense of atmospheric stirring that is at once intriguing and alarming. But that heightened sense of something happening had already been set in motion by a telephone call with news that a newly admitted patient was interested to learn about our study of the course of schizophrenia among Mexican Americans (Karno et al. 1987; Jenkins 1988a, 1988b, 1991; Jenkins and Karno 1992). I entertained, then quickly dismissed urban lore that drew an association between the winds and news of ill portent. After all, it was always a source of hopeful anticipation that a new person might be included in the study. Nonetheless, getting to know Sebastián over the next eighteen months in fact proved a source not only of fascination but also of disturbance.

I found Sebastián at the end of the hall on the locked unit of the university neuropsychiatric hospital. He appeared anxious yet glad to see someone "from the outside." My concern that he thought I could help him leave the hospital was confirmed when he began by telling me he had been there two days and needed to leave. I replied by saying I was following up on a recommendation from a doctor on the unit who had spoken with him about possible participation in our research project. He said he had spoken with a doctor about it and that he might be interested if it had to do with "science." I told him about the study and made sure he knew I was not a physician or clinician but a researcher, an anthropologist working with a team that included a research psychiatrist and a psychologist. As customary, I continued by telling him that the research team did not play any part in his treatment. Wondering if that clarification might conclude our conversation, I was relieved when he sighed and became visibly less agitated. With the issue of discharge apparently off the table he turned to other things on his mind, prominently among them how bad the food was.

Sebastián was twenty-three years old, with gleaming dark brown hair cut in a shag style and alert and kind chestnut eyes. Slender and of medium height, he was a nice-looking young man even if at the time I met him he had a serious case of "bed head," his hair matted along one side of his head. A nurse had just whizzed by to say he should not nap anymore. I explained to him about the research we were doing with Mexican-descent families in Los Angeles and Ventura Counties. We wanted to understand illness experience in the context of routine family life. I did not know how that might or might not qualify as science in his estimation. I continued to explain that if he agreed to participate, there would be a research diagnostic interview by a clinical psychologist and visits by me to his home following discharge from the hospital. I would want to visit and conduct interviews with him and his family over the course of the next year.[1] Though we spoke in English initially, he switched over to Spanish and I followed his lead. Unlike most other participants in the study, Sebastián was thoroughly bilingual. Like others in the study, he was not happy about being in the hospital.

This was his first hospitalization, and he insisted he was there only "to satisfy my mother." Unsurprisingly, when I later spoke with his mother she insisted that she had brought him to the hospital because *"sabía que no estaba bien y tengo fé que los doctors puedan curarlo"* (I knew he wasn't well and I have faith that the doctors are able to cure him). After flipping through a magazine featuring a story on Natalie Wood and talking about the Academy Awards ceremony, he began to talk about who were the best guitar players. He said no one could match Carlos Santana, and I had to agree. Then he looked around his room and asked if I wanted something to drink. I said I was okay but thanked him for asking. He began to tell me that even though he had had some trouble over the past two years, it was a mistake that he was in the hospital. He didn't get along with his father and had had trouble at work and studying for his college courses in science and math. He heard voices that were puzzling. Over time, I learned a great deal about these voices.

The voices started out benignly enough. Sebastián couldn't figure it out but thought perhaps the upstairs neighbor was trying to talk to him. He was not bothered by this and in fact thought it was kind of "cool." However, over a period of about three months the voices changed in mood and content. They became increasingly dictatorial and cruel, taking delight in controlling his every move. Preoccupation with the voices and their commands led him to leave his job at a local aeronautics laboratory and later to drop out of the community college he attended. He had completed more than two years of coursework in chemistry, calculus, and physics. In recent months, however, he found he had to stay up all night studying just to make Cs. Sebastián had long been enthralled with science but also saw college as a way to avoid being stuck forever in a minimum wage job. He wanted to do something he liked. One idea was to combine his love for children and his interest in engineering to design day care centers. He thought such a center should be well supplied with computers to match children's minds, which he likened to "little computers" since "you can put information in their heads and they learn so quickly." The voices, however, held out other plans for him. They instructed him to make a new type of carburetor for a different kind of gas combustion engine. He complied by charging $400 on a Mastercard to buy the parts and undertake the experiment, dropping out of school to work full time on the project. He said that in the earlier stages of the project he was asked by the voices what he intended to do with the millions he would make and how he would safeguard his invention with a patent. Sebastián asked the voices whether or not he should do something for God, and God replied in the affirmative that an enormous glass church would be quite nice. So he agreed that if he made money that is where it would go. But the project flopped, entirely. He told the voices that he was disappointed, and they responded in kind.

## FAMILIAL SITUATION AND DECISION TO HOSPITALIZE

Born in Mexico, Sebastián Sanchez lived in Juárez for about five years while his mother commuted across the border to work in Texas. Gabriela Sanchez, a slight but pretty woman of forty-five, completed eleven years of school and worked full time at an assembly plant where she cut material for mattresses. She disclosed that she became pregnant prior to the father's divorce from his first wife. Growing up in Mexico, Sebastián was raised primarily by his maternal grandmother before his move to Los Angeles at age six, after his parents married. This was the first time he had lived with his father. According to him, his mother and grandmother were doting and overprotective. Oscar Sanchez, a slightly overweight man of forty-five, wore the little hair he had in thin pieces pasted across his scalp and forehead. He had completed three years of public school education. His view of Sebastián's problem differed from his wife's idea that Sebastián was ill. When I met Señor Sanchez, he was secure in his conviction that the voices his son claimed to hear were some clever fakery designed to get attention. The trouble, according to him, was that Sebastián was stubborn and spoiled, with license to do whatever he pleased and a mother willing to cover up any misdeeds. All agreed that his father was strict and hit him regularly for perceived misconduct. "I grew up at the end of a stick," as Sebastián put it. As later became clear, this punishment sometimes took the form of severe beatings. His teachers described Sebastián as not sitting still, as wanting to play. His mother indicated that while he learned English very quickly, he had difficulty finishing tasks. According to both parents, there was no history of mental illness in the family, save the mother's paternal grandmother who at age eighty-seven was said to have become senile and apparently paranoid, "acting real crazy." Other than that, there was nothing to report.

As is common for a psychiatric admission, the decision to seek hospitalization, while contentious, was initiated by the family. After months of taking Sebastián to a minister and a psychiatrist, his mother was desperate to get help for a problem she considered serious but did not understand. She acted on her own initiative, aided by the urging of the community psychiatrist, family, and friends. While Sebastián's father devised a ruse to have his son hospitalized by instructing his wife to tell him he was going "only to talk," he claimed that he participated in this plan despite his conviction that the only problem was his wife's failed child rearing and his son's stubborn streak. He also believed marijuana played a part in the development of his son's condition. In an attempt to get Sebastián to stop using marijuana, his mother had taken him to a Protestant church that convened weekly meetings for young male drug users. The minister had insisted that Sebastián suffered from a "bad spirit." Although Sebastián's mother was reluctant at first, she told me, "I'm Catholic, but it didn't matter to me [if they were Protestant] if they cure him." The meetings failed to bring about any improvement and proved disturbing by eliciting trancelike states in the youths who prayed in militaristic fashion, appearing as if *"en otro mundo"* (in another world). Señora Sanchez saw this one day when she arrived early to pick Sebastián up and was scandalized: "I was afraid because I hadn't seen anything like that. Like an army. I don't believe it, because I go to church. We are Catholic! We don't do anything like that!" They never went back.

At the time he was admitted to the hospital Sebastián said that it was very important to never show anger "no matter what gets done to me." Sebastián's mother initially visited him daily in the hospital, but the commute across town and her work schedule made that increasingly difficult. And her own difficulties with *nervios* were exacerbated. Still, she visited regularly, fretting over whether her son harbored anger toward her about the hospitalization, whether that decision had been the right thing, and whether Sebastián was getting better. In contrast, her husband never visited, staying away out of hostility and fear. He was defensive about not going to see his son, angry and fearful that Sebastián would display anger or perhaps even violence toward him. He claimed one such incident as justification for not visiting.

The ruse devised by the father to have Sebastián hospitalized indicates, however, as he later admitted to me, that he was involved with the decision because he knew his son was in critical need of help. Nothing else had worked, not even kicking him out of the house. Señor Sanchez had complained that since he never knew where his son was, but assumed he was somewhere out on the street, he decided Sebastián might just as well live there. Sebastián came home one evening to his clothes tied in a bundle, along with a sleeping bag left outside. His father explained the bundle as a thoughtful act since he did not want him to get pneumonia. "I thought of that," he told me, pleased for having done so.

Señora Sanchez did not think Sebastián was mentally ill. She thought perhaps he had a problem of *nervios* since he clearly was not crazy (*loco*). He knew what he was saying, spoke well, answered when you spoke to him, did a great many things, including studying. She was deeply sympathetic to her son and his condition, whatever it might be. In dialogue with other relatives and friends, she struggled to understand what it could possibly be. *What* did he have? While mysterious, the reality of some kind of serious illness requiring medical care was not in question. Although initially the father was dogmatic that his son was "faking it" and that his problem was primarily personality deficits (stubborn, immature) along with the use of marijuana, his conception of the problem changed over the course of time that I spoke with him. Weeks and months after the hospitalization he began to grant the possibility he might have a serious illness for which he wanted his son to receive good care. This possibility was held in tandem with his certainty that even so Sebastián willfully thwarted him whenever possible.

For his mother, the tipping point for the onset of his illness involved Teresa Villalobos, Sebastián's girlfriend. He had met Teresa through his grandmother. He had loved Teresa deeply for many years. With sadness she told me that when Teresa broke off with her son it was absolutely crushing. She felt that it didn't bother him as much to have fights with his father, to be kicked out of the house, as long as he had Teresa to go to. Given the intensity of the attachment, she thought that perhaps he "loved her too much." Following Sebastián's breakup with Teresa, his father would often chide him by saying, "Why don't you go out with girls?," promising to buy him a motorcycle or a set of drums if he did. His mother felt his father shouldn't bother him with that, saying, "There will be plenty of time for that [dating]." These offers to buy things seemed less an enticement on the part of his father than a taunt in the form of bribery.

A primary cause of the illness about which Señor and Señora Sanchez seemed to agree—albeit from different angles—was "spoiling" Sebastián. They both claimed that by the time they realized each other's mistakes, it was too late. While the duel over who was the greater "spoiler" was notable, the father complained about it louder and longer. More striking for the mother was her intense resentment over her husband being "too strict," along with his refusal to grant that their son was truly ill. Further, she was convinced that her husband was jealous of the attention and affection she gave Sebastián. The father did convey resentment of his wife, a point underscored by the departure from the usual practice of completing family interviews in the home. To interview Señor Sanchez, I needed to see him in his most usual daily setting, and that was his store. It was located in northeast Los Angeles in a Mexican neighborhood. With its jumble of miscellaneous items for sale (food, hardware, toys, school supplies, small appliances), it reminded me of small stores in Mexico. We talked in the back of the store, where he had a refrigerator, a mini-kitchen, a bathroom, a bed-cot, an office desk, and a TV. Only rarely did he go to the family home to sleep. That was where his wife and seventeen-year-old son Rodolfo resided. Sebastián lived on his own in an apartment paid for by his mother but that she could not afford. He had a roommate for a while but later lived alone. His mother visited every day for a few hours at a time.

On a visit with the Sanchezes at the store, I found Señor Sanchez domineering and aggressive. For her part, Señora Sanchez looked down at the floor with disdain rather than fear. I had to admit, however, that she appeared deferential, even though I knew she had ways of circumventing his control. Legally divorced and living separately, they remained in daily contact. Señor Sanchez had sought divorce on the basis that his wife "wrecked" both his daughter and son. Though locked in acrimony, however, neither ever mentioned altering the daily contact or routine as currently arranged.

Sebastián and his brother, Rodolfo, did not get on well. Their mother reported that Rodolfo felt hostility and a sense of rivalry toward him. I got the impression that Señor Sanchez considered Rodolfo a model son.

When he introduced me to him, he positively glowed: "Here he is! Here is my son! He helps me, I gave him his own phone." Sebastián's nineteen-year-old sister, Renata, had recently moved out of the house with her husband, a military man, who was stationed in Germany. Prior to this, she lived at home but completed her last year of high school in Texas following her father's discovery of what he termed "playing around with three boys at the same time." He packed her off on a plane the very next day to live with his brother. She didn't have much to pack since her father had cut up nearly all her clothes, saying he wanted her to have to earn money for clothes and other things.

While Sebastián was in the hospital he received a variety of inpatient psychiatric treatments, including brief individual and group therapy sessions. The third day in the hospital, he was also given an antipsychotic medication, fluphenazine (Prolixin), with benztropine (Cogentin) for side effects. These seemed to provide little relief. He was unable to read, concentrate, sit still, hold his hands still, or maintain a conversation, all of which he had been able to do before taking the medication. He disliked the fact he could not go outside and did not believe the medication would help him with the voices since they were from God: "What medication is going to help make God go away? I know it won't work." Further, the painful writhing wrought by the Prolixin (a "side effect") had inscribed an indelible corporeal memory that made him cringe at the mere mention of medication (notable in months and years to come). In the hospital he felt confined and bored, depressed and agitated. He wanted to leave. One month after admission, he returned to his apartment.

ONSET OF TROUBLE: VOICES CALLING

Over the course of several visits with him at home, Sebastián described to me the phenomenology of his illness experience. His thought showed ruminative patterns of scientific preoccupation, such as with machinery and the workings of high-tech space rocket equipment. He also experienced spontaneous prenatal and birth images that coincided with recollections of childhood and household scenes from Juárez that included aunts, uncles, and cousins. In telling stories about his early years, he expressed surprise at remembering all this. Given a typically garrulous Sebastián, it was noteworthy to see him reticent or hedging in some of these conversations and impossible not to wonder about its significance. After all the terror of the voices that he faced and talked about openly, it was impossible to know whether there were painful memories that he was working to keep at bay or if these were things that for him were simply unspeakable.

On the one hand, Sebastián felt he was "just like everyone else, except I hear voices." On the other hand, he thought he was "different because I hear those things. I don't feel it's right. I believe there's something wrong with my mind. It's just really bad. It's terrible." Initially, the voices were indistinct and intermittent, and he thought they were coming from his upstairs neighbor, who was telling him that he could transmit his voice in a way Sebastián initially thought was "neat." The communication was intriguing, and it was almost flattering that a neighbor would go to the trouble to converse in such a creative if cryptic fashion. There were, however, multiple voices—male and female, young and old, crowds. Sebastián regularly heard his name being called by the voices. There was a fluctuation in the voices in that sometimes there would be several talking among themselves. At times, he would reply to the voices, even though he knew these were inside his head (*"oigo en mi cabeza"*).

About two months later this began to change. Now Sebastián thought the voices were possibly coming from a man at the aeronautics lab where he had worked in a clerical position. Later, in a rather specific and dramatic fashion, he decided that the dominant voice was none other than that of God. Following this interpretive decision, the voices evolved primarily (although not entirely) into one voice,[2] that of a middle-aged male that Sebastián was convinced was God. He vacillated on this at times, however, casting doubt on the extent to which he was wholly convinced of his own interpretation. While it was strange to him that God would be talking to him since he did not attend Mass, he thought God had "proven" his identity by "touching" Sebastián on the arm and making him tingle, enabling him to play the guitar in beautiful ways he had previously been unable to do, causing him to laugh and cry at no particular stimulus, and allowing him to influence the behavior of others. God, however, refused to prove himself to others. Initially, the God voice was benevolent, offering guidance and explanation, sending Sebastián to a Bible study group in search of people interested in his experiences. Sebastián told me that he had been instructed by the voices to break off his relationship and to await another young woman—Carmen Hernandez, a remote coworker at the lab where he had been employed—who would be his wife by year's end. This made no sense to Sebastián: how could he expect to marry someone he didn't really know? Compliant with the voices, he sent love letters declaring, "Someday I will be you and you will be me," that stopped short of proposing marriage outright. Being married to Carmen by year's end would prove the voice was God's and he was not wasting his time. At this time, he insisted that were he not to be married to this unattainable object he would no longer pay attention to the voices and go back to what he was doing, working and going to school. Despite the dominance of the God voice, Sebastián described what he heard as inherently confusing since there were dynamic, intermittent fluctuations in the identity of the dominant voice. Indeed, who he would hear seemed to depend in large part on who was around. When others were present whom he did not know well, he might hear someone say, "He's stupid." "Then," he continued, "I hear that other vibration, then another vibration that's saying something else, reading my mind. All attacking at once. Then it will all go away. It's different, better, when I'm alone. Then it's mostly Carmen." We spent many visits together discussing his experiences of fluctuation between certainty and confusion regarding who was talking to him and to whom he should pay attention.

Since at the time I was new to the field and had been trying to learn all I could about psychiatry and psychosis in particular, I took courses and studied the texts that psychiatric residents were using at my university. The standard required text, *Modern Synopsis of Comprehensive Textbook of Psychiatry* (Freedman, Kaplan, and Sadock 1976), seemed particularly important. However, as I began to study it I noted with trepidation numerous photos of patients in bizarre poses with strange grimaces and stranger still drawings and numerology (439–48). I was therefore taken aback to observe not only the extraordinary experiences of the persons I came to know but also the exceptional social skills they could simultaneously possess. For example, once I had a professor of cultural psychiatry come to my office to meet Sebastián. He requested that I arrange the meeting in light of the field notes and conversations I had shared with him regarding Sebastián's experience. To commence the meeting, I introduced Sebastián and the professor. Following the introductions, the professor sat down in one of two chairs in my office. I realized I needed to drag another chair in but not as quickly as Sebastián did. He poked his head into the hallway, saw a spare chair, and asked, "Can I bring this one in?" I assented, embarrassed that I had failed to do this before the meeting. But it seemed to me to also point to a contrast in social skills and graciousness Sebastián was in possession of. I thought to myself, "This is hardly bizarre behavior," but I also recall thinking, "Bear in mind that the professor is not Mexican."

In an attempt to interpret the voices or voice he heard, Sebastián subsequently organized a delusional system that, while complex and eventually rigid, was not without several dynamic aspects. Clearly present was a highly oppressive authoritarian and paternal religious figure, that is, "God." The taunting, control, and cruelty of the voice of God mirrored that of his father. At one point Sebastián expressed his feeling that "the voices are pretty harsh on me, you know. They don't let up." He resented the lack of compassion, the continual manipulation of his thoughts and actions. This was without doubt a malevolent God. The perennial question for Sebastián was why he should listen to him. But how could he not?

While Sebastián spoke easily and often about the mutual affection between himself and his mother, rarely did he speak about his father. It was clear, however, that he thought his father did not like him and did not want him around. He thought it was a problem that his father did not believe in God and cursed his name. While our research was not designed to generate psychoanalytic interpretations (Herzog 1991; Singer 1995), it was impossible for me not to hypothesize that transference filled the caldron of taunting, mocking, and controlling voices with which Sebastián struggled. The structure of his experience is seared in fierce psychic-symbolic power struggles with a father who beat him, resented him, and derided the legitimacy of his illness and suffering.[3] Indeed, the case of Sebastián, and many others from my ethnographic research, has convinced me that the psychodynamic structure of the lived experience of mental illness and extraordinary experience is irreducible to random neurosynaptic misfires of auditory perception. Sebastian ultimately interpreted his experience of the voices as *the* voice of God. This was a God who manipulates, derides, and controls his every move. Try as he might to propitiate him, Sebastián realized that "there's no way to make him happy." The meaning seemed unmistakable: he had parallel experience, or more precisely the same experience, regarding his father. Meaning and experience are anything but a matter of happenstance.

## PHENOMENOLOGY OF VISIONS, EMOTIONS, SENSATIONS

Sebastián saw lights of various colors everywhere (*"Veo luces de distintos colores por todos los lugares"*). He understood these lights, as well as shadows, as "some kind of an *emotion,* like an arc above me, like an *emotion.* I can *feel* it." He would also see twinkling lights on a finger, white and black, "like when you rub your eyes," he explained to me. His olfactory sense was altered in various ways. Sometimes he would smell perfumes, other times rotten odors. "Like when meat gets rotten," he said. "And sometimes I smell like I am a girl."

Gendered confusion regarding his own identity and his relations with women he loved—Teresa, in particular—were salient in his phenomeno-logical and social experience. He remained in touch with Teresa after their breakup and at one point asked me if he could come by my office with Teresa to get some career counseling: "She's interested in what you like. She wants to understand people and their problems. But I think she wants to be a psychologist, not an anthropologist, maybe." He was adamant that to do this properly we needed to meet not as we regularly did, in his neighborhood or home, but in an "official" setting like my office because then Teresa would take him (and possibly me) seriously. Teresa stayed with him at his apartment over Christmas for reasons that were never explained to me. He described this as very difficult because he felt like he was "tearing Carmen's heart apart, grinding my whole body apart. It gets real intense. If I try to get closer to Teresa, it all goes wrong. If things just hang loose, then Teresa will come by, and it's like I'm killing Carmen. Two days ago I went to look for her, didn't find her. It makes no sense that I should try to see her. She's a stranger, really." The real (ex-)girlfriend and the fantasy voice–arranged fiancée were at odds, and he felt guilty for not being able to resolve the conflict. He was certain that this was all, inexpli-cably, his unwitting doing. He loved Teresa but was "supposed" to be with Carmen according to God: what in the world was going on?

This conflict intensified for him and seemed to be followed by the disturbing bodily preoccupation with the sensation of smelling "like a girl" that coincided with the preponderance of his sense that the voices were becoming Carmen's "feelings." He even assigned a number to it: 80 percent. The quality of the voices changed again. God told Sebastián that Carmen was starting to hear voices too. It began to shape up as a contest between God and Carmen, when previously the matter had seemed settled. Sebastián was more confused than ever. He noted that sometimes Carmen would say, "Well, I'm on the rag," and then, "I feel like I'm on my [menstrual] period." Sebastián indicated that God seemed to want to stay out of this but enjoyed watching what for him felt nothing short of psychic conflagration. Additional new things started happening that truly frightened him.

Sebastián began to have the occasional sensation of someone touch-ing him, like pressing an index finger on his arm or the top of his head, while the voices would be telling him something undecipherable. He began to feel that he had no control over his life: "*Yo soy un zombie* [I'm a zombie]," he said. "Those voices are driving me crazy. I can't get on to any kind of schedule. There's nothing for me." While the voices had never done so, he worried that they might ask him to kill someone. "I wouldn't want to do it, but like a zombie, I'd go do it. It's not what I want to do." He said that if he started to get into an argument with the voices, they would find other voices to back them up. This thoroughly confused him in terms of what to do: Study? Find a job? Go out on a date? It all seemed impossible.

## MAGNITUDE OF THE STRUGGLE: GOD AND SUICIDALITY

In the months following Sebastián's hospitalization, the voices became more dictatorial, taking delight in controlling his every move. He resented this lack of compassion, the continual manipulation of his thoughts and actions. The magnitude of the suffering inflicted by the puppeteer, which Sebastián described as having a hard heart, delighting in the fact that mere human beings, unlike God, never know what will happen next. These voices spoke mostly when he was lying down and alone, although by that point they were pretty much always present. In an exceptionally vicious taunt, they might have him lay down and "think about everything bad you did" for about three hours, then switch to "think of what good things you did now." This he described as absolute torture and as ludicrous that he would have to comply rather than do something he wanted. He accepted the malevolent God as legitimate for the most part and had no competing explanations for these extraordinary experiences. I sensed that he feared that any serious display of disbelief on his part might result in harm to himself. Sebastián's tale of this cruelty sent a chill up my spine then and now, bringing to mind Jaspers's comment on the quality of the "fact of psychoses" as that which "not only gives us pause but makes us shudder" (Jaspers [1963] 1997: 778).

Sebastián asked my advice about what he should do, if it made sense to wait for a girl who didn't seem like a good prospect. I told him that I agreed with him that it was good to wonder whether this made sense and that I was struck by how excited he was when he initially told me about his interest in chemistry and physics despite the difficulty of the work. As I did on most occasions when he sought advice from me, I said that it's hard to figure out what to do, but therapists and doctors might be really helpful. I routinely mentioned two doctors whom he could telephone on his own, or if he liked, whom I would be happy to call with him. It was painful to me that he never took me up on the offer, even though I did accompany him and his mother to some clinical appointments following his hospitalization. I also routinely mentioned medication to him, though I was acutely aware that the mere mention of medication reminded him of the painful reaction he had had to Prolixin. I saw him throughout that period and observed the physical pain it caused and its failure to ameliorate the voices. Again and again I said that there were other medications and a different one might have different effects. But we also knew it was more than the physical pain and lack of therapeutic effect: for Sebastián, if this was God, what medicine could out-God God?

Faced with this powerful and merciless God this prospect was preposterous. Sebastián summarized an exchange with the voice of God precisely as follows.

> *God:* Sebastián, what pleases you?
>
> *Sebastián:* You do.
>
> *God:* You can't kill yourself because I like to watch you like this! If you kill yourself you'll go to hell.
>
> *Sebastián:* What worse hell could there be than hearing these voices?
>
> *God:* Oh, this is nothing. We can make it worse than you could ever imagine.
>
> *Sebastián:* That's what you enjoy, God? Why have everything the way you have it?
>
> *God:* [silence]
>
> *Sebastián:* He doesn't answer me."

This sort of chilling exchange apparently occurred frequently. For example, Sebastián reported hearing, "I'm God, and you exist, but you are nothing compared to me." He conveyed his response as follows:

> It's just terrible, but [laughs] I'm afraid to do anything to make God mad. I think about killing myself and the voices laugh: "Go ahead! See what happens!" By them saying that I don't know what to do. God would put me through hell. I think this is hell now. God says he could make it a lot worse . . . sometimes I say, "I'll just think of God. But I won't listen to the voices." But I still hear the voices . . . God makes me feel lower, better. I just want to feel the same. Sometimes I feel like a whisper is coming.

The intensity and unrelenting qualities of the suffering led Sebastián at various points to speak of suicide.

I'd like to kill myself, but I can't. I think I'm afraid. But can you imagine if I kill myself? That would be the best state to be in. Sure, my mom would feel sad, but then my dad wouldn't give a shit. He never has. Anyone who came to my funeral might feel sad or disappointed, but it would pass. Don't you think I know that? It would pass. As far as other people here [in this world] it would make so little difference. Now, to me, personally, it would make all the difference. If you take it logically, step by step, and I have, suicide is the *best* idea. And yet those voices won't let me. They keep me locked inside here with no way out. I want a way out. I've tried and I've tried and I've tried, believe me. I don't know. Maybe I am really crazy. I just know I can't take it anymore. I just can't take it anymore. Why is God putting me through this hell? If you want to know what I think, maybe God does exist, but I think God is a pain in the ass to have everything the way it is.

He elaborated.

God says that our suffering is nothing compared to his suffering by being alone, so alone, existing apart. Suffering and love and pain are not different entities to God—only to people—he doesn't distinguish. I ask him, "Pain or sadness doesn't matter to you? Then why do we exist?" Then saying that feels like I'm gouging his heart out.

After relating this, Sebastián said that God had just told him, "Don't tell her [referring to me]. I feel God doesn't want me to explain it to you. *He'll* explain it."

I tried with only fleeting success to get him to see a particular doctor I knew and have a new trial of medications (other than Prolixin and Cogentin). I pleaded for him to give it a chance. But he insisted he was terrified of the bad side effects. If medication remained out of the question, I begged him to let me take him to speak to a clinical psychologist with whom he had spoken before and seemed to have a reasonably good rapport. He declined and started to get testy with me. He said he thought I understood. I told him I thought I did, to an extent, but was very worried about him and his ideas about hurting himself, which I insisted was not a good idea, no matter what. He reiterated that he felt like a zombie, that he had lost much of himself. "In the end," he said, "something is controlling me. It's either the medication or the voices. I can't stand either one."

After this discussion we shared a long silence. Then he spoke: "Oh, maybe I'll just meet you later." "Where?," I asked. "Would you like to try to meet somewhere else, later this afternoon?" His response was heartbreaking; "Oh, no, Jani, not here. Not today. Maybe I'll just meet you somewhere else, some other time. You may not believe me, but there's an existence beyond death. There's got to be. I'll see you there."
I had trouble breathing but managed to ask him to please call or to let

me call him later in the afternoon. He said it would be fine if I called him. I left and got into my car, tears welling up. I drove around the block, wondering when would be a good time to try to talk to him again. I also called his therapist at the local community clinic and explained I was very worried about Sebastián. The therapist asked me if he had a specific plan to hurt himself. I said I did not know of a specific plan, but I thought the concern was quite real and serious and we should consider it as such. The therapist told me I could call the police. I felt that would risk betrayal of Sebastián, yet it was something I considered since maybe that was best in the end. I waited and worried. He was telling me his most private painful thoughts. Was I to "report" him for that and have him taken away in a police car, most certainly drugged with medications I knew had previously had seriously adverse effects on him? If I did, would he regard such a betrayal as reasonable grounds for actually putting together a "specific plan"? Two hours later I called him, and strangely he seemed fine. I didn't believe him. I asked if I could stop by very briefly. He said sure. He made indirect reference to our earlier conversation about suicide by saying that he told me about "it" because he thought I was trying to understand him: "So now you know." He also saw how worried I was and responded compassionately, "Look, I would [commit suicide], but I can't. God won't let me. So I'm stuck in this hell, and not going anywhere. There's nothing you or anyone else can do about it. I can't." Later that evening, I wrote in my field journal:

> Documenting a special human being's extreme suffering, demise, broken dreams, and lack of control over things ranging from what cereal to eat for breakfast to the logicality and consequence of their own suicide is inordinately difficult, if not impossible, without enormous personal despair, frustration, and awareness of the painful inadequacies of (1) what we as "professionals," as "researchers," can offer as true or meaningful assistance as balm for the insufferable; (2) the state of psychiatric care available as it fails to help some significant proportion of those who get it; and (3) the human condition itself.[4]

## MAGNITUDE OF THE STRUGGLE: WORK AND PERSONAL RELATIONSHIPS

In the several months following his hospitalization in August, Sebastián regularly searched for work. It bothered him immensely to receive money from his mother, saying he did not want to be a "leech." He had done some odd jobs at his father's store, but unsurprisingly that did not work out for long. By the following February, he had found a full-time job with the city working on voter registration. He was able to do this for about four months until he was let go for not accomplishing a sufficient amount of work. Loss of that job was a blow to him. He was depressed about being unemployed, saying, "I guess in this society if you don't work you're just a bum. That's how I feel." His mother reported that his voices became worse in the wake of being let go from his job. Further problems arose when interacting with neighbors, who he said he could tell were making fun of him for either being "stupid" or "crazy." He sought solace in smoking marijuana, which he said he enjoyed, although it didn't really help with any of his problems. He didn't consider marijuana "bad," though, like he did "angel dust" (PCP). Speaking of the latter, he said he had done a "bad thing" by taking it two times, "a few months ago." The only drug that he had used with regularity since his teenage years was marijuana. He did this only occasionally now, whether due to lack of money or interest, it wasn't clear. Once when I visited him during this period he giggled wildly when I arrived, blurting out, "I am so stoned!"

A week after this encounter he decided to keep an appointment that I had talked him into at a community mental health clinic in East Los Angeles. There he started taking Haldol, which proved ineffective, and then Mellaril along with Artane for side effects. He said he felt the Mellaril made him "high." The voices were no different. Still, he took two gymnastics classes at a local community college. But he stopped because he felt people were reading his mind: "I get all tense and uptight and want to leave." He felt he could read their minds too. "Telepathy, sort of. Sometimes the whole class will say, 'You asshole.'"

Sebastián's case study suggests that the core of the experience of mental illness is better indexed as *struggle* than as symptoms. This is true at the level of personal and familial struggle but also with respect to romantic relationships, work, and education. That these struggles are invariably intertwined and that they can in turn be traced to the development and course of illness are critical to my argument that in the situation of mental illness there can be no such thing as individual pathology.[5] In the current case study, in the absence of effective relief from antipsychotic medications, the magnitude of Sebastián's personal suffering was great. He regularly fought with his father and the voices and struggled actively to meaningfully interpret his experience. He never lost his desire to work, to create, or to study, yet his dream of successfully completing college was thwarted by his illness.[6] The negative cognitive effects of the medication that prevented him from reading were particularly frustrating. Being involved in a happy romantic relationship eluded him. A psychologist he saw twice considered (somewhat ungenerously, I thought) that he had given up the struggle by becoming "dependent" on his voices to "perform" for him. On the other hand, had Sebastián's illness onset and treatment occurred at a later time and place he might have been exposed to the recent discourse of persons who have recovered through self-discovered and well-practiced techniques of keeping voices at bay (Deegan 2005; Longden et al. 2012).

As we have seen, a primary way in which the cultural content of Sebastián's symptoms was manifest was through religious rumination on the existence of God and how to be a good supplicant. The cultural content of his symptoms also included the desire to be as famous as certain popular musicians. Some of this involved fantasies of success and wealth. These exceeded the commonly shared desire to be educated and have a good job. Prior to the onset of his illness and never completely discarded, his own occupational yearnings incorporated not only social mobility but also intellectual interests along with introductory training at a local aeronautics laboratory. In the social domain of dating, Sebastián definitely embodied cultural expectations regarding gender through his assumption that men must take the initiative. This had worked out for him for several years, and he had a girlfriend that he loved dearly. However, the breakup of that relationship was (according to his mother) particularly hard on him given the fact that it served in part as a refuge from his father's harsh treatment. Attempts to rekindle that relationship proved confusing in light of the demands of the voices that he felt blocked him from reuniting with her. Mysteriously, he was to await a virtual stranger to whom he would miraculously be married by the end of the year. In this respect, Sebastián was not able to realize certain social and cultural yearnings through which to embed his sense of self and social life.

In Sebastián's struggle there were clearly points at which he appeared to be flirting with simply giving up. However, his suffering was existentially fraught and in the broadest sense was nothing short of a matter of life and death. As he struggled daily with symptoms that were as severe as they were cruelly inflected, the central problem was how to go on without knowing how to go on. Yet he did. It is estimated that the lifetime risk of suicide for persons with persistent schizophrenia is approximately 5 percent (Hor and Taylor 2010). Throughout the years of many research projects with such persons, I have known only one case in which that actually transpired. In that situation, it was a man who felt "raindrops" pelting his head continuously and could no longer withstand the pain. His suicide devastated his loving wife and adult children, yet they fully understood it. Given the magnitude of the suffering possible in sustained conditions of schizophrenia, it would seem that the most pressing question is not why 5 percent tragically take their own lives but why it is only 5 percent who do so. In my research experience, immense suffering in psychosis does not drive persons to suicide owing to two strong and equally interactive tendencies: the biologically based propensity for survival and culturally invariant propensities for social engagement and attachment.

I must emphasize that a great many persons afflicted with psychosis do not suffer a fate as outlined here for Sebastián. Their symptoms are less severe and recurrent, and the course of their illness is marked by spontaneous improvement over time and efficacious response to treatments prominently including psychotropic medications. In this instance, many researchers, including me, would argue that if his illness had been treated during a later period (after 1992), he might have responded better to the second generation of antipsychotics, the so-called atypicals. (see also Jenkins and Carpenter-Song 2005). Certainly Sebastián qualified as having been treatment refractory as he had had significant negative responses to the first-generation antipsychotics Haldol and Prolixin. Atypicals do not always help, but in any case they were unavailable at the time Sebastián was treated. It is also possible that the later medications would have more effectively ameliorated the voices. On the other hand, he might never have been interested in or responsive to any kind of medication, or he may have been unsatisfied with the atypicals on the basis of negative side effects (weight gain, among other serious metabolic problems). Indeed, a symbolic system of meaning when compressed into a cruel God offered little respite and in effect amounted to a cultural and psychodynamic trap from which he could not be freed. Recent developments by occupational therapists in "wellness training" and peer support groups for Voice Hearers may well have helped him.[7] But as for medications, nothing had proved tolerable or helpful.

## MAGNITUDE OF THE STRUGGLE: FAMILIAL AND SOCIOEMOTIONAL PROCESSES

The magnitude of suffering on the part of Sebastián's parents, albeit in qualitatively different forms, was also great. It stemmed from the differing modes of relating to Sebastián characterized by devotion on the part of his mother and rejection on the part of his father. These differing socioemotional attachments led to distinctly differing conceptions of what the problem was and what to do about it. Sebastián's mother interpreted the problem in a way that was common among Mexican mothers in the larger study of seventy families: a clear case of serious and perhaps severe *nervios* for which a cultural logic of sympathy and care were warranted. His father claimed to doubt the veracity of an explanation of the problem as one of *nervios* or illness, figuring instead that Sebastián's situation could be characterized by annoying personality characteristics such as willfulness, stubbornness, and laziness. In this respect, his response seemed more akin to that of low-income Euro-Americans I had studied. Nevertheless, each of their interpretations was subject to change, and both struggled to understand the problem and how to handle it. Should he be supported financially, socially, and emotionally? Clearly they had opposing views and practices in this regard. The constant conflict in which Sebastián was embroiled seemed to mirror the marital strife between his parents.

Sadly, Sebastián's father's emotional tone of harshness and control seized Sebastián's unconscious psychological processes and reproduced that dynamic in the formation and experience of his symptoms. Our research documented and rated his father's emotional tone according to the Camberwell Family Interview for "expressed emotion" (Vaughn and Leff 1976; also see chapter 3). The empirical data from this interview revealed Señor Sanchez as both highly critical and hostile.

> He has a mind of his own, and wants to do what he wants to, likes to do what he pleases. Doesn't listen to me, walks out and does exactly what he wants. That creates a lot of problems for us in the family. When he was young he always wanted to do things his way, he cannot take reason; he'll take his feelings. Through my life, he damaged my life in a lot of ways so I had to turn around and ask my wife for a divorce.

And, later in the interview, he encapsulated the tension with his son as follows:

> If he gives a kiss to mother, to me he won't even say, "Hi," he'll turn around and look at me like I was a dog. A dog, you go and pet the dog, to me, he'll see me like an enemy. He tries to fight me.

Señora Sanchez was rated as moderate on the scale for emotional overinvolvement. In other words, while she showed some signs of being overprotective and self-sacrificing, from a Mexican cultural perspective much of this was unavoidable and to be expected. During the interview, she cried or was sniffling and teary-eyed, distraught, wringing her hands.

Her distress was clearly evident. She rented an apartment she could not really afford for Sebastián after her husband kicked him out of the house, insisting, "He's my son. I can't leave him. I feel sorry for him. I can't let him go, just outside, he doesn't have anything, no food, no place to sleep. I can't do that. So I rented him an apartment, but I can't afford it. My husband can't afford it either. I can't let him go and die of hunger." Her daily visits to cook for him and to walk with him in the neighborhood proved a difficult routine to maintain given her full-time job across town. She was not critical of her son with but one exception: "I don't want you to smoke [marijuana]." She did not interpret Sebastián's habit of sleeping most of the day as a source of annoyance but as good because he usually stayed up through the night: "I know that those voices bother him terribly, and he doesn't sleep well. I think that is better that he rest, because then he doesn't hear the voices."

While it is not possible to determine the extent to which Sebastián's illness was socially produced by his familial history and circumstances, I do not doubt that these played a substantial role in the onset and formation of his illness. Whether Sebastián would have developed this illness regardless of his family background is entirely unknown, as are possible biogenetic factors. On the other hand, there is a great deal of recent empirical evidence that physical abuse (and other forms of abuse) is significantly related to the onset of psychosis (e.g., Jenkins and Good 2014). Also, there is a substantial body of evidence to demonstrate that negative "expressed emotion" in the form of criticism and hostility is predictive of poor course and outcome (see chapter 3). This would be one significant factor to account for Sebastián's sustained psychosis and poor prognosis.

## WHAT DOES STRUGGLE AGAINST MENTAL ILLNESS TELL US ABOUT STRUGGLE AS A HUMAN FORCE?

In emphasizing the centrality of struggle rather than symptoms in the lived experience of mental illness, I do not wish to downplay the obvious importance of symptoms for clinical diagnosis. My emphasis on struggle as central to the daily and long-term experience of mental illness is intended as a frame to identify the quality of experience as an active process. The dominant place of struggle in the face of sustained severity and discontent, vivid in the narrative of Sebastián, is not invariably the case among those with mental illness. On the other hand, the core stance of struggle in situations of mental illness is often relevant with respect not only to extraordinary experience but also to the ordinary and mundane. Close attention to the worlds inhabited by persons such as Sebastián demands recognition that everyday routines to create what I have elsewhere called "the rhythm of life" (Jenkins 1997) are sites of struggle no less than the management of tortured and florid experience.

From a methodological standpoint, my emphasis on struggle emerges directly from the nature of the ethnographic encounter and the value and the limitations of listening and understanding. The excerpts from my field notes record my observation that documenting the suffering of an extraordinary human being is difficult for the researcher herself. I cannot say how difficult my presence was in Sebastián's life, whether he found it interesting, supportive, or to some small degree comforting that he could speak about his experiences without negative judgment. It seemed that way to me, but the question of what he got out of the research task I set for myself, to try to understand his experience, I simply cannot say. I did not set out to "document suffering," but his experience was so thoroughly suffused with it that this is what the enterprise became. It was not a sentimental pursuit or an attempt to look voyeuristically into the pain of another but an attempt to understand truly extraordinary human experience and to enter, albeit to a limited extent, the lifeworld of a person whose encounters with reality were not ordinary. The sense in which I use the term *suffering* here is as a mode of experience through which the ethnographer finds occasion to analyze extraordinary experience, power, meaning, emotion, and illness (Kleinman, Das, and Lock 1997; Das et al. 2001; Bourdieu, Accardo, and Ferguson 1999; Singer 2005). Ethnographically, I regard it a methodological imperative in the study of mental illness to begin with the concrete experience and raw existence of human beings and not jump immediately to social, cultural, political, and economic forces. Indeed, an ethnographic approach affords the ability to obtain data that are both valuable and unavailable through any other method.

While I do see Sebastián as a person who was substantially hurt and harmed by his father, he was not a passive victim, and it was through the immediacy of the ethnographic encounter that the notion of struggle came to replace that of suffering in my understanding of his experience. His effort and striving, though often failed, encompassed resilience, resistance, and agency. Once during the course of my visits Sebastián asked me, "Jani, remember you told me you're doing studies about people and you write things? I wonder what kinds of things you write about me?" At that point, I didn't have any manuscripts but thought perhaps I should show him the field notes I wrote, recording whatever was said with poor penmanship at lightning speed, along with my observations and transcribed interviews. I worried. What if what I showed him made him depressed? What if he felt my writing about him objectified or dehumanized him? Would this make the voices intensify? Or might he find satisfaction that things were being (to the best of my ability) accurately recorded? Accuracy was very important to him, and since I felt I had done a good job of it, maybe showing him the notes would make him feel good. I debated this and could not decide. Then one day on a visit to his house, almost on a whim, which I felt bordered on recklessness, I took in one of the larger notebooks I had kept and set it down on the table after I arrived. We sat across from one another in chairs. I slid the notebook and a manila file folder holding everything in it across the table to him. He laughed. As he opened it, I felt I was fighting a losing battle to control my own anxiety. He sat quietly, reading (I thought) the first page, then flipped to the next, then closed the file and slid it back across the table to me, saying, "I thought you were probably doing a good job. You write a lot."

Although I feared that he would be upset at seeing himself as a subject of study he instead seemed concerned about me: Was I was doing a careful job? I felt relieved yet strangely disappointed. Didn't he really want to read all this stuff? Wasn't he worried about what I had written? I had to admit it didn't seem to take much to satisfy him. Then I realized the obvious: what was really at stake was not the content but the act of whether or not I would show him what I was writing. Once that issue was off the table (metaphorically and literally) we proceeded to talk as we usually did. He launched into a story about a new scheme he had to make glass-encrusted lights that he hoped would be of particular interest to Carmen.

Sebastián's request to see the notes was an act of agency and my showing of them an act of respect. Agency and respect point more to the capacity for struggle than to suffering but even more important point to the common human predicament that the mentally ill share with everyone else. But if we grant the centrality of struggle to all humans, as we must, what is so significant about struggle in this case (and others) of mental illness? The salience of struggle is significant in several ways. First, that it emerges so strongly despite the presence of disorienting and disturbing features of illness illustrates that such conditions are not so disabling that the human capacity for striving is eclipsed. The intact and active process of struggle lays bare mistaken notions of the mentally ill as passive and incapable. Indeed, the determined efforts to survive and to make sense of such conditions are in many cases nothing short of valiant. Second, treatment that is primarily or exclusively biomedical, focusing on symptoms and psychotropic medications, is not only reductive but also counterproductive in that it fails to acknowledge and support an active struggle in which persons have the capacity to develop strategies for living. Third, the great suffering that humans experience in situations of mental illness is often met with equally immense endurance in the face of this suffering. Anthropologically, this endurance despite acute distress suggests that the capacity for struggle may be the most remarkable feature of *Homo sapiens*. This is true in neurobiological and cultural respects alike. We are neurobiologically wired for survival in the face of struggle, whether quotidian or titanic. Moreover, persons enduring immense suffering are hosts to an equally remarkable social and cultural capacity for creative strategies to tolerate and manage profoundly disorienting and disconcerting alterations of experience. Indeed, there exists an inherent sociality through which people—with or without psychosis—remain engaged (both in and outside their own minds) and actively involved in the cultural creation of symbolic meaning in their lives.

## CHAPTER 3

# Expressed Emotion and Conceptions of Mental Illness

## Social Ecology of Families Living with Schizophrenia

Every science, like every person, has a duty toward its
neighbors, not perhaps to love them as itself, but still to lend
them its tools, to borrow tools from them, and generally, to
keep the neighboring sciences straight.

—Gregory Bateson, "Minimal Requirements for a Theory of
Schizophrenia"

Persons like Sebastián who are diagnosed with schizophrenia-related
disorders undergo alterations of perception, thought, and habit. Their
parents and other family members go through a complicated process of
trying to come to grips with what is happening to their loved ones. In
chapter 1 I explored the "cultural chemistry" constituted by the cultivation of desires, conceptualizations, and practices surrounding drugs and
illness. Here I am concerned with a similar process situated in the lived
experience of kin-based social relations and constituted through the
confluence of (1) the inchoate and spectacular features of schizophrenia
as subjective experience and (2) the daunting challenge for kin trying to
make sense of and care for relatives in the throes of this experience.
These two intertwined positions can produce a powerful cultural chemistry in the crucible of the household. What is often involved for persons
diagnosed with schizophrenia is an exquisite sensitivity and alteration
of bodily perception, auditory voices, anxiety, and fear about what is
going on as a matter of the self in the world. What is often involved for
the family is an alteration of social relations and functioning, including

anxiety about the disturbed state of a loved one and awareness of the toxic social stigma attached to a condition perceived as a form of mental illness.

Despite the differing perspectives, there are points of intersection in the reciprocal creation of meaning and action between the afflicted and their kin. First, this social situation cannot be understood as generated by or confined to home settings but involves an array of cultural, biological, psychological, and political-economic factors that shape subjectivity. Second, there is a cultural repertoire of conceptions, explanations, emotions, and strategies—what anthropologists call an ethnopsychology—for how to experience and to interpret the world, and this repertoire shapes accounts and actions (Jenkins 1994). Drawing on this cultural repertoire is contingent not only on the subject position (persons hearing voices or kin living with such persons) but also on the temporal criteria of experiencing the situation (initial or long-standing) and exposure to competing discursive social fields of interpretation (biomedical, advocacy, religious, and myriad other social groups). Third, both the afflicted and their family members often describe the situation as bewildering, maddening, or insufferable. Equally striking, however, are the determined, dedicated, and even heroic responses to such conditions by caretakers and afflicted alike.

Inhabiting such a complex social ecology clearly constitutes an extraordinary condition. The case study of Sebastián in chapter 2 provides a painful close-up illustration of the emotional atmosphere of intimate communication among kin in the context of a psychotic process. This chapter examines these emotional atmospheres by addressing what I have formulated as interlocking findings: culture shapes kin conceptualizations of conditions that are diagnosed as psychiatric disorder *and* shapes familial emotional response to those conditions; these two factors in turn significantly influence the course and outcome of schizophrenia and other mental illnesses—that is, who improves and who does not. The classic interests of anthropologists (i.e., how people culturally conceive and inhabit their worlds) and psychiatrists (i.e., how to diagnose and treat those with disorders) converge to shed light on clinical outcomes.[1]

Another way to appreciate the significance of the problem is to consider that, despite the reality that millions of mentally ill persons are homeless, abandoned by kin, or disproportionately incarcerated in prison, from a global perspective families—not "communities," neighborhoods, hospitals, or religious sites—constitute the most common living situation for persons with mental disorder. Among many ethnic and immigrant groups in the United States, including Latinos, kin residence prior to and following hospitalization for an acute psychotic episode is typical. Moreover, in the wake of deinstitutionalization and inadequate community residential programs, kin residence following psychiatric hospitalization has become increasingly common. This trend means that relatives are increasingly finding it necessary to cope with the day-to-day realities and difficulties of living with kin who are diagnosed with mental illness (Jenkins 1988b; Jenkins and Schumacher 1999).

## CONDITIONS OF SCHIZOPHRENIA AND CROSS-CULTURAL VARIATION

Schizophrenia is often spoken about as a single disorder, but properly speaking there is a heterogeneous group of schizophrenias (Bleuler 1978). In the field of psychiatry, schizophrenia has long reigned as the queen of psychiatric disorders, portrayed in textbooks as mysterious, multifaceted, and bizarre (Freedman, Kaplan, and Sadock 1976: 439–48). The semantic network surrounding schizophrenia involves hallucination, delusion, chaotic thinking, and experiencing the world as unreal. Infelicitously, the term *schizophrenia* often appears as a cultural trope for a society out of control or is misused to mean torn in two incommensurable directions. When used to refer to persons it is considered offensive in a way that the term *diabetic*, for example, is not.

While there has been a long-standing controversy over whether schizophrenia is caused by neurobiological and genetic factors *or* by traumatic and adverse events during childhood and adolescence, current research offers evidence for both and suggests that risk is considerably amplified when both sets of factors co-occur (Read et al. 2001; Wicks, Hjern, and Dalman 2010). Studies of monozygotic twins show that rates at which schizophrenia appears in both siblings (concordance rates) vary widely (15–75 percent), but on average the concordance in monozygotic twins is not what one would expect if you take genetics as primary, since concordance rates account for only roughly 50 percent of cases (Insel 2010). On the other hand, there has been a wealth of recent data demonstrating the significant relationship between adverse and traumatic childhood experience (neglect, maltreatment, physical abuse, sexual abuse, severe bullying) and subsequent development of psychosis and schizophrenia (Cutajar et al. 2010; Kelleher et al. 2013; Read et al. 2005; Van Winkel et al. 2013), as well as PTSD, depression, and bipolar disorders (Daruy-Filho et al. 2011; Lu et al. 2008; Quarantini et al. 2010; Nanni, Uher, and Danese 2012).

Impressive as these recent studies are, what will be required in future are integrated genomic approaches that incorporate neurodevelopment, lived experience, and individual and cultural variation. These sources of complex variation remain startlingly undertheorized in light of available empirical evidence. Specifically, theoretical formulations of the development of mental illness must prominently incorporate the adverse living conditions of poverty (Lende 2012) and gender inequality. Thinking on this level must be broad and deep—not reduced to individual "risk factors." For example, worldwide women and girls disproportionately struggle daily against a barrage of events and conditions that can seriously compromise psychological integrity (Jenkins and Good 2014).

Beyond neuroscientific and epidemiological levels of analysis, with respect to empirical evidence of cultural variation for schizophrenia two issues are central: (1) whether there is a universal set of pathognomonic symptoms and (2) whether the course of schizophrenia(s) is invariant. I will address the first only in passing as an introduction to the second, which is the focus of my discussion. Data addressing the first question, that of pathognomonic and universally invariant symptoms of schizophrenia that can be uniformly found across world cultures, are mixed. My reading of the evidence, the details of which are documented in reports by the World Health Organization (1973, 1979), is that there is empirical clinical evidence for the similarity of symptom profiles at the same time that there is evidence of significant cultural variation and specificity of symptoms across countries.[2] However, to the extent that schizophrenia can be reliably identified in different settings, there were early reports in the cross-cultural psychiatric literature of significant cross-cultural variability in course and outcome of schizophrenia even prior to the WHO studies (Murphy and Raman 1971; Waxler 1977).

The larger-scale WHO findings, however, were unexpected since the established clinical literature had long typified schizophrenia as an inevitably chronic and deteriorating disease from which recovery was all but impossible (Kraepelin 1919). From the outset the results of these studies were compelling. Better outcomes in the form of relatively less psychotic symptomatology and higher social functioning were observed in Nigeria and India compared to Denmark, Russia, Czechoslovakia, the United Kingdom, and the United States (WHO 1979). For example, at the two-year follow-up the ostensibly pathognomonic symptom "flat affect"[3] was observed among only 8 percent of the Nigerian sample, compared to 50 percent of Russian subjects (WHO 1979).[4]

Yet the WHO studies could only serve as the basis for hypothesis generation as they required far more extensive and rigorous methods and geographic range. A major anthropological complaint about the original studies is that to account for the unexpected better outcome in "non-Western" countries there would need to have been carefully collected ethnographic materials. In contrast to the systematic research reliability of the clinical data collected by WHO, there was scant sociocultural material with which to work. Fortunately, since the original work, over three decades of WHO studies on the course of schizophrenia have been conducted across nearly thirty research sites spanning nineteen countries that have participated in one or more of the research protocols (Hopper 2004: 62–63).

The WHO analytic designation of sites as "developing" and "developed" has been problematic, however. What the dichotomous group really appears to mean is that research subjects from Africa, Asia, and Latin American have, overall in a statistical sense, better course and outcome compared to subjects from study sites in Europe[5] and the United States. Further, it is crucial to bear in mind that these differences—important as they are—are statistical differences and thus do not address considerable individual variation or potentially significant variation across sites within the same country. Neither place nor "people" equals culture, and the myriad other specific contextual features that comprise cultural orientation are not reducible to factors or geographic locales. Nor can the critique be allowed to stand that evident cultural differences simply amount to unexplained variance (Edgerton and Cohen 1994).[6]

Critical interrogation of the multiple original data sets and their interpretation (Harrison et al. 2001; Hopper and Wanderling 2000; Hopper et al. 2007) has found that when potential sources of bias are analyzed (differences in follow-up, grouping of centers, diagnostic ambiguities, outcome measures, gender, and age), "none of these potential confounds explains away the differential in course and outcome" (Hopper and Wanderling 2000: 835). The most recent analysis of recovery from psychotic illness at fifteen- and twenty-five-year follow-up confirms international variability in course and outcome, and while treated cases have favorable long-term outcome the observation remains robust that sociocultural conditions appear to modify long-term course. The finding of good long-term outcome for a significant proportion of treated cases of schizophrenia suggested that early intervention programs would do well to focus on social as well as pharmacological treatments to enhance recovery (Harrison et al. 2001). In sum, the finding of "consistent outcome differential favoring the 'developing' centers is remarkably robust" (Hopper 2004: 71). Since neurophysiological and natural history explanations of disease are insufficient to explain these findings, the WHO investigators themselves have urged the examination of cultural and social factors (Sartorius, Jablensky, and Shapiro 1977). In sum, the existing body of research clearly indicates that any thoroughgoing understanding of the course and outcome of mental illness must seriously take cultural processes into account.

## SCHIZOPHRENIA AS SITUATION: SULLIVAN, SAPIR, BATESON, AND BEYOND

In my analysis, the process of shaping cultural conceptualizations of mental illness and attendant social emotional responses is reciprocal. Ethnopsychological definition of the problem may suggest a particular cultural emotional repertoire of response. If a person is lovingly attached to an ill family member he or she may choose to adopt a relatively more sympathetic and forgiving cultural conceptualization of the problem. Such was the case with Sebastián's mother. Defining the problem as some kind of clever fakery or manipulation, as did Sebastián's father, may occur in tandem with marked hostility. Moreover, the relation between defining the problem and emotional response can be inflected in a number of ways.

First, though one might expect that most persons struggling with mental illness would be influenced by the affective bent of their relatives, not all are. Second, there can be routes of escape from a potentially harmful family emotional milieu, particularly for those with the financial resources to change residence or secure access to psychotherapy and psychotropic treatments; treatment can offer considerable protection even for those who continue to reside in difficult family situations. Third, the adverse affective kin response has been shown not to be reducible to the severity of illness: negativity in the emotional milieu does not correspond directly to the behavior of the ill person, nor does the sensitivity of the ill person correspond directly to the intensity of negative emotion. Nevertheless, it is also the case that a complex interpersonal dynamic is in play such that persons with illness can wreak havoc on their kin and significantly strain the familial system. No one size fits all in these formulations, and the dynamic is further inflected by individual and group variation in biogenetics, social status, and psychological functioning. To my mind, it is simply impossible to overstate the significance of these specific social and cultural processes for the lives of persons affected by mental illness. Such processes play a profound role in daily experience and possibilities for improvement or recovery from the torment of serious mental illness.

My strategy for examining this issue entails a conceptualization of schizophrenia as an interactive situation rather than as a discrete disease entity. This approach was established by Harry Stack Sullivan and Edward Sapir, who in collaboration considered schizophrenia a paradigmatic case for the analysis of fundamental human processes (Sapir 1961; Sullivan 1962). The anthropological contribution was Sapir's (1961: 151) well-known identification of the locus of culture in the dynamic interaction of specific individuals and the symbolic meanings that they abstracted for themselves from those interactions. From the psychiatric side, Sullivan's (1953: 283) contribution was to understand mental disorder as any interpersonal process inadequate to a particular situation, tracing a continuum from everyday momentary slips of memory to psychotic fixed delusions. This conceptualization was integrally connected to an understanding of the self-system as a configuration of interpersonal devices for protection against emotional distress and for seeking emotional comfort (Chapman 1976: 95), thereby highlighting the importance of emotional atmospheres reciprocally created in the interpersonal space of related selves (Sullivan 1962). Sullivan and Sapir agreed that a person with a mental disorder must be evaluated in the context of his or her interpersonal and social situation, with particular attention to the emotional atmosphere.

The work of Gregory Bateson is equally a pillar of this tradition, for his influential concept of the "double bind" focused on the reciprocal construction of interactive settings, offering a powerful hypothesis about the perception and consequences of disordered communication within families (Bateson et al. 1956; Bateson 1960a, 1960b, 1972, 1979). For compelling reasons, Bateson's notion that the family environment can be "schizophrenogenic" is currently neither favorably regarded nor empirically defensible.[7] Families do not "cause" conditions of schizophrenia. More interesting for anthropologists regarding Bateson's formulation, however, is the curious lack of connection between his work on schizophrenia and his work on emotional atmosphere encapsulated in the concept of ethos (1958). To roughly summarize the contrast between the two concepts, "ethos" refers to the emotional environment of a cultural setting, whereas the "double bind" refers to the communicative environment of a family. Ethos has a more explicitly affective slant, while the notion of communication underlying the double bind concept leans toward the cognitive. Developed in the context of a small-scale society, ethos is descriptive and pertains more to a theory of culture, while the double bind, developed in a Euro-American context, was erroneously understood as causal and addressed to clinical practice. It is unfortunate that Bateson never explicitly integrated the two lines of thought to examine modifications of cultural ethos within the emotional atmosphere of families afflicted with mental disorder. That this integration could be achieved is evident when we observe that the notion of ethos was itself elaborated with data from close interpersonal interaction in particular social situations (Bateson 1958: 119–20). Yet, like Bateson, subsequent researchers have not made the synthesis, and the historical consequence has been a disciplinary segregation of his ideas: anthropologists thought about ethos; psychiatrists and psychologists thought about the double bind.

As a result, anthropology was left without a rigorous way to describe and to examine the emotional atmospheres that exist among the self-systems engaged in any interpersonal situation, let alone those critical situations involving mental disorder.[8] Impetus for developing an appropriate approach finally came from the florescence of theorizing about emotion and the self (Abu-Lughod 1986; Shweder and LeVine 1984; White and Kirkpatrick 1985). Although work such as that of Catherine Lutz on the Ifaluk (1988) shows that the locus of emotions may be primarily in *situations* rather than in the psyche, little cross-cultural work has concerned the emotional atmospheres that characterize such situations. Instead, it has often been concerned with the density of lexical elaboration in ethnopsychological theories of emotion (Lutz 1982) or the degree to which emotions become "hypercognized" (Levy 1984). Anthropologists have less frequently studied emotion in a way that incorporates experience and feeling (M. Rosaldo 1984) or the cultural force of emotion (R. Rosaldo 1989: 2). In Renato Rosaldo's view, the notion of force refers to the kinds of feelings one experiences on learning, for example, that the child just run over by a car is one's own and not a stranger's. Rather than speak in general about emotion as an abstract cultural system, one must consider the subject's position within a field of social relations in order to grasp the meaning of emotional experience. From this perspective the locus of disruptive emotional force in families of the mentally ill could be sought in the rupture of a particular intimate relationship and the violation of the self-systematic capacity for emotional protection.[9] It is in order to move our thinking about self and emotion in this direction that I have made use of "expressed emotion," a research construct specifically developed to take such factors into account.

## EXPRESSED EMOTION AND FAMILY MILIEU: METHODOLOGICAL ORIGINS

In the 1960s in England, the sociologist George Brown and the psychiatrist Michael Rutter initiated a series of studies of the relationship between an individual's living situation following psychiatric hospitalization and patterns of recovery from conditions diagnosed as schizophrenia (Brown et al. 1962). They had observed that persons who returned to live with family were rehospitalized more often than those who returned to live in non-kin settings. Their work was explicitly framed in terms of a shift *away* from prevailing psychiatric assumptions concerning the etiological relevance of *psychopathological* family features to the identification of *everyday* family features that might affect the course of major mental illness. Beginning with a distinctly exploratory approach, Brown adopted an intuitive-inductive approach to identification of qualitative aspects of family interaction and relationships that might be important in pathways to recovery (Brown 1985). Like Bateson, he was particularly attuned to tone of voice as a metacommunicational feature of family interaction.

Brown and colleagues conducted repeated, lengthy (four-hour) in-home naturalistic observational studies that were remarkably open-ended for the simple reason that at that point they had no idea what to look for or what might matter. They did what any anthropologist would do: they paid attention to everything in detail to see what might crop up as salient. Their home observations resulted in development of an open-ended interview, dubbed the Camberwell Family Interview (CFI) after the London township where it was first used. The interview evolved into a semistructured interview guide designed to elicit narrative accounts. The interviewer did not try to elicit any particular information from a respondent, instead allowing him or her to speak in detail and specificity about everyday aspects of family life. Especially noted were family patterns of interaction and relationship, including accounts of irritability, quarreling, intimacy, and affection, as well as events leading up to the recent acute psychotic episode and psychiatric hospitalization. Following the interview, these narrative accounts were analyzed using emotion-rating scales.[10]

Brown assumed that nothing particularly unusual (i.e., pathological) would emerge from his research endeavors; rather, anything of importance was to be discovered in the ordinary (nonpathological) features of family life and communication.

> But such [pathological] families were in fact uncommon, and it seemed most unlikely that they could provide a general explanation for what we were observing. . . . [I]t seemed important that the occasional presence of *deeply* disturbed or unusual relationships between parents and patients should not be allowed to dominate our thinking. If I had any hunch about what was going on, it was that it often involved something a good deal less fundamental, indeed commonplace. Therefore one way forward would be to develop an instrument capable of recording the range of feelings and emotions to be found in ordinary families. Indeed, the family instrument used to record "expressed emotion" was not developed with the families of schizophrenic patients, and it did not occur to me that there was anything amiss in this. (Brown 1985: 22; emphasis in original)

Implicit in this development of method is a parallel to the aforementioned work of Sullivan: just as for the latter there was a continuum between everyday mental disorder and serious psychopathology, for Brown there was a continuum between the feelings and emotions recorded in ordinary families of persons with schizophrenia.

Over two decades, this work became increasingly focused on a particular research construct for better or for worse dubbed "expressed emotion" (EE). The primary features of EE were identified as criticism, hostility, emotional overinvolvement (EOI), warmth, and positive comments expressed by close kin to an ill relative. In the wake of repeated empirical findings in the British studies of a significant relationship of the constellation of criticism, hostility, and EOI with clinical relapse in the course of schizophrenia, the construct of EE was in practice narrowed to these three. The accumulation of cross-cultural studies over several decades has in part reversed this trend such that all five EE factors are more frequently being taken into account. In general, however, it is widely reported that persons who live in households with high degrees of (negative) EE are significantly more likely to suffer a clinical relapse of psychotic symptomatology than are their counterparts in homes rated low on these factors (Brown, Birley, and Wing 1972; Vaughn and Leff 1976; Vaughn et al. 1984; Karno et al. 1987; Leff et al.

1987; Hooley 2007). The best outcomes were observed for persons who lived in low EE households *and* regularly took prescribed psychotropic medications. This was the finding for the Mexican-descent study my colleagues and I conducted, and while both factors were statistically significant, interestingly, EE was even slightly more predictive than was medication use (Karno et al. 1987).

As the EE method became increasingly prominent it generated controversy both in the research world and for its clinical implications. Many research psychologists complained that the method was far too time-consuming and burdensome since research was conducted in the home, insisting on more convenient and highly abbreviated measures.[11] Others were impressed with the research but were either indifferent or tone-deaf to family-based concerns. Psychiatrists and psychologists utilizing these methods often neglected to take into serious consideration the substantial role that culture plays both in theoretical elucidation of the EE construct and in the empirical variation that exists in emotional response. Some cultural anthropologists had a semiautomatic objection based on discomfort with a systematic methodology that includes rigorous training, research reliability, and quantitative techniques.[12] With respect to clinical implications, some family advocacy groups regarded EE research with suspicion, concerned that it presumed there are deficiencies in families; they felt (appropriately or not) attacked by this research paradigm and mounted a counterattack. Receiving political heat, program personnel at the National Institute of Mental Health in the United States quietly determined that perhaps funding this research was problematic.[13] Since then, through better communication and efforts by researchers to develop relevant interventions and respond to legitimate family concerns, the National Alliance for the Mentally Ill (NAMI), the largest family advocacy group in the United States, has undertaken significant efforts to integrate an understanding of EE into its psycho-education programs, particularly in the area of family communication with respect to criticism and hostility. Activists living with conditions of schizophrenia cite the importance of avoiding criticism in situations both inside and outside the family. Integration of EE into psychoeducational and advocacy efforts can be achieved through collaborative efforts to understand the potential therapeutic value of modifications in the content and tone of family communication.

Given this scenario, the synthesis of expressed emotion and psychocultural analysis has promise as a systematic paradigm for understanding the range of emotional experience and response across widely different cultural settings as well as within intimate family environments where in many respects there is the most at stake with respect to emotional well-being. Supplemented by careful case studies of experience and intersubjectivity, this synthesis has the potential to generate a comprehensive account of fundamental human processes associated with mental illness. A first step for an anthropological contribution to the EE work is to identify the forms in which the construct's principal components might appear in other societies. A second step is to assess whether in fact they are the most salient affective domains in other cultural contexts.

For example, in considering British data, the psychologist Christine Vaughn (1986), one the earliest British collaborators and the primary trainer in reliable use of the method, offered a formulation that differentiated relatives on the basis of four factors, in the following terms: (1) respect for an ill family member's relationship needs; (2) attitudes toward the legitimacy of the illness; (3) level of expectations for functioning; and (4) emotional reaction to the illness. Thus a relative is considered low in EE (low criticism) if he or she generally respects the ill relative's need for social distance or nonintimate communication, considers the problem to be illness-related and therefore outside the control of the individual, holds reduced expectations of functioning due to perceived disability, and displays a concerned but "cool," "easygoing," or "flexible" response to the problem (Leff and Vaughn 1985). That such dispassionate traits are held in high esteem in English cultural contexts is well known.

From an anthropological standpoint this culturally specific interpretation of "low expressed emotion" cannot be expected to provide a template for cross-cultural analysis that could elucidate the central features of the EE construct. As a colleague once remarked to me, "Leave it to the English to decide that emotion is a problem." Certainly it is tempting to conclude that construing the expression of anger as socially bothersome is a distinctively British problematic, but in fact across cultural settings the expression of anger is often configured as problematic. Provisos regarding "too much" or "too little" anger are commonplace. The expression of anger generates cultural trouble, be it Inuit, Ilongot, or turn-of-the-century Viennese trouble. In many Latin American traditions, anger and hostility, whether expressed among intimates or in witchcraft, are believed to cause serious, sometimes life-threatening, illness. The question is what counts as anger and, further, what counts as too much anger in a particular cultural setting.

A selective integration of EE into anthropological research, therefore, requires careful analysis of its conceptual components, for behind the questions about implicit and explicit theoretical underpinnings lies the issue of the scope of its potential validity for comparative work. Although the researchers in British and Euro-American studies felt that their work constituted a cross-cultural comparison (Vaughn et al. 1984), the value of this work invited replication across greater cultural distance. Our study of Mexican-descent families was the first such replication, and in the remainder of this chapter I describe this work, briefly discuss EE research in other cultural settings, and consider the importance of cultural variation in the conception of schizophrenia. I conclude with a summary of the critical features of expressed emotion that define its theoretical status in cross-cultural research.

## THE COURSE OF SCHIZOPHRENIA AMONG MEXICAN AMERICAN FAMILIES (COSAMA)

COSAMA was a longitudinal study in California of predominantly monolingual Spanish-speaking immigrant Mexicano families in which one member was under treatment for schizophrenia. Sebastián's family, described in chapter 2, is one of seventy families who participated in this study.[14] Throughout the literature on culture among Mexican, Chicano, and Mexican American populations, no single observation is more often made than that of the overwhelming importance of a strong family orientation (*familismo*) for self, identity, and well-being (Canino 1982; Calderón-Tena, Knight, and Carlo 2011; Calzada, Tamis-LeMonda, and Yoshikawa 2013; Gaviría and Araña 1987; Murillo 1976; Keefe and Padilla 1987). Indeed, as is more broadly true of Hispanic/Latino groups (Murillo 1976), an individual's sense of self may be construed in broad brush strokes as "indexical" (Gaines 1982) or "sociocentric" (social/kin-based, interconnected, interdependent, contingent) versus an "egocentric" (individually based, separate, autonomous, independent) orientation of the self (Shweder and Bourne 1982). Mexican-descent families have been characterized as generally protective of their members. Interpersonal relations characterized by *dignidad* (dignity) and *respeto* (respect) are considered vital to the maintenance of family functioning (Murillo 1976; Keefe and Padilla 1987), although such values can hardly be expected to comprehensively "typify" kin social practices. Further, familial hierarchy and inequality of social power based on age and gender means that such values do not apply across kin with equal force.

During the fieldwork, it was common to hear Mexicans and Mexican Americans comment that they fully recognized that living with an ill relative entailed substantial suffering. Such comments were often made with equanimity and quite notably without relinquishing hope of recovery, or more precisely, cure. In fact, relatives often reported expectations of cure and faith in doctors that mobilized their help-seeking efforts. They also sought out *curanderos* (healers) but not as often as medical doctors. However, these general observations only go so far given the substantial intracultural variation within Mexican-descent populations and within our specific study, and thus must be qualified to avoid essentializing, romanticizing, or bluntly missing the mark where commonly there is variation, divergence, and contestation within and across groups. That said, if a family-based method such as "expressed emotion" were to play a significant role in illness process, we felt that it would be of relevance for this particular ethnic group. As noted in the introduction, "culture" is neither place nor people, not a fixed or necessarily coherent set of values, beliefs, or behaviors, but an orientation to being-in-the-world that is dynamically created in the process of social interaction and historical context.

## CRITICAL MILIEU WITHIN FAMILIES

No ambition. Doesn't care for anything . . . The way I said it was to emphasize that worthlessness of his. Useless.

—Patrick, 42-year-old Euro-American father of Henry, age
20, sitting together in family living room, two weeks after
inpatient hospitalization

*Portándose muy mal con nosotros ella, ya nos perdí por completo el respeto, y entonces eso era muy mal que estaba haciendo ella.* (She was behaving very badly with us, lost respect for us completely, and that was very bad what she was doing).

—Consuelo, 43-year-old Mexican American mother of
Zenaida, age 25, speaking in hushed tones at her kitchen table

In the expressed emotion method, criticism is identified on the basis of the content and/or vocal characteristics of speech (Brown et al. 1978). To qualify as a critical comment an utterance must include a clear and unambiguous statement that the respondent dislikes, disapproves of, or resents a behavior or characteristic. Vocal characteristics that index critical comments are rated using tone of voice, pitch, and intonational contour. Such vocal markers, though their use varies cross-culturally (Irvine 1990), are observed to function in many languages as what Goffman termed "keying devices" to mark specific activities, distinguishing, for example, between teasing and criticism (Ochs 1986: 4–5). In Spanish, as in English, both content and vocal characteristics of speech may convey criticism. We therefore found it appropriate to focus on these features for the display of critical affect. One striking tendency emerged. During the pilot year of administration and rating of the CFI, we observed a common way to convey criticism by reference to anger, typically *me dio mucho coraje* (it made me very angry), although we noted other variations, such as those using the verb *enojarse* (to be annoyed, angry). The frequent use of these phrases to communicate criticism is indicative of the role of anger in Mexican family contexts to signal strong disapproval or annoyance. Such comments were also almost invariably made in a critical tone of voice. We therefore considered anger-related statements to be culturally specific ways of communicating critical affect in a way unparalleled by the British or Euro-American studies of criticism. Among those cultural groups, investigators reported that a typical way for relatives to make a criticism was to express dislike without necessarily making direct reference to anger (Brown, Birley, and Wing 1972; Vaughn and Leff 1976; Vaughn et al. 1984).

Criticisms are recorded and tallied on completion of each interview. In most research to date, the cutoff score for qualifying as "high" in expressed emotion has been derived empirically in relation to outcome.[15] The mean number of critical comments for Mexican American relatives (3.3) was significantly lower than their British (7.5) and Euro-American counterparts (6.9). These differences in the numbers of critical comments suggest cross-cultural variations in levels of criticism in the homes of persons with conditions diagnosed as schizophrenia. However, to understand these variations, the substantive domains in which criticism is expressed must be specified in order to determine whether, in cross-cultural perspective, relatives are critical of the same kinds of things (e.g., hearing voices, laziness, disrespect). Researchers from the original British studies argued that all critical comments could be subsumed under only two categories: "enduring personality traits," which in their analysis accounted for 70 percent of all criticisms, with the remaining 30 percent analyzed as "symptom behaviors" (Leff and Vaughn 1985). In our analysis, we found the empirical need for many more categories to describe the content of relatives' critical comments. From our perspective the type and limit of categories in the British analysis was problematic since (1) the analysis was embedded in Euro-American ethnotheory that tends to explain cultural rule violations (as recorded in criticism) with reference to personality attributions; and (2) the category of symptom behaviors describes the perspective of psychiatrists, not that of family members and their definitions of what might merit criticism.

Our content analysis of interview data for the low-income households of Mexican American and Euro-American families yielded a total of 22 categories for the Mexican Americans and 31 for the Euro-Americans (Jenkins et al. 1986). In the sorting process I found that some categories of critical comments were shared across the two groups, but some were specific to one group only. Moreover, there were major cultural differences in what relatives complained about. Among the Mexican American relatives, 39 percent of all critical comments were aimed at behaviors that relatives considered disruptive or disrespectful of the family, as compared to 27 percent of critical comments by Euro-American relatives. Also, relative to their Euro-American counterparts, Mexican American relatives displayed a lesser concern with negative personality traits and what relatives considered illness-related behaviors (hearing voices, unusual ideas, social withdrawal). The latter point can be taken as empirical support for the proposition that Latinos/Hispanics tended to be comparatively tolerant of behaviors that are diagnosed as psychotic symptomatology (Fabrega et al. 1968; Rogler and Hollingshead 1975; WHO 1979). We also found an important cross-cultural difference in criticism of inactivity and unemployment. Mexican Americans who were critical of the relative's unemployment stated flatly that they wanted or needed the person to work in an income-producing job. Euro-Americans often made the same basic request with statements that were often accusatory regarding what they took to be character deficits such as laziness; a lack of ambition, motivation, or achievement-orientation; or the inability to "settle down to one thing." Although the majority (72 percent) of the Mexican American relatives were not highly critical, the following case study illustrates the type of critical comments among those who were.

## Case Study: Zenaida Serrano

The parents of twenty-five-year-old Zenaida Serrano exemplified the concern for a smoothly functioning family unit. This ideal was sorely tested in the face of the difficulties generated by Zenaida's behavior. Her father made seven critical comments about Zenaida during the course of the interview. All his criticisms focused on various actions that from his perspective can be considered cultural rule violations, in the specific context of a parent-(adult) child family setting. He said she was argumentative, destructive, disrespectful, and deviant, and he complained that she seemed to nag him about a great many things, especially questioning his love and affection for her. This he regarded as silly, and while he would snap at her about such accusations, he nonetheless took the time to reassure her that she was indeed loved and wanted. We cannot know, but it is possible that explicit statements might have been experienced as mollifying by Zenaida. Other behaviors were more disturbing to the father, however. These included Zenaida's tendency to throw objects around the house, the fact that she slapped her mother on one occasion, and that she would go outdoors in her bathrobe. Worse still, she would insult him with rude and obscene language: *"¡Y me sacó a mi madre, y me dio mas coraje!"* (And she insulted me [with reference to my mother] and made me angrier!)

Zenaida's mother made five critical comments during the course of her interview. These were similar to those made by her husband. She criticized Zenaida for slapping her, for quarreling or fighting with the family, for behaving in a disrespectful way, and for behaving in a very strange *(raro)* way. When Zenaida once questioned her mother as to why she was scolded more frequently than were her siblings, her mother replied, *"¡Siempre estás peleando con los demás! ¡Por eso, hay más motivo para regañarte!"* (You are always fighting with the others [siblings]! Therefore, there is more reason to scold you!). Señora Serrano considered Zenaida's lack of proper respect for the family a source of consternation. She narrated an example of *raro* behavior that she found astonishing: *"¡Ella quiere besar el niño de dos años y besarlo en la boca! ¡Le dije que no era correcto besar a un niño en la boca!"* (She wants to kiss the two-year-old child and kiss him on the mouth! I told her this wasn't right to kiss a child on the mouth!). This unusual behavior clearly mortified the mother, who demanded an account of her daughter's strange act. Zenaida replied that she was desirous of knowing the sensation of kissing a man and wanted to try it out with this young child. The mother's response reflected her consternation and incredulity: *"¡Ay, Dios mío!"* (Oh, my God!)

Despite these trying behaviors, this family considered it their responsibility to care for their ill family member. For example, Señor Serrano disagreed with professional staff who had repeatedly advised him that Zenaida should be placed in a board-and-care facility, given their professional perception of the trouble she had caused for the family. Señor Serrano, on the other hand, viewed the care of his daughter as his family's responsibility. Señora Serrano voiced her concern that Zenaida needed "a mother's love" and that certain unscrupulous persons might take advantage of her daughter. She explained to me that people who are very ill with *nervios*[16] can become debilitated and vulnerable and in need of protection. Señor Serrano agreed, adding that the possibility of Zenaida becoming pregnant were she to live outside the household would only add to his financial burden since, in his view, the child would be his responsibility.

Interestingly, the staff at the psychiatric facility where Zenaida had been treated took a different view: as far as they were concerned, the Serrano family had repeatedly "sabotaged the treatment plan" by failing to agree to her placement outside the family. The staff particularly complained that Zenaida's parents seemed unable to comprehend that their daughter, "a chronic schizophrenic," was unlikely to improve. This idea, let alone the specific language of "chronic" or "schizophrenic," made no sense to the parents. Zenaida's family maintained that despite their daughter's strange and upsetting behaviors, they missed her when she was gone (for brief hospitalizations). Even so, they felt that hospitalization, with close care by doctors for brief periods, made sense. They were also convinced that only God knows if and when she would improve. They held fast to their hope and faith that she could. Zenaida's situation illustrates the complex social ecology that constitutes an intrafamilial atmosphere. For example, despite the fact that her father was more critical than most of the other Mexican-descent relatives in the study, he simultaneously expressed warmth and affection. He displayed no hostility toward his daughter but seems to have become exceedingly firm when he felt his daughter had crossed the line of acceptable moral comportment in the family context.

## Criticism as Objections to Cultural Rule Violations

The behavior of persons diagnosed with schizophrenia can violate a host of cultural norms and proscriptions, and kin can often reasonably object to such violations. This is perhaps why, in some societies, the same term is employed for the mentally ill and for young children, indicating that acutely distressed persons are not fully in command of cultural rules (Geertz 1959; Myers 1979). Such social designations might not necessarily involve moral culpability. Even so, the perceived violation of cultural rules can still engender social trouble. Edgerton (1978: 466) has observed that while societies may allow for acceptable diversity in human conduct, one knows "when the limits of acceptable variation have been exceeded because the result is 'trouble' in the form of complaints, disputes, accusations, recriminations, and the like." Critical comments may be viewed in this light as complaints about the perceived violation of rules. In this regard, note that Bateson and colleagues (1956) argued that confusion about rules is central to schizophrenia. Shweder (1980: 86) has underscored Freud's identification of "criticism (and related activities such as accusing and accounting) as the primary activity associated with rules." Also relevant is Lutz's (1982) analysis of emotion words among the Ifaluk in Micronesia; her data show that situations are emotionally evaluated with reference to which cultural values have been violated.

I am convinced that the critical comments component of EE research is valid for cross-cultural research only if grounded in a generalizable definition of criticism as negative affective response to perceived cultural rule violation. In Leff and Vaughn's (1985) conceptualization, the Euro-American cultural preoccupation with personality was already embedded in the theoretical presuppositions, such that their informants' emphasis on personality as a domain of criticism was taken for granted, and both data and analysis were couched in terms of personality. These researchers then concluded that personality traits of relatives (e.g., tolerant-intolerant, good-bad) lead them to make personality attributions (e.g., lazy, stubborn) about their ill family member. The one-dimensional and tautological reasoning is framed by the overarching explanatory construct of personality. This is entirely consistent with Euro-American ethnotheory, which tends to explain things gone wrong with reference to personality traits. While a significant proportion of the critical comments made by the English-speaking relatives do appear as negative personality attribution, careful analysis reveals this is only a partial account of the problem. This example serves to underscore how in the absence of empirical cross-cultural comparative analysis conceptual analysis can amount to little more that the reification of cultural categories (Kleinman 1988b).

My analysis of criticism as kin objections to cultural rule violations is based on the definition of a rule as "shared understanding of how people ought to behave and of what should be done if someone behaves in a way that conflicts with that understanding. Rules, then, prescribe or proscribe behavior . . . and have a regulatory sense" (Edgerton 1985: 24). As Edgerton has pointed out, rules may be understood in terms that are definite or indefinite, explicit or implicit, grave or trivial, simple or complex. They may be formulated as personal routines, conventions, secular regulation, moral principles, or supernatural injunctions. For the anthropology of criticism, however, we must focus only not on the content of rules per se but also on the context of their violation.

Parents of an adult child with mental illness may also launch criticism, for example, in an attempt to elicit behavior change. Euro-American ethnopsychology holds that people can (and should) be direct in expressing themselves and their feelings. Further, parents may even intend their criticism as a motivational exhortation or an attempt to alter a culturally unacceptable behavior. Such exhortations may not necessarily be mean-spirited. Well intended or not, the expressed emotion research appears to indicate that heightened sensitivity to social-emotional stimuli among persons with mental illness means that exhortations or frequent criticisms are counterproductive.[17]

There seems to be a wide range of cultural settings in which some degrees and types of criticism are present, including Ireland (Scheper-Hughes 1979), China (Lin and Lin 1981; Wen pers. comm. 1988; Yang et al. 2004), Puerto Rico (Rogler and Hollingshead 1975), and Sri Lanka (Mendes pers. comm. 1987). A suggestive example of an unaccepting and possibly critical or rejecting affect, despite a sociocentric sense of self and strong cultural prescriptions for love and compassion toward kin, appears in Fred Myers's (1979) work with Pintupi Aborigines in Australia. He noted the overwhelming salience of the concept of *walytja* (compassion for kin, or shared identity) and a specific view of the self based on shared identity connected with a "web" of significant others that European observers would describe as external to the self. In this context we might imagine that a person with mental disorder would be the object of compassion and integrated within the community. However, he reports an example of an individual's strategic use of this cultural orientation to his own personal advantage.

> That the concept of "compassion" is best understood as the notion of being moved by another's wishes or condition is expressed by one man's hope that the doctors would take away his insane wife. They should not, he said, feel sorry for her *(ngal turrinylja wrya)*, but should do what *he* wanted (i.e., have compassion for *him*). (1979: 356; emphasis in original)

In this incident, we may detect traces of a critical attitude, even though compassion is the predominant affective ideal and even though a sociocentric self would seem to preclude self-interest. While this may not be the strongest form of evidence, it suggests that if it were looked for, criticism might even be found among such a compassionate people as the Pintupi.

The issue of the relativity or universality of forms and types of criticism is a matter for empirical determination, and I can suggest three guidelines for such an inquiry. First, if criticism is defined in terms of rule violations, are there rules that exist universally? Edgerton (1985) suggests that there may be some, such as proscriptions of violence and prescriptions for cooperation. Shweder (1980) has also outlined types of rules that may be universal. Second, we need to know the full range of response to rule violation, such that we can identify not only the presence or absence of criticism in a particular society, but its cultural salience or "weightiness" in particular settings. Criticism culturally defined as berating, as punishment, or as normative mode of interaction may not be comparable at all. Third, criticism cannot be understood apart from cultural definitions of the self. With respect to rule violations, the critical issues are agency, autonomy, and accountability for behavior, as well as beliefs about the possible effects of one's actions on others. In sum, a thoroughgoing anthropology of criticism is necessary for further cross-cultural elaboration of ideas generated by the EE paradigm.

## SELF AND EMOTIONAL OVERINVOLVEMENT

Emotional overinvolvement is a type of kin response to an ill family member defined by relatively extreme degrees of self-sacrificing, devoted, protective, and intrusive behavior. In the Mexican American study, our methodological assumption was that for cultural validity in the identification of such behaviors, cultural meaning and definition was paramount. For example, we presumed as normative a high degree of involvement in family affairs in Mexican and Mexican American households. We expected that this would be no less so in a situation of serious family illness. This led us to infer that the way in which high degrees of EOI were manifest among Mexican-descent relatives would not be the same as reported for the British or Euro-American families (Brown et al. 1972; Vaughn and Leff 1976; Vaughn et al. 1984). According to the British criteria, for example, behavior would be considered exceptionally devoted if a relative made daily visits to the hospital and brought homemade food to the patient. However, Mexican Americans would not judge this similarly. Family members do not regard daily visits to the hospital as excessive or self-sacrificing, and such visits often are expected of mothers and female kin. Among our predominantly Spanish-speaking immigrant participants, mothers reported that frequent hospital visits were important, since this may have been their son's or daughter's first overnight stay away from home. They expressed concern about the experience of being sick in an English-speaking American hospital facility. They felt that bringing familiar food to patients was a minor favor that could provide an ill relative with great comfort at a time of extreme distress.

The most notable finding for emotional overinvolvement in our study (as well as others),[18] is that only a small number of kin were considered "high" or "overly" emotionally involved when using the 0–5 point scale: only 11 (or 11 percent) of 109 relatives were rated as excessively or intrusively involved in culturally unusual ways.[19] Our results do not support ethnographic or clinical stereotypes of Latin American women as typically "overprotective" and "self-sacrificing" (Canino 1982). These data are also important because they do not provide support for the notion that disturbed or pathological interpersonal relations typify families of persons diagnosed with schizophrenia. Far from being the norm, our data, as well as those of the British and Euro-American studies, indicate that such characterizations are specious.

Among those relatives who *were* considered unusually or excessively involved, qualitative features of self-sacrificing and overprotective behaviors were culturally distinctive compared to previous studies (see Vaughn 1986). The characteristic features of EOI among Mexican-descent families can be specified precisely as follows: (1) contemplation of suicide or death wishes specifically in reference to concern over the illness; (2) endangering one's own life by risking or enduring extremely threatening or abusive circumstances (e.g., physical violence); (3) extreme somatic distress associated with reports of *nervios,* depression, insomnia, and weight loss specifically in relation to the illness; (4) constant complaints of extreme suffering; (5) living in chronic states of extreme fear, anxiety, and worry over the relative; (6) significant changes in family activities and caretaking patterns (i.e., loss of family orientation and adoption of a nearly exclusive dyadic orientation with the ill relative); (7) cessation of previous social activities to remain home at all times to "protect" the ill relative in the absence of circumstances warranting it; (8) vigilant or intrusive involvement with the ill relative in the absence of dangerous circumstances; and (9) extreme dramatization and emotional display in the narration of events.

It is important that the interpretation of the foregoing behaviors as "extreme" was not confined to the ratings obtained through research interviews. During home visits, it was not uncommon for siblings, spouses, and other kin to convey their concerns that such a relative had "lost it" or was behaving far differently than others in the family expected. One mother, for example, described her relation to her son as follows: "Alejandro and I have always gotten along well because we are very *afinados* [in tune with one another]. In nearly all situations we don't even need to speak because we already know what the other is thinking. This is because we are exactly the same, in all things in life. It's very normal." Referring to such statements, other family members said that she was "not herself."

## Case Study: The Mother of Francisco

Francisco's mother was rated as extremely emotionally involved with her son's illness. She reported being so distressed by her son's illness that she had contemplated suicide in numerous ways, including shooting herself with a gun, throwing herself into oncoming traffic, and throwing herself down a staircase at home. She maintained that she was unable to bear *(aguantar)* the situation for one more day. Throughout the interview she was tearful and emotionally distraught while talking about her son, despite the fact that he had recently experienced a dramatic improvement and had come home from the hospital.

Prior to that, there was no doubt that Francisco, who was twenty-one, was experiencing problems with several hostile voices talking to him. He also believed people were trying to kill him and was very fearful of going into crowds or leaving through the front door of his home. He also reported difficulty with his thinking: he would become confused and disorganized easily and frequently, was unable to concentrate, and believed he could influence other people with his thoughts. When I first met Francisco in the hospital I asked him what kind of trouble he had been having. He responded by telling me he had a "social problem" and that he was not the "sociable" type. He also complained that he had a problem with his thinking because he had a lot of thoughts and feelings that made him feel "stuck." After I explained the study to him, I asked if he thought it would be possible for me to come to visit him at home and also to interview some of his family members. He agreed to this but asked me if I wouldn't mind telling his mother and oldest sister that they should leave him alone and stop bothering him. He claimed that it didn't help him to know that they were always worrying about him, listening in on his telephone calls, following him down the street when he would leave to buy cigarettes, and refusing to let him see his friends.

Francisco's mother described herself as having enjoyed music, singing, and socializing with others prior to the onset of her son's illness, but her interest in these activities had now faded. Suffering (*"sufrir, puro sufrir"*) had come to occupy a central role in her life, and she made it clear that her life had been dramatically altered. She told me that her sole task in life now was to take care of Francisco, saying, *"Yo lo cuidaba como una perla o un diamante"* (I take care of him like a pearl or a diamond). This involved following him around the house and never letting him out of her sight. She claimed she did this to ensure nothing "bad" would ever happen to him. If he was late on a routine errand or a visit to a friend, she would fall to the floor in an *ataque de nervios* (severe attack of nerves; see Guarnaccia and Farias 1988), during which she wailed loudly and talked rapidly and unintelligibly about how unbearable her life has been. Other family members told me that they considered their mother's behavior unusual and extreme. While *ataques* can commonly be expected to occur in response to serious situations (such as death, very bad news, severe family conflict), they considered their mother's frequent episodes in response to minor incidents odd.

### Case Study: The Father of Gabriella

Another case of high emotional overinvolvement is that of Señor Vasquez, the sixty-nine-year-old father of eighteen-year-old Gabriella. The onset of his daughter's illness reportedly began in her early teens, when she would cry and scream throughout the night. On several occasions her father took her to Mexico to see *curanderos* in the border city of Tijuana. The *curanderos* agreed that her condition was due to "female trouble" and was specifically related to the onset of menstruation. Her trouble included hearing voices, irritability, insomnia, and violent and destructive behavior (e.g., breaking a window, hitting and shoving family members).

Señor Vasquez lived in East Los Angeles with his daughter and four younger children. He described himself as "both mother and father to my children," since the mother "deserted" the family. He expressed his view that his daughter suffered from mental illness partly because she has a *"fuerte de naturaleza"* (strong sexual or physical nature). However, Señor Vasquez also understood his daughter's problem as the result of having grown up in a home environment where her mother had various lovers who would "hold and kiss her" in front of Gabriella. According to him, his daughter would be much better off if she were married because he felt it was important for her to be active sexually. During the course of the home visits, he mentioned several times that Gabriella had asked him to make love with her and that he had had to push her away because she clung to him and kissed him in a way that is inappropriate for a daughter to behave with her father.

Despite Gabriella's relatively serious troubles, she had been able to go to school and was particularly interested in friends and in social and church activities. Her father cautioned against all such activities, insisting that she stay home and that he take care of her. Even though a young girl came daily to help with cooking and child care, he said he also felt that his daughter should be at home to take care of him since he was almost completely blind. He reported that the way he took care of *her* was to keep his arm around her all day (*"todo el día la traía del brazo"*). He stayed with her constantly; he helped her dress and eat and especially insisted on helping her go to the bathroom. (His rationale for this kind of "shadowing" was that Gabriella had once thrown a sanitary napkin down the toilet and clogged it up.) He also slept with her at night, his arms around her constantly. His reason for doing this, he asserted, was to prevent her from leaving the house and possibly getting into trouble, despite the fact that she had never attempted to do so. He was explicit in claiming that he slept with her to protect her and certainly not to abuse her sexually. The sixteen-year-old sister, who was also interviewed, reported that she thought her father's behavior was strange, since most of her friends' fathers did not sleep with or dote on their daughters like he did. Throughout his narration of events he was very dramatic, frequently punctuating his points with *"Ay Dios," "¡Válgame Dios!" "Es mi hija, yo la quiero. Me apuro por ella"* (Oh God; Give me a break, God; It's my daughter, I love her. I have suffered because of her). He reported that he had lost sleep worrying about her, thinking of ways to control her and keep her from leaving the house. He dramatically narrated a number of stories; for example, the time eighteen-year-old Gabriella failed to hold his hand when crossing the street, he nearly had an *ataque de nervios*.

## Reflections on Emotional Overinvolvement

The notion of emotional overinvolvement focuses on overprotective and self-sacrificing behaviors. In actuality, high degrees of these behaviors are less frequent than are high degrees of criticism among relatives.[20] When such instances do occur, however, the behavioral portrait appears to resemble constructs in the family therapy literature, such as "enmeshment" and "symbiosis" (Goldenberg and Goldenberg 1980; Minuchin 1974). These terms presuppose a culturally specific notion of the self as a bounded entity, but the defining characteristic is that these boundaries have been surpassed. Aside from the conceptual domain they cover, however, concepts such as enmeshment differ from emotional overinvolvement in two important ways. First, EOI is an empirically derived measure based on evidence gathered in a research interview rather than on clinical judgments made in therapeutic situations. Second, and perhaps more important, these concepts differ substantially in how they have been applied: enmeshment and the double bind were formulated to account for presumed family *etiological* features of schizophrenia, whereas emotional overinvolvement has been applied to features that have been empirically associated with the *course* of illness.

Here is the arena in which the cross-cultural validity of the EOI concept must be scrutinized rigorously, for in order for the required transgression of boundaries to be possible, let alone constitute a disturbance, the cultural psychology[21] of a people must include some kind of bounded self. In approaching this problem, several points must be made. First, in relation to emotion, kin relationships can be understood as constituted precisely with respect to such boundaries, say, in contrast to a jural viewpoint that defines them in terms of rights and responsibilities. Second, it is doubtful that there exists a cultural orientation in which the self is entirely without bounds in some minimal sense. For example, fieldwork with Salvadoran refugees in Boston (see chapters 4 and 5) and the clinical presentation of refugees and torture victims from all parts of the world suggest that trauma and torture are invariably events for the self (Jenkins 1991b; Jenkins, Kleinman, and Good 1991; Mollica, Wyshak, and Lavelle 1987). Third, the existence of an incest taboo argues for the presence of boundaries for the self. Finally, though EOI typically occurs in a small proportion of cases, it exhibits a remarkably similar constellation of features across the cultural settings in which it has been documented. Given these observations, examination of the concept must still address the nature of the self in particular cultural contexts before proceeding to detailed documentation of cross-cultural variability in EOI.

One hypothesis is that EOI will be found only in societies where nucleated households structure the emotional atmosphere. Studies of expressed emotion in India, where extended kin households are prevalent, show the virtual absence of high degrees of EOI, though the methodological adequacy of this work remains in question (Wig et al. 1987a). However, Scheper-Hughes's (1979) data on schizophrenia suggest that EOI is very likely present among the Irish, and Briggs's (1987) data on attached-rejection behavior (*siqnaaniq*) toward vulnerable children suggest the same for the Inuit. Moreover, both these societies appear to possess the kind of repertoire of ethnopsychological concepts necessary even to respond to a research protocol like the CFI. Above all, culturally informed analysis must be alert to evidence of EOI in idioms other than those familiar in Euro-American cultural contexts, such as witchcraft or demonic possession.

A key methodological point about EOI on the part of relatives is that it is not linked to, or explicable by, the objective severity of the ill person's behavioral disturbance. Instead, it has more to do with relatives' subjective perception of how heavy a burden the illness places on the family (on "family burden," see Jenkins and Schumacher 1999). The relative rated high in EOI might say, for example, "I am completely overwhelmed by this," or "My whole life is looking after Juan," whether or not Juan objectively requires such looking after. Relatives who were highly emotionally overinvolved would complain to us that their lives were miserable and filled with suffering. Indigenous recognition of such an attitude and its accompanying behavior as pathological is clearly critical to the cross-cultural validity of the concept. It is, accordingly, important that in our study other household members did not praise emotionally overinvolved behaviors with statements like "She's a saint." Rather, they were likely to tell us things like "That's too much" or "My mother's lost it." This indigenous identification of EOI-related behaviors as unusual provides support for the cross-cultural validity of the concept.

Finally, social-ecological features such as household size, isolation, and economic dependence may be implicated, as suggested by a study showing that high EE level more accurately predicted relapse in one-parent households where there was a poor premorbid history (Parker, Johnston, and Hayward 1988). Moreover, in our study nearly all relatives considered to be high on this factor were female and all subjects male, not surprising insofar as it taps elements such as degree of affective involvement and caretaking that parallel cultural prescriptions for women. Recall that the one Mexican father who was considered high on this factor was a single parent who described his role in the family as "both mother and father" to his children. Given that we observed this kind of dynamic only in cross-sex family relations, there exists the possibility that it is in some instances related to sexualized gender confusion since, as noted in chapter 1, one-fifth of our participants struggled with gender confusion or the question of whether they actually were a man or a woman.

## CROSS-CULTURAL VARIATION IN EXPRESSED EMOTION

The early studies of EE and schizophrenia were carried out in England (Brown et al. 1972; Vaughn and Leff 1976), in California among Euro-American (Vaughn et al. 1984) and Mexican-descent families (Karno et al. 1987), and in India (Wig et al. 1987a, 1987b; Leff et al. 1987). When collapsing the criticism and EOI scores to yield overall household "high" or "low" EE ratings, striking cross-cultural differences emerged: 67 percent of California Euro-American households were classified as "high" (Vaughn et al. 1984), compared to 48 percent of British (Brown, Birley, and Wing 1972), 41 percent of California Mexican-descent (Karno et al. 1987), and 23 percent of Indian (Wig et al. 1987a, 1987b) households. In addition to overall differences in expressed emotion profiles, the studies also reported significant variation in the distribution and mean scores for criticism, hostility, emotional overinvolvement, and warmth.

Eventually, EE became one of the most thoroughly investigated psychosocial research constructs in psychiatry. This research continues and has been extended from schizophrenia to an array of conditions, both psychiatric and nonpsychiatric, across continents and diverse populations (Patterson 2013; Sonuga-Barke et al. 2013; Ogbolu, Adeyemi, and Erinfolami 2013; Rashid, Clarke, and Rogish 2013; Cechnicki et al. 2013; Bhavsar and Bhugra 2013; Gómez-de-Regil, Kwapil, and Barrantes-Vidal 2014; Ellis et al. 2014; Roseliza-Murni et al. 2014; Bader, Barry, and Hann 2014; Duclose et al. 2014).[22] A selective review of subsequent cross-cultural EE studies can highlight features of cultural variation in family emotional milieus.

In comparison to the earlier work cited above, a Japanese study found high EE scores among 37 percent of relatives, higher among mothers than fathers because of a hypothesized greater burden of care on Japanese mothers (Mino et al. 1995: 41). The study replicates the association between high EE and relapse for conditions diagnosed as schizophrenia at periods of nine months and two years. This result is more robust than in comparable studies from Britain, Spain, and India (Mino et al. 1997: 337). In direct comparison to a sample from the

United Kingdom, British relatives registered significantly more critical comments while at the same time were rated higher in the component of warmth (Nomura et al. 2005: 568). The researchers attribute these findings to an overall greater cultural reservation in expression of both positive and negative emotions among Japanese. Also relevant is what they see as a more circuitous expressive style along with reluctance to criticize those with whom they have strong relationship expectations (Nomura et al. 2005: 565, 568).

A multisite Chinese study conducted around the same time as the Japanese one shows an overall slightly higher rate of high EE, 42 percent, but with a dramatic reversal insofar as fathers rather than mothers and wives rather than husbands exhibited elevated rates (Phillips and Xiong 1995: 56; Mino et al. 1995). This difference was especially pronounced with respect to criticism and hostility. Parent EOI varied both insofar as Chinese rates were higher overall and Chinese fathers were equally likely as mothers to be high on this component. However, whereas high EOI is strongly predictive of relapse in Japan (Tanaka, Mino, and Inoue 1995), such is not the case in China, where protective and self-sacrificing behavior by parents is more positively sanctioned (Yang et al. 2004: 600). From a cultural standpoint, in the Chinese case there appears to be less criticism on the part of parents than spouses, and the authors interpret this in terms of the parental relationship's basis in moral obligation and the spousal relationship's basis in contract without the necessity of an affective bond. In this study relapse risk was less for Chinese patients from high EE households who were part of the intervention group than the control group, but there was no greater or lesser risk for participants from low EE households in either group.

A separate Chinese study in Chengdu (Ran et al. 2003) reported overall high EE rates of 33.3 percent in an urban and 22.9 percent in a rural setting, with all components somewhat lower and a complete absence of EOI in the rural group. The combined overall high EE score was 28.2 percent, which the authors identify as intermediate between those in the well-known studies in London and Chandigarh, India (Ran et al. 2003). In both Chengdu and Chandigarh some relatives exhibited hostility without criticism, and sometimes high criticism was accompanied by high warmth, neither of which was the case in London. The authors suggest a love-hate continuum rather than a dichotomy in Chinese cultural orientations, citing the saying "the deeper the love, the greater the criticism." When critical comments occurred they tended to focus on poor work and household ability or serious illness-related behaviors.

Elsewhere in Asia, a study in Kaula Lumpur, Malaysia (Roseliza-Murni et al. 2014), found that relapse rates among the major local ethnic groups were 61.4 percent for Malays, 50 percent for Chinese, and 30.8 percent for Indians. Overall, Chinese were marginally higher in EE at 50 percent, while Malays were 47.7 percent and Indians were 38.5 percent. Chinese were marginally highest in critical comments and Indians in EOI, but none of the differences was significant. High EE robustly predicted relapse for conditions of schizophrenia among all the groups, particularly with respect to criticism. Like the Chengdu, China, study, EE was higher when compared to a rural sample in Kelantan and Terengganu, which the authors attribute to traditional rural social cohesion and collectivism, with extended families distributing the burden of care and related stress. They also suggest the relevance of an indirect communication style and predilection for subjectivity over objectivity and emotionalism over rationalism.

The logic of rural-urban comparison was extended to a study comparing Bali to Japan (Kurihara et al. 2000). High EE was reported as 36.4 percent for Japanese in Tokyo and 12.9 percent for Balinese, which to my knowledge is the lowest reported. Notably, Japanese key relatives were more often females and Balinese key relatives males. Again, the researchers attribute lower Balinese EE in part to a distributed extended family burden of care compared to the relative prevalence of nuclear families in Japan. They also invoke cultural conceptions of causality by uncontrollable supernatural forces such as witchcraft or divine curse that relieves the stress of blame within families, as well as a tendency to suppress the expression of strong feelings, which is said to be even more pronounced in Bali than in Japan. Perhaps because of the prominence of low EE in the Balinese sample, this study did not demonstrate a relationship between high EE and rehospitalization.

Three studies from Spain indicate variability across sites in the same country. In Galicia, where the population was rural, high EE was 34 percent, with criticism at 16 percent, hostility at 6 percent, and EOI at 16 percent (Gutiérrez et al. 1988). An urban sample from Madrid exhibited high EE at 58 percent, with criticism at 34 percent, hostility at 15 percent, and EOI at 25 percent (Arévalo and Vizcarro 1989). In Valencia a mixed rural and urban sample had high EE at 48 percent and criticism at 25 percent but relatively high rates of EOI at 30 percent and hostility at 22 percent, with 9 percent exhibiting the phenomenon of hostility and low criticism. These studies did not address variation in the rates of relapse.

In Italy an urban sample from Milan highlighted the role of EOI in determining household emotional climate (Bertrando et al. 1992). Given what the researchers describe in relation to a particular Italian emotional style, hospital readmission for persons living in households rated high in EE was significant. Interesting in this study was the role of warmth, where 23.8 percent of households rated high and 76.2 percent rated low. The high EE/low warmth group had the highest readmission rate, while no subjects were readmitted from the high EE/high warmth group. All relatives in the "warm overinvolved" group were high EOI and were predominantly mothers.

In Iran a study including Tehran and the smaller agricultural city of Hamedan found 56 percent of relatives to be high EE, with more persons from high EE household relapsing but not at a significant level unless subjects with no symptomatic change were added to the relapse group. There was no difference in EE rates between the two cities. Notable results were that warmth and positive comments were both more prominent in urban areas. Hostility, found among 80 percent of high EE relatives, was the most common component contributing to those in the high EE category. The authors attribute the relatively high rates to the emphasis in Iran on hospital care and little community care, placing significant stress on families.

To summarize, across a broad range of cultural contexts (African settings appear to have been largely overlooked, but see McGruder 2004), the most robust finding is that the emotional milieu within the family is associated with relapse of persons living with conditions diagnosed as schizophrenia who have already been hospitalized for the illness. A prospective study from Poland has demonstrated that this association can persist for at least as long as twenty years (Cechnicki et al 2013). Overall rates of high EE in these studies vary from a reported high of 77 percent in the United Kingdom (Tarrier et al. 1988) to a low of 13 percent in Bali (Kurihara et al. 2000). Yet these gross comparisons are of limited value for cross-cultural generalization given that studies in the same country have shown variation across sites, 48–77 percent in the United Kingdom and 34–58 percent in Spain. Where comparisons become more relevant is at the level of the five EE components. For example, whereas in the original studies hostility was regarded as ancillary to the major components of criticism and EOI, subsequent studies have identified cultural settings in which these are highly predictive of relapse and furthermore may occur in the virtual absence of criticism. EOI has been shown to be subject to significant cultural variation in the expected degree of intimacy among family members and to bear intriguing but ambiguous relation to warmth and positive comments.

However, one cannot simply assert that greater or lesser degrees of criticism, hostility, emotional overinvolvement, warmth, and positive comments are characteristic of different cultural orientations. The proportion of these factors is not the same cross-culturally, nor is the volatility within families or the degree of sensitivity among those afflicted. Moreover, what counts as criticism, hostility, and emotional overinvolvement has to be defined for each cultural context, along with the styles determined by the class habitus and socioeconomic circumstances in which they are expressed. As we have seen, for example, criticism within Euro-American family settings can focus on allegations of faulty personality traits (e.g., laziness) or psychotic symptom behaviors (e.g., culturally unusual ideas). Among Mexican-descent families, criticism tends to focus on disrespectful or disruptive behaviors that affect the family but not primarily on perceived illness behaviors or individual personality characteristics. Thus, culture plays a role in creating the content or targets of criticism. Perhaps most important, culture is influential in determining *whether* criticism is a prominent part of the familial emotional atmosphere. Ethnographic analysis probes these issues, but takes even a further step of asking how people understand the nature of the problem they face in the first place. It is to this issue—the cultural conceptions deployed by families in everyday life—that I now turn.

## CULTURAL CONCEPTIONS OF MENTAL ILLNESS: LAZINESS, *NERVIOS*, AND SCHIZOPHRENIA

Twenty-one-year-old Sergio reclines on the well-worn couch placed centrally against the back wall of the family living room. Lying on his back with legs crossed, he taps one foot vigorously in the air as he stares at the ceiling above. Now and again, he mutters softly, unintelligibly. His mother enters the room, giving him a start. He snaps at her for coming upon him so suddenly. His mother exhales deeply, saying, "*Ay, mi hijo, no más que es los nervios*" (Oh, my son, it's just your nerves).

—Jenkins, "Conceptions of Schizophrenia as a Problem of Nerves"

While clinical diagnosis is neither easy nor straightforward, the task cannot begin to compare with the struggle that families engage in as they attempt to make sense of what is happening for an afflicted relative with whom they live. While recognition of a problem when the onset is sudden and severe might be relatively straightforward, more commonly there is a gradual, sporadic, and indeterminate process of onset and correspondingly of recognition that there is a problem. Such was the case for Sebastián and his family (chapter 2). Moreover, the interpretive social process of culturally puzzling through what the problem might be is mediated differently for each actor through psychological defense mechanisms such as denial, projection, or sublimation (Freud 1962; Vaillant 1986). This process may incrementally affect decisions regarding treatment over months and often years, including struggle over choices between psychological, religious, or biomedical care. While these subjective processes are entangled, the afflicted and their kin do not necessarily share their underlying assumptions. Within and beyond particular households, families are often far from harmonious regarding how to interpret or respond to the problem. This can make for a conflictive and arduous pathway for seeking treatment, as indeed I have shown in the preceding chapter.

Although it is possible to utilize research diagnostic criteria for what can be classified as schizophrenia across diverse cultural settings, commonality of symptom profiles offers little insight into similarities or differences in cultural conceptions of mental disorder or of how those conceptions may in turn relate to illness experience. This is so because indigenous concepts of psychosis embody several orders of cultural knowledge concerning affliction and personhood. Illness labels incorporate a variety of beliefs about the nature, causes, course, and treatment of the problem. Meanings associated with indigenous labels for what is diagnosed as psychiatric disorder have symbolic implications for the social and moral status of persons who suffer such conditions and their families (Edgerton 1966, 1969, 1985; Townsend 1978; White 1982; Fabrega and Silver 1973; Whyte 1991). Identifying a problem in a less stigmatizing way, as one of "nerves" rather than as some form of "mental illness," for example, may differentially allow for the continued incorporation of the ill person in social groups. Variations in cultural usage of illness categories may involve not only differing degrees of stigma (Phillips et al. 2002; Jenkins and Carpenter-Song 2008) but also different attributions of personal responsibility for the illness and controllability of symptoms (Hooley and Campbell 2002; López et al. 1999; Yang et al. 2004; Weisman et al. 1993). Thus, the difficulties families face understanding and labeling a relative's distress are made problematic not only by variations and fluctuations of illness but also by their desire to adopt the most socially acceptable and least stigmatizing culturally available labels for the problem (Edgerton 1969). These processes are not only of social consequence but also of psychological importance insofar as they shape individuals' notions of self and others' degree of identification with the ill individual. Psychocultural differences in attitudes toward and conceptions of psychiatric disorder may also influence the course and outcome of illness by mediating social support and decrement to self-esteem (Murphy 1982; Waxler 1977; Jenkins and Carpenter-Song 2008). I will elaborate this point with a comparison between Mexican-American participants in the study and Euro-American participants in a related study (Nuechterlein and Dawson 1984). The comparison focuses on responses to (1) an open-ended question as to "What kind of problem is it?" and (2) a forced-choice question, "Do you think it could be a problem of nerves/*nervios,* mental illness, or something else?"

In response to the open-ended question, the Mexican American relatives used *nervios* as the most common term for the problem (36 percent); among those who did not, (12 percent) cited specific behaviors or problems typically associated with *nervios.* Thus, 48 percent of the Mexican American relatives conceptualized the problem as one of *nervios.* The majority of the Euro-American relatives responded with a specific term referring to a psychiatric disorder such as schizophrenia, psychosis, or depression (55 percent) or characterized the problem as being associated with mind or brain (34 percent). Thus, the vast majority (89 percent) of Euro-Americans mentioned some type of mental or psychiatric disorder. Only one Euro-American specifically mentioned nerves, and this isolated response is completely noncomparable with those given by the Mexican Americans. Whereas Mexican American notions of *nervios* involve an understanding of the problem as beyond the control of the individual, the non-Hispanic notion of nerves incorporates core Euro-American cultural values of individual initiative and personal control. In addition, Euro-Americans mentioned "nervous breakdown," but the infrequency of this response suggests that this once popular folk and medical term is falling into desuetude. Indeed, the mother of one research subject reported, "I used the term 'nervous breakdown' for a time before I realized that mental illness was the situation." Other mentions of the terms *nervous breakdown* and *nervous reaction* indicate that, unlike biomedical terms, which often focus on neurochemical bases of disease, problems associated with nerves more often incorporate psychosocial etiologies, as in "We felt guilty that we may have pushed her too far, over the edge, to a nervous breakdown."

TABLE 5 CONCEPTIONS OF THE PROBLEM BY MEXICAN AMERICAN AND EURO-AMERICAN RELATIVES

| | Mexican Americans ($N$ = 61) | | Euro-Americans ($N$ = 47) | |
|---|---|---|---|---|
| | N | % | N | % |
| Nerves only | 29 | 47.5 | 2 | 4.3 |
| Nerves and mental illness | 5 | 8.2 | 2 | 4.3 |
| Nerves and other | 7 | 11.5 | 0 | 0.0 |
| Mental illness only | 10 | 16.4 | 25 | 53.2 |
| Mental illness and other | 1 | 1.6 | 4 | 8.5 |
| Other only | 9 | 14.8 | 13 | 27.7 |
| Nerves, mental illness, and other | 0 | 0.0 | 1 | 2.1 |
| Totals | 61 | 100.0 | 47 | 100.1* |
| ($x^2$ = 39.43, $df$ = 5, $P$ = 0.000) | | | | |

*Due to rounding error, percentages do not necessarily total 100.

It is also important that Euro-Americans did not invoke the notion of "craziness," and neither did Mexican Americans invoke the parallel "*locura.*" To be precise, people sometimes used terms like *crazy* and *loco* to describe the behavior of their afflicted relative but never as a label for their problem. For most families it appeared that to be truly crazy or *loco* means that the person has lost all reason, is totally out of touch with reality, completely out of control, and potentially unpredictable and violent. Terms for these states can sometimes imply that there is little or no hope, no possible recovery, and no cure.

Analyses of responses to the follow-up forced-choice question, "Do you think it could be a problem of nerves/*nervios,* mental illness, or something else?," show that significant differences exist between the two groups (table 5). The majority (67 percent) of Mexican Americans considered the problem to be one of *nervios,* whereas only a minority (11 percent) of Euro-Americans thought it might be a problem of nerves. While the majority (68 percent) of Euro-Americans affirmed that mental illness was the problem, only about one quarter (26 percent) of Mexican Americans did so. For this item, ethnicity alone seemed to account for the differences (x2 = 6.94; $P$ = 0.008); social class differences proved nonsignificant. However, the content of these miscellaneous responses revealed differences in the sorts of things that Mexican Americans and Euro-Americans considered problematic. Mexican Americans mentioned assorted issues, including physiological problems, witchcraft, personality problems (overly ambitious, stubborn), destiny, trauma, drugs, family problems, or the current absence of any problem. Euro-Americans mentioned personality deficits (laziness, immaturity), stress, drugs, inactivity, or the current absence of any problem.

The fact that the Mexican Americans mention *nervios* more often in the forced-choice item than in the open-ended response may be related to the cultural appeal this category holds once introduced. It may be that relatives overcame an initial suppression of what they regarded as a culturally appropriate term for the illness. Similarly, the Euro-Americans may be more likely to choose the open-ended "other" category when it is offered since it affords them a chance to give their views about other things they consider problematic. In addition, while it was possible for respondents to cite more than one kind of problem, the vast majority of both the Euro-Americans (85 percent) and the Mexican Americans (79 percent) were likely to consider only one kind of problem.

When we asked relatives to describe the meaning of *nervios* /nerves, there were again both similarities and differences in the responses given by the Mexican Americans and Euro-Americans. *Nervios* is generally considered to afflict weak or vulnerable persons. Two major types were mentioned most often. The first is a person who is easily angered or often irritable (*corajuda*), touchy, sensitive, volatile, or hotheaded. The second is characterized by symptoms such as tension, anxiety, worry, agitation, feelings of insecurity, fear, frustration, desperation, trouble sleeping or eating, shaking and trembling. Less commonly mentioned troubles associated with *nervios* included sadness, depression, or feeling dispirited, somatic effects (e.g. dizziness, feeling pain in the brain or neck), and confusion. Euro-Americans and Mexican Americans shared the two most common descriptions of nerves. In the first, the person is said to be prone to emotional outbursts and to be frequently irritable, short-tempered, easily upset, touchy, likely to fly off the handle, and possibly aggressive. Also like Mexican Americans, Euro-Americans were equally likely to describe a problem of nerves as one of being highly anxious, fearful worried, insecure, jittery, on edge, uptight, or tense. However, other descriptions of nerves varied. Euro-Americans were twice as likely as Mexican Americans to describe a problem of nerves as an inability to cope or function. Some emphasized that a problem of nerves creates trouble "getting on top of the situation" or "being able to cope with what's on hand or whatever comes up." Another ethnic difference was that Mexican Americans were more likely to describe a problem of *nervios* as one in which the person felt sad or suffered from certain somatic symptoms (e.g., dizziness, back pain). In contrast, Euro-Americans were somewhat more likely to mention fear as part of a problem of nerves. Finally, several Euro-American relatives made a point of saying that what they were describing was not their relative's problem, and several declined to give descriptions of nerves, stating they did not really know or that they did not understand why they were being asked such a question because it bore no relevance to their relative's condition. In other words, for many of the Euro-American relatives, questions concerning a problem of nerves fell on deaf ears; they asserted they either had little or no conception of the term or considered it inapplicable or tangential to their own views of the nature of their relative's problem.

Several factors in addition to ethnicity may contribute to these differences. The Mexican Americans had been hospitalized more often and had been ill longer than their Euro-American counterparts. Thus, the Mexican American relatives had significantly more time living with a disturbed family member and reflecting on the nature of the problem. However, although Mexican Americans often conceive of a developmental sequence in which *nervios,* if severe enough and chronic, may develop into mental illness, these family members retained the concept of *nervios* regardless of length of illness or number of hospitalizations. There was also major socioeconomic status (SES) variation: nearly all of the Mexican American relatives were low income, whereas the Euro-Americans were broadly distributed across various socioeconomic levels. However, statistical analysis confirmed ethnic differences independent of social class. It was also the case that variation between the two groups was related to differing degrees of influence by or congruence with the clinicaldiagnosis reported to families. It appears that many of the Euro-Americans held highly medicalized conceptions of the problem, such that over time the professional nosological discourse became incorporated in their lay discourse (Fabrega 1979). Indeed, many of the Euro-Americans' views of the problem were phrased in specifically clinical terms, for example, "a disease, and a full-blown schizophrenia with paranoid overtones."

Despite the similarity in symptom descriptions of nerves/*nervios,* the application of this term revealed striking cultural variations. On the one hand, the similarity of descriptions provides evidence for some commonality in folk medical traditions, as well as in the biological and psychophysiological bases of "nerves" that are manifested in symptom behaviors. On the other hand, the lack of common application of these folk categories stems from a host of culturally distinctive factors. It seems that nerves and *nervios* possess culturally distinctive meanings for Mexican American and Euro-American families. As we have seen, Euro-Americans are in strong accord that nerves is not the problem afflicting their family member and their orientation to the problem is shaped by clinical emphasis on symptom profiles. *Nervios* refers to a wide and diverse range of emotional states, life circumstances, and illness phenomena that go well beyond the symptoms of schizophrenia. Specifically in contrast to Euro-American notions of nerves, a central element in the Mexican American definitions of *nervios* is the individual's loss of control in the face of trying circumstances. And while being mentally ill may also, in some sense, be understood to be out of the person's control, it is not only still subject to being stigmatized, but it is also unrecognized as a state in any way continuous with the experience of others who are not so afflicted and hence less accessible to empathic response. Although it is likely that there are Mexican Americans who are disposed by situation or personality to blame relatives for their own illness, the availability of a concept culturally defined in a way that buffers such attitudes can enhance the positive affective valence of an emotional milieu.

In this respect, essential to understanding the use of *nervios* for conditions diagnosed by psychiatrists as schizophrenia is the centrality of family bonds in Mexican and Mexican American cultural orientations. Needless to say, cultural ideals are rarely achieved in practice. Even so, relative to the Euro-Americans, emotions expressed by Mexican American relatives were more often characterized by warmth and acceptance (see also Weisman et al. 1993). In contrast, the Euro-Americans displayed significantly more criticism and hostility toward their disturbed family member, though some of these relatives may be acting on the ethnopsychological assumption that high *unexpressed* emotion may lead to adverse effects on health. Moreover, not only are levels of warmth as an EE factor higher for Mexican Americans than for Euro-Americans, but lower warmth strongly predicts relapse for Mexican Americans while it appeared less crucial for Euro-Americans. Furthermore, Mexican American relatives have greater amounts of contact time with their ill family member, and this family contact is for them associated with less relapse, while it is not related to relapse among Euro-Americans (López et al. 2004; Vaughn and Snyder 2004).

Relatives' attempts to identify with the ill family member may induce them to adopt the culturally acceptable illness term *nervios* in order to maintain strong self-other connections in the family context. Ill family members are perceived as experiencing a range of both normal and abnormal states not characteristic of someone who is "truly crazy" (*loco*). Many of the Mexican American relatives mentioned that they too had suffered from *nervios*—albeit in a milder form—and therefore had some understanding of their relative's illness. In this way, conception of the illness as *nervios* enables the maintenance of close identification among family members by fostering the view that the relative is "just like us, only more so." A similar finding is reported from China, where some relatives attribute the cause of the family member's affliction to the person's "narrow-mindedness" (*xiao xin yanr*) or conceptualize the problem as narrow-minded character instead of mental illness (Yang et al. 2004). For the Chinese this is not a criticism but a recognition of an uncommon trait, which, like *nervios* for the Mexican Americans, makes the person more like other normal people in the relative's mind. Moreover, the Chinese study showed that invocation of narrow-mindedness helped to predict lower relapse rates, possibly producing a protective effect (Yang et al. 2004: 600).

What appears to be involved is a reciprocal relation between cultural dispositions toward lower levels of EE and a cultural conception of mental illness that disposes family members to a milder and more benevolent attitude toward the afflicted (Jenkins et al. 1986). Such affective attitudes may induce Mexican Americans to make a more empathetic interpretation of the illness than do the Euro-American relatives. Cross-cultural variation was evident, for example, in the relatives' interview responses. Mexican Americans highlighted emotions of sadness and pity and at times an aura of tragedy. Their descriptions of *nervios* were more likely to focus on sad affects and dysphoric emotions than those of the Euro-American group. Their style of interpreting the problem often included elaborated expressions of anguish and sympathy for the ill person, as well as a desire to protect and shelter her or him. In sum, not only may Mexican Americans be warmer in the context of this extraordinary condition, but availability of the cultural concept *nervios* also may be conducive to reinforcing a cultural emphasis on protection of kin affective bonds.

Certainly other psychological and social forces serve to shape cultural conceptions of mental illness. We cannot doubt that psychological defense mechanisms such as denial are at work to ward off social stigma. The relative willingness of the Euro-Americans to entertain clinical labels must be understood against the backdrop of professional attempts to destigmatize schizophrenia by virtue of a scientific approach to it as a biochemical deficit or imbalance (see chapter 1). The Mexican American immigrants in our study were less likely to be aware of this bio-medical information, making *nervios* a plausible category for the illness condition. Preferred illness categories are therefore not entirely determined by "symptom profiles" but rather by the social relations, moral standing, and emotional well-being of the person (Good and Good 1982; Edgerton and Karno 1971) and in turn are among the cultural factors that play into expressed emotion. Yet there is more.

## WHAT'S IN THE BLACK BOX OF EXPRESSED EMOTION?

As I have shown, the relevance of expressed emotion to the course of illness is widely recognized, and although individual variation in the association between EE and outcome exists, it is reasonably regarded as a major risk factor in the course of a mental illness (Kuipers 1979; Goldstein 1987; Falloon 1988; Bebbington and Kuipers 1994; Hooley 2007). The EE paradigm's most serious shortcoming from an anthropological point of view has been its capacity for "prediction without meaning," identified decades ago by George Brown (Falloon, Boyd, and McGill 1984). Empirical approaches in psychiatric research typically do not concern themselves with questions of validity, interpretation, or meaning, and little was done to articulate a theoretical framework for this research. To my anthropological surprise, far too little of the wealth of available data from the Camberwell Family Interview was examined in detail beyond their use for the valuable yet reductive measures of EE. Cultural analysis was either ignored or remained superficial. Research invoked unexamined ethnotheories and the language of psychological and psychiatric approaches that privilege what can be measured (symptoms, personality and attributional factors), thus largely reproducing British and Euro-American ethnopsychology.

In order to avoid this shortcoming, empirical investigation of relatives' subjective experience and response requires a theoretical bridge from behavior to meaning in specific cultural contexts. Providing such a bridge was my intent in a special article in the *American Journal of Psychiatry* that addresses the problem of "prediction without meaning" and specifies theoretical parameters of the global construct of expressed emotion (Jenkins and Karno 1992). This framework for thinking about expressed emotion and the emotional milieu of families remains relevant, and against the background of this chapter's discussion I present it here in updated form.

1. *Cultural interpretations of the problem.* Relatives' interpretations of the problem are their views of its nature, cause, course, and treatment. These interpretations mediate relatives' emotional responses to what is (or is not) conceived as a problem, illness, disease, or affliction.

2. *Cultural meanings of kin relations.* Relatives' responses to an ill family member are formulated in the context of culturally defined possibilities for family life. These involve the stability or fluctuation of kin attachments as matters of belonging, identity, obligation, and separation, as well as patterns of residency and household composition.

3. *Identification of cultural rule violations.* Cultural orientations provide guidelines for how to define what counts as actions deserving of legitimate criticism. Identification of cultural rule violations varies in relation to values, desires, and expectations according to culturally defined statuses that may legitimately exempt or temper familial criticism.

4. *Repertoires and vocabularies of emotion.*[23] There are differential modes of emotional attunement within which relatives' experience may incorporate longing, loss, love, anger, and anguish. The cultural articulations of such modes are conditioned by styles of embodiment, linguistic registers, and moral prescription, all of which may contribute to shaping how individuals might or should feel in a given situation (e.g., Myers 1979).

5. *Relatives' psychobiological predispositions.* Variations in individual personality, temperament, and attributional style are common partial explanations for why relatives might display varying degrees of expressed emotion (Hooley and Campbell 2002). Responses indicative of high levels of expressed emotion may also be partially explained by some degree of shared, possibly genetic psychobiological dispositions of autonomic reactivity.

6. *Symptom severity, heightened perceptual arousal, effects of medication, and psychosocial interventions.* Variation in symptom severity has been hypothesized to account for differences in relatives' expressed emotion, though empirical studies show this relationship is weak. Autonomic intensification and perception of environmental stimuli for persons *and* family members living with mental illness have not been adequately studied. These interpersonal processes may be neurobiologically mediated by medications and/

or psychosocial interventions. Work within interpersonal and cultural neuroscience or dynamic phenomenology[24] may help to shed light on these processes (Raballo and Krueger 2011; Lende and Downey 2012; Critchley et al. 2013; Choudhury and Kirmayer 2009; Docherty et al. 2011).

7. *Family interaction dynamics.* Family patterns of communication, social hierarchy and power, and interpersonal processes can also be expected to shape relatives' emotional responses to an ill family member. The socialization of family dynamics may be both culturally and individually mediated.

8. *Attempts to socially control a relative perceived as "outside" the ordinary.* Expressed emotion can be considered a social strategy among others employed by families that are implicitly or explicitly intended to restrict what they regard as objectionable activities and actions on the part of an afflicted family member.

9. *Availability and quality of social supports.* Not only household composition, including size and kin type, but also presence and frequency of contact may alleviate or exacerbate levels of expressed emotion. Extra-household support from peers, religious involvement, community services, or treatment providers may also mediate EE.

10. *Historical and political economic factors.* It has been suggested that explanations for variation in expressed emotion profiles may change over time. Changing social and economic conditions may influence the emotional climate of a society in general, with repercussions for how families reflect societal attitudes toward individuals identified as ill (Warner 1985). In this regard, the portrait of Mexican-descent immigrant families living in California during the 1980s may differ from that of recent migrants in 2015. Differences in expressed emotion in relation to social class and economic resources are also relevant.

As demonstrated in this chapter, much of EE is rooted in culturally constituted features of kin response to an ill relative. Culture, as a system of meanings and symbols that is deeply taken for granted, offers the most powerful explanation for observed variations in expressed emotion in different populations. Attitudes, affects, and actions on the part of family members toward their ill relative are the culturally constituted features indexed by EE. I have argued for a synthesis of expressed emotion research and psychocultural analysis of the reciprocal effects of family attitudes and illness behaviors. This line of analysis has pragmatic consequences for assisting families in their struggle with mental illness. It also has promise as a systematic paradigm for understanding the range of emotional experience and response across widely different cultural settings as well as within intimate family environments for what arguably is most at stake with respect to emotional well-being. Supplemented by careful case studies of experience and intersubjectivity, this synthesis has the potential to generate a comprehensive account of social, cultural, and psychological processes associated with extraordinary conditions of mental illness.

# PART TWO

# Violence, Trauma, and Depression

## CHAPTER 4

# The Impress of Extremity among Salvadoran Refugees

You think this mountain is beautiful? I hate it. To me it
means war. It's nothing but a theater for this shitty war.

—Response of Comandante Jonas to a foreign journalist's request to
take pictures of the mountains, eastern front, El Salvador, 1983
(Manlio Argueta, *Cuzcatlan: Where the Southern Sea Beats*)

Although violence and civil warfare were common in El Salvador throughout the twentieth century, the most intensive sustained conflict to plague
the country was the civil war that took place between 1979 and 1992.
This wave of warfare and terror, prolonged by U.S. governmental aid to
El Salvador's right-wing government amounting to $1.4 million per day,
decimated the population by death and emigration. A letter sent by Archbishop Oscar Romero of San Salvador beseeched President Jimmy Carter
to cease aid to and intervention in the Salvadoran government.

> According to reports, your government is studying the possibility of (further)
> economic and military support to the present government. . . . Because you
> are a Christian and because you have shown that you want to defend human
> rights, I make a specific request of you: forbid military aid be given to the
> Salvadoran government and guarantee your government will not intervene[,]
> . . . avoiding greater bloodshed in this suffering country.[1]

Carter ignored the plea, and five weeks later, on March 24, 1980, Archbishop Romero was assassinated with a single shot to the heart.[2] A
month later a quarter million Salvadorans came for the funeral, and
four thousand mourners huddled inside San Salvador's cathedral as
bombs exploded and bullets flew outside in the plaza. Snipers from the
National Army fired from the tops of buildings during the funeral, killing forty and wounding many more.[3]

During the civil war, at least 75,000 persons were killed and several thousands more were *"desaparecidos"* (disappeared); 500,000 were displaced within the nation's borders; and an estimated one million more fled to Mexico, Honduras, Panama, the United States, Canada, and other countries. In a nation that as of 1979 had a population estimated at only 5.2 million, one begins to realize the large-scale decimation of the Salvadoran people (United Nations Truth Commission 1993; Wood 2003). Subsequent to the war's end the nation's economy was dramatically transformed by forced migration. In 2013 Pedersen wrote, "El Salvador has shifted as a whole from being oriented around growing and exporting high-quality coffee beans, especially to the United States, to being a country that now is much defined by the circulation of over two billion US dollars annually remitted by more than one-quarter of its population that has migrated to live and work in the United States" (xvii). As part of the two-way flow of people and dollars, American street gangs have thoroughly penetrated Salvadoran communities in the United States as well as in Salvadoran society (Arana 2005; Hume 2007). As of 2014, two decades after the peace accords of 1992 and despite the narrow electoral victory of Salvador Sánchez Cerén (former guerrilla commander and recent minister of education), El Salvador remains deeply polarized politically. Along with postwar animosities, criminality, and the migratory circulation of gang violence, it is as unsurprising as it is disturbing that the recent *Global Study of Homicide* (UNODC 2011) ranks El Salvador among the highest worldwide.

This chapter and the next are based on research I conducted among Salvadoran refugees in Boston during 1987–90, an especially dark period in the conflict. In November 1989, there was a major guerrilla offensive, the largest coordinated attack in almost ten years, aimed at dozens of targets throughout the country, including the capital, San Salvador. Counterattacks on the part of the Salvadoran army were swift and pervasive, escalating in intensity to extensive daily bombing and strafing of villages and neighborhoods. I remember all too vividly the month of November 1989 as I watched my Salvadoran friends and research participants, inseparably connected to their telephones, desperately seeking to learn the fate of their parents, children, grandparents, and other family members. Not surprisingly, the escalation in the violence at home coincided with a pronounced increase in all kinds of exacerbations of distress. November 1989 also saw the assassinations of six Jesuit priests and their housekeeper and her daughter. The priests, faculty from the National University in San Salvador who supported a negotiated peace, were also widely regarded as leading intellectuals in the country. Among them, Ignacio Martín-Baró was a prominent social psychologist interested in the mental health consequences of long-term civil war in his country. As a research scholar, Martín-Baró was particularly interested in the psychological rehabilitation of children orphaned by the war, displaced or traumatized by the endless violence. The manner of the Jesuits' assassination, which apparently included torture and extreme brutality, refocused attention on the widespread human rights abuses that occurred with impunity in El Salvador.[4]

## POLITICAL ETHOS AND *LA SITUACIÓN*

My goal in this chapter is to contribute to anthropological thinking on the relation between subjective experience and broader social process, in this case the nexus between the role of the state in constructing a political ethos, the personal emotions of those who dwell in that ethos, and the mental health consequences for refugees. By "political ethos," I mean the culturally standardized organization of feeling and sentiment pertaining to social domains of power and interest.[5] Recognition of the essential interrelations of the personal and the political has long been central to feminist scholarship (see Rosaldo and Lamphere 1974; Lutz and Abu-Lughod 1990; Harding 1991, 2011).[6] Mary-Jo DelVecchio Good and colleagues introduced the problem of state control of emotional discourse, defined as "the role of the state and other political, religious, and economic institutions in legitimizing, organizing, and promoting particular discourses on emotions" (Good et al. 1988: 4). In a study of Iranian immigrants to the United States, M. Good, B. Good, and Moradi (1985) documented the interplay of cultural themes, sociopolitical events, and depressive disorder. Kleinman (1986) has presented a similarly convincing case for the social production of affective disorders in China during the Cultural Revolution. Feldman (1991) and Aretxaga (1997, 2003) have examined the experiential consequences of conflict and state violence in Northern Ireland, while Theidon (2012) has examined the dialectic of forgiveness and reconciliation in post–civil war Peru. Anthropological study of the emotional climate of populations under martial law or other forms of violent siege can illuminate analyses of the specific transmutations of grief, anger, and paranoia in countries where "disappearances" have been institutionalized (Scheper-Hughes 1990; Suárez-Orozco 1990; Robben and Suárez-Orozco 2000; Scheper-Hughes and Bourgois 2004; James 2010; Nordstrom 2004; Farmer et al. 2013).

The theoretical concern with state control of emotional discourse and the state construction of affect advanced by M. Good, Good, and Fischer (1988) became compelling in the course of my fieldwork with Salvadoran refugees seeking help at an outpatient psychiatric clinic. Anthropological discourses on culture, self, and emotion were not adequate to the task of interpreting the sentiments of persons whose lifeworlds are framed by chronic political violence, extreme poverty, unrelenting trauma, and loss. It became apparent that the role of the state and other political, religious, and economic institutions must be examined to interpret the dominant ethos of a people. In the context of Salvadoran lifeworlds, I understand the state construction of affect in relation to a pervasively dysthymic political ethos and a culture of terror. In the refugees' narratives of their emigration from El Salvador, they often speak of escape from *"la situación." La situación* was the most common way of referring to the intolerable conditions within the country and condenses a set of symbols and meanings that refer to a nation besieged by both devastating economic problems and violence. Particularly among undocumented immigrants who moreover could not be certain of the political affiliations of those surrounding them and who were in regular contact with family remaining in El Salvador, it was a circumlocution that allowed recognition of an intolerable circumstance without requiring the speaker to adopt a position or engage in political discussion.[7]

The political ethos of *la situación* was constructed by a variety of actions and practices. During the offensive, strict enforcement of a curfew from 6:00 p.m. to 6:00 a.m. ensured that no one could be on the streets or in any public place. Failure to adhere to this injunction often had fatal consequences. In the private sphere, no socializing of any sort—family gatherings, parties, religious sessions—could be convened. Cross-cutting the public and private domains were disappearances and the ever-present evidence of violent death: decapitated heads hanging from trees or on sticks, mutilated dead bodies or body parts on the roadside or on one's own doorstep. Nearly all of my informants spontaneously narrated their personal experiences of everyday encounters in a landscape of violence. Habituation to *la situación* amounted to a denial of its reality: a bomb going off could be interpreted as a car backfiring. The reality of *la situación* is noteworthy for its profound sense of *unreality*. Mistrust abounded on all sides, and people commonly said, "You can trust no one." A sketch of the situation and habituation to it is only a first step, however, toward inferring a political ethos, which must be fleshed out by considering both preexisting ethnopsychology and the phenomenology of psychopathology in situations where the defense of habituation fails. A repertoire of affective themes and strategies for constructing the emotional atmosphere is more directly evident in the onslaught of media communications that was an important tool in the state programming of sentiment. For a poor people with little formal education (90 percent nonliterate or semiliterate), the principal media sources were radio and television. These sources suggest to a people how they might or ought to feel about *la situación*. Under conditions of civil war and martial law, the state-controlled media conveyed rigid and dogmatic messages that left little doubt about which affective sensibilities were being communicated and why a truly moral person should justifiably feel them.

Quite revealing in this respect is a sample of regular programming from an audiotaped radio broadcast on the official Radio Nacional, San Salvador, on November 16, 1989—the very day during the guerrilla offensive that the Salvadoran military assassinated the Jesuit priests. Both moral/political and affective rhetorics (explicit and implicit) are operant in the broadcast. In response to the repeated rhetorical question, *"¿Porque lucha la fuerza armada?"* (Why are the armed forces fighting?), several sociocultural, nationalistic, and capitalist values were cited. Most saliently, these included a right to "keep on believing in God"; the preservation of the "nuclear family as the center of the Salvadoran social life"; "the right to live in liberty and freedom"; "the right to 'equal opportunity' in work, education, health and development"; "the right of citizens to have the right to choose." Appeals were made to the personal and societal value of capitalism and the evident need for a military response to the opposition forces that would overturn the very fabric of society. Subtly distributed among these overt patriotic declarations were messages alluding to the emotional substrate of these values as they were imperiled by *la situación*. The Salvadoran military forces were fighting to put "friendships without mistrust into practice." Repeated again and again was the emotional theme that fear was fomented by guerrilla forces. Proper sentiments of hatred and disgust toward the rebels and loyalty and love to one's *patria* (country) were also salient. A generalized feeling of insecurity was inculcated by constant reiteration that the armed forces "are protecting you, providing for your security, that everything is under control, that the armed forces exercise total control over all the national territory." Such messages would doubtless be unsettling even if there were no immediately perceptible threat and must have been doubly so when they were so immediately contradicted by destruction, aggression, and assassination in all quarters.

The Salvadoran populace was pointedly instructed not to listen to competing discourses—so-called clandestine radio broadcasts of the opposition, the Farabundo Martí National Liberation Front (FMLN)—on the grounds that these illicit radio stations seek only "to create confusion and uncertainty" in the Salvadoran family.[8] The state construction of the eminently evil "other" (implied or stated as the FMLN and "Marxist" doctrines) was accomplished through reference to "savages" and "mental illness." Indeed, the listening audience was informed that adherence to Marxist doctrine causes mental illness. Religious officials were interviewed to relate the barbarism and hideous crimes against humanity that the FMLN was accused of committing. They asserted that these crimes (alleged to include placing bombs in hospitals) were worse than anything Christopher Columbus may have committed when he "discovered" America. Announcements of the assassination of the Jesuit priests attributed the murders to the FMLN and denounced as irrational acts of savagery committed for the purpose of destabilizing the democratic process. In the foreign press, these attributions of blame to the FMLN were later retracted and ultimately replaced with admissions by the president that the national armed forces had, in fact, committed the atrocities.[9]

The importance of analyzing the state construction of affect is evident in the case of El Salvador, *una población asustada* (a frightened population). Activities of the state, economic conditions, and the domestic environment must be understood not as independent factors but as coordinate dimensions of a single political ethos. As Martín-Baró (1988) wrote, the entire nation could be characterized as one in which state induction of fear, anxiety, and terror was elaborated and maintained as a means of social control. Warfare is thus waged through all possible avenues: tanks roll down the streets, bullets fly, and minds and hearts are occupied by arresting affects that similarly immobilize. Through long-term exposure to this political ethos the experience of the "lived body" is shot through with anxiety, terror, and despair (see Feldman 1991).

## FORCED MIGRATION: POLITICAL, DOMESTIC, AND ECONOMIC VIOLENCE

Migrants are typically considered in two categories: immigrants and refugees. While "immigrant" implies some degree of choice concerning the decision to leave one's natal country, the designation "refugee" is meant to signal that departure from one's native country is involuntary and repatriation all but impossible. Although the flight of refugees is not a new phenomenon, the dimensions of this problem have recently intensified. Whether we look to Cambodia, Liberia, Haiti, Argentina, East Germany, or Syria, the world's populations are relocating in vast numbers. A recent report from the United Nations High Commissioner for Refugees (2015) shows record high increases of more than 59.5 million forcibly displaced people worldwide, including over 13.9 million refugees, 38.2 million internally displaced persons, and some 1.8 million asylum seekers. Many of these refugees leave their homelands under the press of conditions that threaten their personal, familial, and cultural survival. This was true for Salvadorans. The Central American situation of long-term economic conflicts and political violence often compelled them not only to leave their natal country but also to live with little or no prospect for safe repatriation. Continued human rights abuses and the fear and upheaval caused by the offensive at the end of 1989 led even more Salvadorans to seek to leave the country. In December of that year, officials at immigration offices in San Salvador said that more than two thousand people a day were applying for passports.

Refugees arrived in the United States from El Salvador through a variety of means, ranging from arduous and dangerous journeys led by *coyotes* to the relative comfort of airline flight. Popular destinations points for Salvadoran refugees in the United States included Los Angeles, San Francisco, Washington, DC, New York City, and Boston. Following passage of the Immigration Law of 1986, under which 165,000 Salvadorans sought legal residence in the United States, such status became particularly difficult to obtain. Many Salvadorans sought political asylum from the U.S. government. These court cases were largely unsuccessful: in 1985, for example, only 3 percent of applicants won their appeals. This is so because despite the well-documented and widespread human rights violations in El Salvador, the U.S. government did not consider their emigration to be based on a flight from political violence. Rather, such cases were typically considered "economic" in nature. The official view was that refugees came merely to enhance their economic future. They were not acknowledged to be in personal danger, and there was no recognition that the destruction of infrastructure and deterioration of the economy due to war was responsible for a good deal of the economic desperation. As Alvarez (1990: 61) summarized, "The official stance of the U.S. government and the societal attitudes prevalent in this country are characterized by massive denial, invalidation and indifference towards the collective experiences of violence which the Central American community has endured. . . . The ever present threat of deportation and their ongoing exploitation leads many refugees to live lives marked by invisibility, frozen grief, and despair." Not until late 1990, by an act of Congress, were Salvadorans in the United States able for the first time to gain temporary legal status and avoid the threat of deportation.

In the late 1980s the Boston area was particularly hospitable to refugees, dissenting from the official position of the conservative U.S. government led by President Ronald Reagan. On April 8, 1985, the Cambridge City Council (citing the examples of Berkeley, California, St. Paul, Minnesota, and Chicago, Illinois) adopted a resolution declaring Cambridge a "Sanctuary City," with special mention of refugees from El Salvador, Guatemala, and Haiti who had come to the city by the thousands. The resolution decreed that no city official should interfere with the activities of organizations providing help to refugees or inquire about refugees' immigration status and in general should not participate in "compounding injustice" or the "federal government's persecution" of Central American and Haitian refugees. Similar resolutions were passed in neighboring Brookline and Somerville.

A significant infrastructure of religious and secular community organizations existed (and still does) to support the growing refugee community. The Old Cambridge Baptist Church in Harvard Square housed several groups opposing U.S policies in Central America and during this period followed the old tradition of churches as literal sanctuary sites by publicly harboring a Salvadoran refugee who from the standpoint of the government was in the country illegally. A magnet for controversy, the church was subject to seven doubtless politically motivated burglaries in an eighteen-month period. The Concilio Hispano, founded in 1969, provides educational and health services such as language and literacy training, GED preparation, translation and interpretation, HIV/AIDS prevention, and substance abuse counseling to the area's Latino population (Puerto Ricans, Dominicans, Salvadorans, Guatemalans, Colombians, Hondurans, Nicaraguans, Cubans, and Mexicans) and is "dedicated to progressive social, economic, political change, and to the promotion of active citizenship." Established in 1981, Centro Presente is a Latin American immigrant organization "dedicated to the self-determination and self-sufficiency of the Latin American immigrant community of Massachusetts," led primarily by Central Americans and focusing on immigrant rights as well as social and economic justice. Sarah Willen

(2012) has recently provided a critical anthropological examination of health-related "deservingness" among "illegal" migrants.

Finally, the Latino Mental Health Clinic is a special program of the Cambridge Hospital with a bilingual staff providing a full range of mental health services in the fields of psychiatry, psychology, social work, and family therapy. When I arrived there as a researcher primarily interested in Latino mental health, my intent was to supplement my familiarity with the experience of Mexican Americans gained from previous work in California with an understanding of the circumstances of the full range of Latin American communities present in this East Coast locale. I quickly became aware of the compelling situation of a substantial group of Salvadoran women who had come to the clinic for treatment, and with the collaboration of Marta Valiente, a Salvadoran staff psychologist, decided to work primarily with them.

### The Salvadoran Women's Study: Nervios *and* Calor

I had a *susto* (fright) when a man was dying. Already the man couldn't speak [but] he made signs to me with his eyes. . . . I have seen various dead bodies. Since then, I became sick from *nervios*.

—Lucrecia Cañas, thirty-five

Suffering *(el sufrimiento)* is to hope for something and never see it happen, and sadness is to know that you had it and it's gone . . . it's very different.

—Marina Espinoza, twenty-eight

We interviewed twenty women at least two times each, though with several key informants I met as many as fifteen times in clinical, family, and community settings. In two cases, the frequency was higher (weekly or monthly) over the course of two years. The women in the study were twenty to sixty-two years of age and primarily of rural background and with little formal education, and most were monolingual Spanish speakers. Most had been in the United States for at least one year and had family, including young children, still living in El Salvador. Most worked very long hours—sixty or more—in two jobs, in vigorous efforts to make as much money as possible to send back home to relatives. In spite of these strong economic motives, the reasons given for their flight from El Salvador fall equally under three categories: escape from political violence, escape from domestic violence, and escape from economic conditions. However, all three reasons for leaving are closely bound up with the overarching political ethos of *la situación*. Nearly all of the women reported that they had regularly encountered brutal evidence of the war: mutilated bodies lying on the roadside or on the doorsteps of their homes, family and friends who had disappeared, and the terror of military troops marching through their towns shooting at random and arresting others who were then incarcerated. The women's narratives of fleeing political violence are often suggestive of the relationship between state-constructed affects of fear and anxiety, on the one hand, and indigenously defined conditions of *nervios,* on the other. These narratives also vividly portray everyday encounters with and habituation to truly horrific lifeworlds (see also Farias 1991).

A thirty-eight-year-old woman, mother of two, had survived a series of tortures subsequent to three arrests and imprisonments in the early 1980s.[10] At the time of her first imprisonment, her husband was also taken away by the military, his head covered with a black hood, and assassinated: "When they told me that my husband was dead, for me it was like, like a dream, like something unreal. Yes, there are times he comes into my mind, but I know it's something that will never exist. He's a person that doesn't exist. It's something that I have to try to do, to forget him." On another occasion she told me, "I think about him, I dream about him. I hear his voice calling to me." She now resides with their two children and had come to the clinic to seek assistance for intense psychological suffering that has remained with her, in the form of major depression, anxiety, and trauma. She also reported that her eleven-year-old daughter has *un problema de los nervios.* Although the daughter's doctor told her it was probably nothing and not to worry about it, she was not reassured. Whenever her daughter becames angry her nose would bleed profusely. This problem began in El Salvador but now recurred most often when she saw movies or TV about war or violent situations. She said, "Whenever possible, I don't permit her to watch this. Another thing I think is related to her *nervios* is that she laughs uncontrollably for a long time—for an hour or two—laughing to herself. She can't stop laughing. Afterward, she cries." When I asked her what she thought might have caused this problem, she provided a thoroughly embodied account.

> I imagine that it probably happened while I was pregnant [with her]. I had a lot of psychological problems. When one is very fearful, a nervous tension that the army is going to come, they're going to come through the streets, you're going to get hit by a passing bullet or the army is beating someone and taking them away—all of this affects a little baby you have inside. I feel that when you're pregnant all the nervous things, all the things that are

important to you, all the things you see, the baby feels too. Because it's something inside. I think that everything I went through while I was pregnant is now part of her nervous system. When I was pregnant and we had a strike at the factory, the army would arrive, begin shooting, and throw bombs of tear gas to make us leave. Yes, all this affects you. The tension we had. We had seven months without working, without receiving a salary, so much worry.

Many of the women also reported that they had fled their homelands to escape family violence. The words of a twenty-seven-year-old married mother of two provides a sense of how both societal and familial representations of violence become part of the embodied experience of women: "[I have felt *un susto*] when my husband was drinking a lot, already before he would arrive home. Then I would feel my heart, pum, pum, pum. If you are fearful it can make you sick because it can cause you a *crisis de nervios*. I feel that my body isn't me. It can cause a person to go crazy. It makes me have stomach pain, shaking of my body, and it makes me cold." A thirty-four-year-old married mother of two said:

> I was pregnant at that time [expecting my second baby], when he [my husband] started drinking . . . [and] he beat me. I was "very fat" [in an advanced stage of pregnancy], and he mistreated me. But later, he regretted it because the baby was born unhealthy, with a problem of *nervios*. He mistreated me for no reason when he was drunk. He was treating me like that because his mother told him very bad things about me, but the truth is that his mother never loved him, she was always telling him that I was very bad for him, that she paid his studies so he would marry a "worthy woman," not somebody like me because I was *nothing*. . . . [H]e mistreated me and beat my stomach and then, when the baby was born, he had like a yellow color in his skin, and the doctor told me it was necessary for my baby to remain in the hospital for some time because he was ill. But when my husband found out about the baby's illness he blamed me as well; so you know, I was guilty for everything . . . so I began having problems with my *nervios*, since I was pregnant, because his mother as well was treating me as if I was an animal, never like a person . . . and then when my baby was born I started to have nightmares. . . . [M]y daughter was ten years old by then, and I was suckling my baby and when he arrived home completely drunk then . . . she noticed all what was happening and she cried, she became sick from *nervios*, she became very ill. My daughter, sick with *nervios*, was screaming, throwing things around . . . it made *me* sick but I couldn't say a word to him because he would beat me, so that I knew that I just had to cry and keep quiet.

Domestic violence and abuse are the bodily experience of many of the Salvadoran women refugees in the study. Indeed, some of them reported that they ran for their very lives from husbands and fathers they feared would kill them if they did not escape their regular physical, and often sexual, abuse. The ways in which societal representations of violence are embodied and reproduced in family settings is a topic of great importance and something that, at present, we understand very little about. Future studies on this topic should comparatively and historically consider the prevalence of domestic violence (and cultural and sociopolitical values that surround it) in situations of both civil war and its absence. The women who spoke about their personal experiences of domestic violence did so with great shame and apparent reluctance. In this regard, they have much in common with countless other women worldwide who are regularly subjected to acts of violence by male kin within family settings (Campbell 1985; Counts 1990; Levinson 1989).

Finally, escape from unrelenting hunger and poverty exacerbated by the destruction of infrastructure and deterioration of the economy also impelled refugees to leave their country in search of income-generating work. A fifty-four-year-old woman, mother of four, gave this account.

> In El Salvador it was very hard. I used to wash clothes at the river by the dozens. I would do five dozen. I would get up at 5:00 a.m. and go to the bakery where I got leftover bread I used to take to the *mercado* to sell until 9:00 a.m. Then I would go to the river. I had no help. I didn't like it because I was hungry and sometimes I wouldn't get paid on time. And I would worry because I wouldn't have enough to feed my children. I came here because the situation wasn't good, there were strikes by the teachers, there were no classes, and then the teachers got together with the students and started to protest. After that, you would find dead bodies without heads and eyes on the roads. In 1980, on my own doorstep, I found many people dead. My son was here [in the metropolitan area], so I came.

A thirty-eight-year-old mother of two said:

> As immigrants in this country, the conditions of life are very different. There are so many economic problems, like health care. Employers don't pay Medicaid, and we can't afford it. We don't have good [enough] jobs to pay for it. The bills add up and add up. It's very difficult, life and health, these days in this country. [Back home] sometimes we say to ourselves, "Fine, I'm going to the U.S. I am going to earn money, to work." But it isn't easy. I know persons who come and pass 3 to 5 months without working. They're new, and especially because of the language they are not able to speak. If you want to work in a restaurant washing dishes or work in cleaning, sure, it's an honest job, but sometimes it's really difficult. Because it's the *only* thing you can do as an immigrant. To clean, wash dishes, or work in a factory, where they pay minimum wage, $4.25 an hour. And it's little pay for so much work. It's very difficult. In one factory, for example, they don't give benefits, health

care, nothing. Sometimes out of necessity you, as an immigrant, have to accept it. If you're a parent, it's very difficult. We come here from our country [El Salvador] because of the conditions of living there, the same situation, always through persecution, bombings, and the rest. For so many things that perhaps someone hasn't seen and at other times for others they have lived it, *en carne propia* [in one's own flesh, or lived bodily experience].

The events of political, domestic, and economic violence that constituted *la situación* could be either episodic, as in the witnessing of an assassination or undergoing torture and interrogation, or recurrent, as in repeated beatings by a spouse or violent nightmares. Following immigration to the United States, the women's lives continued to be dominated by *la situación*. Nearly all had family, including young children, who still resided in El Salvador (see also Horton 2009; Yarris 2011). In addition, the terror of *la situación* came to be overlain by new fears associated with life in the United States, including dread of deportation by immigration authorities, discrimination, economic exploitation by employers and landlords, and the need to accept jobs in restaurants, factories, as maids, or as nannies that were often below their level of qualification. Coming from a culture of male dominance, impunity, and heavy alcohol consumption, Salvadoran men who could not find jobs and were being supported by their wives became increasingly volatile. The 1992 settlement between the government and guerrilla forces was met with a mixture of skepticism and uneasiness, leaving unresolved the question for refugees of whether and how to repatriate. Across all the cases, however, the overweening factor remained the violence of *la situación*, and in the next section I focus explicitly on how violence was experienced by these women.

## EXPERIENCE OF POLITICAL VIOLENCE: EXTREME AND MUNDANE

All of the women reported suffering from a variety of problems related to *nervios*, a cultural category that has wide currency throughout Latin America (Low 1985, 1994; Jenkins 1988b; Guarnaccia and Farias 1988) and refers to distress of mind, body, and emotion. In the Salvadoran context, complaints of *nervios* were embedded in conditions of chronic poverty and unrelenting exposure to violence. What I am concerned with here—pathogenic events and conditions of political violence—can be categorized as follows: (1) generalized warfare and terror; (2) poverty; (3) violence against women; (4) death of kin due to political violence;

and (5) torture and detention. These must be understood not as independent factors but as coordinate dimensions of a single political ethos. Specifically, the women were subjected in different proportions to these dimensions of political violence that defined *la situación:* twenty had witnessed violent death or evidence of violent death; nineteen were living in poverty; eleven had been physically and/or sexually assaulted; ten had experienced the death or disappearance of kin; and one had undergone three separate instances of torture and imprisonment. I want to focus here on narrative responses that address two questions. First, how can we account for the fact that some of the women experienced and represented these situations as "extreme" while others appeared either to deny or minimize the impress of extremity under conditions of political violence (Jenkins 1996b)? Second, in what respect can these dimensions be characterized as evoking traumatic emotional responses regardless of whether they are represented as extreme or mundane?

## *"Everything Trembles, It's So Horrible"*

Gladys, a forty-year-old married mother of five, came to the clinic with severe problems of *nervios.*

> I have seen so many dead bodies. It fills me with great terror and dread, when you leave to go out on the highway, you see them without heads . . . everything [in my body] trembles, and it's so horrible. And at night I am not able to sleep thinking about it, because I live with so many ugly, horrible things. When I was pregnant with my second child I saw things so close to the house. I would see people with sacks over their heads [being taken away to be assassinated] . . . I feel the right side of my face all numb and my lips go to sleep.

Gladys decided to leave El Salvador to join her husband in the United States after the following event.

> It was New Year's Eve, and they came to the house of my brother-in-law. He is from a very humble family and hasn't been involved in anything and they came to his house, knocked on the door, and because it's the custom that on the 31st of December at midnight neighbors and all of your friends arrive to give you a hug for the New Year, he thought that when the knock on the door came it would be some friend or relative. He opened the door and someone fired a shot straight in his head and he died and they never knew who or why. He died and we never knew who or why and then my husband told me that with all this he felt ill. With the money that he already had from being in the U.S. he preferred that we come . . . I didn't want to come, but life was so difficult there, more than anything I had to think of my children,

to avoid also having them drafted into the military or being taken by the guerrillas, to lose their lives. I had such strong fear that something would happen to them. I consulted with a lot of people, to get their advice, and [they] told me you have to do something . . . I came here [to the United States] not to be alone, because my husband was already here. And as I said, the children had suffered, the children were so nervous because of everything that happened. In the nights they didn't sleep because of the shootings here and there. They would throw bombs and destroy houses. The father of my husband was the landlord of a lot of places, and they would extort a certain amount of money they had to give, and it was too much. It was the danger of the war. The children were so nervous. When they would go to sleep, they didn't want to be alone. They would cry when they would hear all these things—bombs, shootings—they would say, "Mommy, if we die here alone, without our father, what then?" It was the same problem for them [as for me], a serious problem of *nervios*. (Jenkins 1996b: 282–83)

### "My Terror Was That My Children Would Study Too"

Elsa, a thirty-five-year-old married mother of two children, had arrived alone in the United States just six months before the time of the interview.

[I have seen] many dead bodies. Many, for example there in [name of town], many dead bodies, we went walking looking for a cousin, they had made him "disappeared," and . . . we never found him dead or alive, in any place and his mother also went out looking for him and we never found him and there were many young people who were persecuted, the students, and that was my terror that my children would study, too, if I could have taken them with me I would have, but I couldn't . . . seeing all the dead bodies has affected me terribly, from that I am sick, too, especially one time when I saw a woman that they killed right in front of me, this made me sick, and I felt very ill, desperate really . . . They shot her in the head with me in front of her, I saw her fall and everything, then I became, like paralyzed, like I couldn't move to see that, then at that time lots of persons were killing people, and one time when I saw them kill that woman it made me afraid to go outside, at night we were used to locking the door, and I was used to thinking that they would come and knock on the door because I had seen this woman killed, right? [I was] thinking that they would come and knock on the door to get me too, and this for me made me ill with *nervios* and I was afraid for my husband, for my brothers and sisters, because I have nine brothers and sisters. (Jenkins 1996b: 283)

### "He Would Have Hit Me at That Moment"

Lucrecia was thirty-five years old and a married mother of two children who were still residing in El Salvador with her mother. Lucrecia's experience of *la situación* as extreme derived from her regular encounters with violence both within and outside the home. She recounted an experience of *calor* (heat; see below, this chapter) and *susto* in response to *la situación* prior to fleeing El Salvador.

> In my country I had a *susto* when a man was dying. Already the man couldn't speak [but] he made signs to me with his eyes. It was during the daytime, and I was going to get some chickens for a baptism. He could barely move his eyes. He had been shot in the forehead. It was the time of the fair in November. When I came back he was already dead. I returned home with a fever, and it wasn't something I'd ever experienced. Since it was carnival time, strangers came. They kill strangers. They saw him throwing away some papers. Yes, I have seen various dead bodies. Since then, I became sick from *nervios. Nervios,* upon seeing the dead bodies.

Recurring events of violence were also part of her experience in her new home in Massachusetts.

> I dropped a casserole dish with dinner in it and then the *nervios* came on because my husband was right in front of me. When I dropped the casserole dish it gave me a shiver throughout my body and I felt immediate pain and then, so my husband wouldn't see that I was afraid, I didn't say anything. . . . He had seen I dropped the dinner and since he is really angry, so he would see that I'm not afraid I said nothing to him. I had the heat attack in the moment I dropped the dinner. I felt an electrical charge was put inside my body. It was because of the fear I have of him, it's because he would have hit me at that moment, he would have beat me because I dropped the food. . . . When he goes out drinking on Fridays, he comes back at three in the morning on Saturday, then I feel my face is on fire, really numb, the middle [of my face] only, and the agitation in my chest, I feel desperate, with an urge to leave [the apartment] running, and running, running to get far away. . . . I feel the desire to run away, but I don't actually do it . . . there's the same pressure when he goes out drinking and returns irritable. Then I want to focus my attention and not be afraid of him, be strong, but I can't.

This response of fear and trembling, under the press of *la situación,* is one of the modes of *extreme* experience, as also illustrated by following examples of psychopolitical repression (see also Jenkins 1996b).

### *"It's the Kind of Injury That Remains on the Brain and Can Be Difficult to Heal"*

Julia was a thirty-three-year-old mother of three whose husband had been assassinated and who was herself imprisoned and tortured three times for activities as a union organizer.

I have suffered a lot because of the torture. It is the reason I have the *nervios*, all the different experiences I've had, it results in a kind of injury that remains on the brain and can be difficult to heal. All the trauma over the war, the bombings, the arrests, the mutilated bodies produce a constant tension that cannot be gotten rid of. Ninety percent of the people are traumatized and since it can begin at a very young age it is very difficult to erase. . . . My baby was born at the height of the strikes and violence and he was born with *nervios*.

In dramatic contrast to the reports of extreme violence experienced and narrated as trauma, the following are descriptions of political violence as mundane parts of a daily grind.

### *"But That Was Clear Across the Street"*

A divorced mother of five, fifty-seven-year-old Luz had been in the United States for three years. She explained that she enjoyed working in her own *tiendita* (little store) making cheese in El Salvador because it kept her busy. Further, "no misery or suffering" had befallen her. She maintained that she had come to the United States to be with her sons (who had emigrated earlier) and that *la situación* played no role in her decision to come. She then went on to claim that she really had not witnessed any violence in her country and that no one in her family had been affected. Later, when she narrated an event of violence in which eighteen persons were killed, I gently reminded her that she had said earlier that she hadn't really seen any violence in her country. She responded, "But that was across the street from my house . . . and I had only lived there for nineteen days. I didn't know them." Five of those eighteen had been lined up in front of the house directly across the street from where Luz was living and shot dead (Jenkins 1996b: 284–85).

### *"I Liked My Job"*

A second example of *la situación* construed as mundane is the case of Diana, a thirty-six-year-old middle-class woman with no children. Educated at one of the principal Salvadoran universities, she received an advanced degree and worked as a public health official in cases requiring identification of dead bodies. Her job involved cases of criminal action, often requiring her to collect evidence from medical investigators concerning the often-mutilated bodies of victims. She reported feeling pressured by her supervisors, on the one hand, and relatives of victims, on the other. She received death threats, she was often followed, and her home was ransacked on one occasion. Following these events, she arrived in Boston with complaints of depressive and anxious feelings that she articulated in terms of *nervios*. Noteworthy in her narrative presentation was how much she enjoyed her job in El Salvador, claiming the problem-solving dimensions of identifying dead bodies held great intellectual interest despite the fact that "the bodies are decomposing" and "there is a lot of putrefaction."

> [The type of work I did] had always attracted me, but then in El Salvador, the judicial system has problems. . . . Sometimes the corpses are lost, or there is not sufficient personnel or adequate instruments [for examinations], the paperwork is not carried out at the time when it should be done. . . . Many times they destroy the victims [bodies].

Thus she enjoyed her job despite the bothersome irregularities of missing dead bodies and missing paperwork and appeared not keenly interested in precisely why or how the bodies had disappeared. Although Diana appropriately represented the process of identifying mutilated dead bodies as but part of the professional duties she carried out, she simultaneously showed signs of having been marked by the process, saying she was haunted by thoughts of the dead bodies requiring her scrutiny (Jenkins 1996b).

### "We Never Had Any Problems"

A representation of *la situación* as mundane, indeed virtually nonproblematic, came from forty-nine-year-old Antonia, a married mother of four. Despite having come to the United States in 1979, a time when political violence had escalated tremendously in El Salvador, she made the unusual claim that *la situación* played no part in her decision to emigrate. Citing health and medical reasons primarily—she would see doctors for severe headaches—it was her expectation that the standard of living in the United States would be better. At the time of the interviews, she regularly traveled back and forth to El Salvador to visit relatives. Her most recent visit, three months in duration, was made just weeks after one of the bloodiest rebel offensives (November 1989), which coincided with the government-sponsored assassination of the Jesuit priests, their cook, and the cook's daughter. Claiming it was easy to travel and live in the country, Antonia stated:

I have not lived tortures and I go to El Salvador, I come and go and I don't have problems. . . . You may perhaps have heard that we had the last war in El Salvador just lately, and during this time I would go out at 9:00 a.m. and supposedly this trouble began at 11:00 a.m., but I never saw anything. My husband was head of a government campaign against [a particular disease] and he never had any problems.

In these examples we are presented with two modes of representing the experience of the various dimensions of *la situación* as a political ethos. Despite their apparent difference, my argument is that both are representations of traumatic experience. That such experience is sometimes represented as mundane can be accounted for by a combination of political constraints on expression and the psychological suppression of response—more precisely, by the overdetermination of repression in both its primary senses of political process and psychological defense. This dual sense of repression corresponds with terror and violence, on the one hand, and dissociation and denial, on the other (Jenkins 1996b).

This formulation leads directly to my second question, about the sense in which the phrase *la situación* is evocative of traumatic emotional response. A clue to how it can be said that women typically experienced pronounced response following exposure to discrete events of violence to themselves or others regardless of whether they reported it as extreme or mundane is present in the psychiatric definition of posttraumatic stress disorder as having an "active" and a "numbing" phase. This suggests as a preliminary hypothesis that the extreme and the mundane may be different expressive modalities for the same severe emotional responses. On the one hand, forceful emotion is actively and explicitly acknowledged; on the other, emotion is "numbedly" and implicitly acknowledged through denial, minimization, and withdrawal.

The questions I have been considering with regard to the emotional consequences of existing within a political ethos of violence can be reduced to the single question of whether, when the extreme is common, its very commonality defines it experientially as not extreme. The disturbing adaptability of human beings was given chilling reality in Arendt's (2006) account of the banality of evil during the Holocaust, though in Nazi Germany much of the suffering was hidden behind the scene in ghettos and concentration camps rather than being out in the streets in the form of dead bodies and overt acts of murder. Certainly from the Salvadoran women's points of view, the situation is other than it was in the past. However, the recurring political violence and the regularization of life under such circumstances suggests that though in one sense they are abnormal, in another they have become the norm. The circumstance of extremity comes to be thought of simply as "the way things are."

Perhaps it is most productive to recognize that from these women's standpoint, the extreme and the mundane are not necessarily alternatives but simultaneous states of affairs that are lived with as a persistent existential contradiction. When this contradiction cannot be sustained, either with respect to living in the political ethos or with respect to living with psychological trauma, the survival strategy is a dampening of awareness and expression. Such a strategy is not only the direct consequence of repression operating simultaneously in both the political and psychological senses of the word, for between these repressive poles there opens a continuum of phenomenological shadings of experience and expression along which we can identify emotions of fear, terror, dread, anxiety, and anger (Jenkins 1996b). In the next section I examine one of these phenomenological shadings.

## EL CALOR: IN THE HEAT OF THE MOMENT

*El calor* is an experience of intense heat that suddenly pervades one's whole body. Its emotional dimension is existentially isomorphic with anger and fear, and is grounded in personal encounters with the political violence of *la situación* and the domestic violence perpetrated by males—who of course are themselves also subject to *la situación. Calor* may actively engage an unjust world of violence through justifiable anger but may also reactively engage this same world through fear and trembling. Personally and culturally unwelcome, anger, fear, and heat engage the intentional body. Yet this engagement is clearly problematic. On the one hand, it is described under the rubric *nervios*, a condition to be suffered through with forbearance or healed through therapy or spiritual means (see chapters 3 and 5); on the other hand, women speak specifically of the need to actively control themselves and harness their anger. In the Salvadoran context, women's narratives of *nervios* are deeply embedded in the life situation of chronic poverty and exposure to violence, and *calor* is but one among several bodily phenomena associated with *nervios*. Other such phenomena include *escalofríos* (shivers, chills), *un hormigueo en la piel* (sensation of a swarm of ants on the skin), *un adormecimiento* ("sleepiness" or numbness) localized on one side of the face or body, *choques eléctricos* (electric shocks), and feelings of being *inquieta* (agitated), often with *ganas de correr* (the urge to run). Because it is of value for anthropological and medical understanding of culture, emotion, and embodiment, and the majority of women reported the experience of *el calor*, it deserves special consideration here.

Excerpts from the narratives provide evidence of the polysemous, multivocal nature of discourse on *el calor*. Gladys, a thirty-nine-year-old woman living with her husband and five children, said, "'Heat' is something like fire that you can feel from toe to head ... throughout your body ... nothing more than a vapor that you feel and then it passes ... a hot welling up." Adelina, a fifty-six-year-old Salvadoran living with her daughter, grandchildren, and three other extended family members, had a more elaborated description (see Jenkins and Valiente 1994).

> I used to feel hot currents rising up inside of me, hot, I felt like I was suffocating, and that despair that comes when the heat rises up, something hot, I couldn't [resist it] and I didn't feel well and my vision blurred. . . . [The heat] rose upward inside from my feet to my head throughout my body ... throughout my body, I felt like the fire was shooting out of me, from here and here, and my eyes felt like they were being pushed out by the fire, like they were going to come right out, and from the ears I felt it coming out of me . . . and in my mouth I could begin to taste . . . vapor, my own breath. I felt like it was fire, a flame, and it was inside of me . . . I was desperate, the heat, a terrible thing . . . I felt like I was suffocating and that I was dying [and] I went and turned on the cold water to take a cold shower. . . . [T]he heat feels as if, you know, with a match [you light] a sheet of paper and then swallow it, and inside the heat that feels so terrible, those flames of fire welling up.

Elsa, thirty-six years old, whose family still resides in El Salvador and who lives with a Euro-American couple as a maid and caretaker for their children, said:

> *Calorías* [heat attacks], that's what we call them here in El Salvador, my mother also had them and they say it has to do with the blood, apparently it becomes irritated and well, my hands and neck become . . . as if I had fever and I get real hot, but only in my hands and neck . . . it's a type of heat, yes, that they call "the urge to bathe," yes, it doesn't matter what time, the heat you feel, even though it's cold . . . it comes from worries, more than anything worries about important things, one is startled by one's nervous system and blood that are stirred by bodily memories.

A final example comes from Dora, a thirty-year-old woman separated from her *compañero* (partner) after his repeated violent assaults on her.

Heat, like some kind of vapor that rises upward from the feet, I don't know, I feel hot, I'm not sure how to explain what it's like. As if it begins in the feet and moves up until it reaches my head, at least that's what it was like before, but it's been a while since it happened . . . [it happened] when I was back in my country, and also here a few times, but more back home—from time to time, I would feel bad and my body would feel like it was getting hot, as if I were to suddenly become very chilled [but] with sweaty palms, I think that it could be because of all the problems I had that I couldn't vent, and the only thing I did was cry, and that didn't do me any good, also I didn't want people to see me crying, and I think that was the cause of all of this, the fact that I had so much pent up inside of me which I wasn't able to vent . . . from the feet upward, something hot that made my face and head feel hot and then it dropped down and my hands began to sweat and shake nervously.

Some women reported a particular site of the body, such as the head (face, nose, and mouth, including taste and breath), neck, back, leg, stomach, chest, and hands, as an intense "centering point" from which *el calor* emanates. The onset of *calor* is rapid. It may commence in the feet, progressively intensifying and rising to the head. Other accounts, however, describe *calor* as beginning in the head or neck and then spreading throughout the body. Although the experience is perceived as occurring *inside* one's body, it is thought to originate from without. It may be fleeting (a few minutes) or sustained (several days). While some of the women affirmed only occasional experience of *el calor,* others cite their episodes as too numerous to count: the range in my study was from four or five episodes in total to daily occurrences. The frequency and severity appear interrelated, such that the greater the number of episodes, the more intensely dysphoric the experience. While some women said that they had known *calor* only a few times and in ways that were inconsequential and less than debilitating, others' more frequent episodes were recounted as virtually unbearable (Jenkins and Valiente 1994).

Thus the seriousness of *calor* varies considerably: for some it is perceived as a mild occurrence that is a normal part of everyday experience; for others it is a frightening event with potentially fatal consequences. In the fourth example cited above, Dora recalled that following her relatively inconsequential *calor* experience she resumed her daily household activities without difficulty. In Adelina's narrative, *calor* was described *"como que era fuego"* (as though it was fire) and the experience as a whole in terms of a dissociative state: *"Yo me sentía que no era yo"* (I felt that it wasn't me). So terrifying was this *calor* experience that she feared she would surely die, saying, "I felt a burning flame . . . I felt

I was dying. I felt an agony. I felt death was just above, with that heat." In her frequent encounters with *calor,* she would typically feel compelled to take off her clothes, shower in cold water, and consult with both a psychotherapist and a *santero* for healing. During one especially bad episode in which she thought she might asphyxiate, she ran out of her apartment and into the street. Upon recovery she remembered nothing. This case example falls within the indigenously defined cultural category *ataques de nervios,* a phenomenon more fully described among Puerto Ricans (Guarnaccia, Kleinman, and Good 1990).

*Vapor* (vapor), *corrientes* (electrical currents/surges), *fuego* (fire), and *llama* (flame) are common tropes for describing *el calor. Un vapor* is a steadily rising sort of steam heat that is felt throughout one's body. Although qualitatively intense, the experience nonetheless may have an insubstantial, fleeting quality that ultimately leaves the body, "evaporating" as would steam. *Vapor* thus represents *calor* as a kind of incarnate substance. The sometimes "electric" movement of *calor* is captured by *los corrientes* flowing through the body. This sense of fluidity may also be expressed as waves of fire or flame: "The heat is like fire in your whole body." One woman described *calor* as the sensation of rolled up newspapers that were set ablaze in her chest. Yet another described it as *un vapor* like *el aliento* (the breath), felt as *un fuego,* or *una llama* causing heat inside her body. In still other cases, *calor* can be colloquially described as *un fogaz*—a flame that shoots up through the body. Finally, the experience was also occasionally referred to as *calorías* (calories, heat units) or even *ganas de bañarse* (the urge to take a bath).

The women's attempt to communicate the feeling of *el calor* raises the perennial problem of the relation between language and experience. There is little doubt that *calor* is a cultural phenomenon for Salvadorans, but it is only a partially objectified one. We are constantly shifted among what appear as direct description, simile, and metaphor. Different informants may use the same word, for example, *vapor,* as a simile (expressing similarity) or as a metaphor (expressing shared essence) for *calor.* In one of the examples just cited, we found *calor* to *be* a vapor that was *like* a breath *felt* as a flame *causing* heat. Fernandez (1986) has given us the notion of the play of tropes and Friedrich (1991) the term *polytrope* for such examples of metaphor upon metaphor upon simile. Friedrich (1991: 24) notes that all tropes contribute to both ambiguity and disambiguation, and paraphrases Tyler to the effect that "a trope may mislead in exact proportion to the amount it reveals, but that is the price of any revelation." My example of *el calor* suggests not so much the masking of experience by linguistic representation as the indeterminate flux of bodily existence. The indeterminacy of these tropes reveal them not so much as cultural meanings imposed on experience as fleeting, evanescent disclosures of inexhaustible bodily plenitude. Metaphor and simile emerge from this plenitude in, to borrow Kirmayer's (1992: 380) phrase, the body's insistence on meaning, which is "to be found not primarily in representation but in presentation: modes of action or ways of life." This tropic movement is best described not in terms of Fernandez's (1986) dimension of inchoate to choate but as a movement from preobjective indeterminacy to inexhaustible semiosis (cf. Daniel 1994; Csordas 1994).

In addition to the reliance on simile and metaphor to partially communicate a largely incommunicable bodily experience, this indeterminacy is evident in the women's linguistic confusion over the best way to refer to *calor*. Quite in contrast to their use of the culturally salient category *nervios* (Jenkins 1988b; Low 1985, 1994; Guarnaccia and Farias 1988), many fumbled or varied in the use of the definite or indefinite, feminine or masculine article prior to the nominal *calor*. For this reason, we inquired about their knowledge of *calor* as *"lo que le llaman"* (what they call) *el calor* or *la calor*. (To be grammatically correct, the masculine *el* would be preferred.) Nevertheless, the women disagreed even on this point. Some readily used the term *el calor,* but a few claimed unfamiliarity with it even though they went on to describe the experience itself in ways that were relatively indistinguishable from those who did. These considerations suggest that while *calor* is a *cultural phenomenon* insofar as it is by no means universally reported cross-culturally, it remains only *partially objectified* in the experience of Salvadorans.

Emotions associated with *calor* are nearly all dysphoric: *miedo, temor, susto,* and *preocupaciones* (fear, dread, fright, and worry); *desesperación* (despair, desperation); *agonía, muerte* (misery, death agony); and *coraje, enojo, enojado* (anger). All these diverse affects are strong, to be sure, and were generally mentioned in relation to forceful experiences of *calor*. Milder experiences generally were not accompanied by this particular vocabulary of emotion. Experiences perceived to be "lighter" in character were noteworthy for their failure to evoke certain emotion words in narration. The possibility also exists, however, that some women simply eschewed specific mention of emotional terms on the grounds that these were unnecessary, inappropriate, or even unthinkable (Jenkins and Valiente 1994).

During the narrations of *calor* experience, some women offered examples of specific contexts, often the last time it had occurred. Gladys, thirty-nine and living with her husband and five children, said:

> We were in El Salvador when my mother-in-law died and they called me to give her some water when she was dying. I felt my body very hot and numb but I had to face up to it. Then a neighbor was there too in those days. I had felt it too, because I had a nine-year-old son with a broken leg. I told him to get up, but then I saw that he was in pain—he had lost his color—and that his heart hurt from the force he exerted with the crutches and just at that moment I felt a hot surge. I said to myself, "He died."

In this example, Gladys provides two intimately intertwined family contexts of *calor* experienced as intense fear of actual and imminently imagined death. Faced with the real or potential loss of a family member, she responds bodily with what she thinks of as *el calor*. Reina, a forty-seven-year-old married mother of three, said:

> It happens to me if I feel bored, or it happens to me most when I am walking to the store with my husband, in the store, because with him it's so boring to go out. Because nothing entertains him, nor does he say anything to me if I buy something or if something fits me well. He never says anything to me and then all of a sudden it grabs me, my leg goes to sleep, almost a side [of my body] like painful or my knee goes out, or my ankle.

This darkly amusing example of the body taking itself literally by actually "going to sleep" from sheer boredom is unique in the *calor* narratives. In terms of the emotional context of *calor* experiences, it fits neither with the prosaic, unemotional occurrences of mild impact nor with the intense emotional experiences of anger or fear. Interpretively, it might only be assimilated to one of these types if we were to consider it an example of "angry boredom." Finally, a powerful example of anger associated with heat, though not part of a *calor* experience per se, was narrated by Dora when she was torn over whether to separate from her physically abusive husband.

> It is as if your blood . . . it's like putting water in a pot that's being heated and then letting it boil, it's as if your blood were boiling, and I feel as if I want to wreck everything [the world] if it were possible, but at the same time I can't control myself a bit, because when my world is dominated by anger I prefer not to say anything [to hurt others] because I don't want to use angry words to express or reveal myself. I never know if such reactions are good or bad, for example when my husband becomes violent and mistreats me I fill up with anger [become rabid]. I feel angry, but at the same time I overcome it and I say nothing, and if he comes up to me and threatens to hit me, I tell

him to go ahead, and it is this manner which I believe allows me to control my anger.

How might these diverse accounts of bodily experience be interpreted? *Calor* is an ethnographic example from a phenomenological world neither recognizable nor widely shared across cultural groups. Within the realm of personal experience, *calor* can be conceived as a form of emotional engagement with social and political realities. Specifically, it is a somatic mode of attention (Csordas 1993), a mode of attending to and with the body in an intersubjective environment. Cultural variation in the elaboration or suppression of such somatic modes of attention is a potentially valuable dimension for examining cross-cultural variation in experiential and communicative worlds of emotion. We must insist that it would be a mistake to regard concepts such as *calor,* which only point to or outline a mode of attention, as sorts of bodily analogs of elements in the conceptual "belief system" of traditional cultural anthropology.[11] As Ots (1990: 22) has observed, "This problem becomes even more acute when the concepts of others are not just a different mode of thought but can be viewed as created by a different kind of bodily perception, e.g., the concept of *qi* in Chinese culture." In this context, difference in bodily perception does not refer to the observation that different cultural orientations tend to locate emotions in particular body sites or organs. The problem with organ-specific descriptions of emotion is a failure to link body (or bodily pain) to the social world, such that in fact they remain modeled on an intrapsychic conception of emotion (Lutz 1988). Ots (1990) considers bodily organs such as the "angry liver, the anxious heart, and the melancholy spleen" as evidence of the body's role in generating culture. In a critique of the notion of somatization (which he views as relegating bodily processes to psychological mechanisms presumed to be of a higher order), he argues that bodily manifestations can be considered correspondents or equivalents of emotion (24; see also Ots 1994; on pain as an emotion, see Jackson 1994). This intriguing idea repositions the construct of emotion within the lived body, quite the opposite of the more typical psychosomatic strategy that describes transformation of an essentially psychological event into a secondary somatic expression.[12]

Along these same lines, we can understand that *calor* is existentially isomorphic with anger and fear, with variations in the degree to which it is configured as primarily anger or fear or an admixture of the two. One significant contextual basis for these emotions is personal encounters with violence: violence of male kin and the immediate conditions of civil war represented as *la situación*. Each of these contexts contributes to the political ethos of a culture of terror in which brute violence is regularized. Cultural proscriptions of outwardly directed verbalizations of anger and rage by women are of obvious importance here.[13] Our analyses of refugees' narratives revealed that certainly not all or even most explicitly associated their experiences with either anger or fear. *Calor may* actively engage unjust worlds of violence through justifiable anger, but it may also reactively engage these same worlds through fear and trembling. Personally and culturally unwelcome, the anger and fear that construct *calor* experiences engage the intentional body. In their accounts of *nervios*, on the other hand, these Salvadoran women speak specifically of their perceived need to control themselves, to harness their anger and fear. In this regard, they are not unlike most other women worldwide who, relative to men, feel a disproportionate need to suppress their passions (Lutz 1990). The need for the domestication of emotion was in evidence, for example, in the use of *vapor* as a metaphor, a term more normally employed in the domestic context of ideal cooking time *(al vapor)*. One woman described the experience of *calor* as the "stirring" of bodily memory throughout one's nervous system and blood, perhaps again an oblique culinary reference to the domestication of raw female emotion.

While images of *vapor* and stirring evoke the notion of domestication, that of bodily memory evokes the engagement of affect associated with trauma and incorporated in what Casey (1987) has called habitual body memory. Casey notes that traumatic body memory risks the fragmentation of the lived body such that it is "incapable of the type of continuous, spontaneous action undertaken by the intact body ("intact" precisely because of its habitualities, which serve to ensure efficacy and regularity). The fragmented body is inefficacious and irregular; indeed, its possibilities of free movement have become constricted precisely because of the trauma that has disrupted its spontaneous actions" (155). In the close-knit family atmosphere of Salvadorans, such trauma may be equally poignant if it occurs to immediate kin or if it occurs to oneself. There is ample narrative evidence for the importance of actual or near-death experiences of family members that may elicit the bodily sensation of *calor*. In sum, *calor* is the bodily channeling of emotions seen as emanating from without that must be thrown off, not only to regain a comfortable stance of being-in-the-world, but, indeed, to ensure one's very bodily integrity and survival.[14] As an existential phenomenon associated with *nervios, calor* is a vivid example of what Low (1994) has described as an "embodied metaphor" of trauma that constitutes the habitual body memory of *la situación* for these women.

This understanding of *el calor* is in accord with current work on embodiment that critiques conceptualizations of the body as a tabula rasa on which cultural forces inscribe their codes, pointing instead to the intentionality and agency of the body in creating experience (Csordas 1994, 2011). Some anthropologists and psychologists (e.g., Levy 1984; Frijda 1987) suggest an operational separation of "feeling" (sensation) and "emotion" (cognized interpretation). Others herald "complex" emotions such as the Japanese *amae* (Doi 1973) at the expense of "simple" sensationally and bodily based emotions such as "angry livers" in China (Ots 1990). From the vantage point of bodily experience, these distinctions are problematic, and one wonders whether they are at root predicated on the traditional dualist idea that the closer we come to the body, the farther away we must be from culture.

This approach is compatible with the premise that social domains of power and interest are constitutive of emotional experience and expression (Corradi, Fagan, and Garreton 1992; M. Good, Good, and Fischer 1988; M. Good et al. 2008; Jenkins 1991b; Lutz and Abu-Lughod 1990; Kleinman 1986; Scarry 1985; Swartz 1991). While recognition of the essential interrelations between the personal and the political has long been central to feminist scholarship (Rosaldo and Lamphere 1974), this point has yet to be adequately integrated in theories of culture and emotion/affect. To this end, Abu-Lughod and Lutz (1990) have proposed a theoretical basis for analyzing sociopolitical dimensions of emotion in everyday discourse. Suárez-Orozco (1990: 353) has proposed examination of the formal structures or "grammar" of collective terror such as has been widespread in Latin America. In sum, what is at issue is the cultural and sociopolitical basis of bodily experience not merely with respect to the sociopolitically "inscribed" body but also with respect to the body as seat of agency and intentionality through resistance, denial, and reactivity (Shweder 1990; Scheper-Hughes 1992).

The clinical and existential relevance of understanding *el calor* is all too evident in the following incident. While waiting for the resident to come into the hospital examining room, a patient was overcome by intense heat throughout her body. To relieve herself she took off her blouse and soaked it in cold water from the sink. When the resident entered the room and saw she was not only distressed but also half-nude, he apparently assumed she was "psychotic" and immediately transferred her to the local state psychiatric hospital, where she remained without the benefit of an interpreter for several days until her family discovered her whereabouts. Indeed, clinical confusion over how to biomedically diagnose and treat *calor* was abundant in the women's narratives. Several of the Salvadoran women reported what they regard as common misdiagnoses, including menopause or high blood pressure. The inadequacy of an explanation based on menopause is evident from the fact that *calor* is commonly experienced well before the onset of menopause (age range in the twenties and thirties) and the fact that men can also experience *calor*. Although we cannot entirely rule out the interactive effects of menopausal symptoms among some women in the study, the overarching point is that the phenomenology of *calor* varies substantially from and is not reducible to symptoms of menopause. In addition, *calor* (not unlike pain) is not clinically observable or measurable. The frustration surrounding clinical encounters was captured in one woman's comment, "I tell the doctors to look for something inside of me, but they tell me it's only what I feel."[15]

## TRAUMA, RESILIENCE, AND PSYCHOPATHOLOGY

Identifying the mental health concerns of refugee populations poses a substantial challenge for anthropologists and mental health professionals who seek to understand and treat these populations. Clinical literature on refugee mental health often concerns the fundamental question of how a relationship between refugee experience and mental health status can be demonstrated empirically (e.g., Allodi and Rojas 1985; Postero 1992; Marsella et al. 1994; Summerfield 2000; Kinzie 2007; Kagee and Naidoo 2004). That decades of research has been required to establish this relationship is the case for reasons scientific and political. First is the historical context of the currently dominant paradigm that privileges biochemistry over contextual features of experience. Second, research that seeks to investigate the health consequences of war-related experience has been the subject of political controversy. It was not until 1980, for example, that the Diagnostic and Statistical Manual (DSM-III) of the American Psychiatric Association included the category PTSD. The establishment of PTSD as a psychiatric diagnostic category was intended in large measure to address the cluster of symptoms that has plagued many Vietnam War veterans (Young 1997). From the point of view of many of those veterans, the slowness of this acknowledgment generated numerous psychosocial and economic problems for postwar adaptation and reintegration.

Consistently in the intervening years, symptoms of specific disorders including major depression and PTSD have been documented among refugees from political violence (Kinzie et al. 1984; Mollica, Wyshak, and Lavelle 1987; Westermeyer 1988; Jenkins, Kleinman, and Good 1991; Rousseau 1995; Boehnline and Kinzie 1995; Hinton, Um, and Ba 2001; Fazel and Stein 2002; Fazel, Wheeler, and Danesh 2005; Kinzie 2007; Kirmayer, Lemelson, and Barad 2007; Porter and Haslam 2005; Tol et al. 2010; El-Shaarawi 2015), and this is no less the case among those from El Salvador (Alvarez 1990; Farias 1991; Jenkins 1990a, 1990b; Young 2001; Fortuna, Porche, and Alegría 2008). While forced uprooting and displacement are sources of distress, political oppression and turmoil also clearly have an effect independent of migration. In addition, the refugees experience great psychic and bodily suffering in the aftermath of having fled their homes, whether they have left their countries or are internally displaced and whether they are warehoused in refugee camps or living independently. Despite life in what ostensibly one may have hoped for as a "safe haven," the rupture in the fabric of their lives remains vivid in dreams (often nightmares), is constitutive of memories, and is present in the apprehension of everyday life.

Clinical and research diagnostic data using DSM categories measured by the Schedule of Affective Disorders and Schizophrenia (SADS) developed by Endicott and Spitzer (1978) revealed that the women with whom I worked commonly reported symptoms of affective disorder (primarily major depression and dysthymia) and anxiety disorders (including PTSD, panic attacks, somatization disorder, and generalized anxiety). Nearly all of the research participants in the study had experienced at least one major depressive episode in their lifetime. Most had suffered one or more major depressive episodes within the past two years, and some had struggled with either chronic depression or dysthymia. They often suffered from sleep and eating disturbances, irritability, difficulty concentrating, loss of energy, sadness, helplessness, and hopelessness. The women voiced sadness and sorrow in relation to loss and bereavement. Loss and mourning, however, are often communicated through somatic means such as insomnia, lack of appetite, fatigue, or psychomotor agitation or retardation. As Kleinman observed (1986, 1988b), somatized expression of depressive disorders is very common for most of the world's population.

Among the women who reported symptoms of PTSD, the majority would not meet full diagnostic criteria for the syndrome. However, the criterion of an extreme stressor that threatens one's life, results in sudden destruction of one's home or community, or consists in witnessing the injury or death of another person was present in all cases. Earlier I noted that traumatic events reported by these women could be episodic or recurrent, and I must add the chronic presence of warfare and destruction as a sustained traumatic background feature of daily existence. Symptoms included recurrent nightmares of traumatic violence, a sudden feeling that the traumatic event (or events) is recurring, intrusive memories and feelings associated with the traumatic event, sleep disturbance, and avoidance of stimuli associated with the trauma. Autonomic features include increased arousal, irritability, outbursts of anger, and hypervigilant monitoring of the environment. They commonly reported highly disturbing memories and reexperiencing of traumatic events in the form of nightmares about violent scenarios and generalized fear for the safety of one's family. Less observable among these women were attempts to avoid feelings and memories of trauma. Psychiatrists refer to these "active" symptoms as part of the "intrusive" phase of PTSD, whereas symptoms such as restricted range of affect, feeling of estrangement from others, and efforts to avoid feelings associated with the trauma are part of the "numbing" phase.

In this context, what are possible psychiatric renderings of *el calor* experience? First, we note that the experience of "central heat" has been observed among depressed patients in societies such as Nigeria (Ifabumuyi 1981). The dynamics of this phenomenon in depression have yet to be fully appreciated in North American clinical practice. The *calor* component of the depression picture, however, may warrant identifying this phenomenological type of depression as "engaged" versus "withdrawn," insofar as the women's subjective response during the interview sessions did not, for us, have the "feel" of clinical depression. Relevant to PTSD, the occasional presence of dissociative states, numbness in the face or other body part (paresthesia and akathesia), and "vigilant" startle response all represent varying degrees of the fundamental human tendency to "fight or flight" in response to threat. The *calor* experience occurs under conditions in which such a response is not only appropriate but also vital and possibly inappropriate or personally oppressive. This being said, it is important not to lose sight of the fact that *calor,* like *nervios* (Jenkins 1988b) or depression (Kleinman and Good 1985), can in some circumstances be understood as normal, nonpathological experience. As one Salvadoran woman put it, *"No pienso que es enfermedad"* (I don't think it's illness).

Writing on the relation between passion and delirium, Foucault (1973: 85) mused that "the savage danger of madness is related to the danger of the passions and to their fatal concatenation." A contemporary parallel of Foucault's observation is our simultaneous understanding of, for example, depression as an emotion and as a disorder (Kleinman and Good 1985). The problem of understanding the pathogenic consequences of trauma and the character of the resulting disorder is thus compounded by variations in the psychocultural bases of emotional life (see Kirmayer, Lemelson, and Barad 2007). In the present context, I can offer only the briefest summary of the Salvadoran ethnopsychology of emotion that underlies response to traumatic stimuli (see also Ministerio de Cultura y Comunicaciones 1985):

1. In terms of what would be clinically categorized as the "chief complaint" or presenting problem, nearly all the refugees in the study reported suffering from a variety of problems related to *nervios*. The cultural category *nervios* is deeply embedded in the life contexts of chronic poverty and exposure to violence and refers at once to matters of mind, body, and spirit (see chapters 3 and 5).

2. Salvadorans can in general be characterized in terms of a strongly kin-oriented and relatively sociocentric (Shweder and Bourne 1982) or referential (Gaines 1982) sense of self, with the experience and expression of symptoms framed in reference to the family context.

3. Spanish provides a rich lexicon for emotions of sadness and sorrow. Suffering may be reported through language rich in descriptive detail, and with a distinctly existential flavor. In Salvadoran cultural orientations, ethnopsychological elaboration of *tristeza* (sadness) or *pena* (sorrow) and an underlying sense of life's tragedy invariably color *la situación*.

4. On a phenomenological level, Salvadorans describe their emotional experiences in terms of bodily sensations. The body sites are often both specific and generalized. It is not uncommon to describe one's suffering as a totalizing bodily experience. Reports of various bodily sensations may be interpreted as signs of malevolent spiritual influence, and one's suffering could thus be related to spirit activity.

5. Also common is the preoccupation with protection from the malevolence of others, as manifest in the ethnopsychologically salient themes of *envidia* (envy) and witchcraft (see chapter 5).

6. Salvadorans evidence a great deal of involvement in dream life, and this serves as a means for communicating with distant, missing, or dead loved ones. Sometimes these communications are reported as comforting experiences, as dream memories focus on past family fiestas and Salvadoran love of the land and nature. The dysphoric and distressing quality of dream life becomes evident, however, in the alarmingly high incidence of dreams of disembodied and mutilated bodies, knives and other weapons, and a full array of war-related horrors. Especially noteworthy is the fact that most of the dream life situates Salvadoran refugees back home, not in the United States.

7. Salvadoran ethnopsychology incorporates the belief that anger and hostility, whether expressed directly or covertly (through witch-craft), may lead to serious illness or, in extreme cases, death.

Pierre Janet's work on trauma has undergone a renaissance because it takes us a step beyond the question of whether trauma bears a causal relationship to illness. With the publication of his work *Psychological Automatism* in 1889, Janet began to specify the internal dynamics that organize trauma and the processes that turn trauma into illness. He observed that "traumas produce their disintegrating effects in proportion to their intensity, duration, and repetition" (quoted in van der Kolk and van der Hart 1989: 1536). The initial response combines what he termed "vehement emotion" and a cognitive interpretation resulting in dissocia-tion of memory or identity processes and attachment to the trauma such that the person has difficulty proceeding with her life (van der Kolk and van der Hart 1989).

Martín-Baró (1988, 1989) argued that individualized accounts of trauma and illness are insufficient in the context of long-term political violence. Although the trauma is manifest in individual psychic suffer-ing, dysphoric affect, and psychopathology, it is more appropriate to speak of psychosocial trauma or "the traumatic crystallization in per-sons and groups of inhuman social relations" (1988: 138). Psychosocial trauma is particularly evident in the collective experience of anxiety, fear, paranoia, terror, and, above all, denial of reality. Martín-Baró (1990) interpreted the constellation of state-constructed affects, ills, and defenses as a potent means of psychological warfare. His insight is that, through its own peculiar dynamic, war unfolds into a more global phenomenon and is the dominant process that subordinates all other social, economic, political, and cultural processes. Moreover, this process affects all members of a society, either directly or indirectly. To a greater or lesser extent, all members of the society may experience the war *en carne propria* (in their own flesh). The point is that no one remains untouched, or unchanged, by *la situación*.

Understanding the human meaning of trauma, especially as it affects refugees from political violence, is frequently clouded by failure to distinguish between a relatively enduring traumatic situation and relatively discrete traumatic events. I would suggest that this distinction is relevant in two critical dimensions, namely, the state construction of affect and the phenomenology of affect. In the first of these dimensions, the conditions of trauma established by the state and resistance to it come under the distinction between the situation of terror and events of torture. In the second, the modes in which those conditions are taken up into human lives come under the distinction between the situation of distress and events of disease. Torture is different from terror and disease from distress, by degree and by self-reference. With regard to degree, we might posit that there is a simple continuum from the diffuse effects of the generalized situation to the intensely focused effects of the discrete event. However, torture and disease take on their unique configuration in contrast to terror and distress as a result of what Marx termed the "transformation of quantity into quality," the amplification of a phenomenon until it undergoes a transformation in character and consequences. This understanding is parallel to that of biological psychiatrists regarding the existence of a threshold the crossing of which constitutes a pathogenic alteration of neurological biochemistry. Related to this process is another, more distinctly qualitative threshold associated with the shift in the immediacy of self-reference. The generalized situations of terror or distress bear a relatively diffuse reference to the self, which is precisely the condition for the possibility of denial so characteristic of a political ethos such as that of El Salvador. Stated another way, one may be terrorized by a situation that includes the torture of others, and distressed in a situation that causes mental illness in others, but these can also become immediate events of torture or disease for the self.

Despite the profound differences in degree and self-reference, the essence that terror and torture, disease and distress retain in common is their fundamental dependence on the problem of meaning, sense, and representation. Taussig (1987), in trying to define the culture of terror that existed during the rubber boom in colonial Colombia, discovered that "terror provided only inexplicable explanations of itself and thrived by so doing. . . . [T]his problem of interpretation is decisive for terror, not only making effective counter-discourse so difficult but also making the horror of death squads, disappearances, and torture all the more effective in crippling of people's capacity to resist" (128). If, as Taussig says, terror nourishes itself by destroying sense, Scarry (1985) shows that this is doubly so in the structure of torture. Interrogation and the infliction of pain, the two basic features of torture, are both language destroying and hence destructive of the three principal loci of human meaning: world, self, and voice. Pain creates a "discrepancy between an increasingly palpable body and an increasingly substanceless world" (Scarry 1985: 30), as even familiar objects such as walls, doors, or furniture become weapons. Interrogation is not designed to elicit information but to destroy the voice, creating expressive instability in its conflation of interrogatory, declarative, and imperative modes and the exclamatory of each (29), until every question becomes a wounding and every answer regardless of its content becomes a scream. The self's complicity in its own destruction is represented as self-betrayal in that a transformation occurs between the experience that "my body hurts" and "my body hurts *me*," and as betrayal of others in the signing of an unread confession. The effect of the confession is compounded since it is understood as a "betrayal" by the general populace (47).

The same essential dependence on representation is true of distress and disease. Persons in a situation of terror are not necessarily in a situation of distress unless the terror is represented as such: distress is a particular stance toward the situation, a consequence of the construal of terror as terror. When the political structure of terror is recognized for what it is, the only self-preserving stance is either to take up arms or to flee. The only other solution is to find collectively acceptable ways not to recognize it. Thus, it is no accident that Salvadorans used precisely the vague term *la situación* to refer to the state of affairs in their country, for it is of necessity rhetorically neutral in its nonacknowledgment of distress. This is especially relevant because the acknowledgment of distress was itself considered a subversive act by the authorities. Jennifer Jean Casolo, the American church worker detained and interrogated by Salvadoran authorities in 1989, reported that when she cried upon hearing the moans of detainees in neighboring rooms her captors quickly asked if she was "crying for her subversive friends." Her insistence on the human legitimacy of distress was summarized in her response that she would cry for her interrogator if the same were done to him.

Disease too is bodily representation, a constellation of symptoms constituting a clinical entity that may occur in episodes—and with respect to refugees, what counts as disease is a rhetorical and political issue. A study of Latin American refugees in Toronto and Mexico City and of families of the disappeared in Santiago and Buenos Aires found that "victims of torture and refugees from violent political persecution within a period of ten years following the traumatic experience are impaired by psychosomatic and mental symptoms" (Allodi and Rojas 1983: 246). Moreover, families of *desaparecidos* experienced more symptoms than did refugees, not only because of the stress of uncertainty, but perhaps because they still lived in the mode of terror that stifles resistance and expression of distress. In other words, the authors suggest that families of *desaparecidos* have more symptoms than do refugees because, unlike those who have escaped, they must continue to repress even their distress for fear the authorities will construe its expression as a sign of subversiveness and possibly kill the *desaparecido*. This study has methodological flaws and does not arrive at particular diagnoses, but I cite it as an example of a struggle to represent the consequence of political violence as disease in the face of the ease of denying that someone in distress is persecuted, or even that persecution is wrong. Someone who is distressed might still in some way be accountable for that distress, but, as Young (1982) has noted, someone who is sick is relieved of culpability.

The distinction between distress and disease can also be used to delegitimize the relation of suffering to disease, as has been shown by Brown and Harris (1978). They argue against those who would consider depression a disease only if caused biologically and not by stressful life events. They point out that depressive symptoms are prevalent in the general populace as well as among psychiatric patients, and the former may never reach treatment or be cared for by general practitioners precisely because the origin of their illness is understandable as depression originating in stress, or distress. Emphasis on biological causes can misrepresent the impact of distress and trauma by opening the claim that those who develop pathology had a biological predisposition to the disease or had preexisting pathology. This problem of distress and disease is all the more tenacious because it is not only relevant to the refugee situation, but is inherent in medical thinking. As Kirmayer (1989: 327, 328) argues, "The definition of discrete disorders

remains an artifact of sometimes arbitrary criteria that leave the classification of milder and intermediate forms of distress ambiguous. . . .
[B]oth the lay and medical diagnosis and treatment involve selective
interpretations that hide some causes and consequences of distress while
revealing others."

Questions about the parameters of human nature are inherent in studies of refugees from war-torn countries. What are the limits of human
endurance, suffering, and tolerance for conditions and practices (such as
torture) that can, by any standards, only be characterized as horrific?
How do we come to know and understand the human capacity for
extraordinary strength and resilience in the face of human horrors?
These basic existential queries have been quite striking to me, a middle-
class North American female anthropologist, who has imperfectly
attempted to know my informants' worlds of phenomenal suffering, on
the one hand, and resilience, on the other. Martín-Baró also concerned
himself with the paradox that the suffering inherent in war offers to some
people the opportunity to further develop what we are fond of calling
our "humanity" and strength. This process seems to almost completely
elude social science concepts of adaptation, adjustment, and assimilation. These seem wholly inadequate to the task of understanding how
refugees attempt to reconstitute their lives and construct new meanings.
The kinds of personal, existential, and cultural losses faced by refugees
virtually guarantee a (potentially unresolvable) reaction of profound sorrow and anger. It also seems to me that if, as Obeyesekere (1985) has
argued, culture provides for the working through of grief that guards
against depression, then the work of culture may at times simply not be
adequate in the face of circumstances so extreme.

Yet this is not always how it goes. The persistence of strong love of
life, family, and native land, in the face of what would seem from a
North American point of view overwhelming circumstances, constitutes
a puzzle in understanding bodily and spiritual resistance and resilience.
For example, despite a sometimes dizzying array of losses, traumas,
somatic symptoms, and life crises, Rosa managed to find the proverbial
light at the end of the tunnel. Things had not been going well. Her apartment building was burned to the ground (there was the strong suspicion
by many residents that the match was tossed by the owner of the dilapidated unit for insurance purposes). The new city-owned building she
had moved into was populated mostly by *norteamericanos* (Euro-
Americans) whom she perceived as considerably less than enthusiastic
about having Latinos in the building. Moreover, she had just learned that

her daughter-in-law was again engaged in a "job" (i.e., witchcraft) against her, causing her no end of difficulties. Her therapist, empathetically frustrated and at her own wit's end, said, "Ay, Rosa, I just don't know what you can do. I say it's time to get the candles out and light up as many as you can." (Candles are religious objects with spiritual powers that provide protection and good luck.) Rosa responded by saying, "But doctor, don't you know, I've already tried it! I want to, but I can't. If I light the candles, it sets the smoke detector off!" At this, both patient and therapist burst into peals of laughter. Humor and perseverance in the midst of disaster and misfortune serve as powerful tools for survival (see also Argueta 1987 on this point.)

Having examined the distress and illness linked with political, domestic, and economic violence, contrasted cases in which women construe conditions of political violence in ways that can be described as extreme and construed as mundane, and emphasized the nexus of body and emotion in the phenomenon of *el calor*, it is important to make a broader observation about these groups of Salvadoran women as a whole. Given the common condition of enduring and surviving such adverse conditions, their overall resilience and resistance is striking. Surviving such circumstances, often with a palpable grace and dignity, raises fundamental questions regarding gendered adaptations in the face of extreme circumstances. In the final analysis, while refined understandings of the emotional distortion that occurs subsequent to traumatic experience are needed, it is clear that accounts of the sustained emotional integrity and resilience of persons surviving horrific human circumstances must equally compel our attention.

It would be an error to claim that the experience of these women was typical of all Salvadorans or of all Salvadoran women in Boston. That is definitively not the sense in which the extraordinary conditions of mental illness are valuable for understanding fundamental human processes of culture and self. It is, however, reasonable to suppose that experiences typical of Salvadorans who inhabited *la situación* occurred in more highly concentrated form and frequency among the group of women I encountered in the clinic. Not everyone exposed to the ravages of war becomes symptomatic, and certainly not all refugees end up in the mental health clinic. By the same token, not everyone in treatment at the clinic is necessarily there primarily because of the war, though the war was prominent in the experience of these women.

Indeed, we must take the mental health consequences of *la situación* seriously, even though the symptoms of many of these women were "sub-threshold," for their distress was palpable. Yet even though these women came to the clinic for treatment and even if they were willing to accept a psychiatric diagnosis, mental illness and diagnostic labels did not define what Alfred Schütz (1945) called the "paramount reality" for them. Especially for refugees trying to make a new life in a new land with changes in personal relationships accompanied by continued connection with their struggling homeland, the "world of working as a whole stands out as paramount over against the many other sub-universes of reality. It is the world of physical things, including my body; it is the realm of my locomotions and bodily operations; it offers resistances to overcome which requires effort; it places tasks before me, permits me to carry through my plans, and enables me to succeed or to fail in my attempt to attain my purposes" (Schütz 1945: 549). The last thing I would want to suggest is that my interest in mental health and illness among Salvadoran women refugees translates into their preoccupation with it or their orientation of their lives around it. This is in large part why I did not begin this chapter with a medicalized account of how many women had how many diagnoses but only came to the question of psychiatric disorder at the end, after an account of how the women responded to *la situación*. Furthermore, *la situación* is only one of the overlapping multiple realities they inhabit, and in the next chapter I introduce another—the reality of religion and magic.

## CHAPTER 5

# Blood and Magic

*No Hay que Creer ni Dejar de Creer*

In the preceding chapter my discussion highlighted the relation between violence and mental health among Salvadoran women immigrants in treatment at the Cambridge Hospital Latino Clinic during the darkest days of civil war in their homeland. Political violence was more or less salient depending on the extent to which they had been personally exposed, the year and circumstances of their emigration or flight, and the degree to which family members still in El Salvador were perceived to be in danger. Only a portion of them can be said to be suffering primarily from PTSD resulting from the war. Domestic violence was likewise more or less salient depending on whether it was ongoing, its severity, and whether it was more associated with life in El Salvador or the United States. The inversion of employment opportunities in the United States that made women the more viable breadwinners in the face of highly entitled male dominance was conducive to turning many households into emotional tinderboxes. *La situación* and the conditions of immigrant existence at the very least created a background level of tension in the lifeworld of all these women, as indeed can be presumed of Salvadoran immigrants who were adapting without recourse to mental health treatment.

In this chapter I turn from the relation between violence and mental health to that between religion and mental health. Here we shall also see a greater or lesser degree of salience, while for the most part there is at least a background of spiritual belief, practice, and experience in the lifeworld of these women.[1] In a manner distinctive from that explored in chapter 1, this chapter suggests the importance of bringing magic/religion to the forefront of our thinking about mental illness cross-culturally.

Following on my reference to Schütz (1945) at the end of chapter 4, the world of religion can best be understood as one among the multiple realities inhabited by the Salvadoran women with whom I worked. By far the most common phrase uttered by the women with regard to this domain was the one that constitutes the subtitle of this chapter, *"No Hay que Creer ni Dejar de Creer."* This *dicho* (common saying) has a broad range of applications in everyday discourse.[2] While not easily translated, one rendering is "You can't believe nor stop believing."[3] The phrase is paradoxical and polyvalent. With reference to witchcraft, for example, there's no way to believe it, yet how can you not believe it? While unknown and impossible to pinpoint, one hardly does well to ignore that which *might* transpire without risk of personal or familial peril. In this regard, there is an implicit moral imperative: while you can't believe it, perhaps you *better* believe it just in case, since it is better to be safe than sorry. Ultimately it is simply impossible to know. In this respect, the phrase effectively means that it makes no difference whether one believes; the religious/magical/witchcraft is just there. Its prevalence in everyday speech provides a fascinating illustration of Byron Good's (1994) penetrating critique of the category of belief in anthropology and the health sciences. Good argues that to de-privilege belief requires a rethinking of rationality in a manner that incorporates a deep appreciation of subjunctive realms of experience, meaning, illness, and healing. In the fantastic tangle of the present case, I find this formulation relevant to the narrative interpretation of extraordinary experience.

Moreover, just as it was critical to distinguish political and domestic violence while acknowledging that they quite likely amplify one another, the domain of religion broadly defined is distinguishable into more than one sphere. This will become evident as I describe how women talk about Catholicism, *espiritismo, brujería,* and herbalism. To properly frame the account that follows, I must emphasize that unlike many discussions of religion and mental health it is not focused on the practice of a particular healer and the question of whether it counts as an equivalent of psychotherapy. Moreover, unlike many accounts of medical pluralism and alternative healing it does not attempt to describe a generalized system of practices in the ethnographic setting of metropolitan Boston. Instead, what follows is a grassroots perspective drawing on the concrete manner in which Salvadoran women with whom I talked invoke religion in the broad sense, encapsulated in ideas such as devotion, harm, protection, damage, evil, devotion, prayer, and cure. Sometimes the relevant data are in the form of general statements, more often in the context of significant episodes that have occurred to them and people they know. Drawing on ethnographic and life history materials, I first discuss two women whose experiences were among the most explicit and conclude by placing them in the context of the larger study of Salvadoran women.

## MARIELA

Spiritual means and magical interpretations may be woven into the fabric of life, as are personal problems and elements of social pathology, and the two domains can be teased apart only delicately. This is especially relevant with respect to the permeable boundaries of closely linked selves, which are both the existential locus of spiritual practices and the locus of disordered relationship for borderline personalities. Such is the circumstance of thirty-two-year-old Mariela, whose troubles focused on the triangular relationship with her mother and spouse. She came to the clinic on referral of her common-law husband, who was already in treatment there because of their marital problems. From a methodological standpoint, it is evident that the case study would have a different interpretive valence if he rather than she was its protagonist, or if my work had focused on male rather than female immigrants. Likewise, it would be different if I had adopted a primarily clinical rather than existential standpoint, since her clinical diagnosis of postpartum depression with psychotic and borderline features would skew understanding both toward symptoms and syndromes rather than life circumstances and toward the birth of her second daughter as the temporal focus of her difficulties.

My account, however, is oriented by the manner in which spiritual and magical elements are folded into the fabric of Mariela's life and affliction from an early age. She had been raised by her aunt (*madre de crianza*) since the age of ten months but remained in contact with her mother, a businesswoman with her own bakery (*panadería*). Mariela's mother went on to start a family and had eight sons. One day in her childhood Mariela and her mother had shared a tamale for lunch. She noticed a strange taste, and sure enough someone had put something in it to harm her mother (such magical poison does harm only to the person targeted by the evil, so the young girl wasn't affected). They laid down for a nap together as is the custom after lunch, and when Mariela awoke she was alone, hearing her mother say in a fury that something like a kind of snake (*culebra*) was there to kill her. Friends came to restrain her because she was hitting herself, and Mariela's aunt took her away. It was only years later after she had come to the United States that Mariela learned her mother had subsequently become a spirit medium in order to protect herself from the harm done to her by people who had attacked her out of envy (*envidia*) of her business success, though she kept her spiritual activities within the family and did not take on clients as a practicing medium.

Mariela had been married before leaving El Salvador and had a daughter before moving to Los Angeles, where several other family members lived, in 1978 when she was nineteen. As her mother had done with her, she left her daughter behind in El Salvador at the same early age. By the time her husband and daughter joined her two years later, the young girl did not recognize Mariela and referred to her as aunt. Also by this time she had taken a new boyfriend, and domestic relations became so strained that her husband and daughter returned to El Salvador. Mariela became ill after removing a copper birth-control device, her stomach growing and swelling with pain and inflammation, such that she went through a series of medical examinations to determine whether she had a cancerous tumor. After an initial false positive it was determined that she had no cancer, but when her mother arrived in Los Angeles to help her she determined through consultation with her spirits that Mariela's sister-in-law had executed a magical work (*un trabajo*) to do her harm (*daño*). The illness was caused by a ball of flesh (*carne*) spiritually inserted so as to make her grow as if she were pregnant, but through her mother's intervention and the help of her mother's spirits she was able to survive this and other attacks during her separation. These included gifts from her husband that had been taken to a woman who put a spell on them, which her mother would always remove, and a shirt that had been kept by this woman an inordinately long time and when Mariela sent it to be cleaned ended up with a mysterious dark stain that indicated a work of harmful magic. She was convinced by her husband to reunite, though she did not want contact with his family, and they eventually separated permanently.

Subsequently Mariela became romantically involved with her aunt's son, Javier, and they entered a common-law marriage (*acompañados*) despite being first cousins. This incestuous relationship intensely displeased both mother and aunt, and to escape their disapproval the couple moved to Boston along with another couple. Mariela had promised to send money to help her mother, but after a while she stopped sending the money and communicated less frequently with her mother. She became ill in a way she described as like when someone is inflicting magical harm (*"como cuando una persona le hacen daño"*), feeling generalized fear as well as fear of being alone, hopelessness, inability in her body to understand what is happening, and thoughts of all her problems while at the same time not wanting to think about everything that was in her head. When she contacted her mother, she was told that the illness occurred because she had let her promise of sending money lapse, for "if one does not observe something, one receives some kind of punishment" (*si uno no cumple algo, algún castigo recibe*). She resumed helping her mother but hid it from her husband because they were not getting along.

I must pause in the narrative to observe that there is an implicit classification of explanations for affliction in play here. Mariela and her mother attributed the legal trouble they faced on their move to Boston to bad luck (*mala suerte*). Some of Mariela's troubles were identified as punishment (*castigo*) for her behavior, including failing to keep her promise to send money to her mother and being in an incestuous relationship with her first cousin. It is unclear whether such punishments are considered spontaneous moral consequence or sent directly from God; perhaps there is no real difference between the two. However, punishment can be interpersonal and cause damage without being intentional in the sense of being brought about by a magical act, and in this sense Mariela reported that this was something that cannot be avoided within families. She indicated that her mother surprised her when she reported having been punished by Mariela, probably in the sense of "you have made me suffer." Mariela said that she had experienced punishment in the form of waking in the morning with bruises on her body, perhaps in her case a stigmatic corporal reminiscence of bruises recalled from childhood inflicted by her aunt. Affliction can also be attributed to an explicit work of magic with the intent to cause harm (*trabajo para hacer daño*). This can be done through physical means such as magically poisoning the victim's food or drink but apparently also by invoking spirits to afflict someone, as suggested in Mariela's comment that in one instance she was unable to see any overt sign of being cursed. Finally, it appears that evil spirits can cause harm of their own accord, as in the following circumstance under which Mariela's mother gave up her mediumistic practice.

This is an episode in which a serious affliction comes into play, as described by Mariela (translated from the Spanish):

I felt hopeless and crazy, and this is what caused me to neglect the house, my daughter, and him. He asked me what was happening and I couldn't tell him anything. I was like what they call the "living dead," at times I went around as if I was sleepwalking, I didn't feel desire to have relations with him when he wanted to. I felt obligated, but felt so bad, so I always said I'm tired, I feel sick, and I rejected him. Then I got fat, gained a lot of weight, and he said I'm going to look for another woman if you continue like this, and that's what happened. He got tired of begging me and began going out with his friends and started getting involved with this Puerto Rican girl. This is when I reacted and realized the damage I had done, but I was so sick from my *nervios* and I suffered a lot from him as well because the way he carried on with this woman was open, he didn't hide anything from me, he called her from the house and she called him, too. I took the call and passed him the phone. I knew I was to blame, but not for everything, because sometimes I didn't realize I was doing harm.

The result of all this was a decision, apparently taken in consultation with doctors, to separate. Their young daughter tried to reunite them, knowing that something was wrong, especially when she was taken out by her father and his girlfriend. She asked plaintively for her parents to give her a little brother and was hospitalized on more than one occasion with unexplained fever and later an eye infection that posed the danger of spreading to her brain.

To understand the full significance of this episode, however, one must observe how Mariela frames it in the interview in both spiritual and clinical terms. Immediately before this description she discusses not being able to talk to her husband about magical harm and his mistrust of her mother as a spiritual practitioner. This suggests that her withdrawal from her husband, for which she clearly blames herself, is also the result of magically perpetrated harm. Immediately after the description she recounts how her husband took the initiative to come to the mental health clinic and later asked her to come as well. She agreed, feeling that she had some kind of complex (*un complejo*). Mariela described the benefit of treatment as transitioning from not being able to express her feelings for fear of harming the other person and thereby becoming hopeless to an ability to say, "You may not like this, but it's how I feel and I have to say it"—a change she said helped a great deal. She feels that she had made an error in keeping her suffering to herself, and Javier agrees that things could have been different if they had communicated on an intimate level.

Mariela said that during this period Javier completely ignored her and her daughter out of revenge. As hard as she worked to support her daughter and as much as she suffered with *nervios,* he got pleasure from their suffering because he is the kind of person who when hurt does not care about the other's suffering, his pride outweighing the suffering he saw in his wife and daughter. According to her, Javier was behaving like a typical Salvadoran in that when someone does another harm, one doubles the harm in return. However, as he later told her, during this period when there was virtually no communication between them he was spending sleepless nights and suffering from *nervios* as well, such that his doctors wanted to hospitalize him for two weeks of inpatient psychiatric treatment, which he refused. His drinking increased, and he would dramatically put on a "show *de nervios*" that he would not remember afterwards, insisting he wanted to stay together while her injured pride insistently said no. At one point he was in fact hospitalized for a drug overdose (*"como que se enveneno con tanta pastilla"*). During the worst of these troubles Javier would sometimes sleep in the car or the street, later describing the experience as if he had died momentarily (*"como que una persona como que se meure por un instante"*), with his mind completely blank. Mariela described Javier as someone who had been quite dependent on his parents and who could not easily manage and resolve problems on his own. As the eldest of seven sons, Mariela related that he was treated as the best to the point of being spoiled, and his parents having everything done for him, it made it even more difficult for him than for the typical Salvadoran man who comes to this country hardly able to take care of himself. He was familiar with mental health care even in El Salvador, where he had been in treatment and on medication. Mariela told the kind of story about Javier that is repeated and becomes part of one's identity in a circle of intimates, about a time in El Salvador when he had three or four girlfriends (*novias*) at once, going to work in the morning directly from one or another of them and not sleeping for six months, a long-term event that she regarded as debilitating and that from a clinical perspective has the flavor of a significant period of manic behavior.

Although much of their conflict could be attributed to Javier's drinking and Mariela's own withdrawal, an element of spiritual disagreement existed over her mother's role as a medium. While Mariela stated several times that she believed strongly in her mother, Javier disagreed, saying that one had to study in order to be a medium and observing that in Los Angeles she had often had the spiritual help of a friend or visited another medium, even having to pay this person. Javier evidently interpreted these instances not in terms of assistance or apprenticeship but in terms of Mariela's mother not having sufficient knowledge of her own. Indeed, when Mariela experienced the effects of magical harm she suffered them alone without telling her husband. Two factors are relevant here: the antipathy that existed between Javier and Mariela's mother and the circumstances under which spiritual influences are acknowledged as real and efficacious. Mariela held that people who had strong minds or who did not believe were those who could best avoid harm; she did not think Javier was particularly strong-willed, nor did he appear generally skeptical except with regard to her mother. In general, the rule of thumb with respect to efficacy of and vulnerability to magical harm was that regardless of attitudes of skepticism or acceptance, there was an inherent reality that must be contended with. We very often heard people say, *"No hay que creer ni dejar de creer"*—it doesn't matter whether one believes or refrains from belief.

While for Mariela and Javier this situation could be summarized as a case of postpartum depression that led to severe relationship problems between two psychologically fragile people and while they were both actively engaged in psychotherapy, the existential significance and interpersonal meaning of their circumstance goes well beyond clinical understanding. The emotional background was one of anxiety and foreboding created by their respective mothers' disapproval and warning of punishment for their incestuous relationship. The mothers made it clear that because of this incestuous relationship they would always have problems, would never be able to get ahead or go forward (*salir adelante*), would always be without money, and so forth. This must only have been exacerbated by the birth of a child into the incestuous relationship. Indeed, when Mariela became ill her mother indicated that the warning had been warranted and that the punishment had ensued. It remains unclear whether from Mariela's standpoint this punishment was divinely or humanly inflicted, since with reference to not having sent money to her mother she says they gave her the punishment (*"ellas me dieron un castigo"*) Moreover, Mariela's mother and aunt, both of whom were recognized to have mediumistic capabilities, had a motive for trying to disrupt the spousal relationship of first cousins. Mariela's mother pointed out that when Javier was unemployed before they moved to Boston, his mother blamed Mariela because she was supporting him and he was no longer helping his own mother. She also said that Mariela only started with him in order to have a man. Mariela said that women were more easily blamed because Latinos think that a man never says no (*"el hombre nunca dice que no"*) and that men can in general do what they like with women. For his part, Javier thought Mariela's mother was responsible and that she would not rest until they were separated. Indeed, her mother had admitted at one time being the kind of person who could commit magical harm and would respond to a request to do so but attested to having "woken up" and changed. Mariela was willing to entertain the possibility that her mother was to blame, though she did not think and did not want this to be the case.

Ultimately the question of whether her mother could have intentionally done Mariela harm was superseded by a development that in effect allowed what appears to be the best compromise solution: her mother did it but unintentionally. Specifically, the damage was due to her mother's involvement with spirits that she thought were good but were not, damage that extended to Mariela because she so thoroughly believed in and was influenced by her mother's practices. She said explicitly that although her mother had not done bad things, this involvement had caused great damage to her self (*"me hizo mucho daño a mi persona"*). The man who discerned this problem was not identified as a priest, but Mariela explicitly refers to the action he took upon her mother as an exorcism. On learning of this Mariela became fearful, her *nervios* began acting up, and she began having a lot of dreams, as if the vengeful evil spirits were attacking her after their exposure by the exorcist. This turn of events gave her an important insight into the origin of the relationship problems with her mother and with what she described as a change in her own character whereby she became unhappy, fearful, anxious in gatherings of people, and neglectful of herself, leading to the severe problems with her husband. It deeply shook Mariela's confidence in her mother's spiritual abilities.

The situation between the spouses was ameliorated under the influence of mental health treatment and spiritual intervention quite independent of Mariela's mother and aunt. The latter took the form of a ritual cleansing (*limpieza*) by a spiritist from the Dominican Republic. It is noteworthy that Mariela framed her narrative of relationship with this healer by comparison to another healer whose help she rejected because she did not like the way she worked and because the woman did not convince her of her authenticity and efficacy. Along with a friend she visited this other healer, described as Spanish (*española*), to ask for divination as to whether Javier's Puerto Rican girlfriend had cast a spell on them (*"había hecho un trabajo"*). It was said of this Spanish woman that in the course of performing her work she produced a spider from her belt, a practice the Dominican healer later said she would have nothing to do with. The price asked by the Spanish woman was $2,000, and when Mariela countered that of course she did not have that much, the price was reduced to $100. The healer also required that the evil she removed be buried along with pledges in the form of $600 worth of gold jewelry. Mariela observed that the consequence would be virtual slavery and wondered whether the medium might later unearth the buried pledge. At this point the woman who was with Mariela said, "Look, let's go to my friend's mother," which they did immediately. This woman divined for her with cards (*lea las cartas*) for only $10 and convinced Mariela of her legitimacy by telling her things about herself that were true, such as that her husband had a son with another woman in El Salvador.

This sixty-two-year-old medium had her own chapel in Santo Domingo and a center in New York and in visiting her daughter in Boston every six months was beginning to develop a reputation and a following in Boston. Mariela described her as typically wearing brightly colored kerchiefs folded and tied to her belt, as well as a set of rosary beads (*camándula*). The woman instructed her to pray the rosary daily with a glass of water, a candle on a small plate, an old frying pan or tin can in which to burn incense, and some orange scented water to sprinkle through the house. Every year she held a festival for her patron saints at her Santo Domingo chapel, during which her followers gathered and at which many people sponsored Catholic masses. Mariela took pride in being one of her first clients in Boston, having met her because the medium's daughter was a friend of her friend. After a cleansing ceremony (*limpieza*) in her home Mariela began to follow (*acompañar*) this medium, who put her in direct contact with spirits. The medium's primary spirit also told Mariela that her own mediumistic talents and precognizant dreams could be developed.

Mariela and Javier had determined that something was wrong that required spiritual help both because of their relationship problems and because certain unusual disruptions were occurring in their material affairs. They observed changes in their mood (*humor*) so that when she was in a good mood and acting affectionate toward Javier, he was in a bad mood and didn't want to talk about it, and vice versa ("*si no era él era yo*"). They also observed that when their affairs seemed to be going well money problems suddenly occurred, that there was never enough money, and that when money came in to the household it immediately went out to some new necessity and things became worse on a daily basis. She would feel unhappy and fearful in the house and sometimes experience the sensation that someone or some presence was there behind her. In particular, problems kept occurring with the car they had recently purchased such that several times they had to leave for work without it, and when they took it to the mechanic there was nothing out of order. Comparing notes on all the things they observed as abnormal, they concluded that someone had perpetrated a work of maleficent magic. Mariela said she did not want to go for help, but Javier convinced her to do so because he believed it was her mother who was at fault.

When the spiritist arrived she made preparations at the kitchen table, where there was sufficient space for her paraphernalia. This included incense, candles, a glass of water, and, spread out in the middle of the table, her rosary. Once the preparations were complete she began to pray (*orar, rezar*) and entered a moment of deep concentration in which the spirit entered her. Mariela noted that a person who pays close attention can observe that a spirit is present instead of the person because the eyes become a little brighter and the voice and style of speaking change. She said, "The spirit was a woman who seemed happy, and was speaking and taking care of the incense herself, having us take turns sprinkling water, and I began feeling something saying, 'Don't be upset by what you are going to feel.'" Indeed, Mariela described feeling as if she was walking on clouds (*"en las nubes"*), while Javier only felt an upset stomach.

During the household cleansing the Dominican through her accompanying spirit expressed what Mariela felt was an accurate (*cierto*) understanding of the situation—that although the couple was together things were unclear between them and that a magical work (*trabajo*) had been perpetrated in order to separate them. The spirit revealed (*"me salió"*) that it was Javier's Puerto Rican mistress who had perpetrated the magical harm by giving him a cold drink when he was lying in bed. When Javier protested that the Puerto Rican woman was now married and expecting a baby, the spirit explained that this had occurred when the two of them were still together so that she could dominate him and make him do what she wanted, so that he would be like a baby and she would be the man. The spirit pressed Javier to remember the cold drink, and he recalled that she had given him some food that had done him harm. The spirit continued to say that when a person cannot remember, that is how it is done and how the harm is transmitted, and again he said he did not remember. The spirit finally revealed that it was a beer that the Puerto Rican woman had given him and that whether it was ultimately the food or the beer that had upset his stomach, it was most certainly something she had given him. Evidence of the ongoing effect was that at times Javier's stomach became bloated, that certain foods caused him harm, and that he suffered with stomach gas. The healer addressed these internal effects by performing a cure on Javier, taking up a cross and some small candles that she extinguished with his saliva by passing them across his tongue, thus extracting the evil from him, and following this by giving him some specially prepared tea to drink. This outcome was likely to his chagrin, since it would have been to his advantage if Mariela's mother was to blame and his disadvantage to acknowledge an enduring effect of his unfaithfulness. On the other hand, confirmation of her mother's innocence and the guilt of the other woman likely consolidated Mariela's belief and loyalty to the spiritist.

Later the healer prepared items that she would leave with the family, such as a bottle with water to sprinkle through the household, a tiny bottle containing liquid that smelled like cleaning fluid to sprinkle only at the door, and a plastic bottle (as for juice or shampoo) for each member of the household. This larger bottle contained a pleasant-smelling green liquid for washing the entire body in a bath three consecutive nights until it was used up. They then conducted a blessing of the entire house, first with a penny placed under a chair and on which the healer placed a small stick of white wood, explaining that the penny raised the stick up. Mariela, Javier, and the healer took turns passing the penny and stick throughout the house, first holding it low, then high, then low again as they went from room to room. They did the same with the two specially prepared waters and the incense. The spiritist then grabbed Javier's hands and pressed them very tightly in order to cure his stomach. Prayers for all the evil to leave the house was followed by the healer giving Mariela a little seed called *mate* to be used as protection. Finally, they made the sign of the cross (*santiguar*) and blessed or baptized (*bautizado*) the car, since the healer recalled even at the first card reading having seen something in the car, and Javier acknowledged not having been able to drive without being distracted by the problems they were having. She instructed them not to let anyone else use the car without first saying prayers. The entire cleansing lasted about an hour, a duration that Mariela said indicated the seriousness of the problems.

In the aftermath the healer prepared, in case anyone else tried to harm Mariela, a protective amulet to keep in her wallet made from braided cloth in a rainbow of colors, including the *mate*. Mariela observed that Salvadorans refer to this seed as "deer's eye" (*ojo de venado*). In biological nomenclature, the deer's eye seed is recognized as *Mucuna pruriens* and is known to contain the psychoactive substance L-Dopa. In this instance there was no indication that a preparation of the plant was administered internally but only used as the centerpiece of the protective amulet. Javier also received one that was placed in the car; another was placed in the house; and each of Mariela's brothers-in-law had one to keep in his pocket. She was instructed that whenever she sensed someone wanted to do her harm she should grasp her wallet and utter a specific prayer to repel the malevolent person; Mariela had forgotten the exact words but planned to ask the healer at their next encounter.

The spirit told Mariela that the maleficent magic had not been successful in separating her and Javier because she was under the protection of the spirits of her father and grandmother and that now that the cleansing had been performed things would begin to change and improve in the coming month. Mariela attested that things were already better and reported that the spiritist also told her that things were already better, acknowledging that both the healer and the client had to believe in order for the work to be effective. For his part, although Javier did all the things required of him, Mariela reported that he didn't want to believe. He stubbornly and contrarily said instead, "The spirit believes in me." It is likely that in this instance skepticism was combined with an element of truculence over having been proven wrong about the identity of the perpetrator. In discussing this "I told you so" scenario, the spirit later reassured Mariela that given his pridefulness, the statement "The spirit believes in me" was in fact an acceptance of the spirit's existence and by extension an acceptance of what the spirit had said. In fact, Mariela had been risking nothing in this respect, for even in the preliminary card reading the spirit had identified the perpetrator as one of Javier's two previous lovers, and given the timing she was convinced that it was the aforementioned Puerto Rican woman. More important, she felt satisfied because she had made Javier believe in that everything the spiritist had revealed was true. In this respect and because in direct contrast to the Spanish healer who wanted to make money, Mariela "liked the way she works."

Mariela's belief, if not Javier's, appeared to be strengthened further by a frightful event that occurred while they were in bed one night: Mariela's mind went blank, something began turning in her head, and she felt someone touch her stomach. Although she knew more or less that it had to do with spirits, she was confused as to whether she was awake or asleep while they were talking in her head. She asked her husband to turn on the light, and she went to the bathroom to wash her womb (*limpiar la matriz*) with herbal waters given her by the healer. Returning to bed, she felt the cold of death, because as the healer said the spirit enters and one feels the touch as if it is removing something, so that the next morning one awakens feeling a bit ill and as if one had been pricked or given an injection in a vein. That morning, she reported, she saw a puncture mark and then began feeling pricks all over her body, but she remained calm because she thought perhaps the spirits were administering a tranquilizer and also felt something leaving as one feels air blowing from a passing car. The healer later affirmed that the spirits often perform a cure by working on one directly during the night while one is in bed to remove the evil of the work that has been perpetrated; she instructed Mariela not to be afraid of them. Javier, who during the incident accused his wife of being theatrical (*"creía que lo mío era teatro"*), could not sleep at all that night and was quite afraid. Mariela was of the opinion that he was feeling what the spirits were doing and that after this event he believed in the experience.

Things eventually settled down for Mariela and Javier. Within a year she was pregnant, reporting no problem with *nervios*, a good appetite, and sleeping well. Throughout their troubles they had managed for the most part to maintain their employment and adapt to the contingencies of everyday life. Even prior to the momentous healing event in their household they had been forced to leave their Cambridge apartment after allowing a brother-in-law who had separated from his wife to stay in an empty apartment in their building. They moved across the river to Chelsea, where the couple, their little daughter, and the husband's two unmarried brothers lived. A lot of Salvadorans were settling there because it was cheaper and one could share the apartments without being asked how many people would be living there, as was done in Cambridge. She regretted that her own half brothers refused to acknowledge her as their sister but felt compensated by the fact that she got along so well with her brothers-in-law. The point is that life goes on in a variety of dimensions, and the account I have given of Mariela's spiritual experiences does not preclude alternative narratives that might focus on her experience as an outpatient in the Latino Mental Health Clinic, her economic circumstances and work life, being part of a migrant and refugee community, and the reality of ongoing political violence in *la situación* back in El Salvador.

Indeed, Mariela had come to the United States in 1976, which she described as the year when people first began to see things like students starting to have demonstrations and beginning to disappear, but she saw nothing of the war herself. As others began to come to Boston telling stories and as she continued communication with people back home in El Salvador, the war became a palpable part of her lifeworld, especially because deportation was a constant possibility for those who had fled. According to some, the people who fled are those who are inherently nervous and fearful and who drink; they were afraid in El Salvador, and they remain afraid (for example, of being robbed) in the United States, while people who remain in El Salvador are not afraid. According to others, those who come have experienced people being killed and thus with good reason to tend to be nervous, fearful, and prone to drink. Mariela was willing to arrange an interview with a brother-in-law (*cuñado*) who was a recent arrival, a student involved in election campaign activities who had fled the week before the vote and was very familiar with the situation. Javier's two younger brothers who lived with them were among the class of youths who were subject to being coercively recruited to one side or the other in the conflict, and their presence was also a constant reminder of the war.

## CERES

Ceres was fifty-one years old when I met her, and she had already been in Boston for eighteen years. Though she had worked as an elementary school teacher in El Salvador, her primary occupation during the course of our interviews was in a factory making suitcases. She had come to Boston in 1971, six years before Mariela, when El Salvador was under a military government but prior to the civil war when there were only a handful of Salvadorans in the city. Her two sons and daughter (the boys eventually came to the United States as adults) remained behind as she followed a man who had immigrated, leaving behind his own wife. Arriving alone by plane, she anxiously sought out an older taxi driver who might by virtue of age be trustworthy. She vividly described her fear as they drove through the tunnel into the city and her gratitude when on handing over the fare of "four-fifty" the driver returned all of the $450 except a $5 bill.

Ceres was a high-strung, somewhat overweight, and good-humored woman who described her childhood as unstable, bouncing around like a ball to different living situations without emotional protection. She described herself as proud (*soberbia*), contradictory (un caracter bien contradictorio) and not an easy person (*"no soy una persona fácil"*), made that way by a hard life (*"como mucho rigor"*). Like Mariela, she was raised by an aunt who was harsh but who taught her the value of hard work and made certain she had training in a sewing school that served her well after her migration. Also like Mariela, she maintained relations with her mother, though on an emotionally closer and less fraught basis, with conversations in which she asked for advice, visits between El Salvador and the United States, and presents given by Ceres even though her mother never asked for anything. She reported that all her life she had been anxious whenever she went out in public, to the point of nausea and vomiting. Being sick to her stomach and having diarrhea, dizziness, headaches, and insomnia often bothered her. A critical event was her pregnancy after being beaten and raped by her boyfriend at the age of eighteen; this was his revenge against Ceres for having discovered him making love to her best friend at a picnic. She said she was never the same afterwards and moreover was no longer allowed to eat at her family table because her pregnancy was a disgrace.

Ceres had been referred to the clinic in 1985 by her general practitioner for multiple somatic complaints, including vomiting when nervous and irritability. She first received the diagnosis of somatization and later adjustment disorder with mixed emotional features. After learning with relief that a feared breast tumor was benign and having no means to pay for care, she stopped going to psychotherapy. She was referred again for similar symptoms in 1987 and was in treatment when I met her in 1989. She complained of arthritic pain in her leg that made it difficult to work and the feeling of pins and needles along with her headache (*"hormigueo en la cabeza"*), as if little animals were moving under her skin. She reported relief at a doctor's conclusion that there was nothing wrong with her brain but that the problem was in the bones of her skull. Having been in therapy for several years she attested to considerable improvement over time through monthly individual therapy. She was reticent regarding group therapy, however, noting that because of the group she and another woman from her hometown who had never been friends or acquaintances know more about one another than was comfortable and that their respective relatives both in the United States and El Salvador seemed to be in the know as well.

She and her husband had visited El Salvador annually, taking the opportunity to bathe in a river for ritual cleansing. Her husband, who worked in a hospital, observed that basic supplies had become increasingly scarce in Salvadoran health care facilities. At the time of our interviews in 1989 Ceres expressed reluctance to return because of the danger; when one goes out to buy food one doesn't know if one will return or when the shooting will start, she said. She also said that neither side wanted peace because if they did so many people would not be dying; neither did they want equality or jobs because if they did they would not be destroying factories and communications systems. In her view both sides were out for their own interests. Ceres and her husband were somewhat cynical about the demands for equality in their country: one needed adequate preparation before one could claim equality in employment, yet the educational infrastructure in her country was being destroyed, and besides inequality existed in all countries anyway, including the United States. The latter was evident in the racism expressed on an everyday basis against Latino people such as themselves, even in things overheard on the bus when people assumed one couldn't understand English or when people refused to sit next to someone who had a Latino-looking face. Equality is illusory in any case since some people have more advantages, or are better prepared by education, or have inherited resources. A decade earlier she and her husband had been arrested twice. Each time they had to pay fines and were told to leave the country voluntarily within three months, but they had managed to stay until an amnesty program was instituted, and at the time of our interviews she was enrolled in civics classes to consolidate her legal status.

Ceres's three adult children all had different fathers. Her current husband was a quiet, somewhat asocial (*apartado*) man who did not like to go out as much as she did, character traits Ceres attributed to a harsh childhood. He was from the same Salvadoran town as Ceres's mother, but they had met in Boston after she separated from the man she had followed from El Salvador. Six years earlier he smoke and drank excessively, requiring surgery for blood vessels in his nose, and gambled as much as $100 a week on the lottery. Since then he had for the most part reformed, retaining only the habit of spending $10 on the lottery. The only major and enduring tension between them appeared to be with respect to the monthly remittances they sent to their respective families from their respective wages, since they both had separate sets of children from prior relationships. Ceres in particular felt obligated to help her mother, aunt, and sister and brother-in-law and their children despite her husband's objections that both her sister and brother-in-law had good, stable employment and that she should contribute more to their own rent and food expenses instead. Meanwhile, his ex-wife and daughter were a source of tension in that Ceres was convinced they were intent on either separating her and her husband or killing one of them by witchcraft. A Guatemalan friend of her husband was suspected of doing harm as well, causing headaches and stomachaches. Another source of interpersonal tension was her daughter-in-law, who apparently was cheating on her son, leading to Ceres's tacit approval of her son beating her.

Living conditions were also stressful. Ceres and her husband rented two unconnected rooms in one side of a building, one serving as their bedroom and the other as their living room. The building was occupied by six other unrelated people who shared a single kitchen and bathroom. Ceres complained that no one else cleaned the kitchen and that the food remains of other tenants frequently clogged the toilet and that they often found drug paraphernalia left behind. They had been robbed twice on successive days, and the landlord refused to make repairs in general and was particularly lax with respect to a dangerous stairway. When the building burned they finally moved. Work in the suitcase factory was also stressful, in part because the owners were inconsiderate, indeed barely civil to their employees, and in part because her back and arthritis made it difficult for her to work at all. Finally, her greatest sadness (*tristeza*) came from feeling underappreciated and unloved by her two egoistic sons, who rarely visited except to ask for something. It was her own force of will (*fuerza de voluntad*), along with God's help, that allowed her to carry on (*salir adelante*).

As we begin to outline the shape of the spiritual milieu that Ceres inhabited, one of the first elements that emerges as salient for her is the distinction between white and black magic. White magic is for protection and black magic to do harm to another. The latter would include the *prueba del puro,* in which pins are inserted in the form of a cross into a cigar in order to attract someone of the opposite sex or to make a wandering lover return. However, along with her husband she told me about the existence of red magic as well. They responded negatively to my query about whether red magic was somehow "between" white and black, saying that it was more powerful than either and could be used to help or to harm. It appeared to have special efficacy in matters of sex, either to attract someone or to retrieve someone who had strayed. Its critical feature, however, is that its practices make use of blood. Ceres and her husband did not elaborate in detail but referred me to the Dominican healer—the same woman Mariela saw and whom Ceres also frequented—because she was known to have studied such things. Ceres insisted on taking me to see her on several occasions. From what I have been able to determine red magic is distinct from animal sacrifice as practiced in rituals to venerate deities in African traditions in that it uses human rather than animal blood. Whether its effects are positive or negative appears to be related to whether the practitioner uses his or her own blood or the blood of another. Ceres and her husband observed that there was significantly more magical activity in the United States than in their home country because so many groups from other countries were mixed together, particularly those from African or Yoruba traditions that conducted rituals by night under the moon, including what they had heard were rites in which they killed and ate people as if they were chickens.

Herbal remedies found in the various *botánicas* that had been established to serve the growing Latino community in the Boston area, and which we visited together on Saturday afternoons, were of considerable importance to Ceres. She and her husband showed me a book about herbalism and Aquarian healing, and she had spent considerable time studying such remedies. These included simple herbal teas such as cinnamon, apple, chamomile, mint, and orange blossom used for calming the nerves or soothing inflammation. Among anti-inflammatories she mentioned the dinasa seeds (*semillas de dinasa/hialuro-dinasa* is an enzyme with anti-inflammatory properties), chan or chia seeds (*Salvia hispanica Lamiaceae*), and a cold tea of rue (*Ruta graveolens*) used as a remedy for earache. One can talk every day with one's plants, and even though one might not know all their specific properties they can help to maintain a clean (*limpia*) household environment. Plants in general can absorb or take on bad influences and wither on that account, and likewise a ring of silver ritually prepared to absorb such influences will become black with tarnish.

Ceres was aware of the spiritual need for a ritual to accompany administration of herbal treatment, and of the practice of praying and drawing a circle in the earth around a medicinal plant prior to cutting or uprooting it. She also kept a small aloe vera plant above the door to her apartment, not for ingestion or topical use, but to absorb potentially maleficent influences from people who entered. Such influences belong in the familiar genre of the evil eye (*mal de ojo*), conceived not only as like a laser from the eye in the form of a hard look or stare (*vista*) but also as an ambient force of personality emanating from the person, regardless of their own intention, in the form of an overall mood or humor. Ceres mentioned that when a child vomits or has diarrhea and cannot be cured the reason is exposure to a person charged with a lot of influences (*"cargadas de muchas influencias"*) and with a very powerful type of blood (*"muy fuerte su tipo de sangre"*). Such a person, in addition to harming a child, can cause an animal such as a snake or a scorpion to fall immediately somnolescent and motionless. The person may be ignorant of their own power and without meaning to or without anyone noticing can leave the influence in one's house, where subsequently things start to fall apart and problems arise in the family. She was acutely aware of this from an earlier experience in which the wife of the man she followed to the United States became ill. Ceres became deeply worried that she was the cause of this illness and prayed intensively that nothing bad would happen to the woman.

Notably, she expressed no interest or desire to cultivate any abilities of her own. She acknowledged that when she dreamed her dreams came true and that this frightened her, apparently because she was concerned that her dreams might not only predict but also cause events to happen. Foremost in her mind was the fire in her house, about which she had dreamed but had told no one. Dreams are also a medium of communication, to which she attested in noting that on Mother's Day that year she and her mother had dreamed about one another. She also acknowledged occasionally having the unconscious sense (*inconsientemente siente*) that someone was calling her, as when she might be out walking. She recalled that as a child of eight to ten years old she saw blurred shapes (*bultos*) of people who said that they were dead but that others had also seen these dead people (*muertos*). Later, as a young woman, she typically ate in the house of a woman who died in childbirth and was unable to stay at this house for the prayers (*oraciones*) in front of the coffin because she had to tend to her sister's young child. However, that night in bed she felt the touch of the dead woman's hand lightly on her arm that remained uncovered by her blanket, and she quickly got up and began to pray.

Ceres distinguished between emotions such as sadness (*tristeza*), suffering (*pena*), anger (*cólera*), happiness (*felicidad, alegría*), or fright (*susto*) that were situational and could pass, and envy (*envidia*) understood as an illness (*enfermedad*) that could result in killing someone (hasta matar a uno) through witchcraft. Hence the value of the aloe at her doorway is to absorb negative influences before they enter the house. Not only is aloe known as a topical treatment for burns, but as a succulent plant it has the capacity to retain fluid and thus implicitly to absorb ambient humor. Ceres was explicit that this is not spiritual, although according to books she has read the reason some people and not others have such force may be due to having been reincarnated as the powerful spirit of someone previously deceased. The influence itself and the aloe's effect can thus be understood as absorption of humor both as harsh mood in the form of a look (*vista*) and as material bodily emanation in the form of sweat (*sudor*) or odor (*olor*) that can linger in the environment. In the same vein, a glass of clean water mixed with alcohol and camphor kept in one's kitchen can absorb and neutralize such harmful influences.

Ceres expressed her understanding of the difference between *santería* and *espiritismo* in recounting two consecutive events she attended. She described the *santería* temple as a room in which everyone was praying and at whose front there were numerous figures of saints, including Anthony and Martin, as well as Jesus and the Virgin. There were lit candles, a fountain of water in front of the altar, and another fountain on a table where prayers were being read. She observed that the people were disposed (*despojarse*) of bad influences by invoking their guardian angel using blessed water from the earthen bowl or gourd, taken in the palm of their hand and sprinkled from head to foot ("*de arriba para abajo*") and then thrown into the gourd as if ridding oneself of something ("*como que se quitara algo*"). One woman was seized by a spirit and kept stepping backward as she continued to dispel the influence, until she came to the table where people were reading prayers. Without anyone raising a finger, the water bowl shattered into a thousand pieces, the water splashed everywhere, and the glass fragments scattered over the floor.

By contrast, when Ceres consulted a spiritist in El Salvador, the healer told her she was ill but that a medical operation would make it worse and that she would operate spiritually instead. Ceres noted that spiritists use medicines from the pharmacy and that she was instructed to purchase several. Then she was told that the operation would take place during the night and that she should place at the head of her bed a glass of water and a frying pan with a scoop of salt and a lemon cut in half. In the middle of the night Ceres felt afraid and as if she was going to fall into a well. She heard the voice of the healer, who was in another city, telling her not to be afraid and fell soundly asleep. In the morning she did not feel much of anything, except for the feeling of having been given an injection in the arm.

Ceres testified to the existence of *brujería* and magic from a childhood episode in El Salvador, which led to her grandmother's death. It was the kind of episode, she said, that one never forgets, though it happens when one is very young. When she was four her father entered into a common-law marriage with a woman who had attracted him by means of *brujería*. Their servant woman at the time told Ceres's grandmother that she should warn her son not to drink water from the bedside pitcher. When her grandmother subsequently saw the woman's dirty sanitary napkins mixed in with her son's clean clothes in the dresser, she was taken with such an extreme attack of rage (*cólera*) that it eventually caused her to die. She became gravely ill and wanted to leave that house to live with a daughter in San Salvador, who meanwhile had come and was caring for her mother day and night. One night during a thunderstorm with lots of lightning those caring for her fell asleep, and when they opened their eyes she was not in bed. They found her among a collection of African medicinal plants that was in the house, her arms in the form of a cross, and told her to be calm (*tranquila*), promising to take her to San Salvador when she recovered. They did so, but during that period the house was constantly disturbed at certain hours of the night by the creaking of doors, which, when opened, let in an odor of cypress. This was evidence of the suffering of her spirit, and not only caused considerable fear among the caretakers but also left an indelible impression on Ceres. As if this was not evidence enough, the ungrateful woman did not allow her husband to die in peace, not behaving at all like a grieving widow. As he was on his deathbed she was chatting with people without emotion, in the afternoon following his funeral she went off to relax at a nearby lake rather than mourn, and soon afterward she sold everything in their house as well as the house itself. Moreover, when the new owners planted a garden all the plants either failed to grow or withered. Someone who lived nearby advised them to dig up the earth and replace it, and during the excavation they found numerous dolls (*muñecas*) buried and pierced with thorns all around (*"con espinas clavadas por todos los lados"*). They burned the dolls and put in new soil, after which the garden was beautiful. As Ceres said, "This is why I say, yes, witchcraft exists" (*Por eso es que te digo yo que si, la brujería existe*).

Ceres says she has never wanted to harm another by magic, only to defend herself, though she admitted having "impulses" (*impulsos*) to do so or to pay someone else to do so. Though she has been harmed herself in many ways, she recounted feeling such an impulse especially because of what was done to her daughter, who lives in El Salvador and is married to a lawyer. The young man was quite appropriate in seeking permission from Ceres to ask her daughter to leave her life as a student to become his wife. However, he did not tell either Ceres or her daughter that there was another woman already involved. The young man was one of two children adopted by a couple who were unable to have any children of their own; he was very close with his adoptive sister, and the woman with whom he had been involved was her closest friend. They did not want the marriage to take place and, according to the healer (*curandera*) who helped her, placed something at a location she usually passed that had the effect of transforming her skin such that it was as if she was flayed (*despellejaba*) and looked like a monster. Notably, Ceres observed that this occurred during the worst period of guerrilla warfare when dead bodies were appearing, but she did not elaborate as to whether this aspect of the situation directly affected or exacerbated her daughter's affliction or whether its relevance was primarily in making it dangerous to travel there since the town was best accessed by light aircraft. A doctor claimed never to have seen anything like it and was unable to cure her, and only the local healer was able to help. That the woman had performed a work of malevolent magic was confirmed when the healer asked to see her daughter's wedding dress, shook it, and numerous pins fell out onto the floor—pins that apparently had severely irritated the bride's skin—and when the *curandera* held a cup in front of the husband he saw the image of the woman reflected on the surface of the liquid inside. Moreover, the local healer in Boston confirmed the act of magic by reading tea leaves. The remedy was for the afflicted young woman to pray at certain hours of the day in the cathedral with her arms extended in the form of a cross, followed by the couple bathing in a river where the current was so swift that it almost carried the husband away. The result was positive; the daughter reported that her husband now cared for her very much and that she had confidence that he would have nothing further to do with the offending woman as long as they remained married, because otherwise she would kill him. Ceres laughed as she recounted the last remark.

Ceres attended Catholic Mass every Sunday and said that when she missed Mass she would typically have a very bad week. She also kept images of saints in her house, as well as of the Divina Providencia. She explained that for Salvadorans Divine Providence was characterized differently than for Puerto Ricans, another prominent Latino group in the Boston area. Specifically, for the latter it is Mary holding the dead Jesus in her arms after he was taken down from the cross, in the figure of the Pietà. For Salvadorans it is the Holy Trinity, Father, Son, and

Holy Spirit. Ceres kept holy pictures, a calendar, and statues in both her living room and her bedroom to protect her home from misfortune. She distinguished the kind of protection offered by Divine Providence and the saints from protection against witchcraft and magic perpetrated by others. Indeed, although she indicated that the fire in the house where they lived was caused by witchcraft from her husband's ex-wife, she attributed the fact that their rooms had suffered only smoke damage to the protection of Divine Providence. The saints in particular intercede for one before God, and she requests their help in asking God to help her with her problems or with what she desires or wants to do, because no one knows what is going to happen.

In response to one of my questions, Ceres indicated her understanding that body and mind are linked (*juntos*) but that they can be separated (*pueden separarse*). For example, one's mind can fall suddenly into a void (*caer de repente en un vacio*) in the case of illness or madness (*locura*) while one's body remained normal. At the same time, when one has a problem or preoccupation it can cause one to lose or to gain weight, and thus one's body is changed by the effect of the nervous system. She understood her own troubles as involving *nervios,* because it is evident that they were creating problems (*los nervios molestan*) when one is unable to resolve one's situation (*su situación*), whether it has to do with emotions, finances, or work. More than two years later, Ceres wrote to tell me that things had improved for her, that she had traveled three times to El Salvador in the previous year, and that she and her husband were in pretty good health (*"bastante bien de salud"*). In fact, on the last trip she had undergone a cure and had an incredible experience (*"tuve una experiencia increíble"*) that she hoped at some point to be able to tell me about.[4] Probably not coincidentally, this was in 1992—precisely when the civil war, *la situación,* officially ended.

## INHABITING THE RELIGIOUS MILIEU

Among the Salvadoran women with whom I worked, Mariela and Ceres had the richest texture of religion woven into their everyday lives. Even in such vivid instances, it cannot be said that religious practice and experience are either the cause or the effect of mental illness. There is no evidence that any of the experiences or ideas reported have the character of psychotic delusion, and the common clinical diagnoses among the women would not lead one to suppose that might be the case. Neither can we generalize that religious and magical means are either primarily forms of treatment or factors that exacerbate psychic distress. They are a feature of the lifeworld for people and in the social environment, and though it is beyond the scope of my study I would hypothesize that little difference could be found in this respect between clinic patients and those in the broader immigrant community.

Studies of pluralism among healing systems often make the point that people do not appear to be troubled by incommensurability or contradiction between alternative practices and systems (Csordas 2000; Singer and Baer 2011; Jütte 2013). The scene that emerges from my work, and particularly from conversations with Mariela and Ceres, suggests that this is neither because differences remain unperceived nor because perceived differences are dismissed as irrelevant. From the ground level of the everyday lifeworld, far more salient is the religious and spiritual lay of the land in the sense of what ideas and practices actually exist and where one stands pragmatically in relation to them. The idea that patients in a specialty mental health clinic might not without conflict or contradiction seek help from spiritual sources should be no more remarkable than the idea that trained physicians and mental health professionals might also be devout churchgoers. More significant is where the line is drawn between, for example, emotion and illness. It appeared more than once in my interviews that whereas sadness (*tristeza*), suffering (*pena*), anger (*coraje*), and happiness (*felicidad*) are emotions, envy (*envidia*) is an illness that can result in either intentional or unintentional damage or harm (*daño*). Likewise, just as the clinic is distinguished from the church, the *centro,* or the *botánica,* Catholicism is distinguished from the practices of *espiritismo, santería,* and *curanderismo* as well as from the negative forms of magic and *brujería* despite the possible presence of the saints across all the forms. Not only does the figure of Divine Providence dominate the sphere of Catholicism and not only does the mode of relation to the sacred here take the form primarily of devotion and petition rather than protection and power seeking, but it appears to exist at a deeper level of taken-for-grantedness. Whereas the saying *"No hay que creer ni dejar de creer"* is an assertion of the reality of spiritism and witchcraft in the face of skepticism, it is not uttered in relation to Divine Providence, the Virgin, or the saints since for the most part these represent a reality beyond question.

In general, with respect to the full range of religious practice and experience we can differentiate between degrees of salience in the lives of these women and degrees of skepticism about the existence of the phenomena or efficacy of the practices. Only four of the twenty women said nothing about religion and/or magic, while at the other end of the continuum four had at some time been active followers of an *espiritista* or *santero*. At the skeptical end of the continuum, only one woman explicitly rejected belief in spiritism, witchcraft, and herbalism, saying that they are superstitious and do not exist (*"esos son cosas supersticiosas y para mi no existen"*), though she had once accompanied her father to a *centro* for treatment of his prostate by means of waters, baths, grain, and tobacco, which did not cure him. Another, a professional whose job in El Salvador had included identifying mutilated cadavers and who was the most highly educated and professionally accomplished participant in the research, described herself as chronically angry at the world and questioning of God's justice and love as articulated by teachers, nuns, and parents.

Several women acknowledged the reality of witchcraft without granting it great salience, as in the case of a woman who said the practice of doing evil deeds existed (*existe el hechicería*) but that no one had ever done anything to her. One woman simply claimed no knowledge of *espiritistas* or other such practices except that orange leaf tea (*hoja de naranja*) is good for the nerves. Her attitude was that spiritual practitioners take people's money and don't cure, and she noted, "they say" that when one cures and it doesn't cost much money, then it's good. Another version is from a woman who made several generalized allusions to God and as for witchcraft said that such harm (*daño*) was never done to her but her mother experienced a big one when her boyfriend's other girlfriend put evil in her head (*malas in su cabeza*) using hair, which was cured by a male *espiritista* who apparently specialized in removing curses. This woman said explicitly, "I don't believe in this, but since this happened in my family, there it is."

Sometimes a significant episode was somewhat more consequential in establishing acceptance of spiritual phenomena, as with the woman who had been sent to Catholic boarding school when she was eight years old and described her own quest for meaning in which she tried every religion and went to healers but for whom the most compelling event was the healing of her brother by a woman in El Salvador. Another instance in which the narrator herself was the victim was the report of being poisoned by her mother-in-law with a chicken dinner that made her very sick. Her mother provided initial help by preparing healing waters, and subsequently in New York City she saw a spiritist who gave her a cure that produced black diarrhea, after which she started feeling better as if something was released (*"fue como que se me desprendio"*). In an instance emphasizing the Catholic idiom, one woman reported having experienced a miracle and the presence of God, along with the help of the Virgin of Guadalupe, the Immaculate Conception, and the Sacred Heart. She commented as well that the strange civil war between brothers was taking place because of things written in the Bible about the end of a world that had meaning on a global level.

A somewhat more elaborate instance of a significant episode was the illness of Malvina, who had witnessed killing and saw corpses in El Salvador, including seeing a woman's head blown off in front of her, and had a cousin "disappear." In El Salvador, her father expelled her from home when he discovered she was pregnant at age eighteen. She was also attacked with a knife by her mother-in-law and beaten by her boyfriend when they discovered her pregnancy. After marriage he beat her again when the baby was born because it had jaundice (though she attributed the condition to the prior beating). She had a dissociative episode after the birth including a suicide attempt by hanging on command of voices. Hospitalization and psychiatric treatment with vitamins and sleep medication did not help, but spiritist treatment every eight days by bathing her head with milk and prepared waters, along with herbs, incense, and lotions, rid her of evil influences (*malas influencias*). The spiritist determined that the illness was due to *un mal* from her brothers' neighbors who were mad at him for being a *cipote* ("prick"). Other than this episode she had no significant family background with magic and little engagement with it in the United States, where upon arrival she was treated poorly as a live-in nanny for a wealthy right-wing Salvadoran family and in a subsequent job with an American family was accused (though later exonerated) of improperly touching their son. Magic is an acknowledged part of her lifeworld but not a strong presence in her experience; it is as if she passively accepts it but does not regard it as a force with which she can personally engage. She regarded it as legitimate in that it is recognized in the Bible. She also invoked the saying that whether or not one believes, one could end up dead without knowing why: *"Está en la biblia. Existe el mal ¿verdad? No hay que creer ni dejar de creer porque ustedes pueden morir y no saben porque."*

The narratives of five other women tend more toward the greater degree of existential salience we have seen with Mariela and Ceres. It is worthwhile to add a degree of detail about the spiritual configuration of their lifeworlds.

1. Alicia came to the United States because of her frequent sightings of hungry children and dead bodies, the difficulty of getting a job, and particularly because of having military-age sons who were severely brutalized. She immigrated with the assistance of a *coyote*. Her alcoholic husband brutalized and kicked her out of their house so she has had to sleep outside on several occasions. She gave a very explicit description of her depression but at the same time expressed her need to get up and go to work. She believes in God and has devotion to la Divina Providencia, always crosses herself (*"Yo me persigno"*) before leaving for work and does not care if people laugh because it is her faith. She asks God for good work and that good people will extend a hand so she can get ahead (*seguir adelante*). She uses herbs like orange leaf tea, spinach, blackberry (*mora*), and verdolada. She does not frequent *centros* or *espiritistas* in the United States, though she believes in spirits and consults two "brothers," Ciriaco Lopez and (San) Simon, the latter of whom helped her cross the border. She engages in Ouija that she describes as a game having to do with spiritism and concentration. She does not consult card readers because she is afraid they will predict something bad or that she will die from the power of suggestion (*"me voy a morir de la sugestion"*). She observed that in El Salvador there are no *curanderos* or *santeros* but spiritists, mediums, *centros negros,* and *centros blancos.* She reported having had many dreams of violence, rivers, poverty, and her mother's ranchito, saying that they are a form of communication or presci- ence (*presentimientos*), but she gave no indication of cultivating them as a spiritual faculty.

2. Cecilia was given into fosterage (*regalada*) at a young age and psychically wounded when she discovered she was adopted. She referred to children dying of hunger and dead people in the streets in the mornings before she left El Salvador but was not politically astute. In the face of a troubled and sexless relationship with her current spouse she romanticizes a teenage boyfriend. She is among three of the women I worked with whose apartment in the Boston area burned down.[5] She does not believe in *espiritistas, santeros,* or *curanderos* but nevertheless maintains that if doctors cannot cure an illness it is probably caused by *brujería*. Magic exists, but no one has ever done anything to her. While this indicates a relatively inactive background level of magic taken for granted in everyday life, it may also indicate her social isolation and a feeling of not

being important enough to anyone to come under attack. She mentioned having had the sensation of a spirit entering her and that she felt like another person. This makes her afraid and she tells herself "this isn't able to exist in me," but it also suggests to her as she looks in the mirror that she will have power. She is devoted to San Antonio del Monte who helped her come to United States and to la Vírgen de Santa Ursula, observing that one has to have faith in the saints or they will not help. She prays to the Virgin day and night that God will grant her return to her country. She uses vitamins but apparently not herbs. She dreams often, especially of her early boyfriend, fish in the sea, and people in the cemetery who scare her when she realizes they are dead, but she does not attribute any significance to these dreams.

3. Melina followed her husband to the United States in 1984, but her children remained in El Salvador. She had witnessed and fled war violence and atrocities, including having seen a man who was dying. In the United States she was subjected to domestic violence and isolation imposed by her husband, despite having five siblings in the Boston area. She remarked on the curability of *nervios* with waters prepared from roots (*aguas hechas de raices*) in El Salvador but reported being told that in the United States *nervios* can only be cured by therapy and went by herself to the clinic. She believes that *brujería* exists, but she relies on psychiatry and the clinic. She did not consult spiritual healers in El Salvador, except that in preparation for emigration she went with her mother to a spiritist who gave her an amulet. Nevertheless, she did use herbal remedies like *ipacina* (Petiveria) for headache, colds, constipation, and congestion. In the United States nothing evil was ever done to her, but she gave a detailed account of a *mal* done to her aunt. Her only sustained engagement for spiritual protection was through God, and she wore a scapular of the Vírgen of Carmen, who protects against bad spirits. Indeed, she had felt the presence of a demon and says they persecuted her father because he had to kill two men. She feels distant from the church since her marriage was civil but believes she can do religious activities herself without a priest.

4. Matilda was a psychology student at the university when her husband and mother-in-law were killed in the war. Less than a month later her three-month-old son died, which she attributed to the evil eye (*mal de ojo*). Following psychiatric treatment for

depression, she got a job and lived with her brother in El Salvador, during which period she was afflicted by a *mal* cast at her sister but which struck her instead. Medical treatment for vomiting and fever failed, and she consulted a spiritist *centro* over the objection of her Evangelical Christian mother. She was treated for three days using (successively) *aguas* of basil and rue, seven cooked heads of garlic, and herbally infused liquor from the pharmacy combined with castor oil. This cure was successful, and the spiritist told Matilda she had spiritual abilities of her own that could be cultivated, so she began attending weekly meetings that began with invoking God and the Sacred Heart of Jesus, praying the rosary, invoking spirits, and integrating New Age thought. Sessions included prayer for the sick and for the war that seemed to constitute a form of communal healing and group therapy. She had out-of-body experiences, as when talking with a woman and suddenly finding herself in Salvadoran President Duarte's office warning him not to sign papers. She also saw spirits across the water as well as shadowy forms (*bultos*) and conversed with Ivon Kafki from Mars. She reported to the spiritist that someone accompanies her and was told it is her father's spirit, but she thinks it is actually the restless spirit of her troubled grandmother. After resuming her university studies, one of her roommates was killed and another disappeared, upon which she fled El Salvador and entered the United States with a coyote. Perhaps because of her recent arrival, she thought that spiritism and herbalism were unavailable in the United States, but she commented that therapy was helping her to see the truth more clearly every day and to accept the pain she has experienced. She also mentioned that she was continuing to develop her spiritual abilities because hate separates dimensions and if more people lived spiritually the world would be a better place. She distinguished *espiritismo* and *santería,* talking about how in the latter animal sacrifice is used to free one from the police and "things like that" and associating it with bad magic.

5. Soledad had considerable exposure to war violence; one of her sons disappeared, and she reported having seen decapitated bodies, as well as having undergone family and economic problems. She reported dissociative episodes and multiple unpleasant physical sensations. She felt spiritual presences and told of an instance in which a spirit took over her body. Her apartment burned down within eight days of her arrival in the United States. During her

participation in my research, between one interview and the next she had seen a healer she called a *santero,* after which she felt relief from multiple physical and emotional complaints. She said a profound change came upon her overnight, so that instead of the feeling of weight in her body and foggy vision she felt a general calmness. Her affect became notably elevated, and she appeared less depressed and defeated. She continued to visit the healer every fifteen days at no charge. This was one of the few instances during my study in which the specific focus of religious healing appeared to correspond with that of her ongoing psychotherapy. Giving her personal guidance and using ritual in the form of incomprehensible speech, contact with spirits/saints, *aguas,* and other magical acts, the *santero* seemed to have given her a new focus on personal well-being and work, relieving her of previous worries about keeping her children close and reliant on her. Despite referring to the man as a *santero,* several factors—the healer's apparent use of glossalalia, Soledad's mention of the importance to her of la Divina Providencia in moments of crisis, and the fact that she hosted a Catholic Bible study group at her house that helped her "clear her mind and forget the things one can't"—suggest that the man may have in fact been a Charismatic Christian healer. Beyond this involvement, however, Soledad said that her habit of drinking with a friend was caused by someone doing a *mal* and reported that her mother was able to cure her with some food. She also has worn a horseshoe amulet for protection since coming to United States. Nevertheless, she had not frequented *centros* in El Salvador like she frequented her healer in this country. In other words, her accept-ance of spiritual realities did not change, but her need and hence her engagement did; she became no more religious but had more recourse to religion.

## PARA SALIR ADELANTE

The final two vignettes have the most in common with the narratives of Mariela and Ceres insofar as the women were engaged followers of spe-cific healers. However, whereas Matilda was involved primarily in El Salvador without continuing in the United States, Soledad became involved in the United States without having had much experience in El Salvador. Indeed, this circumstance of potential change in degree of reli-gious involvement from origin to host country is of equal importance to the change in the religious lay of the land in coming to a place where multiple Latin American and Afro-Latin traditions mingle. The United States in general, and no less in cosmopolitan Boston, is a locale in which ethnic, medical, and religious pluralism are in constant ferment (Barnes and Sered 2011; Csordas and Lewton 1998). With regard to particular practices, the degree of salience and skepticism may not change, but it certainly varies from person to person with relevance to their search for health and healing. Dreams, for instance, may be regarded as evidence of spiritual abilities, forms of communication, nightmares, conduits of pleasant or unpleasant memory, or of little significance at all. A telling grammatical feature is that Salvadorans do not dream about people but with (*con*) people. Spiritists will point to their clients' dreams as much as to their perception of spirits as indications of spiritual talent, whether as simple observation or as flattery to induce their continued participation in ritual activities. Herbs are another example, with some casually using readily available herbal teas and the ever popular orange leaf (*hoja de naranja*), others acknowledging the use of more esoteric plants from herbal pharmacies (*botánicas*) and specially prepared waters (*aguas*), and still others citing the importance of prayers and rites surrounding the harvesting and efficacious use of plants that form the specialized knowledge of herbalists and spiritists. Finally, the degree of immediacy of experience plays into the role of religion and magic in everyday life insofar as relevant episodes may have happened in the past or more recently, or to others rather than to oneself.

What is in question is the manner in which religious reality is related to the paramount reality of the world of work, the political reality of *la situación*, the reality of domestic life and kin relations, and the reality of mental health, illness, and treatment. Given the vivid content of the descriptions offered in this chapter and the manner in which it is woven into the fabric of experience for many of these women, it is doubtless the latter—the relation of religion and mental health—that requires specific attention in conclusion. My data offer no grounds to suggest that religious experience is symptomatic of psychopathology or that religious activity can cause or exacerbate mental illness. Neither can religious involvement simply be said to buffer mental illness since, particularly with respect to vulnerability to malevolent magic, it can be as much a source of distress as a relief from distress. To the extent that the practices we have encountered can be understood as form of treatment or healing, they cannot be considered an alternative to mental health care since all the women in the study were actively engaged in therapy through the clinic. Neither can they strictly speaking be described as parallel or complementary since in only one case was healing by a *santero* clearly addressing issues similar to those being dealt with by the person in therapy.

Yet they are not irrelevant to mental health. The critical point is to distinguish the manner in which these religious practices (1) like the mental health care system, are a resource for healing and an idiom for explaining misfortune and conflict that themselves remain in some sense mysterious and inexplicable; and (2) unlike the mental health care system, constitute a dimension of reality that has an ontological character and a place in everyday life that is existentially broader and deeper for distressed persons and the communities in which they live than the world of symptoms, diagnoses, and therapies. The very fact that religion can be considered separately, as I have done in this chapter, has a kind of paradoxical quality in that it allows either for the perspective of transcendence in which the sacred and profane are so distinct as to be mutually irrelevant or for the perspective of immanence in which sacred and profane permeate and mutually define one another. In more pedestrian terms this would translate as either treating the religious dimension as a remote existential backwater easily ignored and overlooked as of marginal interest (would the reader interested in mental illness have missed this chapter if it had not been included?) or as intimately essential to our goal of understanding subjectivity and struggle among the afflicted.

In my view these women's religious reality is not only essential in this respect, but its otherworldliness offers a clue for finding the common thread that binds together all the multiple realities I have discussed. It invites invocation of the philosophical and literary notion of haunting as an ontological category that encompasses the possible simultaneity of being and nonbeing, reality and unreality, the secret that should be discovered and spoken and the secret that is unspeakable in both senses of that word (Derrida 1993; Davis 2005). In this perspective, the point is not that reality is haunted by ghosts but that it is permeated by the haunting uncertainty captured in the key saying I have highlighted in this chapter about belief and unbelief; both are immaterial to what is most essential. To be sure, this uncertainty has to do with phenomena such as gossip, witchcraft, miracles, and ghosts. Much more, however, it extends to the haunting existence of *la situación* in its dangerous ambiguity and quotidian violence, the existence—or nonexistence—of the political *desaparecidos* who are more ghostly than ghosts in being neither knowably dead nor alive, and the ever present always anticipated possibility of deportation by the host government in the United States. As the common thread linking multiple realities it also provides a means more immediate than periodic encounters with the psychotherapist to support the needs and meet the contingencies of the paramount reality. In fact, the religious domain of the lifeworld I have examined in this chapter plays a major role for better or worse with respect to the primary goal mentioned by these women. For just as often as they say, *"No hay que creer ni dejar de creer,"* it is in the context of talking about the obstacles and opportunities, the threats and protections offered by religion and magic that they most clearly express their deeply held desire simply to carry on and go forward—*para salir adelante.*

## CHAPTER 6

# Trauma and Trouble in the Land of Enchantment

The wide geographic swath of the state of New Mexico, self-described as the "Land of Enchantment,"[1] is well known as a multicultural mélange. Images of this rural state as one of beautiful expansive landscapes and the cosmopolitan tourist mecca of Santa Fe are common, but less widely recognized are its exceptionally high rates of child poverty and historically produced institutional subjugation. The most populous metropolitan areas are Albuquerque and Las Cruces, but the rural character of the state overall is noteworthy compared to the rest of the nation (17.0 vs. 87.4 persons per square mile). As of 2010 the U.S. Census reported the population of New Mexico as just over two million, representing a 13.2 percent growth from the previous decade. Census data represent the population as predominantly Hispanic (46.3 percent), followed by Euro-American (40.5 percent) and Native American (9.4 percent).

New Mexico is one of the poorest states in the nation. According to the U.S. Statistical Abstract, as of 2008 the median household income was ranked low ($43,508, or 44th among the 50 states). The Abstract further ranked the state as having among the highest proportion (17.1 percent, or fifth highest) of persons living below the poverty level. A national survey in association with the U.S. Census found the rate of child poverty in New Mexico to be 30 percent, second only to Mississippi at 32.5 percent (Macartney 2011: 6).[2] The long-standing adverse conditions for survival were exacerbated under the press of the Great Recession at the end of the first decade of the twenty-first century when our research team was conducting the work I describe in this chapter. The economic decline cut deeply and broadly in the form of job loss, home foreclosure, and radical curtailment of health services.[3]

In particular, the lives of the adolescents with whom we worked were by and large marked by residential instability and familial fragmentation. For the most part they belonged to low-income households, with some living on the rough edge of survival. The conditions of their lives were toned by structural violence, including high unemployment, the presence of gangs, violent crime, and a scarcity of social, educational, and health services. One commodity for which there was no shortage is street drugs. Albuquerque and Las Cruces are major points of transmission of heroin and other drugs for the Southwest, Midwest, and Pacific Northwest. Garcia (2010) has captured the nuances of heroin-saturated family life in this state, which has the inauspicious distinction of having the highest per capita rate of heroin-related deaths in the nation. Overall, in New Mexico drug-related overdose was recently reported as the leading cause of unintentional death (New Mexico Department of Health 2011). Use of cannabis, alcohol, methamphetamine, and cocaine, among other drugs, is common among adolescents.

In this chapter I continue the discussion of psychic trauma begun in chapter 4, in the context of life conditions of precarity for adolescents. The extraordinary conditions of their lives are arguably among the most precarious of the precarious, their experience marked by multiple psychiatric hospitalizations. I examine the relevance of PTSD for answering the anthropological question of how to define the "problem." Factors that define the extraordinary conditions under which these youths struggled to live are extreme on a continuum of conditions to include serious distress (minimally defined by diagnostic categories), familial strife and fragmentation, socioeconomic hardship, and severely limited access to health care. I discuss the mental health care system for adolescents and present two case studies of young inpatients, emphasizing the need for dual specification of the conditions of trauma and the structure of experience. Comparing this situation with that of Salvadoran refugees discussed in chapters 4 and 5, I argue for deploying the generalized category of trauma instead of the psychiatric category of PTSD and for understanding patterns of abandonment that shape the raw existence of young people at both the personal and collective levels.

The primary aim of this portion of the book is to analyze the phenomenological, social, and situational features of trauma as the lived experience of children and adolescents. While we know that adaptation in the aftermath of warfare is intricate, far less is known about the process of defense and adaptation of children who are repetitively exposed to traumatic events as the everyday condition of their lives. For situations of trauma that we did observe in the New Mexico study, there is a patterning of conditions of social danger that make events of trauma all but routine. The conditions provide the occasion for regular violation of the dignity and integrity of teenagers with precarious lives. Comprehending this problem, in my view, requires a clear recognition of a social-historical pattern of structural violence (see Antze and Lambek 1996; Farmer 2004a) that conduces to a reciprocal shaping of subjective experience and social structural relations. This reciprocal shaping can create inarguably tangible forms of psychic anguish as a bodily matter of lived experience.

## ADOLESCENT MENTAL HEALTH

Scholarly attention to the mental and behavioral health of adolescents has intensified as a global concern (Hoagwood and Olin 2002; Kieling et al. 2011; WHO 2005; Carpenter-Song 2009a, 2009b; Floersch et al. 2009; Read, Adiibokah, and Nyame 2009; Panter-Brick et al. 2011; Kohrt et al. 2008; Korbin and Anderson-Fye 2011; Anderson-Fye 2004; Gone and Trimble 2012). The reasons for this uptick in concern are not reducible to moral panic, psycho-political projection of societal problems onto youths, or subjection of young people to medicalization and pharmaceuticalization. Critics have pointed to the problem of adolescent mental health as somehow restricted to affluent populations where, for example, performance-enhancing drugs and anxiety over college entrance exams are foregrounded. Yet the World Health Organization (2005: 7) reports a 20 percent overall prevalence rate of mental disorders among children and adolescents worldwide. In the United States, 26.2 percent of adults experience a diagnosable mental disorder in any given year, with an overall rate of 6 percent considered serious and severe (NIMH 2012). Within this adult group, those 18 to 25 years of age rank highest, with an overall rate approaching 8 percent. For teenagers between 13 and 18 years of age, the overall rate of mental illness is reported as 21 percent. As I have argued throughout this book, ethnographically derived empirical data are much needed in order to fully understand the magnitude, urgency, and increasing commonality of these problems worldwide. A full anthropological research agenda would most certainly include identifying the contribution of social problems across socioeconomic groups and elaboration of the cultural meaning attributed to suicide attempts or violent interaction that results in psychiatric hospitalization.

Much current debate within the professional and public mental health sectors revolves less around definitions of mental disturbance that afflict youths and more about what sorts of health services can be demonstrated as "evidence-based" and cost-effective (Hoagwood et al. 2001; WHO 2005).[4] Discourse and practices tend in the main to focus on individual pathology and treatment in the absence of cultural critique or calls for social change. This is clearly an arena in which anthropology has much to contribute, beginning with recognition of the cross-cultural and historical variation in the very concepts of adolescence and psychopathology. The field of adolescent psychopathology and the discipline of adolescent psychiatry/psychology are themselves "recent creations of Western biomedicine" (Fabrega 1995: 4). While underlining the biocultural basis of adolescence, Fabrega and Miller (1995) also endorse the idea that the contemporary form of adolescence is a product of capitalist industrialization and market development the stresses and strains of which generate "adolescent psychopathology." They apply a historical and comparative perspective to anorexia nervosa, dissociation disorders, and social aggression among adolescents and argue for the importance of the interactions between historical and structural forces, experiential meaning, and psychobiological/biomedical changes. Along similar lines, I argue that the mental health of adolescents[5] is best considered in light of the reciprocal shaping of subjective experience and social institutions.[6]

New Mexico and its system of child and adolescent mental health care is a case in point. A series of articles based on ethnographic study of mental health professionals (Willging, Waitzkin, and Lamphere 2009; Kano, Willging, and Rylko-Bauer 2009; Willging and Semansky 2010; Watson et al. 2011) examine the pragmatic, institutional, community, and policy effects of the behavioral health care reforms under way during the course of our research. These included attitudes toward evidence-based therapy and culturally competent treatment among health care providers in the state's "safety-net institutions," the concept of "wrap-around services" provided by multi-institution "clinical homes," and the institutional emphasis on promoting "recovery" from mental illness. Their findings are fully in accord with our ethnographic observations that the impact of managed care on adolescent patients and their families has been

FIGURE 3. Mural of the Virgin and family, New Mexico. Photo by author.

profound (figure 3). At the beginning of our research in 2005, New Mexico had become the first state to contract a health care management company to administer all its Medicaid insurance payments. This began a period of severe contraction of services that lasted for the duration of our project. The radical curtailment of services during the course of our study coincided with the centralization of all mental or behavioral health services managed by Value Options, the largest privately held health care corporation in the country at the time. Through what was said to be competitive bidding in 2005, the state of New Mexico selected Value Options to oversee public funding and delivery of health care throughout the state. The company operated as the state's single managed care entity for the delivery of mental and behavioral health care. Its prevailing philosophy was that extended inpatient treatment is therapeutically ineffective and economically extravagant.

The University of New Mexico Children's Psychiatric Hospital (CPH) where our research participants were being treated is the primary public facility for such care in New Mexico, and children are referred there from all over the state. Under pressure from Value Options, payment for both residential treatment and day treatment was approved with decreasing frequency, and more beds had to be allocated to acute care for the institution to remain financially viable. At the time of our work, a day hospital program had recently been eliminated, one of the regular inpatient cottages had switched from residential to acute care, and a special cottage for girls in legal trouble was also redirected to acute care. Of the six units, each with a capacity for approximately nine patients, by the end of our research only one was for residential treatment of adolescents. As payment for residential treatment was approved with decreasing frequency, the average stay for long-term residential (RTC) patients declined from one year to 30 to 60 days. The approved length of short-term stay for the acutely distressed declined to 5 to 10 days, not even the length of Hendren and Berlin's (1991) "honeymoon period" during which basic therapeutic trust was established.[7] During the six-year period of the study (2005–11) we saw therapeutic time eroded even further. This restriction of services was a source of great dismay to clinicians, patients, and families alike. From the standpoint of clinicians, this meant that patients were often being discharged to disorganized family environments that did not provide sufficient opportunity for their condition to stabilize or to less intensive levels of care for which they were not prepared.[8] Accordingly, they perceived an increasing frequency of adolescents being discharged too soon, and too soon ending up hospitalized again, creating the sense of a revolving door of discharge and readmission for patients whose clinical need was extended residential treatment.

Highly disturbing was the reluctant rationing of high-quality care at CPH that opened other doors to considerably less qualified caregiving due to the corporate takeover of residential behavioral health care at many sites. One example of a site where several of the children from the present study were transferred owing to a shortage of space at CPH was Desert Hills of New Mexico, part of Acadia Healthcare's nationwide behavioral health treatment system. With thirty-four facilities with approximately 2,500 beds across twenty states, Acadia was founded in 2005 as a provider of inpatient services. On December 26, 2012, Acadia Healthcare, Inc., announced options to purchase shares of stock (traded on the NASDAQ Global Stock Market under "ACHC") that had begun on November 1, 2011, after completion of its merger with PHC, Inc., a public company traded on the American Stock Exchange.[9] While it is beyond the scope of this chapter to develop this further, the overall effect of the changing balance between public and private, nonprofit and for-profit mental health care, is a critical background feature of the setting in which we worked.

## SOUTHWESTERN YOUTH AND THE EXPERIENCE OF PSYCHIATRIC TREATMENT: THE SWYEPT STUDY

We began our work in 2005, having arranged with three therapists at the Children's Psychiatric Hospital that they would refer to us patients aged twelve to eighteen who were not so severely cognitively disabled or developmentally impaired that they would be unable to participate in interviews and who were not so emotionally or clinically fragile that their participation would be unduly stressful.[10] Although we initially encountered the young people in an inpatient psychiatric facility, the majority of the ethnographic and research psychiatric diagnostic work was carried out in homes. We conducted anthropological interviews and observations with parents, siblings, and clinical staff. We also collected ethnographic observations of neighborhoods and communities. Research visits with adolescents and parents were conducted at various intervals over periods of between one and two years.[11]

While the study was based in the Albuquerque metropolitan area, the research spanned the state of New Mexico both because the hospital served the entire state and because of a high degree of residential mobility among the youths. Conducting a study of persons in motion does not resemble the more traditional anthropological approach of staying put in one locale, neighborhood, or village (cf. Gupta and Ferguson 1997). While we did live and stay in some places for periods of months, more often than not field-workers ventured out from a base of operation more in the manner of "road warriors," given the great distances we frequently traveled to get anywhere when the "where" was wherever the adolescents went after their discharge from the psychiatric hospital.[12] In both the literal and figurative senses, we went to great lengths to find people, sometimes even crossing state lines. Occasionally we lost track of someone who moved too far afield for us to logistically handle follow-up visits, which were scheduled for six months and one year following our initial interview. A research team member would meet with the adolescent and his or her family (separately, usually) in the home setting, although in some cases we met in coffee shops or the homes of other relatives where they were not residing. The homes were typically poor-quality or low-income housing with few amenities and little space (apartments, trailers, small and often crowded homes).

Often there was a steady flow of persons coming and going amid inter-personal relations that were strained. Residents often did not regard their neighborhoods as spaces in which they could walk about freely or safely, and this may in some instances account for the feeling of crowding or being cooped up.

The most fundamental anthropological question concerns how to define the "problem" for which the adolescents were hospitalized. In an overall sense, the fieldwork was colored by palpable personal anguish and the cultural conditions implicated in its creation: (1) the utility and limitation of psychiatric diagnostic categories used not only as clinical descriptors but also as rhetorical tokens in a discourse of everyday sense-making; (2) the lived experience of serious distress in phenomeno-logical, existential, and dynamic detail across the social settings in which young people and their families interacted; (3) a complex of social, economic, and political conditions that are entrenched in the history of the state and that incise deep and enduring mental and material anguish; and (4) how to formulate a theoretical framework that could take into account the reciprocal relations between immediate social institutions (kin-based homes, foster homes, hospitals, schools, neigh-borhoods) and those at greater reach (economic recession, state and federal health care policies, judicial system, ethnic discrimination, cross-border drug trafficking). This complex of forces would be dizzying enough in its own right were it not for the constant instability of each of these factors in cybernetic interplay. Instability in the provision of health care, housing, employment, and social actors across settings must be taken into consideration in configuring the shifting sands of subjectivity and social world. These considerations pose a challenge for taking the next step beyond understanding the problem that led to their hospitalization, which is to understand these youths' lives in terms of what Christine Korsgaard, drawing on Ricoeur's narrative model, calls practical identity: "a description under which you value yourself, a description under which you find your life to be worth living and your actions to be worth undertaking" (Korsgaard 1996: 101). In situations of exposure to repetitive or sustained traumatic events and conditions, persons might be expected to fundamentally call into question an exis-tential description of life worth living (Nietzsche 1967a).

The project included forty-seven youths, twenty-five boys and twenty-two girls, between the ages of thirteen and seventeen. On average, they were fourteen years old. Participants were roughly equally distributed between Hispanic and Euro-American heritage, with a smaller group of

Native Americans and a number of other combinations of ethnicity that included African American and Southeast Asian ancestry. Almost three quarters of the youths had been hospitalized previously on multiple occasions. Data from the Structured Clinical Interview for DSM-IV (in the version for children known as the KID-SCID), administered by one of two members of the team (a child psychiatrist and clinical psychologist, both trained specifically to reliably administer this research diagnostic interview), are impressive in terms of the co-occurrence of multiple psychiatric diagnoses (table 6).

Depression was the most common of all the research psychiatric categories observed among participants, with 18 of 22 girls (82 percent) and 10 of 25 boys (40 percent) meeting the DSM-IV criteria. As table 6 shows, mean number of diagnoses is 3.1 for girls and 2.3 for boys (2.7 overall), with the fewest co-occurring diagnoses for a single youth being 0 and the most being 6.

Diagnostic criteria aside, however, table 7 shows that these youths had been exposed to or involved in various types of violence. They had frequently committed violent or suicidal acts, had encounters with police and the juvenile justice system, were involved in drug-related violence, had undergone physical and/or sexual violation (an alarming number of girls were raped multiple times), or had engaged in routine self-cutting. Fully 32 of our 47 participants (68.1 percent) exhibited evidence of suicidality; 16 of the 47 admitting incidents that brought them to the hospital for the most recent hospitalization were suicide attempts. Overall, the state of New Mexico ranked sixth in 2010 in the number of suicides among fifteen- to twenty-four-year-olds and fifth in all ages combined (McIntosh 2010).[13]

THE PLACE OF TRAUMA

Ethnographic interviews and observations, along with the KID-SCID psychiatric diagnostic interviews, provide evidence of the prominent place of trauma in the lives of many of the adolescents. This includes experiencing the recent violent deaths of loved ones, heavy use of drugs and alcohol that involved violence, shocking revelations and betrayals (e.g., being disowned or learning of sexual abuse), and abrupt residential moves (adolescent ejected or removed from home, family eviction or flight), among many others. If there is value in using the diagnostic category PTSD where the conditions of life are essentially unstable and traumatic events not uncommon, it is to distinguish those circumstances

TABLE 6  GENDER AND DIAGNOSIS AMONG HOSPITALIZED ADOLESCENTS IN NEW MEXICO ($N = 47$)

| | Major depression/ dysthymia | Anxiety/ panic disorder | Substance abuse/ dependence | ODD/ conduct disorder | ADHD | PTSD | Psychotic disorder | Bipolar disorder/ cyclothymia | Eating disorder | Mean |
|---|---|---|---|---|---|---|---|---|---|---|
| Female (N = 22) | 18 (81.8%) | 12 (54.5%) | 8 (36.4%) | 6 (27.3%) | 5 (22.7%) | 8 (36.4%) | 4 (18.2%) | 4 (18.2%) | 4 (18.2%) | 3.1 |
| Male (N = 25) | 10 (40.0%) | 7 (28.0%) | 9 (36.0%) | 8 (32.0%) | 8 (32.0%) | 5 (20.0%) | 6 (24.0%) | 3 (12.0%) | 1 (4.0%) | 2.3 |
| Total (N = 47) | 28 (59.6%) | 18 (38.3%) | 17 (36.2%) | 14 (29.8%) | 13 (27.7%) | 13 (27.7%) | 10 (21.3%) | 7 (14.9%) | 5 (10.6%) | 2.7 |

TABLE 7  VIOLENCE-RELATED PROBLEMS AMONG HOSPITALIZED ADOLESCENTS IN NEW MEXICO ($N = 47$)

| | Perpetrator of violent acts | Suicide attempt/ preoccupation | Police/legal trouble | Self-cutting | Victim of physical abuse | Victim of sexual abuse | Mean |
|---|---|---|---|---|---|---|---|
| Female ($N = 22$) | 16 (72.7%) | 18 (81.8%) | 11 (50%) | 15 (68.2%) | 11 (50%) | 10 (45.5%) | 3.7 |
| Male ($N = 25$) | 19 (76%) | 14 (56%) | 20 (80%) | 9 (36%) | 11 (44%) | 5 (20%) | 3.1 |
| Total ($N = 47$) | 35 (74.5%) | 32 (68.1%) | 31 (66%) | 24 (51.1%) | 22 (46.8%) | 15 (31.9%) | 3.4 |

in which the response is especially serious and severe. As defined in DSM-IV, PTSD applies when a person directly experiences a traumatic event involving serious injury or death of self or another and reacts with intense fear, helplessness, or horror. This event is subsequently reexperienced through memories, dreams, flashbacks, distress, or physical reaction. The afflicted person avoids stimuli associated with the trauma and exhibits numbing of general responsiveness, along with symptoms of increased arousal such as difficulty sleeping, irritability, trouble concentrating, hypervigilance, or exaggerated startle response. These difficulties persist for more than a month and cause significant distress or impairment in social functioning. Although the core definition focuses on experience of a single life-threatening event, the DSM recognizes that symptoms can result from repeated exposure to events that may be less severe but have a cumulative effect over time.

Later I focus on the experience of a particular boy and girl, but for the moment I want to briefly characterize the entire cohort of eight girls and five boys (13 of 47, or 28 percent) who met the full diagnostic criteria for PTSD. This does not include several more who were diagnosed as having clinically sub-syndromal PTSD. Notably, for all of them PTSD only begins to describe the situation from the standpoint of co-occurring diagnoses. These youths commonly met diagnostic criteria for more than one disorder. In particular, all eight of the girls and two of the five boys were also diagnosed with depression; studies have shown that depression is very commonly correlated with PTSD. It is important to bear in mind the close correlation of PTSD and depression not only as a matter of phenomenological experience but also in theorizing about the social determinants of these concurrent disorders.[14] Moreover, among the cases diagnosed with PTSD, in addition to diagnoses of depression (10), we found, by order of frequency, substance abuse or dependence (7), separation anxiety disorder (5), oppositional defiant or conduct disorders (5), ADHD (4), panic disorder (3), eating disorder (2), psychosis (2), anxiety disorder (2), bipolar disorder (2), and phobia. These are all derived from our administration of the KID-SCID and do not include clinical diagnoses.

In itself, this summary of applicable diagnostic categories does little to capture the diversity of these youths' experiences and social predicaments. It is no surprise that common traumatic experiences in this group were rape and sexual molestation (6 girls, 1 boy), sexual violation of others (2 boys, and 1 girl), and physical or verbal abuse (5). What stands out, however, are various kinds of broadly conceived social abandonment in the home setting (10 children), whether it means a biological or stepparent leaving, already absent, or imprisoned; serial changes in caregivers; death (and associated child bereavement); absence of adequate familial care or emotional involvement; parental suicide attempt; or the need for the child to act as caregiver to one's parent. Abandonment in the present case thus subsumes neglect in a specific sense. Diagnostically, it corresponds to the frequency with which we found separation anxiety disorder to be in play. Existentially, we must point to the nexus of being abandoned (alone) and feeling abandoned (lonely), as well as of abandonment as a condition for trauma (vulnerability) and a traumatic event in itself (violation). Subtle variations based on cultural patterns of family dynamics across Euro-American, Hispano/Hispanic, and Native American groups are beyond the scope of my discussion here, but across groups the exceptions stand out, as for example a boy who ran away from home repeatedly to escape his father's rages but who said his father loved him nonetheless because he always came to find him.

But why subject PTSD to particular scrutiny? Certainly its high profile and cultural saturation in everyday discourse is compelling in itself. Yet there is a need to conceptualize psychic trauma in a way deepened by a framework that takes into account the reciprocal shaping of social institutions and personal subjectivity, and there is an array of notions that are currently candidates to become part of that framework. Dominant in establishing the discursive status quo is the notion of psychiatric diagnosis based on categories that utilize criteria of symptom content, severity, and functionality codified in the classificatory systems of DSM-IV or ICD-10. Generally, among anthropologists there is a good deal of suspicion if not outright disdain for these diagnostic categories as historical inventions, biologically reductive, lacking in cultural validity, biased in relation to gender, ethnicity, and social class, and products of medicalization, potentially pernicious both socially and politically. It is little wonder that this suspicion would lead to outright rejection of the utility of psychiatric diagnostic categories. Nevertheless, I agree with the position outlined by Byron Good (1992) that the psychiatric diagnostic categories provide a useful starting point for cross-cultural comparison by identifying constellations of symptoms that tend to "go together" by virtue of neurobiology, social etiology, and the structure of subjective experience. That said, in this study of troubled youths I experienced a greater degree of discomfort with these categories than in any other study that I have conducted. The co-occurrence of disorders—for example, depression + PTSD + psychosis—confers a degree of complexity that is dizzying if not an outright muddle. How to account for this? Might not some measure of the complexity be due to developmental issues insofar as these are adolescents in (relatively) earlier stages of the onset of illnesses that have not yet fully "coalesced" in a (relatively) more coherent clinical picture?

On the other hand, is this infelicitously termed "co-morbidity" better understood as a mirror of the severity of the charred social, economic, political, and psychological realities of lived experience? If that were true, how should one think about the manner in which such totalizing forces produce subjectivity? A number of works suggest that violence might be the critical master concept in thinking about disease. Scheper-Hughes (1993) has written of the violence of food scarcity and of hunger configured as a madness of impossible choices for maternal decision making in the care of children in northeastern Brazil. There has been little doubt that the fear and reality of going hungry leads to poor mental health since the National Co-morbidity Survey Replication Study (McLaughlin et al. 2012) linked food insecurity to mood, behavioral, and substance disorders among adolescents thirteen to seventeen years of age. Das (1995: 175) has written on subjectivity and violence as "conceptual structures of our discipline" that are necessary yet problematic insofar as they are a "professional transformation of suffering which robs the victim of her voice and distances us from the immediacy of her experience." Drawing on Bateson's notion (1958), I have elaborated the idea of "political ethos" conceived as the cultural organization of feeling and sentiment pertaining to social domains of power and interest for examination of "the nexus among the role of the state in constructing a particular political ethos, the personal emotions of those who dwell in that ethos, and the mental health consequences of inhabiting such a milieu" (Jenkins 1991b; chapter 4 above). Farmer (2004a, 2004b) has argued the utility of a broadly encompassing notion of "structural violence" (built into institutions, practices, and presuppositions), while Quesada, Hart, and Bourgois (2011) sought to refine the potentially overinclusive term *violence* by substituting the term *vulnerability*.

Another master concept is that of precarity, which is valuable in directing attention to the ongoing conditions that give rise to repeated traumatic events (Butler 2004, 2009). I have addressed this theme above in the introduction and in developing the concept of *palpable insecurity* (Jenkins 2013) present in situations like the urban environment of Rio de Janeiro or among depressed women in Ghana. Discussing Sen's distinction between well-being and agency, I reject his critique of anthropology's limitation by the sensory, since the sensory as the ground of social meaning and ill health opens onto the broadest issues of social justice and inequality. Lovell (2013) has provided a formulation of extraordinary circumstances such as what transpired during and in the aftermath of Hurricane Katrina to take into consideration preexisting psychiatric vulnerability and yet a remarkable capacity for action and agency in the face of necessity. Drawing on Arendt's notion of "natality" to account for this capacity, Lovell elaborates a notion of "precarity" that holds particular value by encompassing an experience-near quality of danger while preserving human sociality under the press of extreme and life-threatening circumstances. In an effort to link long-term stress associated with loss of family, jobs, and community, in a context of unsettled life circumstances, Adams, van Hattum, and English (2009: 615) coined the term *chronic disaster syndrome* to draw together the long-term effects of personal trauma, the social arrangements of what Klein (2007) called "disaster capitalism" in which disaster is really a way of life, and the geographic displacement of populations such as the poor of New Orleans following Hurricane Katrina. In such formulations the potential problem is not a myopic individualism mired in the complexity of comorbidity but an unwieldy mélange of everything that begs the question of how a multiplicity of factors and levels of analysis are interrelated.

In short, our studies require a specification of the situations and conditions of trauma in cultural, social, and human development, along with appreciation of trauma as a complex attunement to modulations of raw existence and the structure of experience. The struggle to conceptualize that which is at once totalizing and pervasive—we cannot presume that there is either a definitive temporal "post" or "pre" to a traumatic event or collective traumatic situation—poses threats to the very structure of meaning. What Bateson and colleagues (1956) called the "double bind" for individuals presents itself on a structural level in ironic and fragmentary form as "continuous crisis" and repetitive and predictable cycles of disbelief that defy human cultural and psychological expectations of the possible. Cultural scripts or models (Holland and Quinn 1987) are either lacking, or inadequate, or irrelevant in the landscape of dashed expectations and ethnopsychologies. For example, what are the cultural meanings and development consequences from the perspective of a child when a mother doesn't bake cookies because she was high on meth for three days and went away without notice for months at a time? How does a girl organize her emotional life in relation to a father who has been in prison her entire lifetime, yet whom she feels she "needs" now that she is "getting older" (seventeen) and will graduate from high school, get married, and become a parent herself? Likewise, what is the meaning of home in a circumstance where residential instability is virtually normative? Even the methodological assumption of what it means to conduct interviews and observations in adolescents' homes is rendered tentative in such a situation.

## TRAUMATIC LIVES

To take an initial step toward illustrating this point in relation to existential features of psychic trauma, I provide a description of the situations of Luke and Alisa. While each case has unique qualities, the two presented here are representative of a pattern of precarious relations and abandonment that holds in general for the thirteen participants diagnosed with PTSD.

### Luke: "I don't want to let it go"

At the time he began participation in the study, Luke was fifteen years old and in ninth grade at his local high school. He lived in a low-income neighborhood outside Albuquerque with his mother, two younger sisters, and brother, all of whom have different biological fathers. Luke had received outpatient psychiatric treatment since he was in kindergarten, diagnosed at the time with ADHD, for which he was prescribed medication. Since then, he had had seven inpatient hospitalizations for episodes of explosive anger and was diagnosed with posttraumatic stress disorder and oppositional defiant disorder.[15] The hospitalization during which we encountered him occurred in the wake of a physical fight with his sister. Luke's mother had called the police, who offered the option either to arrest him or to take him for psychiatric hospitalization. He insisted, and there were no indications, that he had ever used drugs or alcohol. He said he had made a solemn promise to his grandmother never to do so. Her brother, an alcoholic, had said something "really mean" to which the (nonkin) party responded by beating him to death with a lead pipe. When we first met Luke, he was quite heavily medicated but managed an apparently well-practiced firm handshake and direct look in the eye. We heard that he did not get along well with peers or his siblings. Although chatty and personable, he was easily distracted and could be fidgety. Overall, the research team and clinical staff found him a quite likable if troubled teenage boy with a body not unlike that of a large St. Bernard puppy. He got on well with adults, being eager to please and congenial. He seemed honest, open, and trustworthy.

Luke's mother, Martha, is Euro-American and divorced from Luke's father, who is of Mexican origin. Luke commented that even though his father, José, left in 1985 when he was three, he would not rule out contact with him at some point, stating that "there must have been a reason" (for leaving). Martha was receiving unemployment assistance through a housing subsidy, and since the divorce had had a series of live-in male partners. The most recent was Chuck, who was working full-time as a truck driver and who Luke thought of as a "cool guy." A previous partner, Kent, the biological father of Luke's younger brother, lived with the family from the late 1990s. Luke recalled, "For seven years, I thought I loved him as my father." Thus it was crushing to him when his younger sisters divulged in 2006 that for a period of approximately four years, when Luke was between the ages of nine and thirteen, Kent had sexually abused them. More, his stepfather handcuffed Luke to a bed and beat him, allowing for opportunities to abuse his sisters without his knowledge or interference. Luke struggled with the handcuffs, breaking some of the bars on his bed but not one of the thicker bars. Following his sister's revelations of sexual abuse, Luke demanded that they tell his mother because he refused to keep such a terrible secret. In the wake of that telling, Kent was arrested and held in custody, pending a trial that particularly preoccupied Luke at the time we met him. Asked what he thought of his hospitalization, he said he was there for his "anger": "Mostly my anger, I have big, erratic blowups. I go from flat-line to straight up." During his diagnostic interview with our research psychiatrist, he said, "The only reason for my anger is I need to distract myself." He is unwavering, however, in his conviction that his problems started with the "trauma" inflicted on him and his sisters by their stepfather, Kent.

In ethnographic interviews his mother recounted an array of Luke's actions that puzzled her, such as poking holes in walls, playing with lighters, and destructive acts. She had been on a long and dedicated quest to find "the right diagnosis" and associated medications. She was free in expressing her frustration with child psychiatry as not an exact science and with receiving a variety of working diagnoses without specific labels or perspectives on the problem: "I'm ready to throw their books at them and leave my child alone." In particular, she expressed her view that a complex case such as her son's clearly called for a brain scan. She was adamant on this point, repeating this several times, seeing the brain as the source for control of anger. By demanding the "right" diagnosis, it can be argued that parents are searching for interpretability of the actions of their children, an interpretability that through language can identify and singularly name the chaotic and disturbing array of problems in condensed form. Unfortunately such a condensation can render an already thick, murky, and complicated situation more rather than less opaque. In this case (and others in the study), arriving at an understanding was complicated by a cultural model (Holland and Quinn 1987) that simultaneously configures trauma as a brain deficit, making it incumbent on young persons to take responsibility for their actions.

In their differing narratives, Luke's emphasis on a moral subjectivity rooted in biographical experience is in tension with his mother's emphasis on a technoscientific account of the problem. Her approach exhibits the cultural proclivity for defining reality in a literal sense of what is visible and what can be believed as authoritative proof, in this case a brain scan. It also exhibits a tendency to downplay the significance of parental and other kin effects on children in an apparent effort to evade implications of culpability. In light of the pervasiveness of violence, abuse, loss, and abandonment, it is striking how biomedical diagnosis but not biographical experience holds such a prominent place in parental thinking. The perhaps ironic moral appeal of diagnosis is that it is determined without regard to moral matters, which occupy no proper place in the scientific task of nosology. Indeed, central to nearly all DSM-based psychiatric diagnoses is the emphasis on descriptive categories without causal inference.

The diagnosis of PTSD is thornier in the case of adolescents when the *events* that are thought to be direct precipitants are emergent from *conditions* in the familial household such as parental presence or absence, action or inaction, that do not directly qualify as traumatic in themselves. Given this, it is hardly surprising that parental narrative self-positioning in relation to the events and conditions of trauma is particularly morally fraught. Over the past century there has been a nearly riotous cultural battle over the blaming of parents for psychosis and nearly all mental illnesses. In the United States and elsewhere, there has been a radical cultural shift away from etiological models of

232 | Violence, Trauma, and Depression

psychopathology based on inadequate parenting (usually maternal) toward scientific brain-based accounts. As we have seen in earlier chapters, the cultural saturation and appeal of the biological brain-based model is patently evident. And while conflict over the role of personal and interpersonal factors versus biological factors is considerable across a variety of mental illnesses, in the case of psychic trauma among adolescents in poor families with intergenerational legacies of structural violence this conflict may be heightened. Moral discourse interpreted as distant, irrelevant, or threatening gives way to a reductionist discourse of biology and brain scans, in the process excluding the discourse of genuine therapy. What is missing is what Parish (2014: 32) has identified as central for the theorizing of moral realms to incorporate "the ways people connect, clash, and experience each other as this is worked out in the 'space between' persons" that can create or negate intersubjective possibilities for persons "being with" or "being together."

In the case of Luke, parental desire to minimize or erase biographical experience was remarkably salient during a set of six-month follow-up ethnographic interviews. During the interim Luke had had another explosive episode in which, according to his mother, he threatened to kill both her and himself. His mother called the police, and he was readmitted for a three-week hospitalization followed by placement in treatment foster care for a six-month period. These arrangements were presented to Luke as an alternative to going to jail. He was prescribed a particularly high dose of Seroquel, 700 milligrams. His speech had a drawl, likely a medication effect. Given the intensity of her earlier emphasis on investigating Luke's problem by means of a brain scan to get to the root of things, her narrative focus shifted decidedly to a position that, trauma or not, Luke needed to "move on" and "get past" what had happened. For his part, Luke was reflective about trying to manage his anger but still convinced that his stepfather's violation was the source of his and his family's troubles, that he simply could not "let it go" and indeed that to do so would be a problem. In his words, "I don't want to let go of this thing" because "that day may come when I need it, and if I don't have it then, I'll have to revert it, something that I don't like to do. Use weapons. Because I don't like using weapons in fights." Luke was fully aware that he retained his anger not only as a defensive strategy to keep him vigilant but also as the fuel for his wish for violent retribution of which he was now physically capable as an older, stronger young man.

## *Alisa: "I had to grow up early"*

Alisa, of mixed Hispano and Mexican heritage, was seventeen when we met. She had scarcely managed to sustain her life in the face of economic hardship and parents who were overwhelmed by histories of addiction and deprivation (see Garcia 2010). Suffering numerous insults to the integrity of her development, she struggled with the pain and confusion of a shattered psyche and limited resources for the crafting of a satisfying life. She had been hospitalized eight times since the age of thirteen. Alisa was open about the relentless buffeting of her identity and evolution as a child with multiple father figures and violation by several unsavory ones. Still, the most profound insult to her, renunciation by her father, loomed largest.

In our initial interview, Alisa attested emphatically that she had been devastated to receive a letter from her father, then serving in the military in Iraq, informing her that he was not her biological father and had decided to disown her. After his return to the Albuquerque area, she attempted to contact him by telephone to no avail. She felt that his refusal to take her call was the last straw, reporting that she "freaked out" and began to cry, feeling abandoned. This experience was the immediate precursor to the hospitalization during which we first met her. She had been given several clinical diagnoses over the years, but the central and enduring one was PTSD. The acuity of the loss of her relationship to this father figure unfolded in the context of a history of having suffered multiple instances of sexual molestation by her mother's boyfriends or partners. The first she recalled had occurred at age eleven, when she was sleeping in the same bed with her mother and her partner at the time while her mother was either asleep or drunk. Adding to the horror of that assault was her family's response to the event; she felt "blamed and unsupported," with her mother and other relatives trying to minimize what had occurred. It was immediately after this event that she began self-cutting on the advice of a friend who had been raped by her father. This became a regular habit in the wake of a subsequent sexual assault as a young teenager by a boy she had "trusted, [and] he took advantage of me." By the time of her father's rejection, her narrative drew the connection all too clearly and literally: "He cut me out of his life." She resumed her habit of self-cutting not only to take away the pain but also in a desperate attempt to draw him back into her life. She pined for some resolution.

Our research psychiatrist thought perhaps this played into a need for a particular connection with her boyfriend and the trouble that led to their breakup. Shortly after turning seventeen, she gave birth to Adan, a healthy baby boy. Yuma, a member of the Isleta Pueblo tribe and her boyfriend of two years, was an active father in the months immediately following the birth. The couple seemed quite pleased with their creation. However, when Alisa confessed that she had a friendship with another boy, Yuma became enraged and broke off the relationship. In response, she swallowed a bottle of the antipsychotic medication Seroquel and at age seventeen was hospitalized, again. Just as she intended the cutting as a means of bringing back her father, she admitted that the overdose was intended to get her boyfriend to return.

According to DSM criteria derived from our KID-SCID interview, Alisa's current diagnoses were enduring PTSD and depressive disorder with psychotic features. The latter diagnosis pertained to a condition that developed postpartum. While breastfeeding she experienced sexual stimulation that, while not uncommon among nursing mothers, terrified her. It brought back her own experience of prior sexual molestation. She developed hostile thoughts about the baby and was plagued by fears she might harm him. Although she stopped breastfeeding "cold turkey," she felt she withdrew but never did actually hurt the baby. Past clinical diagnoses included alcohol abuse and cannabis dependence, an eating disorder, and PTSD. Unlike Luke, Alisa did not easily accept the diagnosis of PTSD, and coming on top of her other diagnoses she experienced it as confusing and having been "thrown" at her.

> I had some weird ones [diagnoses]. I've always been depressed. And then, all of a sudden, they pulled PTSD out of the air . . . I don't know what that is. I don't think I have PTSD . . . I kinda live in the past a little bit, but I don't think all of a sudden I just start having like flashbacks or anything, I, um, was still feeling uncomfortable about things that had happened to me. I was talking about them a lot and writing about them. It's because when I was eleven, I got molested by my mom's boyfriend. So, um, that's when they, they, like, threw the PTSD at me.

By our follow-up with her the next year, Alisa had also received the clinical diagnosis "psychosis." This she experienced with both relief and shame. She felt relief in that the diagnosis made sense to her since she had had frightening hallucinatory experiences. She felt shame particularly in relation to her two older sisters who alternately doubted or derided the diagnosis. Their responses were laden with social stigma as they mocked their sister: was she going to be like the infamous Andrea

Yates from Texas who drowned her children in the bathtub? She was also offended by her sisters' antipsychiatry discourse about how she did not need a pill every day. Through her own disturbing experience of having gone off medications she knew better, and she now took them regularly with conviction.

Her mother, Ramona, a large and rough-hewn woman of Hispanic heritage, had a difficult life growing up in a family of eight where beatings were routine. Her small home was provided through a housing subsidy. She had a history of alcohol and drug abuse for which she was placed in court-mandated rehabilitation programs using the treatment model from Alcoholics Anonymous. She reported that she was raped as a child and that her family did not care about her. She saw this lack of care and protection as an intergenerational repetitive cycle: "I look at cycles and the way I see cycles is you keep doing it, it keeps repeating itself and repeating itself through the generations and I want it to stop . . . I've seen cycles my whole life . . . because that's what I saw my mother do."

In the wake of the accident involving drunk driving that seriously injured Alisa, the judge mandated a residential rehabilitation program for Ramona. She was allowed only supervised visits with Alisa for a period of several months. During that time, Alisa lived with her uncle and then her elder sister. Ramona successfully completed the rehabilitation program, but she could not maintain her sobriety. One event about which she was "horrified" led her back to the bottle. Her brother, the uncle with whom Alisa had stayed for a period while she was in rehab, killed himself. Ramona was so devastated she said she didn't care about anything or anyone, including herself, and she gradually declined back into alcoholism. She said, "[Alisa] saw that. I know she did." When asked how Alisa's hospitalization came about, she cited two reasons that together dealt brutal blows: Alisa's stepfather's rejection and Ramona's own return to serious alcohol abuse.

Her mother's serious problem with alcohol was a lifelong source of torment for Alisa. At around five, she suffered a major injury in a car accident when her mother was driving while intoxicated. Alisa's right arm was very nearly severed. A very pretty young girl with long dark hair and striking brown eyes, she was also notable not only for being overweight but also for the long, deep scars that ran the length of her arm. Dealing with her mother's alcoholism from an early age, she says she had to "grow up early" and be "the adult" from the age of six. Being the adult involved making sure at times that her heavily intoxicated mother was still breathing and being exposed to what she describes as her mother's "bringing different men in the house, being very promiscuous in front of me." With sadness she related that she knew all about sex from the age of four and had nightmares about her mother being brutalized by the men she brought home.

Alisa's intelligence and sensitivity shone through in her narrations, and her attention to others was all the more remarkable given the intensity of her own distress. For example, on a trip to Arizona to collect insurance money related to the car accident, she managed to track down a grown son of her adoptive father who reported that he, too, had been abandoned. This elicited empathy as she wondered how bad it was for him, and she imagined that given his grief as a biological son it could have been relatively worse for him than for her. Given the need to become "the adult" at age six, as Alisa said, it is to her credit that she appeared as a precocious, contemplative, and empathetic person. Two years after we met her, she had moved out of her mother's house, having in fact been expelled, and was living in a small, messy, and dirty apartment with her new boyfriend and two-year-old son. Even though she was wracked by anxiety, she managed to earn a GED. She was in the process of enrolling in courses at the local community college, interested in the possibility of becoming a counselor.

POST-PTSD?

Luke met the lack of social protection with the creation of a self-system in which anger was readily and reliably available. His anger protected him even if his mother and her various boyfriends could not. The emotional response to violent life-threatening events under conditions of the *absence* of social protection was anger at the most visible level. More tender emotions of fear and trembling, and even grief over how alone in the world he is when it comes to his own protection, are camouflaged by barefaced and dramatic displays of anger. Yet Luke has done far more than to devise an elaborate self-system of anger that is at once protective and destructive. His interests in astronomy and other sciences, along with interest in having a girlfriend, helped to protect an estimable if fraught capacity for development, resilience, and even idealism. That he had crafted these under conditions of psychic trauma and adversity is extraordinary.

Alisa's life was no less poignant with respect to breakdown in the provision of protection as the ground for sustained and repetitive events that for her have created deep and enduring psychic trauma. In addition to the serious injuries sustained in the car crash that left her at a young age with indelible marks of precarity, she could not rely on a familial safety net in the face of unrelenting familial crises and residential moves. Her recourse to self-cutting was thus an acknowledgment of the enduringness of this precarity. Alisa's problem was not anger, as with Luke, but being lost in an arid world of misery and misjudgment. Navigating a parched and unreliable social landscape, she had still managed to muster personal resources without succumbing to an otherwise arguably warranted resentment. She lived a mix of sadness and loss that she could not save her relationship with her mother without surrendering her sanity. She had her child and herself to care for, and this constituted her self-created system of self-protection.

Comparing the two young people, several variations on the experience of abandonment are in evidence. A stepfather who for years he thought loved him like a "real father" betrayed Luke, while a father Alisa had been misled to think of as her biological father disowned her. The long night work hours of Luke's mother made her unavailable and oblivious to abuse, while the alcoholism of Alisa's mother rendered her even less available. There is a perhaps stereotypical gender difference in the way Luke engaged his circumstances with anger directed outward in a mode combining self-protection and vengeance, while Alisa did so by means of self-harm turned inward, reflecting age-inappropriate responsibility and vulnerability. Yet both have implicitly strategic elements in their response: Luke's anger serves as a tool to keep him vigilant and forestall him from having to resort to weapons; Alisa used self-cutting and attempted suicide as means to draw her boyfriend and stepfather back to her. There is also a contrast in apparent outcome, perhaps independent of gender as a factor but more related to the three-year age difference, with Alisa seeming ultimately more successful in beginning a transition to maturity and adulthood.

What also comes into play for both youths is in part the ability to envision having a life and hope for the future, and I want to pass once more through the experience of these two with an eye to their own sensibilities in transcending the developmental challenge of trauma. This is important for understanding their experience but also more broadly insofar as discussions of PTSD in general tend to focus little on the possibilities for and subjective conditions of healing.

Luke made two clear statements in this regard, the first directed toward trauma as constraint and the second indicating a vision of the future.

My mom thinks I'm not letting it go. Personally, I'm trying to, but it's kinda more harder than she seems, I know something has happened to her in the past. I don't want to say. But for me, it's different because my sisters were molested, and I was abused. You can't really compare the two. Mine was worse in the abuse, but it hurt their mind. So it hurt me, like, way worse. They didn't get none of that physical trauma that I had. But they have high mental hurt from him. They're not retarded. It just hurt them—they don't like boys. My sister doesn't like boys. She doesn't want to have a boyfriend.

I want to be an archaeologist. Either that or a NASA scientist. And with the scientist, there's a bunch of goals that I want to accomplish in the scientist part . . . I want to create drugs that slow down the aging process, a cure for cancer. . . . Well, first I have to go to college. I have to get my doctorate in science before I do that. And archaeology I have to get, like, math, science, and history.

Luke's mother was optimistic about his future, albeit in a gruff way that expresses her attitude that he needs to "move on."

I think once he basically gets his crap together, he can function like a normal human being. And what I mean by normal is a person without trauma, not normal. Because nobody's *normal,* normal. You know, when my kids do normal things, they throw me for a loop because I'm so used to trauma that when they do something normal I'm like, "Is this okay?" And the therapists are going, "This is normal." I say, "You don't understand. We don't do normal. I don't know normal." So yeah, he's, you know, he has a lot of things that he wants to do. If he did not have those dreams, I would say, yeah, we're in deep trouble.

Alisa was explicit about her future both in its continuity with and mastery of her experience.

Well, after I get my GED I really, really wanna go to school. I am kinda unsure what I want to major in, though, like, I kinda wanna be a counselor or a therapist for teenagers, like how all the things that I have been through. Or, I wanna be a nurse. Something that is helping people.

Her mother expressed optimism but in a different key from Luke's mother.

What do I see? I see her tripping and falling along the way. But I see her getting back up. I don't see her staying on the ground. I see her getting back and saying, "Okay, I messed up, how do I fix this? How can I make this better?" 'Cause she's not dumb. That little girl is *not* dumb. . . . What I would like to see is for her to go back to school . . . and make her life better for her and her son. For her son, mostly.

Again perhaps in a gendered way, for Luke the goal of transcending trauma was expressed not only in a letting go but also in a turning outward toward the creativity of science, toward discovering fossils or a cure for cancer. For Alisa the goal was expressed by internalizing the therapeutic ideal that she recognized as a prime source of her ability to transcend the pain. Their mothers' future orientation likewise contrasted along the lines of Luke's mother's emphasis on getting himself together (responsibility) and Alisa's mother's image of tripping and getting up (resilience).

## PATTERNS OF PRECARIOUSNESS: TRAUMA AND SOCIAL DANGER

The diagnostic conceptualization of PTSD recognizes that it is often not attributable to a single event but rather constitutes a response to recurrent threats to bodily and psychic integrity. Analysis of the foregoing cases, in accord with others diagnosed with PTSD based on research criteria, reveals a pattern with respect to the conditions in which these youths find themselves, a pattern of precarious conditions that lay the grounds for the occurrence of traumatic events.[16] Identification of such a pattern of instability constitutes a parallel if wider-ranging diagnosis of social, psychological, cultural processes in political and historical context. The interviews provide experience-near accounts of conditions of existence made perilous by abandonment and circumscribed protection by kin. In identifying the problem within the proximal space of the family, such relations must be configured within a broader framework of intergenerational and regional legacy.

Many of the parents in this group have themselves had chaotic childhoods ravaged by poverty, drug and gang violence, and neglect or maltreatment. This sequence can be traced further to the tangled colonial history of New Mexico. At its best this history is expressed as pride in identity and diversity, but at its bleakest it is a story of painful coexistence of the oppressed indigenous, the conquered conquistador, and the impoverished pioneer. An elaborated history of some five centuries of conflict among Native American, Spanish, Euro-American, and Mexican populations is beyond the scope of this chapter; however, the set of connections are critical to take into account in order to theorize the precarious conditions that transcend individual or familial households. The historical context of political and cultural instability in the region is manifest in families and communities as the collective casualty of centuries of colonial conflict. Contemporary warring within families and communities tragically reproduces and carries on the violence of the broader theater. It is noteworthy that in addition to ethnographies of indigenous communities, a body of literature exists focused on the Hispano/Hispanic culture of northern New Mexico (Sanchez 1967; Briggs 1987; Kutsche and Van Ness 1988; Trujillo 2009; Garcia 2010). The most recent of these works pay significant attention to the scourge of drug use and impoverishment in this region. However, our research experience is that such conditions are by no means limited to the north of the state, nor are they limited to Hispanics. A work on Albuquerque by an anthropologically trained journalist describes it as a wonderfully diverse place "at the end of the world" with an exotic name akin to Timbuktu, Keet Seel, or Katmandu (Price 2003). The author worries about the city's development potential and water quality but makes virtually no mention of health, poverty, or drugs, and gives no hint that an entire area of the city is labeled the "war zone" because of its endemic gang violence. The view is one that might be expected from any middle-class high school teacher or car wash proprietor, with little sense of the endemic social danger evident from the ethnographic standpoint.

Such are conditions for social inattention and abdication of moral obligation to provide protection and care. The absence of protection may occur in relation to instability of residence and partner, severe drug and alcohol abuse, and emotional volatility. Taken together, these conditions make possible the many forms of violation and neglect of children. Individual agency and responsibility in the ethics of care under such conditions are hazy at best, and the children in this study demonstrated considerable confusion about security, attachment, and who if anyone was morally accountable for such a precarious existence. To be sure, some blamed their parents, whereas others notably did not and indeed struggled to hold tight to a vision of their parents as caring and having done the best they could given their own typically traumatic lives. Yet the recurrent breakdown of human relations fractures the psyches of those whose dignity is violated, both in the sense of the integrity of the body and its boundaries and in the sense of having a place of habitation—a home—for the body. The rupture involved is so disorganizing that symptoms of PTSD develop not only as sequelae of such patterned conditions (consistent chaos) but also in tandem with features of psychosis.

## DYNAMIC PHENOMENOLOGY: THE INEXTRICABILITY OF CULTURE, PSYCHE, AND SOCIAL WORLD

In sum, common elements in the lifeworlds of these teens appeared as alternating modes of attention that I have been thinking about in terms of "dynamic phenomenology." What I have in mind in invoking the idea of dynamic phenomenology may be familiar territory for psychotherapists working from an analytic or psychodynamic perspective; however, for me as a psychological anthropologist this comes to mind as a way of thinking about what I interpret as the intricate crafting of psychological and social processes for self-protection under extraordinarily adverse conditions. Under such conditions, evidence for "resilience" or explicit indicators of "hope" is not widely visible. Like persons with conditions of schizophrenia who have been mistakenly accused of not having "affect," or being "flat" (Jenkins 2004; Kring and Germans 2004), these adolescents may possibly disguise or transform their subjective experience for their own psychological safety.

Dimensions of what I am calling dynamic phenomenology can, in the case of trauma among these adolescents, be characterized in preliminary fashion in the following ways. First, there is an intricate blending of psychologically strategic "hiding" or social withdrawal, on the one hand, and furious if anxious insistence on attachment and connection, on the other. Second, there are conflicts over the sense of erasure and nonrecognition of self and others that contribute to a sense of objectified invisibility. Third, and by far most striking to me in this study as well as others on trauma (Jenkins 1991b, 1996b; Jenkins and Valiente 1994; Jenkins and Hollifield 2008), is the profound bodily and psychic vertigo that is commonly experienced as one's sense of reality being ruptured (often recurrently) by traumatic events of penetrating assault, betrayal, and shock. In the immediate aftermath and subsequently as a distant kind of ghostly refrain, there is a sense (and often the actual words) that "I just can't believe . . . I just can't . . . imagine . . . I never thought . . . it's not real." Reality is defined by the profound sense of unreality in the realm of what is (un)imaginable. Thus this third dimension, deeply affecting and at times totalizing, is the unbelievability, the unreality, the simultaneity of utter doubt and certainty surrounding what really did or possibly could have happened that marks the shady boundaries of what is felt and not-felt as reality. In sum, the phenomenological sense of being-in-the-world that deep bodily and psychic trauma can wield can be summarized precisely as the *unfathomability* of an enduring lived reality.

The array of anguish for which the diagnosis of posttraumatic stress disorder might be applied is vast (Jenkins 1996a; Breslau 2004; Gross 2004; Henry 2006; Kienzler 2008; James 2010; Varma 2012). The question remains whether the category is at one and the same time too broad to be of therapeutic value and too narrow for descriptive purposes, and reasonable arguments can be mounted for both sides of this epistemological quandary. In an account of the range of the institutional genealogy, situational application, and geographic circulation of the term, Fassin and Rechtman (2009) offer a historical analysis of trauma as a discursive "empire" instituted through uncontested claims of the validity and moral value of PTSD, with particular attention to France. Elsewhere, logic of care that defines PTSD as meriting sympathy, treatment, and compensation can be less straightforward and even overtly contested. For instance, the legitimacy of PTSD and access to health care services for men and especially for women has been much disputed by the U.S. Department of Veterans Affairs, with the implication that claimants are trying to manipulate the system of benefits to their advantage (Young 1997; Hoge, Auchterlonie, and Milliken 2006; Hamilton, Poza, and Washington 2011). On the other hand, adolescents in particular are not trying to "get stuff" (i.e., services, statuses, diagnoses). The diagnosis may in fact be experienced as an imposition, as was the case when Alisa said that mental health professionals "threw the PTSD at me," implying a degree of arbitrariness and aggression on the part of mental health professionals. In such an instance, PTSD is neither a descriptive nor a clinical category but a rhetorical token in the performative arena of the polemic and strategic rather than of the diagnostic and therapeutic.

I am less concerned with the ontological, historical, or political status of PTSD and more interested in the lives of adolescents struggling with the raw existence of trauma. The anthropological paradigm of embodiment has made clear the inseparability of soma and psyche (Csordas 1994), and in this case it is abundantly clear that psychic trauma engulfs both, no less than a physical trauma would have profound psychic consequences. Serious injury has occurred either way, whether intended, uncontrolled, or accidental. In both cases it is ultimately a failed project to conceive either psychological or physical trauma as "more" or "less" of the body or mind. An obvious example is sexual abuse, inarguably an instance of both physical and psychological trauma. While it is my methodological position to grant the epistemic value of PTSD as a construct for the organization and comparison of symptoms of psychic trauma,[17] a terminological choice remains as the terms *PTSD* and *trauma* are frequently used interchangeably. Although the above analysis is drawn from cases that met research diagnostic criteria for PTSD, my preference for the broader term *trauma* is based on two cultural and existential factors that define the distinctive forms of this social and psychological experience.

The first is the structure of the experience of psychic trauma as circumscribing one's very being-in-the-world. I use this phenomenological phrase because it focuses our attention on the immediacy of raw existence rather than the objectification of experience implicit in the language of symptoms. In my conceptualization, under enduring and inescapable conditions of psychic trauma, habitual self-processes of protection may occur through *absorption* or *dissociation*. Absorption occurs as preoccupation and dissociation as disconnection and detachment of self and traumatic world. Whether through absorption or dissociation (or both), the taking up of the trauma into psychic structure can provide enshrinement of the traumatic event or respite from its ravages. Drawing on the case of warfare, Kardiner (1941) conceived of such defensive moves as an individual's inability to adapt to the aftermath of the trauma. In chapter 4 this dual possibility was evident in the description by some Salvadoran women refugees of their experience as extreme and by others as mundane. Precariousness is a common denominator for civilians and combatants alike, even the most heavily armored soldiers in contemporary theaters of war (MacLeish 2012). Yet while adaptation following exposure to warfare is notoriously intricate, we know far less about the process of defense and adaptation of children who are repetitively exposed to traumatic events as the everyday condition of their lives often without ever having a baseline sense of security to serve as existential point of reference. The critical observation is that absorption and dissociation—whether in the form of anger as with Luke or self-harm as with Alisa, whether in the form of construing experience as extreme or mundane as with the Salvadoran immigrants, and insofar as they are imbricated in the unfathomability I identified above—are part of the fabric of the lifeworld and not merely a matter of symptomatology. In the present case, the lived experience of these adolescents can be characterized as "essentially unstable."

The second is the question of cultural validity. The constellation of symptoms that make up the clinical category of PTSD can certainly vary in relation to culture and gender. For instance, in my work with Salvadoran women refugees discussed in chapters 4 and 5, participants did not meet DSM-IV criteria for PTSD because there was an absence of efforts to avoid remembering traumatic events. The particular quality of their suffering from the aftereffects of political violence means either that PTSD must be configured differently by sociocultural context or that as set forth in DSM it does not fully apply (Lansen 1992; Jenkins 1996a; Patel 2000). Comparing the Salvadoran situation to that examined in New Mexico, regardless of whether research could document similar symptoms, neurobiological changes, or medication response, the conditions and events of trauma are radically different across the two settings. To take the broadest dimensions, whereas in the Salvadoran situation domestic violence of men against women or children was often accepted or even positively sanctioned, in New Mexico it was negatively sanctioned as action that its perpetrators should not be permitted to get away with even though it is structurally endemic. Again, public violence existed in both situations, but whereas in the Salvadoran situation it was the violence of civil war and death squads, in New Mexico it was the violence of gangs in places like the "war zone" in Albuquerque. Attending to such difference is essential both to interpretive understanding and to effective therapy.

Not included in the DSM criteria but crucial to understanding is the cultural meaning of the injury as within or beyond the bounds of human making. When injury is perpetrated by interpersonal violence, there may be a personal degradation of the psychological and moral moorings of trust, security, and safety. When perpetrated by intimates within households and neighborhoods, the affront goes to the core of psychological conditions for social relations ruptured by betrayal. Betrayal leading to the rupture of trust is reported by some survivors of violence (and those of torture) as the "worst" of all that has occurred (Hollifield et al. 2005, 2006).[18] The social and psychological specification of stressor events is key to analysis of the cultural meaning of psychic trauma.[19] Likewise, observations of the cultural particularity of response to traumatic events provide empirical evidence for the inextricability of culture, psyche, and social world (Shweder 1990).

## CONCLUDING REMARKS

In this chapter I have stressed the reciprocal shaping of (1) subjective experience and social institutions and (2) conditions and events of trauma. Note that in the first instance the conceptual contrast is not between the individual and institutional construed in terms of the distinction between micro- and macrolevels of analysis but between experiential and institutional understood in terms of the relation between subjectivity and structure. When understood as separate levels of analysis, experience and institution both appear abstract and without substance, whereas in actuality they are vitally intertwined in the fabric and the "rhythm of life" (Jenkins 1997). The institutional encompasses the relatively impersonal aspects of state government (including schools and prisons), the managed health care industry, the treatment system (inpatient and outpatient), and the colonial legacy that has resulted in a particular mix of European, Hispano, and indigenous groups coexisting in a milieu of endemic poverty. The experiential refers to the relatively immediate flow of life as young people navigate through the contingencies of family (supportive or destructive), self (coming to have a life), gender (identity and sexuality), education (performance and aspiration), and therapeutic process (psychotherapy and medication). My insistence that they are intertwined rather than separable levels of analysis means that our interpretation must include the experience of engagement with institutions and the institutional constraints on experience; encounters with the treatment system are experienced, and the therapeutic process is institutionally inflected. Even the brief consideration of possibilities in this chapter suggests that such an understanding at both the personal and the collective level is required to apprehend the depth and durability of the problem, and compels us toward a philosophical anthropology and a historical psychology.

Such an approach is necessary not least because the pain of significant changes in public mental health policies contribute to the palpable insecurity of young persons and their families. Over the five-year course of the present study, a strained system became only more so. With Value Options in control of service delivery, we saw residential and outpatient treatment facilities closed across the state and the radical contraction of units, services, and clinical staff, including the best public facility in the state. In the face of dwindling or unavailable mental health services for this population, the human toll can be described as the consequence of "structural violence" perpetrated semianonymously on entire populations or segments of populations (Farmer 2004a). Fassin (2004) has described the identification in France since the mid-1990s of a domain of suffering understood to exist between the social and the individual, constituting "a problem of mental health, even if not a problem of disease" (29) and having to do with "disorders that do not strictly speaking depend on pathology" (32). I would posit that a similar domain of suffering subtends the institutional and experiential aspects of the New Mexican situation that I have examined. In a 1995 administrative report that proved to be a powerful engine of mental health policy in France, "suffering produced by the social situation appeared as the problem, and speech, and by extension listening, as the best adapted solution" (Fassin 2004: 29). The report led to the development of new therapeutic institutions named "places of listening" that belong neither to the domain of social action nor to that of traditional psychiatry. The question remains whether we must create new institutional arrangements in places like New Mexico that can address themselves to the level of raw existence and often-inchoate subjectivity opened up in such analyses or whether current arrangements can be enhanced in their sensitivity to this level of experience.

With respect to the second relation, there is an identifiable pattern of *conditions* of abandonment and neglect that make possible the *events* of trauma. In a process of reproduction where few are left unscathed, cultural patterns of indifference are laid bare as the (il)logic of systematic violation of the psychic dignity and bodily integrity of children. The danger is doubly so for girls. As a matter of oppression, it comes as no surprise that the systematicity of such arrangements is common among the economically and socially disenfranchised. Given the persistence of these conditions, traumatic violation is often routine and repetitive in the lived experience of the young. Resources that could counter such maltreatment within the health care and educational sectors are often either unavailable or inadequate to the task of transforming adverse conditions and events. This can result not only in the breakdown of meaning, but in what Clifford Geertz (1973: 100) referred to explicitly as chaos when he asserted that "bafflement, suffering, and a sense of intractable ethical paradox are all, if they become intense enough or are sustained long enough, radical challenges to the proposition that life is comprehensible and that we can, by taking thought, orient ourselves effectively within it." For children and adolescents, the breaking point brought on by the *incomprehensibility* and unfathomability can threaten their very existence. In this respect it is precisely analysis of the reciprocal relation of conditions and events of trauma that allows us to ask how they are configured either to foreclose the horizons of possibility for youths or to allow them ultimately to have a life in the sense of an existentially grounded and "life-affirming" moral sensibility as described by Nietzsche (1967a).

While ethnopsychological, cultural, and social accounts of traumatic conditions and events are crucial, they are insufficient if they fail to incorporate an understanding of the intergenerational, collective reach of trauma. Here I do not wish to engage the debate about the existence of an intergenerational trauma understood on the model of inheritance of acquired characteristics (Duran and Duran 1995; Kirmayer, Gone, and Moses 2014). The notion of a collective reach of trauma that I have in mind has to do with persistent conditions of essential instability and palpable insecurity—precariousness—conducive to recurrent traumatic events. It is rooted in an appraisal of interrelated social-psychological processes and conditions of adversity: (1) the mental health effects of structural violence (Farmer 2004a, 2004b; Quesada et al. 2011); (2) a political ethos that produces insecurity and the conditions of possibility for recurrent damaging events (Jenkins 1991b; Lovell 2012; Jenkins and Hass 2015); (3) the reproduction and transmission of warfare and political violence as domestic abuse within family settings (Martín-Baró 1988, 1990); and (4) intergenerational inheritance or traditions of loss and longing in a context of ache and disconnection (Garcia 2010). These interwoven processes twist the experiential field of families and individuals to form enduring social-psychic webs of subjugation counteracted by unambiguous ferocity for survival and a being-in-the-world that alternates between agitated and enervated.

# Conclusion

*Fruits of the Extraordinary*

Throughout this book I have emphasized how the extraordinary conditions of mental illness engage fundamental human processes in a situation of existential precariousness, arguing that the experience of mental illness is better characterized in terms of struggle than symptoms and that culture is integral to all aspects of mental illness. This is above all for the sake of understanding and more productively responding to the suffering of those living with mental illness. It is also for the sake of an intellectual agenda in which anthropology does not remain incomplete by turning a blind eye to the world of mental illness and in which psychiatry and anthropology in effect complete one another as complementary approaches to psychic suffering. It is well worth repeating in this respect that anthropology neglects the extraordinary to its theoretical and empirical peril and biomedicine and psychiatry neglect culture to its theoretical and clinical peril. In closing I want to reinforce this emphasis by further tying these themes together across the diverse settings I have described.

In the first place, the extraordinary conditions encountered in each chapter vary not just in terms of the illness and its symptomatic effects. In chapter 1 the extraordinary is constituted by a cultural chemistry the active ingredients of which are conditions diagnosed as schizophrenia, self-processes, and the experience of medication. The persons encountered in the Clozapine clinic had suffered for years under the definition of being "treatment refractory," or nonresponsive to conventional psychopharmaceutical medication. They inhabited an extraordinary moment in which a new class of drugs had been introduced that have significant consequences for fundamental processes of self and identity. In a circumstance where some clinicians questioned whether their patients had a psychological life at all, people I talked with reported distinct before and after experiences, and occasionally claimed the drug "saved" their lives while at the same time acknowledging negative medication effects. They articulated different aspects of their experience, including symptoms, drugs, and change. They talked about medication in terms of both what it does and how it feels in everyday life—the extraordinary within the ordinary.

The discourse of medication experience outlines an existential totality weaving together interrelated levels of meaning and orientational processes that define one's self and one's transformed place in the world. Across the narratives created by these persons it was evident that this totality penetrated to the core of being, touching on bodily sensation, toxicity, clarity and velocity of thought, balance, control, discipline, identity, normality, and everyday life. Insofar as the suffering of psychosis is sometimes precariously held in check, the precise character of this totality for each person has profound consequences for existential coherence and a meaningful life. In this process the element of struggle is never far from the surface. People struggle for normality not only with respect to diminished symptoms but in terms of normal behavior, acutely aware of themselves as appearing abnormal and being subject to stigma. There is a struggle for control not only over their lives, but in a subtler sense over "who is in charge, me or the meds?" There is a struggle over the meaning of illness in terms of paradoxes such as recovery without cure, whether it is better to be crazy or fat, whether one can be a sexual being or is destined to asexual existence, being faced with social and developmental problems without adequate therapeutic resources, and being subject to stigma despite improvement.[1]

While certainly there can be "no health without mental health" (Prince, Patel, and Saxema et al. 2007) and psychotropic medication can play a therapeutic part in short- or long-term care, we have seen that the use of these drugs is a complicated matter for persons and their kin whether in Ghana, India, or the United States. These difficulties cannot be brushed aside and indeed must be taken as a significant challenge for the scaling up and implementation of global mental health services as currently proposed (Lancet Global Mental Health Group 2007; Collins et al. 2011; Escobar 2015). Anthropologically, it is clear that cultural and social issues

surrounding psychotropic drugs will require careful ethnographic attention and clinical engagement. There is a crucial need for culturally competent provision of information regarding drug effects (desired and unde-
sired) along with engaged listening to the satisfactory and dissatisfactory
aspects of their use. These engagements must include dialogue about the
desire for cure, social stigma, and therapeutic strategies beyond psychotropic drugs. Besides drugs, there are local and international collectives
working to help to interpret the meaning of extraordinary modes of experience and to develop strategies for living with these.

Thus the problem of "scaling up" mental health services worldwide
might not be (as some critics have charged) so much a problem of appli-
cability of psychiatric diagnostic categories or uneven results with
respect to treatment as a failure of proponents and critics alike to zoom
in on illness and treatment experience for the afflicted and their kin. To
be precise, experience-near perspectives must inform interventions to
take into account the numerous *quandaries* involved in understanding
the cultural, social, and biological effects of psychotropic drugs. In the
face of this situation, I am convinced of our continued need to reassert
the importance of research at the juncture of anthropology, psychiatry,
psychology, and allied fields. Ultimately, any true scaling up of mental
health worldwide will require economic resources to counteract poverty
and social disadvantage. That formidable fact cannot be taken ethically
as so daunting as to justify failure to improve care now in all ways possible. Mental health care that involves psychotropic drugs must be followed ethnographically to determine the cultural, social, and political
processes that accompany its use.

The cultural milieu and cultural meanings of illness are thoroughly
implicated in this scenario. Science holds overarching symbolic value as
the potential source of "miracle drugs" that address "chemical imbalance" and produce "awakenings." Cultural expectations about the
course of the illness change over time, with improvement if not recovery
coming to be recognized as a viable possibility. The meanings of drugs
to those who take them are highly consequential, including how they
work and what they're for as well as the actuality of incremental effects
in contrast to the expectation of dramatic effects. Ethnic differences
such as those I discuss between Euro- and African Americans come into
play with respect to attitudes to medical knowledge, expectations about
privacy, and whether illness is foregrounded among other features of
everyday life. The meaning of drugs can extend into a kind of social
relationship with them involving attachment or personification such

that the drug can seem to be a knowing presence, an arbiter of reality, a source of power and agency, and even the surrogate for a human therapist. Religious meanings can intervene not only with assimilation of medication to ideas about hexes, magic, or demonic influence but also insofar as people might pray that they will have sufficient medication or that the drugs will work better through divine intervention. Such meanings, finally, are always subject to the curious cultural practice of distinguishing main effects from side effects.

If in the first chapter we were able to construct a collective existential totality across a group of similarly afflicted persons, the case study of Sebastián presented an existential totality for a single human being. Here the encounter of psychopathology and fundamental human processes, including self, emotion, subjectivity, and identity, is vividly immediate; Jaspers's reference to psychoses as the unresolved problem of human life as such has to do with why they exist and not with any presumed experiential opacity. From the classic case of Judge Schreber to the contemporary madness memoir, and in this case as well, the nature of suffering and existential constriction can be intersubjectively engaged, articulated, observed, and described. What is extraordinary here is not just spectacular symptoms and profound suffering, but how these are played out in an everyday lifeworld with a specific context and temporality. There is poignancy in the gradual onset of sensorial changes that at first were not at all unpleasant for Sebastián but led eventually to a hospitalization, both before and after which he incurred a series of losses that included his job, school, girlfriend, and failed attempt to invent a new kind of engine.

If my claim that the core of pathological experience is better indexed by struggle than by symptoms or even suffering is to be borne out, the case of Sebastián is a critical piece of evidence. Whereas symptoms and suffering can be exacerbated or alleviated, not only can struggle intensify or abate but it can be won or lost as well. Struggle is the sign under which Sebastián tried to carry out his failed project to design an engine, had to stay up all night studying just to earn Cs before finally dropping out of school, and underwent the terrifying side effects of antipsychotic medication. He lived in the midst of the struggle in his family between a harsh father and a doting mother who were divorced but still intimately connected, along with alienation from siblings. He was locked in an internal struggle between his real-life love, Theresa, and the extravagant, impossible fantasy about marrying Carmen. His existential precarity was evident in an increasingly desperate struggle over suicide, yet he persisted in a struggle for normality in that even while his illness advanced he acquired and held a job for four months and enrolled in gymnastics classes. In this context it is important to recognize that the evolution of Sebastián's voices was a temporal process corresponding to the constriction of existential horizons and a crystallization of his increasingly malevolent tormentor as God, though he fluctuated between certainty and confusion about this identity and though from a psychodynamic standpoint his struggle with this God was assimilated to the struggle with his harsh and ambivalent father. It was likewise a process of self and identity in that he could define himself both as "just like everyone else except I hear voices" and "different because I hear those things" and in that his body image and gender stability became disturbed.

Mental illness does not just happen to a person, but is an arena in which the stakes are measured in terms of agency and respect, and which require not only resilience but also incredible endurance. This is connected both to my claim about the centrality of struggle and to my claim that there is no such thing as individual pathology because the sociocultural milieu invariably affects subjectivity. This includes Sebastián's subjection to the fundamentalist Christian substance abuse treatment regime, which could have played as much of a role in the apotheosis of his voices as the internalized presence of his father. It is also discernible in his rule of thumb to not show any sign of anger in the hospital, as well as in his mother's definition of his problem as *nervios,* or nerves. Here we open the theme of the cultural and emotional constitution of this Mexican American family and the specific meanings of a situation in which a harsh father and a solicitous mother argue about "spoiling" their child.

This issue of the importance of culturally constituted emotional atmosphere for the course of schizophrenia is precisely the issue that I have addressed in chapter 3. The extraordinary condition under investigation here subsists in the confluence of the illness, how it is culturally conceived, and the power of family/kin relationships—again the result of a kind of cultural chemistry. Within the family, emotional precarity is related to the cultural definition of self, and the degree to which self is understood and experienced as a bounded entity influences the manner in which fundamental self-processes take place. The research I described that combines ethnography and the paradigm of "expressed emotion" allows a fine-grained understanding of emotional struggle that is sometimes destructive and sometimes heroic in a bewildering, maddening, and insufferable situation within a family that includes an afflicted member. It is also a struggle to make sense of what is happening in which not all parties are necessarily in accord. In this context it is of enormous value to be able to determine the presence within families of expressed emotion components of criticism, emotional overinvolvement, and hostility, on the one hand, and warmth and positive comments, on the other. High negative expressed emotion is an extraordinary condition that, while it cannot be said to cause mental illness, has been robustly shown to facilitate relapse among persons with mental illness worldwide.

Culture is a prominent feature here. Twenty-five years of studies by the World Health Organization determined that the course and outcome of schizophrenia vary across cultures, and this is related to cultural variations in the components of expressed emotion. That this is a matter of fundamental human processes of emotional expression and experience in intimate family settings is underscored by the fact that the interview designed to tap these components was developed among families without mental illness rather than those with an ill member, presupposing the importance of everyday emotion for the course of illness rather than the pathogenic effect of negative affect. The discussion also underscores the importance of considering the illness not as individual pathology but as an interactive process within the family, and furthermore of considering the emotional atmosphere of families as connected to the ethos of the surrounding culture.

This process takes place against the background of cultural differences in patterns of posthospital residence, values such as dignity and respect, the importance of family ties, religious commitment, and attitudes toward suffering and endurance. Understanding criticism in cultural context benefits from identification of what counts as a rule violation subject to censure or chastisement and cast in terms of patterned forms of expression. In my primary example contrasting Mexican Americans and Euro-Americans, the former tended to express criticism as dislike and the latter as anger; the former tended to base a criticism about lack of employment in terms of the economic need for a job, while the latter expressed it in terms of a negative character attribution such as laziness. Emotional overinvolvement might be attributed to a Euro-American family member who visited the hospital daily bringing home-cooked food but was entirely ordinary among Mexican American family members. Intimately intertwined with these processes are cultural conceptions of illness as such, including its nature, cause, course, treatment, moral status of the afflicted, illness-related stigma, and personal responsibility of the ill family member. In the case of the Mexican American and Euro-American comparison, this was evident in the different meanings deployed around the concepts nerves/*nervios* and crazy/*loco*. In the final analysis, ethnographically informed expressed emotion research is a prime exemplar of work defining a common ground for the cultural concerns of anthropology and the clinical concerns of psychiatry and psychology.

The extraordinary conditions faced by the Salvadoran women refugees discussed in chapters 4 and 5 are the product of a remarkably complex cultural chemistry in which subjective experience intersects broader social processes. Its components most prominently include a situation of sustained political violence: traumatic exposure to disappearances, the death of kin, public murder, bombings, detention, torture. Societal chaos was evident in the murders of the Jesuit Ignacio Martín-Baró and Archbishop Oscar Romero, the latter of whom three decades later and under a different papacy was a candidate for beatification on account of his courage. Salvadorans were a frightened population—*una población asustada*—living under a political ethos of terror used as psychological warfare and a state construction of affect in which government propaganda included warnings that adherence to Marxist ideas could cause mental illness. The precarity of *la situación* was exacerbated by extreme economic insecurity and the compounding of political and domestic violence with the rupture in families and the fabric of lives as refugees fled the country to find relative safety living with undocumented status in a hostile host country, all the while concerned for the safety of relatives left behind. For the most part, under these conditions what is at issue is not how the mentally ill are affected by war but how war as an enduring traumatic situation punctuated by discrete traumatic events can have pathogenic mental health consequences for those who might not otherwise be sick.

The extraordinariness of their conditions is no less because the clinical severity of their distress did not reach diagnostic thresholds. The symptoms of affective disorders (depression and dysthymia) and anxiety disorders (PTSD, panic, somatization, and generalized anxiety) are in full accord with the struggle they faced to maintain some sense of existential equilibrium. Narrative representation of traumatic experience as sometimes extreme and sometimes mundane corresponds with clinical observations of the active and numbing phases of PTSD. These two expressive modalities of response to trauma should be considered not so much as contradictory to one another but as simultaneously possible styles of confronting persistent existential contradiction. The need to normalize trauma as mundane appeared as evidence of an over-determination of repression in the sense that it was present both as a political process in the government's violence and as a psychological defense in being able to distance oneself from a horror that was manageable because it was "all the way across the street." Again, this is not necessarily pathological in the strict sense but indicative of a deep struggle for psychic adaptation. The same can be said for those women who exhibited what I called an engaged rather than a withdrawn depression. Recognizing the experiential subtlety between living through persistent situations of terror and discrete events of torture, as well as persistent situations of distress and discrete events of illness, helps us understand how meaning, sense, representation, emotional integrity, humor, resistance, and resilience are enacted as fundamental human processes among these women. An understanding of these processes is crucial since throughout the world women and girls struggle daily against the wearing effects of myriad insults to their psychic integrity.

The struggle of these women was culturally conditioned in noteworthy ways, not least of which was the progressive cultural milieu of metropolitan Boston in the 1980s, when a number of municipalities declared themselves "sanctuary cities" for refugees. Culturally sanctioned male dominance, impunity, and high alcohol consumption were severely tested by an economic role reversal in the United States in which it was often the woman who had steady work and became the family provider. For their part, cultural proscription of emotional expression remained in place despite the stress of social and emotional precarity inherent in flight from *la situación*. The Salvadoran ethnopsychology of emotion includes the dominant category *nervios,* which encompasses mind, body, and spirit and is played out in a strongly kin-based social milieu and with a rich lexicon for emotions of sadness and sorrow. Preoccupation with protection from the malevolence of others, often highly developed involvement with dream life, attention to bodily sensation, and the idea that anger and hostility can be pathogenic are equally relevant features of this ethnopsychology. The manner in which the cultural shaping of distress appears as fundamental human process is vividly evident in the phenomenon of *el calor,* a spontaneous bodily sensation of heat isomorphic with anger and fear. Emerging from the indeterminate flux of bodily existence, *el calor* is thoroughly cultural but unevenly elaborated and only partly objectified, applied sometimes as a literal description of experience and sometimes in the form of simile or metaphor.

The continuation of my discussion of these women in chapter 5 highlights the constitution of their lived experience in terms of multiple overlapping realities and also the specificity of how one of these realities, that of magic and religion, is culturally elaborated. In no instance did it appear that religio-magical ideas or practices were contributing causes to mental illness but rather that these practices played a therapeutic or sense-making role, often in a manner that was quite quotidian. Indeed, magic and religion are best characterized as forms of the extraordinary in the ordinary for these women, posing potential danger but not exacerbating precarity with a sense of constant apprehension. In this respect, echoing a theme from the chapters in part 1, the persons utilizing mental health care were perhaps "just like everyone else, but more so." Nevertheless, the struggles of these women were different from those of the persons such as Sebastián. Mariela's spousal conflicts and postpartum depression had clearly distinguished clinical and spiritual dimensions, with both she and her husband in treatment at the Latino Clinic while struggling with evil spirits released by her mother's error and the spiritual consequences of their culturally incestuous relationship. The *limpieza* performed by a Dominican spiritist helped resolve their disagreement over whether her mother or his mistress was the source of harmful magic. Throughout it all they remained gainfully employed and engaged with everyday life as outpatients, relatives, refugee community members. Despite multiple sources of stress and distress, their struggle was successful in the end.

Understanding the mental health implications of inhabiting the religio-magical world begins with its multicultural complexity as a mélange of Catholicism, *espiritismo, brujería, herbalismo,* New Age, *santería,* and other forms of spirituality. It is no accident that women felt there was more magic in the United States than in El Salvador precisely because so many cultural groups were mixed together in the host country. This hardly means that this domain is experientially disorganized or unanalyzable. It appeared, for example, that while Catholicism was taken for granted in a deep sense, spiritism and witchcraft were more likely subject to the ambivalence of *"No hay que creer ni dejar de creer."* With respect to this ambivalence, we observed not only varying degrees of knowledge and experiential immediacy but also varying degrees of salience and skepticism. Moreover, some women became more involved in such practices after arriving in the United States, while others became less involved; some were no more religiously committed than they had been in El Salvador but came to have more recourse to religio-magical practices after arriving. As the chapter's brief vignettes showed especially clearly, therapy and spiritual practices both addressed illness, though that illness might be defined in slightly different terms.

In the context of religious healing and magical vulnerability, for example, the idea that sadness and suffering are emotions while envy (*envidia*) is an illness is not only an element of an ethnopsychology, but one that has therapeutic implications. In the end magic is both a resource and a domain of reality, not a remote backwater of esoteric belief but integral to the ongoing existential struggle. Filled with haunting uncertainty, yet perhaps more knowable and predictable than the ghastly atmosphere of *la situación,* it may serve to bind together the disparate multiple realities of life as a refugee, less a medium of precarity than a mode of holding precarity at bay.

If there is a singular commonality in the extraordinary conditions of the Salvadoran refugee women and the adolescent psychiatric inpatients I discuss in chapter 6, it is the coexistence of ongoing conditions of trauma with multiple discrete events of trauma. Especially in the adolescent case this often takes the form of abandonment as a condition of vulnerability and abandonment as an event of violation. Even though these youths more often meet the threshold criteria for diagnoses with psychiatric disorders, including PTSD and depression, and often have multiple diagnoses, the more general notion of trauma seems better able than the diagnostic category to capture the cultural chemistry of abandonment as a fundamental human process. The components of this chemistry include the illness, potential foreclosures of adolescent development in the face of trauma, poverty and lack of resources, residential instability, familial fragmentation, drugs, gangs, violent crime, and the social institutions of care under a regime of managed care that engenders revolving door hospitalization, often in a series of different institutions. The result is a kind of precarity I can only describe as "essentially unstable."

The outcome is often a compelling struggle between social withdrawal and an insistence on attachment, evident in the cases of Luke and Alisa. Luke, who had in his young life undergone seven hospitalizations under the diagnoses of ADHS, PTSD, and ODD, stood up to the sexual abuse of his sisters even though he had been beaten and handcuffed to a bed. His struggle included whether to hold on to his anger as a defensive weapon or to let it go in order to move on in his life. Alisa had undergone eight hospitalizations under the diagnoses of PTSD, postpartum depression, and psychosis. She had been subject to sexual assault, abandonment by a wounded alcoholic mother, and being left by her son's father and rejected by her stepfather, and she responded with a struggle inscribed by self-cutting and attempted suicide. Yet if Luke's anger and Alisa's self-cutting are emblematic of struggle against an abandonment that we must recognize as a fundamental human process, his nurturance of the goal to become a scientist and hers to become a therapist affirms that hope is an equally fundamental process, integral to a struggle to arrive in a circumstance in which it is even possible to have a life.

In this instance, the manner in which the experience of mental illness is culturally conditioned is not reducible to invoking differences among Hispanic, Native American, and Euro-American ethnic groups that constitute the population of New Mexico. Insofar as these rough categories are relevant, it is not only with respect to subtle differences in meaning and practice but also with respect to the historical forces that construct them in the image of the conquered conquistador, the oppressed indigenous, and the impoverished pioneer. The cultural dimension of mental illness runs even deeper, to a recognition that the very categories of adolescence and adolescent psychopathology are cultural-historical products. It runs to the patterned manner in which troubled adolescents and their families interact with social institutions in their immediate milieu (kin-based homes, foster homes, hospitals, schools, neighborhoods) and how they are affected by social forces at greater reach (economic recession, ethnic discrimination, health care policies, cross-border drug trafficking, the judicial system). The discourse of diagnosis is itself part of the cultural chemistry insofar as specific diagnostic categories applied to young lives at different points in time operate as rhetorical tokens, often with more polemic and strategic import than explanatory and therapeutic value.

If it is the case that an anthropological study of mental illness is necessarily a study of extraordinary conditions, this is predicated on my understanding that there is a continuum between the extraordinary and the ordinary in human experience and likewise a continuum between normal and abnormal, healthy and pathological. Across cultures, families, social circumstances, individual dispositions, diagnostic categories, symptoms, levels of distress, and moments in time, there is no absolute threshold that separates these as dichotomous categories. Indeed, the threshold that one crosses in beginning to hear voices is not the same threshold that one crosses in being unable to work or maintain social relationships, and it is not the same threshold that defines whether one experiences any of this as suffering. The multiplicity of thresholds and the fact that none of these thresholds necessarily occupies the same place for all people is why I continually return to the theme that, with respect to the extraordinary and the extreme, those with mental illness are just like everyone else—only more so.

In fact if there is any question that is relevant about the extraordinary in relation to fundamental human processes it is whether our stance should be that the extraordinary can teach us about those processes or whether in fact the capacity for the extraordinary—to confront it, to survive it, to seek it out—is itself one of those fundamental processes. The thresholds become even more blurred when we stop to recognize that people not uncommonly perceive the extraordinary in the ordinary, not unlike the artist sees the world in a grain of sand or the religious person sees the action of divinity in the mundane. Moreover, if finding the extraordinary in the ordinary is a possibility, it is a finding that is reversible: it is a possibility to find the ordinary in the extraordinary, the kernel of shared humanity that allows an understanding of culture and experience in mental illness. It is only a matter of perspective whether we call it empathy, intersubjectivity, or just ethnography.

If dealing with the extraordinary is a window onto understanding fundamental human processes but at the same time a fundamental process in its own right, so is struggle. Struggle appears from time to time as a theme in anthropological work, yet it is seldom thematized as a main topic in our attempt to understand human being and experience. We encounter class struggle, political struggle for indigenous rights, or the struggle of subaltern communities. A collection of work on contemporary China describes it in terms of "media, identity, and struggle" (Murphy and Fong 2008). Sherine Hamdy (2012) writes of organ transplantation in Egypt in terms of a "struggle for human dignity." Robert Desjarlais (1994) has depicted the life of homeless mentally ill people as one of "struggling along." Paul Brodwin (2013) has portrayed the everyday ethical struggles of front-line mental health clinicians serving the most marginalized groups in the U.S. health care system. Michael Jackson (2005) writes of a "struggle for being" that defines existence in terms of contending forces and imperatives, at times taking the form of a search for oneself or for belonging, attempting to transform the world into which one is thrown into one that one participates in creating. Moreover: "At times it entails a struggle to go on living in the face of adversity and loss. At times it is a struggle for being against nothing-ness—for whatever will make life worth living rather than hopeless, profitless, or pointless" (Jackson 2005: x).

In the situations and for the persons I have discussed in the preceding chapters, struggle is not just *against* an illness and its symptoms but also *for* a normal life, *to* make sense of a confusing and disorienting circumstance, *with* intimate others, and *in* a world characterized by stigma. Yet if struggle is a fundamental human process, it has not always been recognized as characterizing the lives of the mentally ill. Indeed, struggle was virtually moot during the long period in which serious mental illness, schizophrenia in particular, was considered a permanent and progressively deteriorating condition. In recent years recognition of the possibility of recovery has dramatically changed the scene, and in fact this very possibility and envisioning it as a goal implies recognition of struggle. Examining this sea change was my aim in "The New Paradigm of Recovery from Schizophrenia: Cultural Conundrums of Improvement without Cure" (Jenkins and Carpenter-Song 2005). While allowing the reality of struggle on the part of the afflicted to emerge into view, the article identified substantial problems with the "new paradigm" when promoted in policy and services insofar as it can be construed as a neoliberal mandate that burdens individuals with their own recovery in the absence of adequate services. This was especially salient given the unchanged presence of paradoxes of lived experience that prominently include the holding out of "hope" in the context of what constitutes an institutional demand freeing the state from responsibility for care in a way that simply extends the ravages of deinstitutionalization that took place in the 1980s. The ideology of the recovery paradigm and the economic globalization of psychopharmaceutical drugs in the context of neoliberal policy have generated a vexing situation for persons living with mental illness (see Myers 2015).[2]

If it is granted that there is a continuum from extraordinary to ordinary, and from struggle that is heroic to that which is mundane, and further that this bespeaks not only fundamental human processes but a fundamentally shared human condition as well, it does not mean that the furthest ends of these continua are necessarily mutually intelligible or accessible without sustained interpretive effort. The experience of mental illness may be unbearable, incommunicable, unfathomable, incommensurable, inconceivable, inscrutable, and incomprehensible—to those so afflicted no less than to the unafflicted. This is because at the deepest level persons with mental illness never completely abandon the stance of everyday life, and hence the extremity and extraordinariness of their condition does not render people incapable of either struggle or strategy, of endurance or expression. This was strongly evident in the consideration of Salvadoran women refugees (chapters 4 and 5), who despite often serious conditions diagnosed as mental illness were grounded in the stance of everyday life that for them was defined by work, family, healing, magic, and religion. One of the patients in the Clozapine Clinic (chapter 1) described psychosis as "unmitigated suffering" and continued, "I often allude to what the soldiers had to go through in the trenches, uh, during World War I. They're dealing with this illness, there's almost an aspect of horror to it. It's very merciless. It's very cruel." Two decades later the "Voice Hearers" movement is advocating ways to "make friends with" or strike deals with their voices to "limit their airtime" in a less adversarial way. Thinking of this variability in terms of fundamental human processes helps remind us that those with mental illness remain fundamentally human.

Across the diversity of situations I have examined, in addition to the encounter with extraordinary conditions and the engagement with struggle, a common theme has been the reciprocal relationship of culture and mental illness. I have necessarily emphasized how culture shapes mental illness, but it is important to note as well how mental illness shapes culture. Consider, for example, Martin's (2007) brilliant analysis of how bipolar (manic-depressive) illness reveals cultural values. In her American case study the core "symptoms" of mania are highly prized as emblems of cultural cachet and economic productivity: high energy, excessive activity, overly elevated mood (highly optimistic?), fast talking, and hard drinking or drugging. For some stars of the entertainment industry (e.g., Robin Williams, Ted Turner) these are virtually job requirements making the practice of their professions possible. But mania is a feature of public culture as well. In the 1960s Beatlemania swept the Western world as teenage fans "went crazy" for a rock-and-roll band. More recently, Ottomania is not merely a form of political nostalgia, but an active desire to re-create the greatness of Turkish empire. In India, everyday discourse incorporates the language of mania. Political rallies in 2014 for the controversial pro-market prime minister Narendra Modi were represented in the *Financial Times* as being characterized by "Modi Mania," and there were claims that his economic policy propelled India's stock market for the first time into the ranks of the world's ten biggest by value, surpassing Australia amid growing investment.[3] At the risk of romanticizing injurious excess, the cultural capital of these qualities cannot be underestimated. These cases stand in marked contrast to a cultural aesthetics of "staying cool," restrained, or composed, such as can be found in Indonesia (Hollan 1988).

Yet insofar as a goal of this work has been to understand culture and experience in mental illness, it is incumbent on me to acknowledge the limitations of the series of ethnographic studies I have presented. These are persons who sought and received psychiatric treatment. They were not homeless. They were not in prison. Those are whole other life-worlds, which are not represented in this work. Moreover, none of the studies I have presented were done using participant observation of the "usual" sort that includes intensive study of a community and extended interactions with the same group of people. Something is lost as well as gained when one is working among people with some common illness experience but who live dispersed over an indeterminate geographic area and with whom the ethnographer must interact on a periodic rather than a sustained basis.

I would like to say a final word in favor of the power of anthropology as method. The many hundreds of stories that form the substance of this book were possible only by virtue of encounters with persons in their own domestic space. While there were interview guides and particular questions, the format of these encounters was open-ended in terms of subject matter and time in a manner not practiced in psychology or psychiatry. As an anthropologist, I made my best efforts to engage and to understand everyday and extraordinary features of the lives of the persons with whom I interacted. A great many indicated they had never experienced this kind of (anthropological) engagement and conveyed appreciation for being in the lead position regarding the telling of their narrative as they saw fit. While it is a truism that such narratives are invariably co-constructed and have limits as a function of role and social position, I was struck repeatedly by how these anthropological encounters appeared to resonate positively for interviewee and interviewer alike. Not many people—not families, clinicians, or even friends—have the opportunity or willingness to engage in open-ended encounters with the singular goal of understanding life from an extraordinary person's point of view. It might be overwhelming, threatening, or simply too taxing for persons in the absence of anthropological sensibilities to suspend judgment to enter into unfamiliar extraordinary terrain. This certainly has been my great anthropological privilege. I am acutely aware that as a student of the extraordinary I stood to gain much more than the experts with whom I spoke. However, to the extent that anyone can validly judge interpersonal encounters, I have been gratified that in many cases persons I encountered felt they too were touched by the experiential encounter. I do not wish to overstate this point because this is not always the way things went, but my own sense is that not infrequently it was. I therefore stand by my claim that anthropology has much to offer as a powerful method of engagement and understanding in the study of mental illness.

# Notes

INTRODUCTION

1. That these extraordinary conditions can become routine and even ordinary is a matter not only of human irony but also of social pathology. I also note that "extraordinary" can of course be applied to conditions of social advantage and privilege in situations of comfort and health. The latter such conditions are not the primary concern of this research.

2. Georges Canguilhem (1989) examined the divergent intellectual and therapeutic consequences of understanding the normal and pathological as defining two endpoints of a continuum or as defining categorically distinct states. In this respect, each illness or disorder can be understood in terms of its degree of divergence from health or as a distinct entity defined by the crossing of a definite threshold between normal and pathological.

3. Internet sites include what appear as informational websites (often funded by pharmaceutical companies), media sharing sites such as Tumblr and Screen Caps, media sharing sides with video blogs, Web comics, and social networks (forums and blogs).

4. A brief listing includes Ingstad and Whyte 1995; Farmer 2004b, 2006; Farmer et al. 2013; Kleinman 1988b, 2007; Kleinman and Good 1985; James 2010; B. Good 2010a, 2012; M. Good et al. 2008; Good and Good 2012; Patel, Kleinman, and Saraceno 2012; Han 2012; Brodwin 2012, 2013; Rhodes, Battin, and Silvers 2012; Jenkins 2010, 2013; Jenkins ed. 2010; Jenkins and Barrett 2004; Hollan and Wellenkamp 1994; Biehl 2005; Biehl, Good, and Kleinman 2007; Chen 2003; Parish 2008; Carpenter-Song et al. 2010; Estroff 1985, 1989; Desjarlais 1997; Hinton and Good 2009; Scheper-Hughes [1979] 2001, 1992; Garcia 2010; Holmes 2013; Ecks 2013.

5. Hawkins (1999) has called this new genre "pathography."

6. B. Good's (1994) critique of the concept of belief highlights the role of "subjunctivity," the "could be" and "might have been" in human thought and emotion.

7. Yet given the emergence of suffering as a prominent theme of anthropological analysis, it is unsurprising that it has drawn critique that misses its palpable reality or depicts it in distal, theoretically abstract, reduced terms. Robbins (2013) provides a problematic instance of equating an anthropological focus on the various forms of human suffering with the erstwhile anthropological interest in conceptions of the savage. Such a caricature erroneously compares a mode of experience (suffering) with a category of being (savagery) and confuses description (of savagery) with critique (of suffering). His argument also misses the point of scholarly moves toward recognition and understanding of human conditions long ignored in social anthropology in favor of clean and tidy categories such as religion, ritual, culture change, or the good that generally favor public over intimate realms. While he claims equitably enough that the study of suffering and of what he calls "the good" can be complementary, his additional claim that studies of suffering tend to ignore cultural depth and diversity is largely unfounded. Moreover, Robbins's attempt to circumscribe an "anthropology of suffering" has the rhetorical effect of portraying treatment of this topic as a narrow and sentimental pursuit, when for those who actually deploy the concept suffering is a mode of experience through which the ethnographer finds occasion to analyze power, meaning, affect, and illness. Likewise, a concern with suffering is not a glorification of passive victimization or victimhood, both substantively in that it encompasses resiliency, resistance, creativity, and agency and methodologically in that it insists on linking the concrete experience and raw existence of human beings with broader social, cultural, and political economic forces and conditions.

8. Scholarship that anthropologically addresses the cultural-existential question of "that which matters" is represented in B. Good's (1977, 2012) work on "theorizing the subject" and "the heart of the matter" and Kleinman's (2007, 2009) work on what is "at stake" and "what really matters."

9. Lovell (2012) invokes the idea of precariousness to characterize the situation of survivors of Hurricane Katrina in New Orleans and explore their strategies for survival in the aftermath of this natural disaster.

CHAPTER 1

1. See Wallis and Willwerth 1992.

2. Michael Winerip, *New York Times,* September 9, 1992, 41.

3. My approach to the anthropological study of psychotropic drugs has been developed over the course of a series of NIMH-funded projects that have involved persons taking an array of psychotropic drugs: antipsychotics, anticholinergics, antidepressants, anxiolytics, mood stabilizers, psychostimulants, and sedative hypnotics.

4. A report from the Treatment Advocacy Center (2014) found that a high proportion of persons with mental illness are incarcerated in the United States and that "in 2012, there were estimated to be 356,268 *inmates* with severe

mental illness in prisons and jails. There were also approximately *35,000 patients* with severe mental illness in state psychiatric hospitals. Thus, the number of mentally ill persons in prisons and jails was *10 times the number remaining in state hospitals"* (emphasis added). In U.S. state prisons, the prevalence of serious mental illness is two to four times higher than in the community (Cloud 2014).

5. Several recent works have examined the startling rise of psychotropic use in the United States (Healy 1997; DeGrandpre 2006; Whitaker 2010). This historical trend has transpired in relation to the "creation" of psychiatric disorders by pharmaceutical companies in tandem with psychiatric researchers and health care practitioners who have expanded the range of application of diagnostic categories and the drugs to treat them. Watters (2010) has written an elegant journalistic account of this trend as a product of globalization.

6. As a reminder, the names of research participants in the present study (and throughout the book) are pseudonyms. No identifying personal information is provided, in keeping with confidentiality required for the protection of human subjects.

7. A residue of alchemy provides the clearest evidence of this association by linking cultural-historical imaginaries of "scientific" discourse and practice to the realm of the mysterious. A pre-Enlightenment work by the chemist John Rudolph Glauber published in 1689 is described by its author as "containing great variety of choice secrets in medicine and alchemy." As recently as the eighteenth century chemistry was so divided over its proper paradigm as to create a state of flux so drastic that the term *revolution,* in the Kuhnian sense, was routinely invoked to describe it (Chaouli 2002: 118).

8. As a member of the research community concerned with the need for better medications for those who choose to take them, I too was initially taken with the possibilities of hope and improved therapeutic care. My own views have formed over time in the context of carrying out the research project presented here.

9. Copyright restrictions prohibit me from publishing illustrations of pharmaceutical ads. Here, and elsewhere in the book, I describe them.

10. Scull (1984) argued that while it may have appeared that deinstitutionalization was fueled by the appearance of effective antipsychotic drugs, financial gains gleaned by the state from divesting patients were a more significant driving force.

11. Braslow (2013) has argued that this reversal has not been accompanied by a radical departure in treatment policy, but that values and practices of the past continue to shape current recovery-based policies. Review of scholarship in the history of psychiatry and mental health policy is beyond the scope of the present work, but see Braslow 1997; Porter 2002; Sadowsky 1999, 2004; Scull 1984.

12. Conference presentation, Second Meeting of the International Consortium on Hallucination Research, Grey College, Durham University, September 12–13, 2013. See also TED talk by Dr. Longden: www.ted.com/talks/eleanor_longden_the_voices_in_my_head.

13. Early on in this study, I was taken aback when a project consultant, a senior psychiatrist renowned for research on atypical antipsychotics and

schizophrenia, confided, "Really, Jan, I'd be surprised if you find anything of a psychological life of the sort you seem to be looking for with these people. I've never seen it."

14. SEACORA was a collaborative research project funded by National Institute of Mental Grant R01 MH-60232 awarded to the author as Principal Investigator. Professor Milton Strauss, PhD, was Co-Investigator. Several graduate students worked as research assistants for the study, including Holly Hainely, Elizabeth Carpenter-Song, Zee Butt, Elizabeth Ihler, Sarah Adler, and Kate Masley. Jean Berggren, MD, was trained in research reliability for the administration of the Structured Clinical Interview for Diagnosis and Brief Psychiatric Ratings Scale (BPRS) by Joseph Ventura, PhD, Director of the Diagnosis and Psychopathology Unit of the UCLA Center on Treatment and Rehabilitation of Psychosis. The research team had no relationship with a pharmaceutical company.

15. The Clubhouse is located in the university area and 5 to 10 minutes away from the university outpatient clinic. Many study participants frequented the Clubhouse, where members are assigned one or more tasks (e.g., food preparation, management of computer files, orienting new members). There are regularly scheduled group meetings on employment seeking, social skills training, and diverse topics in health and well-being. Levels of involvement and interest in the Clubhouse varied among study participants.

16. Transcribed data were entered into a qualitative software program (Atlas.ti) to organize thematic content for interpretive analysis. Because this analytic enterprise was extensive, organization of the data was accomplished through application of a considerable number of codes (738) defined for specific use in the Atlas program that were systematically coded from interviews and ethnographic observational notes. Taken together, all interview and observational notes yielded a total of 4,722 single-spaced pages of transcribed data for our analysis. This does not include data obtained from the Structured Clinical Interview for DSM-IV (SCID) that appear in table 3. The SCID data provide detailed symptom profiles.

17. The psychiatrist Herbert Meltzer of University Hospitals founded the Clozapine clinic, or the Meltzer Psychobiology Clinic. At the time I began the SEACORA project, both Dr. Meltzer and I were professors of psychiatry at the associated medical school of the university.

18. There are innumerable pharmaceutical ads for antipsychotic and antidepressant drugs in relation to "balance" and "imbalance" in leading academic journals (e.g., American Journal of Psychiatry). These ads are aimed at physicians and appeal to simplified understandings of psychiatric disorder through the cultural metaphor of chemical imbalance. For example, Seroquel (an atypical antipsychotic drug taken by many people in our study) is advertised as restoring balance with images of rocks delicately piled on one another.

19. Over the past few decades, there has been a political shift in preferred language for persons utilizing health care in the United States. Traditional medical practice has and continues to use the term patient, although at the urging of advocacy groups this has changed in line with preferences for "consumer," "survivor," or (services) "user" (Jones et al. 2014). Some groups with first-person

experience of what is diagnosed as mental illness prefer the experiential term *voice hearer*. Indeed, voice-hearing groups originating in Europe have gained increasing popularity through international voice hearing networks: www.intervoiceonline.org/. Deegan (2007) makes the case for the importance of lived experience and the use of psychiatric medication through a shared decision-making process with one's provider while at the same time insisting on personally devised nonpharmacological strategies to enhance well-being.

20. I have defined my use of these terms: "To be precise, if, following Hallowell (1955), we understand the self as the sum of processes by which the subject is oriented in the world and toward other people, then the pharmaceutical self is that aspect of self oriented by and toward other people, then the pharmaceutical self is that aspect of self oriented by and toward pharmaceutical drugs. If, following Castoriadis (1987), we understand the imaginary as that dimension of culture oriented toward conceivable possibilities for human life, then the pharmaceutical imaginary is that region of the imaginary in which pharmaceuticals play an increasingly critical role" (Jenkins ed., 2010: 6).

21. There were no differences between attendees of the university-affiliated Clozapine Clinic (53.7%) and the other community clinic (52.8%) with respect to whether or not they consider their medication a "miracle drug." The lack of discursive "staying power" of clinical ideology inculcated at the Clozapine clinic could be related to notable resistance and critical thought on the part of participants there, or it might reflect the cultural saturation of this ideology in equal measure across the two sites independent of (redundant) exposure to clinical-cultural messaging.

22. For an extended discussion of side effects of atypical antipsychotics among participants, see Jenkins and Carpenter-Song 2005.

23. For ethnography of psychiatrists and the paradigmatic flux of psychoanalytic and biological approaches, see Luhrmann 2000.

24. See www.youtube.com/watch?v=twhvtzd6gXA&list=PLB989432F3EF2CoA9.

25. See www.youtube.com/watch?v=tGymr78FtbU.

26. Among the persons participating in this study, gendered conflicts were similar for persons with and without extraordinary conditions and were remarkably conventional in cultural terms. Gendered confusion as a matter of identity is of course a common human dilemma; however, one-fifth of persons in the present group of ninety expressed serious gender confusion, sometimes to include the question of whether, at different and varying periods of time, they were a man or a woman.

27. In the United States, the situation is dire, with many (perhaps the majority) who need care living on the streets or incarcerated.

28. While biomedical circles share awareness of psychopharmaceuticals, this awareness hardly matches availability in relation to economic scarcity of treatment. Indeed, WHO has recently highlighted this fundamental problem:

> Health systems have not yet adequately responded to the burden of mental disorders; as a consequence, the gap between the need for treatment and its provision is large all over the world. Between 76% and 85% of people with severe mental disorders receive no treatment for their disorder in low-income and middle-income countries; the

corresponding range for high-income countries is also high: between 35% and 50%. A further compounding problem is the poor quality of care for those receiving treatment. WHO's Mental Health Atlas 2011 provides data that demonstrate the scarcity of resources within countries to meet mental health needs, and underlies the inequitable distribution and inefficient use of such resources. Globally, for instance, annual spending on mental health is less than US$2 per person and less than US$0.25 per person in low-income countries, with 67% of these financial resources allocated to stand-alone mental hospitals, despite their association with poor health outcomes and human rights violations. (2013: 8)

## CHAPTER 2

1. Sebastián did agree to participate in the study after reading the Informed Consent form. He said he thought his mother would probably also participate, but that even though he could understood that the study was confidential, he seriously doubted that his father could or would want to talk to me. I let him know I would ask each of his parents separately about whether they wanted to participate. As it turned out, both did.

2. Even though there was a time when Sebastián identified the "voices" as the "voice" of God, he continued to refer to voices and hence the text conforms to this usage. Over time, it seemed there were other voices too. However, it also seemed that all voices were in some way sent *by* God as master controller. There were many fluctuations in the voices over time.

3. I am convinced of the power of psychodynamic interpretations and therapeutic process in the present case of Sebastián and also in the case of Salvadoran women (chapters 4 and 5) who engaged in discussion with me about how events of the past have come to shape their current relationships and how these are represented symbolically in resonant objects and subjects. Further, although most of the participants in the study had very little formal education, I believe that, contrary to common American psychoanalytic assumption, they can engage in and benefit from psychodynamic interpretation. Certainly, Latin Americans are culturally oriented to intellectual, philosophical, and spiritual realms as matters of interest, mystery, and healing. This idea of broad psychoanalytic application is culturally hyper-assumptive in some parts (Buenos Aires) but can be relatively foreign in others (Manhattan).

4. I also tried to imagine how Sebastián's talk of suicide, and the ability to speak about it with me without overwhelming fear, might have been of importance to him. This is true for persons who do and do not carry out suicide, as Staples and Widger (2012: 183) indicate, whereby even completed suicides "can be understood as a kind of sociality, as a special kind of social relationship, through which people create meaning in their own lives."

5. See Morrison 2012 for a literary portrait of social pathology manifest in the hallucinations of an African American war veteran trapped in a tangled biographical web of child abuse, war trauma, and the indivisibility of self and kin.

6. Sebastián's frustration over failure of his scientific endeavors was particularly vexing for him. I was reminded of how such frustrations fueled the onset of psychotic experience in the case of Nobel laureate John Nash. I interviewed

Dr. Nash at the Institute for Advanced Study in Princeton, New Jersey, on June 11, 2012, when he explained to me his theory of schizophrenia as a situation of frustration that can lead to "minds on strike." For Dr. Nash, this can occur when a person, such as Sebastián (or Nash himself), is extremely frustrated and unhappy in a context of societal failure where the social world fails to recognize the experience and talent of the nonordinary (or what in this book I refer to as the extraordinary).

7. See Deegan 1988, 2007; International Voices Hearing Network, www .intervoiceonline.org/ and http://hearingthevoice.org/.

CHAPTER 3

1. The question of how social response to schizophrenic illness varies across cultures has long been of interest to anthropologists (Edgerton 1966; Estroff 1981; Janzen et al. 1978; Jenkins 1988a, 1988b; Kennedy 1974; Murphy 1976, 1982; Scheper-Hughes 1979; Townsend 1978; Wallace 1961; Waxler 1974; Warner 1985).

2. The primary studies include the International Pilot Study of Schizophrenia (IPSS), a large (N = 1202) nine-country study of schizophrenia (WHO 1973, 1979; Sartorius, Jablensky, and Shapiro 1977), the Determinants of Outcome of Severe Mental Disorder (DOSMeD) (Craig et al. 1997) with follow-up periods ranging between two and five (and in several, ten) years, the Reduction of Disability Studies (Jablensky, Schwarz, and Tomov 1980), and the International Study of Schizophrenia (ISoS) (Mason et el. 1996). Taken together, these studies constitute a substantial body of longitudinal WHO-Collaborative Projects.

3. Elsewhere (Jenkins 2004) I have critiqued the clinical interpretation of "flat affect" as a problem of the clash of perspectives (doctors and patients). Persons diagnosed with conditions of schizophrenia may have self-protective behavioral strategies (Corin 1990; Kring and Kerr 1993; Kring and Germans 2004) that challenge conventional notions of the meaning of facial expression and tone of voice as indicators of subjective experience. The representation of persons with schizophrenia as "flat" or as "nobody's home" are not only offensive; they are wrong. The cruel irony is that persons with schizophrenia are exquisitely tuned to the social and emotional environment.

4. Potential sources of bias were examined (differences in follow-up, grouping of centers, diagnostic ambiguities, outcome measures, gender, and age), but none of these potentially confounding factors could explain away the transnational differences in course and outcome (WHO 1979).

5. The inclusion of Moscow in this grouping further complicates this dichotomy.

6. A recent round of critique and response was published in *Schizophrenia Bulletin*. Cohen and colleagues (2007) launched a series of methodological complaints, some reasonable and some mistaken, that had previously been responded to by Jablensky and colleagues (1994), yet oddly omitted in the second publication detailing what the authors regard as methodological problems in support of the overall finding for variation in outcome transnationally. Cohen and colleagues intend their critique as a challenge to what "they claim to

be an 'axiom' (i.e., a self-evident proposition requiring no proof) of better course and outcome in developing countries which has been 'embraced' by international psychiatry" (Jablensky and Sartorius 2008: 343). It is ironic that in many a medical school training program, and the field of psychiatry globally, there is scant awareness of these findings and when introduced psychiatrists and residents are not infrequently skeptical to say the least. Frequently there is a cultural assumption of the superiority of European and American psychiatric biomedicine that is presumed to conduce to better outcomes relative to diagnosed persons and practitioners in the global South.

7. This "schizophrenogenic" research tradition (see Fromm-Reichmann 1948) can be roundly criticized on several grounds. First, the data on disturbed family relations are retrospective rather than prospective. Second, the key concepts in the family psychopathology literature were often diffuse and tended to be applied without precision. Third, the concept of the "schizophrenogenic" mother is properly critiqued on feminist grounds because it assumes a disproportionately noxious influence exercised by mothers; attributions of blame for the illness were attributions of inadequacies in the fulfillment of the maternal role (also see Scheper-Hughes 1979 on this point). And fourth, the dominance of biological paradigms in contemporary psychiatry holds obvious appeal as a significant challenge to family theorists and to theorists and clinicians with now-outmoded claims of family pathology as etiological.

8. LeVine (1990) has proposed introducing the psychoanalyst Heinz Hartmann's concept of "average expectable environment" into anthropological analysis, though the emphasis appears to be on a communicative environment with emotional components rather than an emotional environment determined by expression. Gergen (1990: 594) calls for "refiguring emotional terms (along with the actions indexed by those terms) as components of more extended relational patterns," with a view of relational space constituted by emotion as social performance. Beeman (1985) suggests that Bateson's approach to metacommunicative behavior could fruitfully be applied to the study of depression, where aside from work by family therapists little research on interaction processes is being carried out. The key to determining the value of such suggestions is to assess the methodological significance of relative emphases on cognitive or affective and behavioral or experiential orientations.

9. Literature appearing in the past decade under the label of affect theory tends to understand emotion less in relation to cognition and self than to agency and intensity (Gregg and Seigworth 2010; Massumi 2002; Stewart 2007), but it remains to be seen whether this work can contribute to the understanding of mental illness as extraordinary experience.

10. The Camberwell Family Interview (CFI) generally lasts about two hours, and subsequent analysis using the rating scales takes six to eight hours (Brown et al. 1978). I was trained in an intensive two-week workshop led by highly experienced CFI interviewers (the psychologists Christine Vaughn and Karen Snyder), followed by several months of extensive reliability checks using Euro-American and British training interviews that take approximately six months to listen to and rate twenty-five "master interview" sets of audiotapes for the determination of research reliability. A training manual was developed to define

in detail precisely how to identify and to rate these features of "expressed emotion" (Vaughn n.d.). Interviewers for our Mexican American study achieved high inter-rater reliability scores (above Pearson R of .85) with the original ratings, and maintained reliability through periodic co-ratings of randomly selected interviews. As described later, we spent approximately one year in a pilot study prior to our larger study to adapt this interview and rating system for culturally and linguistically valid use in Spanish with Mexican-descent families.

11. The labor-intensive process, considered by most psychologists as overly time-consuming and costly, led to a demand for development of abbreviated measures, such as a five-minute speech sample (Magaña et al. 1986) to reduce requisite research time. Most anthropologists (certainly including me), operating from a different research methodology, would be loath to impose such restrictions on research time or effort in this manner.

12. One anthropological critique was curious. In a public presentation I made at the annual meetings of the American Anthropological Association, the discussant for the session claimed they just "didn't get" what the value of EE research could possibly be. In my conference paper, I had argued (as in publication) that to be useful for anthropologists (as well as psychiatrists and psychologists), cultural and linguistic adaptations of the method were required to enhance cultural validity. I further argued that to get at what's "inside the black box" of EE as an empirical research construct required anthropological analysis since the elements of the index are inherently cultural. My argument was met by what I took to be a rather startling claim by the discussant that this research effort indicated that I was "erotically attached" to the EE construct. Being an election year in the United States, I replied with what immediately came to mind: "What would Reverend Jesse Jackson say? I think we need to take this to higher ground." It came as news to me that there could be such a thing as erotic attachment to, of all things, a research construct. Not only did this make no intellectual sense to me, but also appealed not in the least by way of fun. Further, I wondered if a male researcher would be commented on in similar fashion or instead as perhaps (too) "productively driven."

13. My understanding of these issues comes from working with program officers for my own studies and attending programmatic-sponsored meetings to establish research priorities. I served as a member of three scientific review groups at the U.S. National Institute of Mental Health over a number of years (1993–2005).

14. The Mexican-descent study was conducted with seventy families. The study was carried out over a period of six years (1980–86). For the total of 70 persons recently hospitalized for psychiatric treatment, we interviewed 109 key relatives identified on the basis of reports regarding which family members had the most face-to-face contact with the ill relative. In some cases two such relatives were identified, whereas in others only one relative had regular close contact (defined as 35 hours or greater). Subjects resided in parental (70%), sibling (10%), and marital (10%) households. The vast majority (94%) of the families were of low-income households, and most were either monolingual (65%) or primarily Spanish speakers (24%). All families were of bilateral Mexican descent. Most relatives (71%) and persons who were hospitalized

(63%) identified themselves as *Mexicanos,* but those born in the United States identified themselves as "Mexican American." These families did not self-identify as Chicano. Subjects were recruited to the study at the time of their inpatient hospitalization for an acute psychotic episode. Over half (57%) were male, and the mean age was 26.1. The mean number of hospitalizations was 3.3, and the mean number of years since the time of onset of illness (initial onset of psychotic symptoms) was 4.5 years.

15. As a starting point, we analyzed our data using the cutoff points for "high" versus "low" EE as derived from the British studies (Vaughn and Leff 1976; Vaughn et al. 1984). A rating of six or more critical comments and/or a (high) score of 4–5 were employed for the scale for EOI. In the Mexican-descent study, we had assumed that if we were to find this significant relationship, it would probably occur through utilization of different cutoff points from those used for the English-speaking groups. Surprisingly, this was not the case and the cut-off points for Mexican Americans were the same, possibly suggesting that although cultural content and styles of criticism and EOI varied considerably, a quantitative threshold for the experience of negative affect by persons with schizophrenia might be similar.

16. See the discussion that follows on *nervios* as a cultural conception of schizophrenia.

17. This is why many contemporary psycho-educational interventions make this matter explicit. This holds the potential for relief all around for caregivers and persons in the struggle to recover from conditions of mental illness.

18. Relatively few relatives were rated high on this factor: none of the Indian relatives, 11% of the Mexican-descent relatives, 15% of the Euro-American relatives, and 21% of the British relatives. These results do not provide cross-cultural support for the idea that families of persons diagnosed with schizophrenia are appropriately characterized as disturbed or pathological in their interpersonal relations.

19. A rating of "high" would be a score of 4 or 5 (on the 0–5 point scale).

20. For example, among the 109 Mexican-descent relatives, 24 (or 22%) were considered high on criticism. Of the eleven (11%) relatives rated high on EOI, 4 were also rated highly critical. One such relative is the father of Gabriella.

21. I distinguish between ethnopsychology as the explicit indigenous theory corresponding to our own notion of psychology and cultural psychology in the sense used by Shweder (1990) to denote actual psychological processes and dynamics observable in a people.

22. The research literature on "expressed emotion" is voluminous, and only a small fraction can be provided here.

23. See Hildred Geertz (1959) for a formulation of "vocabularies of emotion."

24. To account for the complex social and psychological shaping of psyche and culture in relation to trauma (in chapter 6), I tentatively suggest the idea of "dynamic phenomenology" to account for intricate self-processes of protection in the context of inhabiting situations of precarity.

CHAPTER 4

For the subtitle of this chapter, I have borrowed the phrase "impress of extremity" from Forche's (1993) exploration of the poetics of trauma and memory under extreme conditions.

1. Letter from Archbishop Oscar Romero to President Jimmy Carter, February 17, 1980. U.S. Policy & Human Rights in the Salvadoran Civil War, www.csusmhistory.org/atkin008/plea-to-carter-response-from-reagan/.

2. While condemning the murder of Archbishop Romero, the U.S. governmental response was to blame Cuba for generalized violence:

> The United States yesterday accused Cuba of directly contributing to violence in El Salvador by sending weapons and leftist insurgents into the country to try to topple the civilian-military junta backed by the United States. The charge was made by Carter administration officials who sought congressional approval to supply military equipment worth $5.7 million to El Salvador's ruling *junta.* . . . Secretary of State Cyrus Vance said yesterday that the United States still plans to give military and economic aid to El Salvador, noting that the country's rulers recently have taken steps aimed at "healing" the country's wounds and divisions, and that "the junta has been making progress . . . especially in land reform." El Salvador's civilian-military junta has enacted a series of sweeping economic and land reforms with U.S. support and about $50 million in American economic aid. (*Washington Post,* March 26, 1980, A26)

3. Massacre at Funeral of Archbishop Oscar Romero, March 30, 1980. www.youtube.com/watch?v=EN6LWdqcyuc.

4. This chapter is dedicated to the memory of Dr. Ignacio Martín-Baró, a psychologist from El Salvador who personally inspired several dimensions of this essay and research. In what now reads as a painful foreshadowing, Martín-Baró jokingly remarked during a visit to Boston, where he spoke with a health collective involving members of our Latino Team (Cambridge Hospital, Harvard Medical School), "In the United States it's publish or perish. But for professors who speak and write on behalf of social justice in a totalitarian society, it's often publish and perish." Less than nine months after making these remarks Martín-Baró was dead, one of six Jesuits assassinated by the government during a bloody rebel offensive. As a social psychologist, he had been in a unique position to produce a social analysis directly relevant to the life situations of Salvadoran refugees in North America today. His loss to the international community of scholars concerned with the mental health consequences of civil warfare is profound. His loss as a humanitarian working toward a negotiated settlement of the conflict in El Salvador is incalculable.

5. See Bateson (1958: 118) for a definition of ethos as the emotional environment of a cultural setting. My use of "political ethos" with respect to the state construction of affect diverges from the use of that phrase in political science to describe an "orientation toward politics" (Wilson and Banfield 1971).

6. See the edited volume by Lutz and Abu-Lughod (1990) on political dimensions of everyday affective communications focusing on various kinds of "talk" (e.g., narratives, text, speech, aesthetic performances, and scientific discourse). In the context of contemporary El Salvador, it's clear that enforced silence and the absence of talk were equally important in constituting a political ethos.

7. In a psychosocial study of motivation and achievement among Central American refugees who attend U.S. high schools, Suárez-Orozco (1989) also reports common usage of the term *la situación.*

8. Regrettably, audiocassette recordings of the guerrilla radio broadcasts were not available for similar analysis of the contribution these broadcasts make to the political ethos. My partial knowledge of these broadcasts (from approximately the same time period) suggests the broadcast salience of themes of "liberty," "revolution," and "victory."

9. Of course it must be fully acknowledged that *la situación* is not unilaterally constructed by the state but is also constructed by actions in response to and in opposition to the state, such as those of the armed forces or guerrilla resistance. Tragically, the waging of war typically involves criminal and violent actions on both sides of the conflict. This fact has been acknowledged by members of the FMLN (e.g., in recent admissions of the apparent execution of American military personnel subsequent to their survival in a helicopter crash landing) and has also been documented for the military forces by human rights groups compiling data for the United Nations High Commissioner for Refugees (UNHCR). The systematic practice of detention, torture, sexual violence, disappearance, and execution of those suspected of participating or collaborating with guerrillas has been summarized by the U.S. Committee for Refugees (1990a).

10. For a portrait of detention practices in the context of everyday life in El Salvador, see Argueta's novel *One Day of Life* (1983).

11. For a critique of the concept "belief" in anthropological theory, see B. Good 1994.

12. Adequate consideration of the extensive epistemological difficulties with cross-cultural application of the concept of somatization is beyond the scope of the present chapter; see Kleinman 1986; Kirmayer 1984; Escobar et al. 2006.

13. The women who reported personal experiences of domestic violence would typically do so with shame. The cross-cultural commonality of violence by male kin within family settings is alarming (Levinson 1989).

14. Ethnopsychologically, this is likely to be also related to indigenous "hot—cold" theories common throughout Latin America.

15. See Scarry 1985 for a discussion of the relationship between the clinical gaze and the experience of pain.

CHAPTER 5

1. As an anthropologist working in the field of mental health, for me this work involving magic, religion, and witchcraft posed a significant challenge for an ethnographic interpretation of intimate experience.

2. This adage is invoked for realms about which one can never be certain, such as witchcraft, miracles, ghosts, gossip, or even political corruption. This cultural orientation involves the paradoxical acknowledgment of awareness of the existence of such things while at the same time disavowing "belief" in such. For the definitive anthropological analysis of the cultural concept of belief and its use in medical anthropology, see B. Good 1994.

3. For consultations on a variety of translations, I thank Angela Garcia, Victoria Ojeda, Olga Odgers Ortiz, and Paula Saravia.

4. By that time, I had moved out of the state and could visit only occasionally.

5. It was strongly suspected in these cases that the owners tossed the matches to collect insurance money for largely dilapidated buildings.

## CHAPTER 6

1. Upon entering the state, roadside signs and vehicle license plates alike hail New Mexico as the "Land of Enchantment."

2. The child poverty rate is 20% or higher in twenty-four of the fifty states (Macartney 2011).

3. This research was conducted in 2005–11. As of 2013, the situation had deteriorated even further for behavioral health services under state administration of the Affordable Care Act passed in 2010. State officials have enacted provisions that exacerbate access to health care (Willging 2014).

4. Recently these debates have come to prominently include the relationship of mental health and gun violence in the United States. There are numerous instances that can be referenced but one suffices: the now globally notorious killing in Newtown, Connecticut, of twenty-six persons (twenty children and six adults) by Adam Lanza, who is alleged to have had an autism-spectrum disorder. Geneticists were asked to examine the DNA of the deceased shooter in an attempt to identify abnormalities that might somehow shed light on his actions. Given that no such biological markers have been identified that clearly link violence and blood samples, the action may amount to a misguided fishing expedition.

5. There is wide recognition of how the category "adolescent" is culturally and historically constructed (see Hall 1904; Ariès 1965). Benedict ([1928] 2008: 42) noted "from a comparative point of view, our culture goes to great extremes in emphasizing contrasts between the child and the adult."

6. Reviewing the current social and health sciences, the significance of cultural variation appears to be increasingly recognized in relation to (1) conceptualizing "the normal" and (2) attending to "context." Powers and colleagues (1989) provide a psychological approach that appears to have taken to heart the matter of cultural relativity with respect to the threshold for normal and abnormal. A psychological overview article on adolescent mental health takes care to invoke Anna Freud's (1958: 275) dictum that "to be normal during the adolescent period is by itself abnormal," before pointing to the need for "anthropological studies investigating the interaction of biological, psychological, and cultural features of adolescence." The recognition of context in interdisciplinary research appears less with respect to families/households and more with respect to neighborhoods (Aneshensel and Sucoff 1996; Hoagwood and Olin 2002). Yet while instructive, accounts from the social and health sciences can fall flat and seem at a remove from the often-harsh realities of communities when compared to ethnographic approaches to context that can provide deeply eloquent accounts (Lovell 1997; Scheper-Hughes 1993; Goldstein 2003; Biehl 2005; Henry 2006; Garcia, 2010; James 2010). This chapter falls unambiguously on the ethnographic side in its

account of adolescent mental health in light of the notably turbulent lives of persons with whom we worked.

7. Hendren and Berlin (1991) give an account of psychiatric inpatient care of children and adolescents and issues related to cultural diversity at CPH in the 1980s, when it was something of a model for culturally attuned psychiatric care for adolescents.

8. For a detailed ethnography of the experience of clinicians on the front lines of the struggle against mental illness, see Brodwin 2012.

9. Noteworthy to the research team field-workers were the comments of adolescents who stayed at Desert Hills and other facilities. Across the board, they voiced their strong preference for CPH and its "caring" staff, which they perceived as well trained, and a therapeutic environment that they found (despite protestations regarding rules such as bedtime schedules) relatively comfortable and beneficial.

10. This collaborative project was funded by National Institute of Mental Health Grant # R01 MH071781–01, Thomas J. Csordas and Janis H. Jenkins, Co-Principal Investigators. Data collection for the study took place across the state of New Mexico, with major sites of research in the Albuquerque and Las Cruces metropolitan areas (2005–11). The team-based study involved ethnographic interviews and observations of many youths from all parts of the state. As for all such university- and government-sponsored studies, informed consent was obtained, and in this case it involved both a parent or guardian and the adolescent. Along with the principal investigators, the skilled and intrepid fieldwork of doctoral students Bridget Haas and Whitney Duncan (now completed PhDs) extended the reach of this intricate and emotionally strenuous research. Child psychiatrist Michael Stork, MD, and clinical psychologist Mary Bancroft, PhD, artfully accomplished the work of conducting research diagnostic interviews. Data organization and analysis were made possible by the assistance of Heather Hallman and Allen Tran. In addition, we acknowledge the research assistance of Eliza Dimas, Jessica Hsueh, Nofit Itzhak, Jessica Novak, Celeste Padilla, Marisa Peeters, Leah Retherford, and Amy Rothschild.

11. Not all adolescents and parents were interviewed beyond an initial set of visits. Some were lost to follow-up due to geographic moves out of state if we either could not locate them or did not have the logistic capability to do so. We did, however, make repeat visits with trips to Texas, Colorado, and California. For the state of New Mexico, our research team scoured the entire state to locate and carry out ethnographic interviews in the case of (not infrequent) moves that occurred after our initial contact.

12. Although our study of adolescents who had inpatient psychiatric treatment includes a comparison group of nonhospitalized children from a public school district, this chapter draws only from the clinically related component of the study.

13. For youths ages fifteen to nineteen, the U.S. national suicide rate in 2010 was 7.53 per 100,000.

14. Given that depression was the most commonly observed of all disorders, an article that addresses particular dimensions of depression was recently published; see Csordas 2013.

15. See Hinton et al. 2009 for a conceptual and empirical analysis of the clinical commonality of the connection between anger and PTSD within the nuclear family and how family-related anger is generated.

16. For a nuanced application of the notion of ontological "precarity" rooted etymologically in supplication as a mode of subjectivity, see Lovell 2012.

17. It is an anthropological commonplace to critique diagnostic constructs as presumptively universal in the absence of empirical research. I agree with the position articulated by Byron Good (1992) that anthropological research on mental illness does well to utilize psychiatric diagnostic categories as a starting point for analysis and comparison. In careful research in Aceh, Indonesia, Good, Good, and Grayman find PISD to be a "good enough" concept for mental health research.

18. See also Judith Herman's (1997) analysis of the aftermath of trauma in the context of domestic and political violence.

19. As a diagnostic category, is important to keep in mind that posttraumatic stress disorder has the distinction of being the only major mental disorder in DSM-IV that requires a "stressor" as precursor to the development of symptoms. The diagnostic starting point of identifying specific agents or events as etiological and symptomatically criteria is unique in DSM. In PTSD we see vividly the external etiological agent ("stressor") suffused with personal experience manifest as psychopathology.

## CONCLUSION

1. For a treatment of the inherent irony of illness that "stands with endurance, aspiration, and humor as one of the 'transcendent responses' to the resistances humans face in their lives," see Lambek 2003: 17.

2. Braslow (2013: 783) extends the examination of recovery and recovery-based policies in historical context as "an amalgam of culturally determined beliefs, treatment practices, and assumptions about mental illness" that are continuous with rather than radically distinctive from attitudes and practices of past decades.

3. www.ft.com/cms/s/0/fa07a946-e1a1–11e3-b7c4–00144feabdc0.html#ixzz3 IbriG8Vo.

# Works Cited

Abu-Lughod, Lila
  1986   *Veiled Sentiments: Honor and Poetry in a Bedouin Society.* Berkeley: University of California Press.

Adams, Vincanne, Taslim van Hattum, and Diana English
  2009   Chronic Disaster Syndrome: Displacement, Disaster Capitalism, and the Eviction of the Poor from New Orleans. *American Ethnologist* 36(4): 615–36.

Afuape, Taiwo
  2011   *Power, Resistance and Liberation in Therapy with Survivors of Trauma: To Have Our Hearts Broken.* Hove: Routledge.

Allodi, F., and A. Rojas
  1985   The Health and Adaptation of Victims of Political Violence in Latin America (Psychiatric Effects of Torture and Disappearance). In *Psychiatry: The State of the Art.* Vol. 6, *Drug Dependence and Alcoholism, Forensic Psychiatry, Military Psychiatry.* P. Pichot, P. Berner, and K. Thau, eds. Pp. 243–48. New York: Plenum Press.

Alvarez, Mauricia
  1990   Central American Refugees. Paper delivered at the conference Psychotherapy of Diversity: Cross-Cultural Treatment Issues. Harvard Medical School, Department of Continuing Education.

Alvir, J. M., J. A. Lieberman, A. Z. Safferman, J. L. Schwimmer, and J. A. Schaaf
  1993   Clozapine-Induced Agranulocytosis: Incidence and Risk Factors in the United States. *New England Journal of Medicine* 329(3): 162–67.

Anderson-Fye, Eileen
  2004   A "Coca-Cola" Shape: Cultural Change, Body Image, and Eating Disorders in San Andres, Belize. *Culture, Medicine and Psychiatry* 28(4): 561–95.

Andreasen, N. C.
　1984　Scale for the Assessment of Positive Symptoms. Iowa City: University of Iowa.
Aneshensel, Carol S., and Clea A. Sucoff
　1996　The Neighborhood Context of Adolescent Mental Health. *Journal of Health and Social Behavior* 37(4): 293–310.
Antze, Paul, and Michael Lambek
　1996　*Tense Past: Cultural Essays in Trauma and Memory.* New York: Psychology Press.
Appadurai, Arjun, ed.
　1988　*The Social Life of Things: Commodities in Cultural Perspective.* New York: Cambridge University Press.
Arana, Ana
　2005　How the Street Gangs Took Central America. *Foreign Affairs* 843: 98–110.
Arendt, Hannah
　2006　*Eichmann in Jerusalem: A Report on the Banality of Evil.* New York: Penguin Books.
Aretxaga, Begoña
　1997　*Shattering Silence: Women, Nationalism, and Political Subjectivity in Northern Ireland.* Princeton, NJ: Princeton University Press.
　2003 Maddening States. *Annual Review of Anthropology,* 393–410.
Arévalo, Jorge, and Carmen Vizcarro
　1989　Niveles de "emoción expresada" en familiares de pacientes esquizo-frénicos: Datos para una comparación transcultural. *Revista de la Asociación Española de Neuropsiquiatría* 9(30): 437–50.
Argueta, Manlio
　1983　*One Day of Life.* New York: Vintage Books.
　1987　*Cuzcatlán: Where the Southern Sea Beats.* Trans. Clark Hansen. New York: Vintage Books.
Ariès, Philippe
　1965　*Centuries of Childhood: A Social History of Family Life.* New York: Vintage Books.
Ayers Counts, Dorothy
　1990　*Domestic Violence in Oceania.* Honolulu: Institute for Polynesian Studies, Brigham Young University–Hawaii.
Bader, Stephanie H., Tammy D. Barry, and Jill A. H. Hann
　2014　The Relation between Parental Expressed Emotion and Externalizing Behaviors in Children and Adolescents with an Autism Spectrum Disorder. *Focus on Autism and Other Developmental Disabilities:* 1088357614523065.
Barnes, Linda L., and Susan Starr Sered
　2005　*Religion and Healing in America.* Oxford: Oxford University Press.
Barrowclough, Christine
　2003　Attributions and Expressed Emotion: A Review. *Clinical Psychology Review* 23(6): 849–80.

Basu, Helene
  2014  Davaa and Duaa: The Pluralization of Healing Mental Disorders
        at a Muslim Pilgrimage Centre. In *Asymmetrical Conversations—
        Contestations, Circumventions and the Blurring of Therapeutic
        Boundaries*. William Sax, Harish Naraindas, and Johannes Quack,
        eds. Pp. 162–99. Oxford: Berghahn Books.
Bateson, Gregory
  1958  *Naven: A Survey of the Problems Suggested by a Composite Picture
        of the Culture of a New Guinea Tribe Drawn from Three Points of
        View.* Stanford, CA: Stanford University Press.
  1960a The Group Dynamics of Schizophrenia. In *Chronic Schizophrenia:
        Explorations in Theory and Treatment.* L. Appleby, J.M. Scher, and
        J. Cumming, eds. Pp. 90–105. New York: Free Press.
  1960b Minimal Requirements for a Theory of Schizophrenia. *Archives of
        General Psychiatry* 2(5): 477–91.
  1972  *Steps to an Ecology of Mind: Collected Essays in Anthropology,
        Psychiatry, Evolution, and Epistemology.* San Francisco: Chandler
        Publishing Co.
  1979  *Mind and Nature: A Necessary Unity.* New York: Dutton.
Bateson, Gregory, Don D. Jackson, Jay Haley, and John Weakland
  1956  Toward a Theory of Schizophrenia. *Behavioral Science* 1(4): 251–64.
  1963  A Note on the Double Bind—1962. *Family Process* 2(1): 154–61.
Bebbington, Paul E., and Liz Kuipers
  1994  The Predictive Utility of Expressed Emotion in Schizophrenia: An
        Aggregate Analysis. *Psychological Medicine* 24(3): 707–18.
Becker, Anne
  1995  *Body, Self, and Society: The View from Fiji.* Philadelphia: University
        of Pennsylvania Press.
Becker, Anne, and Arthur Kleinman
  2013  Mental Health and the Global Agenda. *New England Journal of
        Medicine* 369(1): 66–73.
Beckett, Samuel
  2010  *The Unnamable.* London: Faber & Faber.
Beeman, William O.
  1985  Dimensions of Dysphoria: The View from Linguistic Anthropology.
        In *Culture and Depression: Studies in the Anthropology and Cross-
        Cultural Psychiatry of Affect and Disorder.* Arthur Kleinman and
        Byron J. Good, eds. Pp. 216–43. Berkeley: University of California
        Press.
Belluck, Pam, and Benedict Carey
  2013  Psychiatry's New Guide Falls Short, Experts Say. *New York Times,*
        May 6. www.nytimes.com/2013/05/07/health/psychiatrys-new-guide-
        falls-short-experts-say.html. Accessed July 22, 2013.
Benedict, Ruth
  2008  Continuities and Discontinuities in Cultural Conditioning. In *Anthro-
  [1928] pology and Child Development: A Cross-Cultural Reader.* Robert

Alan LeVine and Rebecca Staples New, eds. Pp. 42–48. Malden, MA: Blackwell.

Berlioz, Hector, Gérard de Nerval, Almire Gandonnière, and Henry Barraud
1979    *La damnation de Faust.* Paris: L'Avant scène.

Bertrando, P., J. Beltz, C. Bressim, et al.
1992    Expressed Emotion and Schizophrenia in Italy: A Study of an Urban Population. *British Journal of Psychiatry* 161(2): 223–29.

Bhavsar, Vishal, and Dinesh Bhugra
2013    Cultural Factors and Sexual Dysfunction in Clinical Practice. *Advances in Psychiatric Treatment* 19(2): 144–52.

Bhui, K., S. Stansfeld, J. Head, et al.
2005    Cultural Identity, Acculturation, and Mental Health among Adolescents in East London's Multiethnic Community. *Journal of Epidemiology and Community Health* 59(4): 296–302.

Biehl, João
2005    *Vita: Life in a Zone of Social Abandonment.* Berkeley: University of California Press.
2010    "CATKINE . . . Asylum, Laboratory, Pharmacy, Pharmacist, I and the Cure": Pharmaceutical Subjectivity in the Global South. In *Pharmaceutical Self: The Global Shaping of Experience in an Age of Psychopharmacology.* Janis H. Jenkins, ed. Pp. 67–96. Santa Fe, NM: School for Advanced Research Press.

Biehl, João, Byron Good, and Arthur Kleinman
2007    *Subjectivity Ethnographic Investigations.* Berkeley: University of California Press.

Boehnlein, James K., and J. David Kinzie
1995    Refugee Trauma. *Transcultural Psychiatry* 32: 223–52.

Bourdieu, Pierre, Alain Accardo, and Priscilla Parkhurst Ferguson
1999    *The Weight of the World: Social Suffering in Contemporary Society.* Stanford, CA: Stanford University Press.

Bouton, Mark E., and Jaylyn Waddell
2007    Some Biobehavioral Insights into Persistent Effects of Emotional Trauma. In *Understanding Trauma: Integrating Biological, Clinical, and Cultural Perspectives.* L. J. Kirmayer, R. Lemelson, and M. Barad, eds. Pp. 41–59. Cambridge: Cambridge University Press.

Braslow, Joel T.
2013    The Manufacture of Recovery. *Annual Review of Clinical Psychology* 9: 781–809.

Breslau, Joshua
2004    Cultures of Trauma: Anthropological Views of Posttraumatic Stress Disorder in International Health. *Culture, Medicine and Psychiatry* 28(2): 113–26.

Briggs, Jean L.
1987    In Search of Emotional Meaning. *Ethos* 15(1): 8–15.
1998    *Inuit Morality Play: The Emotional Education of a Three-Year-Old.* New Haven, CT: Yale University Press.

Brodwin, Paul E.
  2012  *Everyday Ethics: Voices from the Front Line of Community Psychiatry*. Berkeley: University of California Press.
Brown, George W.
  1985  The Discovery of Expressed Emotion: Induction or Deduction. In *Expressed Emotion in Families*. Pp. 7–25. New York: Guilford Press.
Brown, George W., J.L. Birley, and J.K. Wing
  1972  Influence of Family Life on the Course of Schizophrenic Disorders: A Replication. *British Journal of Psychiatry* 121(562): 241–58.
Brown, George W., and Tirril O. Harris
  1978  *Social Origins of Depression: A Study of Psychiatric Disorder in Women*. New York: Free Press.
Brown, George W., E.M. Monck, G.M. Carstairs, and J.K. Wing
  1962  Influence of Family Life on the Course of Schizophrenic Illness. *British Journal of Preventive and Social Medicine* 16(2): 55–68.
Brown, George W., David Quinton, Michael Rutter, and Christine E. Vaughn
  1978  Camberwell Family Interview: Notes on the Rating of Expressed Emotion. Unpublished (rating manual in author's possession).
Bristol-Myers Squibb
  2011  Televised advertisement for Abilify. ABILIFY® (aripiprazole) Anti-Depressant Add-on Treatment. www.youtube.com/watch?v=tGymr78FtbU&feature=youtube_gdata_player. Accessed March 23, 2014.
Bruner, Jerome S.
  1990  *Acts of Meaning*. Cambridge, MA: Harvard University Press.
Buckley, Thomas C.T., and Alma Gottlieb
  1988  *Blood Magic: The Anthropology of Menstruation*. Berkeley: University of California Press.
Butler, Judith
  2004  *Precarious Life: The Powers of Mourning and Violence*. London: Verso.
  2009  Performativity, Precarity and Sexual Politics. *Revista de Antropología Iberoamericana* 4(3): i–xiii.
Calderón-Tena, C.O., G.P. Knight, and G. Carlo
  2011  The Socialization of Prosocial Behavioral Tendencies among Mexican American Adolescents: The Role of Familism Values. *Cultural Diversity and Ethnic Minority Psychology* 17(1): 98.
Calzada, E.J., C.S. Tamis-LeMonda, and H. Yoshikawa
  2013  *Familismo* in Mexican and Dominican Families from Low-Income, Urban Communities. *Journal of Family Issues* 34(12): 1696–1724.
Campbell, J.C.
  1985  Beating of Wives: A Cross-Cultural Perspective. *Victimology* 10(1–4): 174–85.
Canguilhem, Georges
  1989  *The Normal and the Pathological*. New York: Zone Books.

Canino, Glorisa
    1982    The Hispanic Woman: Sociocultural Influences on Diagnoses and
            Treatment. In *Mental Health and Hispanic Americans: Clinical Per-
            spectives*. R. Bercerra, Marvin Karno, and J. Escobar, eds. Pp. 117–
            38. New York: Grune and Stratton.
Carpenter-Song, Elizabeth
    2009a   Caught in the Psychiatric Net: Meanings and Experiences of ADHD,
            Pediatric Bipolar Disorder and Mental Health Treatment among a
            Diverse Group of Families in the United States. *Culture, Medicine
            and Psychiatry* 33(1): 61–85.
    2009b   Children's Sense of Self in Relation to Clinical Processes: Portraits of
            Pharmaceutical Transformation. *Ethos* 37(3): 257–81.
Carpenter-Song, Elizabeth, Edward Chu, Robert E. Drake, Mieka Ritsema,
    Beverly Smith, and Hoyt Alverson
    2010    Ethno-Cultural Variations in the Experience and Meaning of Mental
            Illness and Treatment: Implications for Access and Utilization. *Trans-
            cultural Psychiatry* 47(2): 224–51.
Casey, Edward S.
    1987    *Remembering: A Phenomenological Study*. Bloomington: Indiana
            University Press.
Cechnicki, Andrzej, Anna Bielańska, Igor Hanuszkiewicz, and Artur
    Daren
    2013    The Predictive Validity of Expressed Emotions (EE) in Schizophrenia:
            A 20-Year Prospective Study. *Journal of Psychiatric Research* 47(2):
            208–14.
Center for Disease Control and Prevention
    n.d.    National Center for Injury Prevention and Control—Injury Center.
            www.cdc.gov/injury/. Accessed October 10, 2013.
Chaouli, Michel
    2002    *The Laboratory of Poetry: Chemistry and Poetics in the Work of Frie-
            drich Schlegel*. Baltimore: Johns Hopkins University Press.
Chapman, A.H.
    1976    *Harry Stack Sullivan: His Life and His Work*. New York: Putnam.
Chen, Nancy
    2003    *Breathing Spaces: Qigong, Psychiatry, and Healing in China*. New
            York: Columbia University Press.
Chiao, Joan Y., Bobby K. Cheon, Narun Pornpattananangkul, Alissa J. Mrazek,
    and Kate D. Blizinsky
    2013    *Cultural Neuroscience: Understanding Human Diversity*. Oxford:
            Oxford University Press.
Choudhury, S., and L.J. Kirmayer
    2009    Cultural Neuroscience and Psychopathology: Prospects for Cultural
            Psychiatry. *Progress in Brain Research* 178: 263–83.
Choudhury, Suparna, and Jan Slaby, eds.
    2012    *Critical Neuroscience: A Handbook of the Social and Cultural Con-
            texts of Neuroscience*. Chichester: Wiley-Blackwell.
Churchland, Patricia Smith
    2013    *Touching a Nerve: The Self as Brain*. New York: Norton.

Cloud, David
  2014  On Life Support: Public Health in the Age of Mass Incarceration. Report by the Vera Institute of Justice. www.vera.org/pubs/public-health-mass-incarceration.

Cohen, A., V. Patel, R. Thara, and O. Gureje
  2007  Questioning an Axiom: Better Prognosis for Schizophrenia in the Developing World? *Schizophrenia Bulletin* 32(2): 229–24.

Collins, Pamela Y., Vikram Patel, S.S. Joestl, et al.
  2011  Grand Challenges in Global Mental Health. *Nature* 475(7354): 27–30.

Corin, Ellen
  1990  Facts and Meaning in Psychiatry: An Anthropological Approach to the Lifeworld of Schizophrenics. *Culture, Medicine and Psychiatry* 14(2): 153–88.

Castoriadis, Cornelius
  1987  *The Imaginary Institution of Society*. Trans. by Kathleen Blarney. Cambridge, UK: Polity Press.

Corradi, Juan, Patricia Fagen, and Manuel Garreton
  1992  *Fear at the Edge: State Terror and Resistance in Latin America*. Berkeley: University of California Press.

Cottingham, Katie
  2009  How Do Psychotropic Drugs Work? *Journal of Proteome Research* 8(4): 1618.

Counts, Dorothy
  1990  *Domestic Violence in Oceania*. Honolulu: Institute for Polynesian Studies, Brigham Young University–Hawaii.

Cozolino, Louis
  2006  *The Neuroscience of Human Relationships: Attachment and the Developing Social Brain*. New York: Norton.

Craig, T.J., C. Siegel, K. Hopper, and S. Lin
  1997  Outcome in Schizophrenia and Related Disorders Compared between Developing and Developed Countries: A Recursive Partitioning Re-Analysis of the WHO DOSMD Data. *British Journal of Psychiatry* 170(3): 229.

Critchley, H.D., J. Eccles, and S.N. Garfinkel
  2013  Interaction between Cognition, Emotion, and the Autonomic Nervous System. In *Autonomic Nervous System: Handbook of Clinical Neurology*. Ruud M. Bujis and Dick F. Swaab, eds. 117:59–77. Amsterdam: Elsevier.

Csordas, Thomas J.
  1993  Somatic Modes of Attention. *Cultural Anthropology* 8(1): 135–56.
  1994  *The Sacred Self: A Cultural Phenomenology of Charismatic Healing*. Berkeley: University of California Press.
  2000  The Navajo Healing Project. *Medical Anthropology Quarterly* 14(4): 463–75.
  2011  Cultural Phenomenology. In *A Companion to the Anthropology of the Body and Embodiment*. Frances Escia-Lees, ed. Pp. 137–56. Hoboken, NJ: Wiley-Blackwell.
  2013  Inferring Immediacy in Adolescent Accounts of Depression. *Journal of Consciousness Studies* 20(7–8): 239–53.

Csordas, Thomas J., and Elizabeth Lewton
   1998   Practice, Performance, and Experience in Ritual Healing. *Transcultural Psychiatry* 35(4): 435–512.
Cuellar, Israel
   1980   An Acculturation Scale for Mexican American Normal and Clinical Populations. *Hispanic Journal of Behavioral Sciences* 2(3): 199–217.
Cutajar, Margaret C., P. E. Mullen, J. R. Ogloff, S. D. Thomas, D. L. Wells, and J. Spataro
   2010   Schizophrenia and Other Psychotic Disorders in a Cohort of Sexually Abused Children. *Archives of General Psychiatry* 67(11): 1114–19.
Cutting, Linda P., Jennifer M. Aakre, and Nancy M. Docherty
   2006   Schizophrenic Patients' Perceptions of Stress, Expressed Emotion, and Sensitivity to Criticism. *Schizophrenia Bulletin* 32(4): 743–50.
Daniel, E. V.
   1994   The Individual in Terror. In *Embodiment and Experience: The Existential Ground of Culture and Self*. I.J. Csordas, ed. Pp. 229–47. Cambridge: Cambridge University Press.
Dao, James
   2013   Drone Pilots Found to Get Stress Disorders Much as Those in Combat Do. *New York Times,* February 22.
Daruy-Filho, L., E. Brietzke, B. Lafer, and R. Grassi-Oliveira
   2011   Childhood Maltreatment and Clinical Outcomes of Bipolar Disorder. *Acta Psychiatrica Scandinavica* 124(6): 427–34.
Das, Veena
   1995   *Critical Events: An Anthropological Perspective on Contemporary India*. New York: Oxford University Press.
Das, Veena, Arthur Kleinman, Margaret M. Lock, Mamphela Ramphele, and Pamela Reynolds, eds.
   2001   *Remaking a World: Violence, Social Suffering, and Recovery*. Berkeley: University of California Press.
David, William K.
   1902   *Secrets of Wise Men, Chemists and Great Physicians: Illustrated Comprising an Unusual Collection of Moneymaking, Money-Saving, and Health-Giving Prescriptions, Receipts, Formulas, Processes and Trade Secrets*. Philadelphia: WK David.
Davis, Colin
   2005   Hauntology, Spectres and Phantoms. *French Studies* 59(3): 373–79.
Deegan, Patricia E.
   1988   Recovery: The Lived Experience of Rehabilitation. *Psychosocial Rehabilitation* 11(4): 11–19.
   2005   The Importance of Personal Medicine: A Qualitative Study of Resilience in People with Psychiatric Disabilities. *Scandinavian Journal of Public Health* 33: 1–7.
   2007   The Lived Experience of Using Psychiatric Medication in the Recovery Process and a Shared Decision-Making Program to Support It. *Psychiatric Rehabilitation Journal* 31(1): 62–69.

DeGrandpre, Richard J.
  2006   *The Cult of Pharmacology: How America Became the World's Most Troubled Drug Culture*. Durham, NC: Duke University Press.
Deleuze, Gilles, and Felix Guattari
  1988   *A Thousand Plateaus: Capitalism and Schizophrenia*. Trans. Brian Massumi. London: Bloomsbury.
DeNavas-Walt, Carmen, Bernadette D. Proctor, and Jessica C. Smith
  2011   Income, Poverty, and Health Insurance Coverage: 2010. US Census Bureau. www.census.gov/hhes/www/hlthins/data/incpovhlth/2010/index .html. Accessed October 17, 2013.
Derrida, Jacques, Bernd Magnus, and Stephen Cullenberg
  2006   *Specters of Marx: The State of Debt, the Work of Mourning and the New International*. New York: Routledge.
Desjarlais, Robert
  1994   Struggling Along: The Possibilities for Experience among the Homeless Mentally Ill. *American Anthropologist* 96(4): 886–901.
  1997   *Shelter Blues: Sanity and Selfhood among the Homeless*. Philadelphia: University of Pennsylvania Press.
Desjarlais, Robert, and C. Jason Throop
  2011   Phenomenological Approaches in Anthropology. *Annual Review of Anthropology* 40(1): 87–102.
Docherty, N. M., A. St.-Hilaire, J. M. Aakre, et al.
  2011   Anxiety Interacts with Expressed Emotion Criticism in the Prediction of Psychotic Symptom Exacerbation. *Schizophrenia Bulletin* 37(3): 611–18.
Doi, T.
  1973   *The Anatomy of Dependency*. New York: Harper and Row.
Duckworth, Ken, Vijaya Nair, Jayendra K. Patel, and Stephen M. Goldfinger
  1997   Lost Time, Found Hope and Sorrow: The Search for Self, Connection, and Purpose during "Awakenings" on the New Antipsychotics. *Harvard Review of Psychiatry* 5(4): 227–33.
Duclos, Jeanne, Géraldine Dorard, Sylvie Berthoz, et al.
  2014   Expressed Emotion in Anorexia Nervosa: What Is Inside the "Black Box"? *Comprehensive Psychiatry* 55(1): 71–79.
Dumit, Joseph
  2012   *Drugs for Life: How Pharmaceutical Companies Define Our Health*. Durham, NC: Duke University Press.
Duncan, Whitney L.
  2012   The Culture of Mental Health in a Changing Oaxaca. PhD dissertation, University of California, San Diego.
  2015   Gendered Trauma and Its Effects: Domestic Violence and PTSD in Oaxaca. In *Culture and PTSD*. Devon Hinton and Byron Good, eds. Pp. 202-239. Philadelphia: University of Pennsylvania Press.
Duran, Eduardo, and Bonnie Duran
  1995   *Native American Postcolonial Psychology*. Albany: State University of New York Press.

Duranti, Alessandro
  2010   Husserl, Intersubjectivity and Anthropology. *Anthropological Theory* 10(1–2): 16–35.
Ecks, Stefan
  2013   *Eating Drugs: Psychopharmaceutical Pluralism in India.* New York: New York University Press.
Edgerton, Robert B.
  1966   Conceptions of Psychosis in Four East African Societies. *American Anthropologist* 68(2): 408–25.
  1969   On the Recognition of Mental Illness. In *Changing Perspectives in Mental Illness.* Stanley C. Plog and Robert B. Edgerton, eds. Austin, TX: Holt Rinehart and Winston.
  1978   The Study of Deviance—Marginal Man or Everyman? In *The Making of Psychological Anthropology.* Pp. 444–76. Berkeley: University of California Press.
  1980   Traditional Treatment for Mental Illness in Africa: A Review. *Culture, Medicine and Psychiatry* 4(2): 167–89.
  1985   *Rules, Exceptions, and Social Order.* Berkeley: University of California Press.
Edgerton, Robert B., and A. Cohen
  1994   Culture and Schizophrenia: The DOSMD Challenge. *British Journal of Psychiatry* 164(2): 222–31.
Edgerton, Robert B., and Marvin Karno
  1971   Mexican-American Bilingualism and the Perception of Mental Illness. *Archives of General Psychiatry* 24(3): 286–90.
Eisenberg, Leon, and Laurence B. Guttmacher
  2010   Were We All Asleep at the Switch? A Personal Reminiscence of Psychiatry from 1940 to 2010. *Acta Psychiatrica Scandinavica* 122(2): 89–102.
Ellis, Alissa J., Larissa C. Portnoff, David A. Axelson, et al.
  2014   Parental Expressed Emotion and Suicidal Ideation in Adolescents with Bipolar Disorder. *Psychiatry Research* 216(2): 213–16.
El-Shaarawi, Nadia
  2015   "Everything Here Is Temporary": Psychological Distress and Suffering among Iraqi Refugees in Egypt. In *Genocide and Mass Violence: Memory, Symptom, and Recovery.* D. Hinton and A. Hinton, eds. Pp. 195–211. Cambridge: Cambridge University Press.
Endicott, Jean, and Robert L. Spitzer
  1978   A Diagnostic Interview: The Schedule for Affective Disorders and Schizophrenia. *Archives of General Psychiatry* 35(7): 837–44.
Escobar, Javier I.
  2014   Global Mental Health and Psychiatric Services. *Psychiatric Services* 65(8): 967.
Escobar, Javier I., A. Diaz-Martinez, and Michael Gara
  2006   Idiopathic Physical Symptoms. *CNS Spectrums* 11(3): 201–210.
Estroff, Sue E.
  1985   *Making It Crazy: An Ethnography of Psychiatric Clients in an American Community.* Berkeley: University of California Press.

1989　Self, Identity, and Subjective Experiences of Schizophrenia: In Search of the Subject. *Schizophrenia Bulletin* 15(2): 189–96.

2004　Subject/Subjectivities in Dispute: The Poetics, Politics, and Performance of First-Person Narratives of People with Schizophrenia. In *Schizophrenia, Culture, and Subjectivity:The Edge of Experience.* Janis H. Jenkins and Robert J. Barrett, eds. Pp. 282–302. New York: Cambridge University Press.

Evans-Pritchard, E. E., and Eva Gillies

1976　*Witchcraft, Oracles, and Magic among the Azande.* Oxford: Clarendon Press.

Fabrega, Horacio

1979　The Scientific Usefulness of the Idea of Illness. *Perspectives in Biological Medicine* 22: 545–58.

Fabrega, Horacio, and Barbara Diane Miller

1995　Toward a More Comprehensive Medical Anthropology: The Case of Adolescent Psychopathology. *Medical Anthropology Quarterly: International Journal for the Cultural and Social Analysis of Health* 9: 431–61.

Fabrega, Horacio, and Daniel B. Silver

1973　*Illness and Shamanistic Curing in Zinacantan: An Ethnomedical Analysis.* Stanford, CA: Stanford University Press.

Fabrega, Horacio, Jon D. Swartz, and Carole Ann Wallace

1968　Ethnic Differences in Psychopathology—II. Specific Differences with Emphasis on a Mexican American Group. *Journal of Psychiatric Research* 6(3): 221–35.

Falloon, Ian R. H.

1988　*Handbook of Behavioral Family Therapy.* New York: Guilford Press.

Falloon, Ian R. H., Jeffrey L. Boyd, and Christine W. McGill

1984　*Family Care of Schizophrenia: A Problem-Solving Approach to the Treatment of Mental Illness.* New York: Guilford Press.

Farias, Pablo

1991　Emotional Distress and Its Socio-political Correlates in Salvadoran Refugees: Analysis of a Clinical Sample. *Culture, Medicine and Psychiatry* 15(2): 167–92.

Farmer, Paul

1997　On Suffering and Structural Violence: A View from Below. In *Social Suffering.* Arthur Kleinman, Veena Das, and Margaret M. Lock, eds. Pp. 261–83. Berkeley: University of California Press.

2004a　An Anthropology of Structural Violence. *Current Anthropology* 45(3): 305–25.

2004b　*Pathologies of Power: Health, Human Rights, and the New War on the Poor.* Berkeley: University of California Press.

2006　*AIDS and Accusation: Haiti and the Geography of Blame.* Berkeley: University of California Press.

Farmer, Paul, Arthur Kleinman, Jim Kim, and Matthew Basilico

2013　*Reimagining Global Health: An Introduction.* Berkeley: University of California Press.

Fassin, Didier

    2004   *Des maux indicibles: Sociologie des lieux d'écoute.* Paris: la Découverte.

Fassin, Didier, and Richard Rechtman

    2009   *The Empire of Trauma: An Inquiry into the Condition of Victim-hood.* Rachel Gomme, trans. Princeton, NJ: Princeton University Press.

Fazel, Mina, and Alan Stein

    2002   The Mental Health of Refugee Children. *Archives of Disease in Childhood* 87(5): 366–70.

Fazel, Mina, Jeremy Wheeler, and John Danesh

    2005   Prevalence of Serious Mental Disorder in 7000 Refugees Resettled in Western Countries: A Systematic Review. *Lancet* 365(9467): 1309–14.

Feldman, Allen

    1991   *Formations of Violence: The Narrative of the Body and Political Terror in Northern Ireland.* Chicago: University of Chicago Press.

Fernandez, James W.

    1986   *Persuasions and Performances: The Play of Tropes in Culture.* Bloomington: Indiana University Press.

    1991   *Beyond Metaphor: The Theory of Tropes in Anthropology.* Stanford, CA: Stanford University Press.

Fisher, Daniel

    2014   Recovery through Voice and Dialogue. Mad in America: Science Psychiatry, and Community. www.madinamerica.com/author/dfisher/. Accessed March 11, 2014.

Floersch, Jerry, Lisa Townsend, Jeffrey Longhofer, et al.

    2009   Adolescent Experience of Psychotropic Treatment. *Transcultural Psychiatry* 46(1): 157–79.

Forché, Carolyn

    1993   *Against Forgetting: Twentieth-Century Poetry of Witness.* New York: Norton.

Ford, Leonard A., and E. Winston Grundmeier

    1993   *Chemical Magic.* New York: Dover.

Fortuna, Lisa R., Michelle V. Porche, and Margarita Alegría

    2008   Political Violence, Psychosocial Trauma, and the Context of Mental Health Services Use among Immigrant Latinos in the United States. *Ethnicity and Health* 13(5): 4335–63. http://works.bepress.com/lisa_fortuna/1.

Fortune, Reo

    1963   *Sorcerers of Dobu: The Social Anthropology of the Dobu Islanders of*
    [1932]   *the Western Pacific.* Rev. ed. New York: E. P. Dutton.

Fosha, Diana, Daniel J. Siegel, and Marion Solomon

    2009   *The Healing Power of Emotion: Affective Neuroscience, Development and Clinical Practice.* New York: Norton.

Foucault, Michel

    1965   *Madness and Civilization: A History of Insanity in the Age of Reason.* New York: Pantheon Books.

1977    *Discipline and Punish: The Birth of the Prison*. New York: Pantheon Books.

1980    *Power/Knowledge: Selected Interviews and Other Writings, 1972–1977*. Colin Gordon, ed. New York: Pantheon Books.

Frazer, James George

1890    *The Golden Bough: A Study in Comparative Religion*. New York: Macmillan.

Freedman, Alfred M., Harold I. Kaplan, and Benjamin J. Sadock

1976    *Modern Synopsis of Comprehensive Textbook of Psychiatry*, II. Baltimore, MD: Williams & Wilkins.

Freud, Anna

1958    Adolescence. *Psychoanalytic Study of the Child* 13: 255–78.

Freud, Sigmund

1962    Further Remarks on the Neuro-Psychoses of Defence. In *The Standard Edition of the Complete Psychological Works of Sigmund Freud, Volume 3 (1893–1899): Early Psycho-Analytic Publications*. Pp. 157–85. London: Hogarth Press.

Friedman, Jonathan

1994    *Cultural Identity and Global Process*. Thousand Oaks, CA: Sage.

Friedmann, Richard A.

2012    A Call for Caution in the Use of Antipsychotic Drugs. *New York Times*, September 24. www.nytimes.com/2012/09/25/health /a-call-for-caution-in-the-use-of-antipsychotic-drugs.html. Accessed July 17, 2013.

Friedrich, Paul

1991    Polytropy. In *Metaphor: The Theory of Tropes in Anthropology*. James W. Fernandez, ed. Pp. 17–55. Stanford, CA: Stanford University Press.

Frijda, Nico H.

1987    Emotion, Cognitive Structure, and Action Tendency. *Cognition & Emotion* 1(2): 115–43.

Fromm-Reichmann, Frieda

1948    Notes on the Development of Treatment of Schizophrenics by Psychoanalytic Psychotherapy. *Psychiatry* 11(3): 263–73.

Gadamer, Hans-Georg

1996    *The Enigma of Health*. Cambridge: Polity Press.

Gaines, Atwood

1982    Cultural Definitions, Behavior and the Person in American Psychiatry. In *Cultural Conceptions of Mental Health and Therapy*. Anthony J. Marsella and Geoffrey M. White, eds. Pp. 167–92. New York: Springer.

Garcia, Angela

2010    *The Pastoral Clinic: Addiction and Dispossession along the Rio Grande*. Berkeley: University of California Press.

Garro, Linda C.

1986    Intracultural Variation in Folk Medical Knowledge: A Comparison between Curers and Non-Curers. *American Anthropologist* 88(2): 351–70.

2002 Hallowell's Challenge: Explanations of Illness and Cross-Cultural Research. *Anthropological Theory* 2: 77–97.

Gaviría, F. Moises, and Jose D. Araña
1987 Health and Behavior: Research Agenda for Hispanics. Simon Bolivar Hispanic-American Psychiatric Research and Training Program, University of Illinois at Chicago.

Gazzaniga, Michael S.
2011 *Who's in Charge? Free Will and the Science of the Brain.* New York: HarperCollins.

Geertz, Clifford
1973 *The Interpretation of Cultures: Selected Essays.* New York: Basic Books.

Geertz, Hildred
1959 The Vocabulary of Emotion: A Study of Javanese Socialization Processes. *Psychiatry: Journal for the Study of Interpersonal Processes* 22: 225–37.

Gergen, Kenneth J.
1990 Social Understanding and the Inscription of Self. In *Cultural Psychology.* J. Stigler, R. Shweder, and G. Herdt, eds. Pp. 569–606. Cambridge: Cambridge University Press.

Glauber, Johann Rudolf, and Christopher Packe
1689 *The Works of the Highly Experienced and Famous Chymist, John Rudolph Glauber: Containing, Great Variety of Choice Secrets in Medicine and Alchymy in the Working of Metallick Mines, and the Separation of Metals.* Christopher Packe, trans. London: Thomas Milbourn.

Goldenberg, Irene, and Herbert Goldenberg
1980 *Family Therapy: An Overview.* Monterey, CA: Brooks/Cole.

Goldstein, Donna M.
2003 *Laughter Out of Place: Race, Class, Violence, and Sexuality in a Rio Shantytown.* Berkeley: University of California Press.

Goldstein, M. J.
1987 The UCLA High-Risk Project. *Schizophrenia Bulletin* 13(3): 505–14.

Goldstein, M. J., and D. J. Miklowitz
1989 Patterns of Expressed Emotion and Patient Coping Styles That Characterise the Families of Recent Onset Schizophrenics. *British Journal of Psychiatry* Supplement (5): 107–11.

Goldstein, M. J., S. A. Talovic, and K. H. Nuechterlein
1991 Family Interaction vs. Individual Psychopathology. *Schizophrenia Research* 4(3): 303–4.

Gómez-de-Regil, L., T. R. Kwapil, and N. Barrantes-Vidal
2014 Predictors of Expressed Emotion, Burden and Quality of Life in Relatives of Mexican Patients with Psychosis. *Journal of Psychiatric and Mental Health Nursing* 21(2): 170–79.

Gone, Joseph P., and Joseph E. Trimble
2012 American Indian and Alaska Native Mental Health: Diverse Perspectives on Enduring Disparities. *Annual Review of Clinical Psychology* 8: 131–60.

Good, Byron J.

1977    The Heart of What's the Matter: The Semantics of Illness in Iran. *Culture, Medicine and Psychiatry* 1(1): 25–58.

1992    Culture and Psychopathology: Directions for Psychiatric Anthropology. In *New Directions in Psychological Anthropology.* Theodore Schwartz, Geoffrey M. White, and Catherine A. Lutz, eds. Pp. 181–205. Cambridge: Cambridge University Press.

1994    *Medicine, Rationality, and Experience: An Anthropological Perspective.* Cambridge: Cambridge University Press.

2010a    The Complexities of Psychopharmaceutical Hegemonies in Indonesia. In *Pharmaceutical Self: The Global Shaping of Experience in an Age of Psychopharmacology.* Janis H. Jenkins, ed. Pp. 117–44. Santa Fe, NM: School for Advanced Research Press.

2010b    Emil Kraepelin on Pathologies of the Will. In *Toward an Anthropology of the Will.* K. Murphy and C. Throop, eds. Pp. 158–75. Stanford, CA: Stanford University Press.

2012a    Phenomenology, Psychoanalysis, and Subjectivity in Java. *Ethos* 40(1): 24–36.

2012b    Theorizing the "Subject" of Medical and Psychiatric Anthropology. *Journal of the Royal Anthropological Institute* 18(3): 515–35.

Good, Byron J., and Mary-Jo DelVecchio Good

1982    Toward a Meaning-Centered Analysis of Popular Illness Categories: "Fright Illness" and "Heart Distress" in Iran. In *Cultural Conceptions of Mental Health and Therapy.* Anthony J. Marsella and Geoffrey M. White, eds. Pp. 141–66. Culture, Illness, and Healing, 4. Amsterdam: Springer Netherlands.

2012    "To Make a Difference . . . ": Narrative Desire in Global Medicine. *Narrative Inquiry in Bioethics* 2(2): 121–24.

Good, Byron J., Mary-Jo DelVecchio Good, and Jesse Grayman

2015    Is PTSD a "Good Enough" Concept for Post-Conflict Mental Health Work? Reflections on Work in Aceh, Indonesia. In *Culture and PTSD.* Devon Hinton and Byron Good, eds. Pp. 387–418. Philadelphia: University of Pennsylvania Press.

Good, Byron J., and Devon E. Hinton

2009    Introduction: Panic Disorder in Cross-Cultural and Historical Perspective. In *Culture and Panic Disorder.* Devon E. Hinton and Byron J. Good, eds. Pp. 1–28. New York: Palgrave Macmillan.

Good, Byron J., and Subandi

2004    Experiences of Psychosis in Javanese Culture: Reflections on a Case of Acute, Recurrent Psychosis in Contemporary Yogyakarta, Indonesia. In *Schizophrenia, Culture, and Subjectivity: The Edge of Experience.* Janis H. Jenkins and Robert J. Barrett, eds. Pp. 167–95. New York: Cambridge University Press.

Good, Mary-Jo DelVecchio

1995    *American Medicine: The Quest for Competence.* Berkeley: University of California Press.

2007    The Medical Imaginary and the Biotechnical Embrace. In *Subjectivity: Ethnographic Investigations.* Joao Biehl, Byron Good, and Arthur

Kleinman, eds. Pp. 362–80. Berkeley: University of California Press.

2010 Trauma in Postconflict Aceh and Psychopharmaceuticals as a Medium of Exchange. In *Pharmaceutical Self: The Global Shaping of Experience in an Age of Psychopharmacology*. Janis H. Jenkins, ed. Pp. 41–66. Santa Fe, NM: School for Advanced Research Press.

Good, Mary-Jo DelVecchio, Byron J. Good, and Michael M.J. Fischer

1988 Introduction: Discourse and the Study of Emotion, Illness and Healing. *Culture, Medicine and Psychiatry* 12(1): 1–7.

Good, Mary-Jo DelVecchio, Byron J. Good, and Robert Moradi

1985 The Interpretation of Iranian Depressive Illness and Dysphoric Affect. In *Culture and Depression: Studies in the Anthropology and Cross-Cultural Psychiatry of Affect and Disorder*. Arthur Kleinman and Byron J. Good, eds. Pp. 369–428. Berkeley: University of California Press.

Good, Mary-Jo DelVecchio, Sandra Teresa Hyde, Sarah Pinto, and Byron J. Good

2008 *Postcolonial Disorders*. Berkeley: University of California Press.

Good, Mary-Jo DelVecchio, Sara W. Willen, Seth Donal Hannah, Ken Vicory, and Lawrence Taeseng Park, eds.

2011 *Shattering Culture: American Medicine Responds to Cultural Diversity*. New York: Russell Sage Foundation.

Greek, Milt

2012 *Schizophrenia: A Blueprint for Recovery*. Athens, OH: M. Greek.

Gregg, Melissa, and Gregory J. Seigworth

2010 *The Affect Theory Reader*. Durham, NC: Duke University Press.

Gross, C.S.

2004 Struggling with Imaginaries of Trauma and Trust: The Refugee Experience in Switzerland. *Culture, Medicine and Psychiatry* 28(2): 151–67.

Guarnaccia, Peter J., and Pablo Farias

1988 The Social Meanings of Nervios: A Case Study of a Central American Woman. *Social Science & Medicine* 26(12): 1223–31.

Guarnaccia, Peter J., Byron J. Good, and Arthur Kleinman

1990 A Critical Review of Epidemiological Studies of Puerto Rican Mental Health. *American Journal of Psychiatry* 147(11): 1449–56.

Gupta, Akhil, and James Ferguson

1997 *Culture, Power, Place: Explorations in Critical Anthropology*. Durham, NC: Duke University Press.

Gutiérrez, E., V. Escudero, J.A. Valero, and M.C. Vazquez

1988 Expresión de emociones y curso de la esquizofrenia: II. Expresión de emociones y el curso de la esquizofrenia en pacientes en remisión. *Análisis y Modificación de Conducta* 14(40): 275–316.

Hall, G. Stanley

1904 *Adolescence: Its Psychology and Its Relations to Physiology, Anthropology, Sociology, Sex, Crime, Religion and Education*. New York: D. Appleton and Co.

Hallowell, A. Irving

1934 Culture and Mental Disorder. *Journal of Abnormal and Social Psychology* 29(1): 1.

1955    *Culture and Experience.* Philadelphia: University of Pennsylvania Press.

Hamilton, Alison B., Ines Poza, and Donna L. Washington
2011    "Homelessness and Trauma Go Hand-in-Hand": Pathways to Homelessness among Women Veterans. *WHI Women's Health Issues,* Supplement 21(4): S203–S209.

Han, Clara
2012    *Life in Debt: Times of Care and Violence in Neoliberal Chile.* Berkeley: University of California Press.

Harding, Sandra G.
1991    *Whose Science? Whose Knowledge? Thinking from Women's Lives.* Ithaca, NY: Cornell University Press.
2008    *Sciences from Below: Feminisms, Postcolonialities, and Modernities.* Durham, NC: Duke University Press.
2011    *The Postcolonial Science and Technology Studies Reader.* Durham, NC: Duke University Press.

Harrison, G., K. Hopper, T. Craig, et al.
2001    Recovery from Psychotic Illness: A 15- and 25-Year International Follow-up Study. *British Journal of Psychiatry* 178: 506–17.

Hawkins, Anne Hunsaker
1999    *Reconstructing Illness: Studies in Pathography.* Lafayette, IN: Purdue University Press and National Center for Health Statistics.

Healy, David
1997    *The Antidepressant Era.* Cambridge, MA: Harvard University Press.

Hendren, Robert L., and Irving N. Berlin
1991    *Psychiatric Inpatient Care of Children and Adolescents: A Multicultural Approach.* New York: Wiley.

Henry, Doug
2006    Violence and the Body: Somatic Expressions of Trauma and Vulnerability during War. *Medical Anthropology Quarterly* 20(3): 379–98.

Herman, Judith Lewis
1997    *Trauma and Recovery.* New York: Basic Books.

Herzog, Patricia Susan
1991    *Conscious and Unconscious: Freud's Dynamic Distinction Reconsidered.* Madison, CT: International Universities Press.

Hinton, Devon, Khin Um, and Phalnarith Ba
2001    A Unique Panic-Disorder Presentation among Khmer Refugees: The Sore-Neck Syndrome. *Culture, Medicine and Psychiatry* 25(3) 297–316.

Hinton, Devon E., and Byron Good
2009    *Culture and Panic Disorder.* Stanford, CA: Stanford University Press.

Hinton, Devon E., Alexander L. Hinton, Kok-Thay Eng, and Sophearith Choung
2012    PTSD and Key Somatic Complaints and Cultural Syndromes among Rural Cambodians: The Results of a Needs Assessment Survey. *Medical Anthropology Quarterly* 26(3): 383–407.

Hinton, Devon E., A. Rasmussen, L. Nou, M. H. Pollack, and M. J. Good
 2009   Anger, PTSD, and the Nuclear Family: A Study of Cambodian Refu-
        gees. *Social Science & Medicine* 69(9): 1387–94.
Hoagwood, K., B. J. Burns, L. Kiser, H. Ringeisen, and S. K. Schoenwald
 2001   Evidence-Based Practice in Child and Adolescent Mental Health Serv-
        ices. *Psychiatric Services* 52(9): 1179–89.
Hoagwood, Kimberly, and S. Serene Olin
 2002   The NIMH Blueprint for Change Report: Research Priorities in Child
        and Adolescent Mental Health. *Journal of the American Academy of
        Child and Adolescent Psychiatry* 41(7): 760–67.
Hoge, Charles W., Jennifer L. Auchterlonie, and Charles S. Milliken
 2006   Mental Health Problems, Use of Mental Health Services, and Attri-
        tion from Military Service after Returning from Deployment to Iraq
        or Afghanistan. *Journal of the American Medical Association* 295(9):
        1023–32.
Hollan, Douglas Wood
 2000   Constructivist Models of Mind, Contemporary Psychoanalysis, and
        the Development of Culture Theory. *American Anthropologist*
        102(3): 538–50.
Hollan, Douglas Wood, and C. Jason Throop
 2011   *The Anthropology of Empathy: Experiencing the Lives of Others in
        Pacific Societies*. New York: Berghahn Books.
Hollan, Douglas Wood, and Jane Wellenkamp
 1994   *Contentment and Suffering: Culture and Experience in Toraja*. New
        York: Columbia University Press.
Holland, Dorothy C., and Naomi Quinn
 1987   *Cultural Models in Language and Thought*. New York: Cambridge
        University Press.
Holland, Dorothy C., and Debra G. Skinner
 2008   The Co-Development of Identity, Agency, and Lived Worlds. In
[1996]  *Comparisons in Human Development: Understanding Time and
        Context*. J. Tudge, M. Shanahan, and J. Valsiner, eds. Pp. 193–221.
        Cambridge: Cambridge University Press.
Hollifield, Michael, Valorie Eckert, Teddy D. Warner, et al.
 2005   Development of an Inventory for Measuring War-Related Events in
        Refugees. *Comprehensive Psychiatry* 46(1): 67–80.
Hollifield, Michael, Teddy D. Warner, Janis Jenkins, et al.
 2006   Assessing War Trauma in Refugees: Properties of the Comprehen-
        sive Trauma Inventory-104. *Journal of Traumatic Stress* 19(4):
        527–40.
Hollifield, Michael, Teddy D. Warner, Barry Krakow, Janis Jenkins, and Joseph
   Westermeyer
 2009   The Range of Symptoms in Refugees of War: The New Mexico Refu-
        gee Symptom Checklist-121. *Journal of Nervous and Mental Disease*
        197(2): 117–25.

Holmes, Seth M.
2013 *Fresh Fruit, Broken Bodies: Migrant Farmworkers in the United States.* Berkeley: University of California Press.

Hooley, J. M.
2007 Expressed Emotion and Relapse of Psychopathology. *Annual Review of Clinical Psychology* 3: 329–52.

Hooley, J. M., and C. Campbell
2002 Control and Controllability: Beliefs and Behaviour in High and Low Expressed Emotion Relatives. *Psychological Medicine* 32(6): 1091–99.

Hopper, Kim
2004 Interrogating the Meaning of "Culture" in the WHO International Studies of Schizophrenia. In *Schizophrenia, Culture, and Subjectivity: The Edge of Experience.* Janis H. Jenkins and Robert J Barrett, eds. Pp. 62–86. New York: Cambridge University Press.
2008 Outcomes Elsewhere: Course of Psychosis in "Other Cultures." In *Society and Psychosis.* Pp. 198–216. Cambridge: Cambridge University Press.

Hopper, Kim, G. Harrison, A. Janca, and N. Sartorius
2007 *Recovery from Schizophrenia: An International Perspective. A Report from the WHO Collaborative Project, the International Study of Schizophrenia.* Oxford: Oxford University Press.

Hopper, Kim, and Joseph Wanderling
2000 Revisiting the Developed versus Developing Country Distinction in Course and Outcome in Schizophrenia: Results from ISoS, the WHO Collaborative Followup Project. *Schizophrenia Bulletin* 26(4): 835–46.

Hor, Kahyee, and Mark Taylor
2010 Suicide and Schizophrenia: A Systematic Review of Rates and Risk Factors. *Journal of Psychopharmacology* 24(4): 81–90.

Horton, Sarah
2009 A Mother's Heart Is Weighed Down with Stones: A Phenomenological Approach to the Experience of Transnational Motherhood. *Culture, Medicine, and Psychiatry* 33(1): 21–40.

How, Sabrina K. H., Ashley-Kay Fryer, Douglas McCarthy, Cathy Schoen, and Edward L. Schor
2011 *Securing a Healthy Future: The Commonwealth Fund State Scorecard on Child Health System Performance, 2011.* New York: Commonwealth Fund.

Hume, Mo
2007 Mano Dura: El Salvador Responds to Gangs. *Development in Practice* 17(6): 739–51.

Humphrey, Nicholas
2011 *Soul Dust: The Magic of Consciousness.* Princeton, NJ: Princeton University Press.

Huxley, Aldous
2006 *Brave New World.* New York: HarperPerennial Modern Classics.

Ifabumuyi, Omotayo Ifagbola
    1981    The Dynamics of Central Heat in Depression. *Psychopathologie Afri-
            caine: Bulletin de la Société de Psychopathologie et d'Hygiène Men-
            tale de Dakar* 17(1–3): 127–33.
IMS Institute for Healthcare Infomatics
    2014    Top Medicines by Non-Discounted Spending. In *Medicine Use and
            Shifting Costs of Healthcare: A Review of the Use of Medicines in the
            United States in 2013*. www.imshealth.com/deployedfiles/imshealth
            /Global/Content/Corporate/IMS%20Health%20Institute/Reports
            /Secure/IIHI_US_Use_of_Meds_for_2013.pdf.
Ingstad, Benedicte, and Sysan R. Whyte
    1995    *Disability and Culture.* Berkeley: University of California Press.
Insel, Thoms R.
    2010    Rethinking Schizophrenia. *Nature* 468(7321): 187–93.
    2014a   Mental Disorders in Childhood: Shifting the Focus from Behavioral
            Symptoms to Neurodevelopmental Trajectories. *Journal of the
            American Medical Association* 311(17): 1727–28.
    2014b   Psychiatry 2024. Grand Rounds Presentation, Department of Psy-
            chiatry, University of California, San Diego.
Insel, Thomas R., and N. Goytay
    2014    National Institute of Mental Health Clinical Trials: New Opportuni-
            ties, New Expectations. *Journal of the American Medical Association
            Psychiatry* 71(7): 745–46.
Insel, Thomas R., and Remi Quirion
    2005    Psychiatry as a Clinical Neuroscience Discipline. *Journal of the Amer-
            ican Medical Association* 294(17): 2221–24.
Institute of Medicine
    2013    U.S. Health in International Perspective: Shorter Lives, Poorer Health.
            Report Brief (January): 1–4. http://iom.edu/~/media/Files/Report%20
            Files/2013/US-Health-International-Perspective/USHealth_Intl_
            PerspectiveRB.pdf.
Irvine, Judith T.
    1990    Registering Affect: Heteroglossia in the Linguistic Expression of Emo-
            tion. In *Affecting Discourse: Language and the Politics of Emotion.*
            Pp. 126–61. New York: Cambridge University Press.
Irving, Washington
    1882    *Rip Van Winkle, and Other Sketches.* New York: Useful Knowledge
            Publishing Co. http://archive.org/details/ripvanwinkleando1irvigoog.
            Accessed March 24, 2014.
Jablensky, Assen, and Norman Sartorius
    1978    Cross-Cultural Differences in the Short-Term Prognosis of Schizo-
            phrenic Psychoses. *Schizophrenia Bulletin* 4(1): 102–13.
    2008    What Did the WHO Studies Really Find? *Schizophrenia Bulletin*
            34(2): 253–55.
Jablensky, Assen, Norman Sartorius, J. E. Cooper, M. Anker, A. Korten, and
    A. Bertelsen

1994    Culture and Schizophrenia: Criticisms of WHO Studies Are Answered. *British Journal of Psychiatry* 165(4): 434–36.

Jablensky, A., N. Sartorius, G. Ernberg, et al.

1992    Schizophrenia: Manifestations, Incidence and Course in Different Cultures: A World Health Organization Ten-Country Study. *Psychological Medicine Monograph Supplement*: 1–97.

Jablensky, Assen, R. Schwarz, and T. Tomov

1980    WHO Collaborative Study on Impairments and Disabilities Associated with Schizophrenic Disorders: A Preliminary Communication: Objectives and Methods. *Acta Psychiatrica Scandinavica* 62(S285): 152–63.

Jackson, Jean

1994    Chronic Pain and the Tension between the Body as Subject and Object. In *Embodiment and Experience: The Existential Ground of Culture and Self*. Pp. 201–28. Cambridge: Cambridge University Press.

Jackson, Michael

2005    *Existential Anthropology: Events, Exigencies, and Effects*. New York: Berghahn Books.

2012    *Between One and One Another*. Berkeley: University of California Press.

James, Erica Caple

2010    *Democratic Insecurities: Violence, Trauma, and Intervention in Haiti*. Berkeley: University of California Press.

Jamison, Kay R.

1997    *An Unquiet Mind*. New York: Vintage Books.

Janzen, John M., and William Arkinstall

1978    *The Quest for Therapy in Lower Zaire*. Berkeley: University of California Press.

Jaspers, Karl

1997    *General Psychopathology*. Vol. 2. J. Hoenig and Marian W. Hamilton,
[1963]  trans. Baltimore: Johns Hopkins University Press.

Jenkins, Janis H.

1988a   Conceptions of Schizophrenia as a Problem of Nerves: A Cross-cultural Comparison of Mexican-Americans and Euro-Americans. *Social Science & Medicine* 26(12): 1233–43.

1988b   Ethnopsychiatric Interpretations of Schizophrenic Illness: The Problem of Nervios within Mexican-American Families. *Culture, Medicine and Psychiatry* 12(3): 301–29.

1991a   Anthropology, Expressed Emotion, and Schizophrenia. *Ethos* 19(4): 387–431.

1991b   The State Construction of Affect: Political Ethos and Mental Health among Salvadoran Refugees. *Culture, Medicine and Psychiatry* 15(2): 139–65.

1994    The Psychocultural Study of Emotion and Mental Disorder. In *Handbook of Psychological Anthropology*. P. Bock, ed. Pp. 307–35. Westport, CT: Greenwood Press.

1996a   Culture, Emotion and Post-Traumatic Stress Disorders. In *Ethnocultural Aspects of Posttraumatic Stress Disorder Issues, Research, and Clinical Applications.* Anthony J. Marsella and Matthew Friedman, eds. Pp. 165–82. Washington, DC: American Psychological Association.

1996b   The Impress of Extremity: Women's Experience of Trauma and Political Violence. In *Gender and Health: An International Perspective.* Carolyn Fishel Sargent and Caroline Brettell, eds. Pp. 278–91. Upper Saddle River, NJ: Prentice Hall.

1997   Subjective Experience of Persistent Schizophrenia and Depression among US Latinos and Euro-Americans. *British Journal of Psychiatry* 171(1): 20–25.

2004   Schizophrenia as a Fundamental Human Process. In *Schizophrenia, Culture, and Subjectivity: The Edge of Experience.* Janis H. Jenkins and Robert J. Barrett, eds. Pp. 1–25. New York: Cambridge University Press.

2010a   Introduction. In *Pharmaceutical Self: The Global Shaping of Experience in an Age of Psychopharmacology.* Janis H. Jenkins, ed. Pp. 3–16. Santa Fe, NM: School for Advanced Research Press.

2010b   Pharmaceutical Self and Imaginary in the Social Field of Psychiatric Treatment. In *Pharmaceutical Self: The Global Shaping of Experience in an Age of Psychopharmacology.* Janis H. Jenkins, ed. Pp. 17–40. Santa Fe, NM: School for Advanced Research Press.

2012   The Anthropology of Psychopharmacology: Commentary on Contributions to the Analysis of Pharmaceutical Self and Imaginary. *Culture, Medicine and Psychiatry* 36(1): 78–79.

2013   Palpable Insecurity and Sen's Comparative View of Justice: Anthropological Considerations. *Critical Review of International Social and Political Philosophy* 16(2): 266–83.

2015   Straining Psychic and Social Sinew: Trauma among Adolescent Psychiatric Patients in New Mexico. *Medical Anthropology Quarterly* 29(1):42–60.

Jenkins, Janis H., ed.

2010   *Pharmaceutical Self: The Global Shaping of Experience in an Age of Psychopharmacology.* Santa Fe, NM: School for Advanced Research Press.

Jenkins, Janis H., and Robert J. Barrett, eds.

2004   *Schizophrenia, Culture, and Subjectivity: The Edge of Experience.* New York: Cambridge University Press.

Jenkins, Janis H., and Elizabeth Carpenter-Song

2005   The New Paradigm of Recovery from Schizophrenia: Cultural Conundrums of Improvement without Cure. *Culture, Medicine and Psychiatry* 29(4): 379–413.

2008   Stigma Despite Recovery: Strategies for Living in the Aftermath of Psychosis. *Medical Anthropology Quarterly* 22(4): 381–409.

Jenkins, Janis H., and Mary-Jo DelVecchio Good

2014   Global Mental Health, Women, and Empowerment. In *Global Mental Health.* Samuel Opakpu, ed. Pp. 264–81. New York: Cambridge University Press.

Jenkins, Janis H. and Bridget M. Haas
2015 Trauma in the Lifeworlds of Adolescents: Hard Luck and Trouble in the Land of Enchantment. In *Culture and PTSD*. Devon Hinton and Byron Good, eds. Pp. 179–201. Philadelphia: University of Pennsylvania Press.

Jenkins, Janis H., and Michael Hollifield
2008 Postcoloniality as the Aftermath of Terror among Vietnamese Refugees. In *Postcolonial Disorders*. Mary-Jo DelVecchio Good, ed. Pp. 378–96. Berkeley: University of California Press.

Jenkins, Janis H., and Marvin Karno
1986 Expressed Emotion, Maintenance Pharmacotherapy, and Schizophrenic Relapse among Mexican-Americans. *Psychopharmacology Bulletin* 22(3): 621–27.
1992 The Meaning of Expressed Emotion: Theoretical Issues Raised by Cross-cultural Research. *American Journal of Psychiatry* 149(1): 9–21.

Jenkins, Janis H., Marvin Karno, A. de la Selva, and F. Santana
1986 Expressed Emotion in Cross-Cultural Context: Familial Responses to Schizophrenic Illness among Mexican Americans. In *Treatment of Schizophrenia*. Michael J. Goldstein, Iver Hand, and Kurt Hahlweg, eds. Pp. 35–49. Berlin: Springer.

Jenkins, Janis H., Arthur Kleinman, and Byron J. Good
1991 Cross-Cultural Studies of Depression. In *Psychosocial Aspects of Depression*. Joseph Becker and Arthur Kleinman, eds. New York: Erlbaum.

Jenkins, Janis H., and John G. Schumacher
1999 Family Burden of Schizophrenia and Depressive Illness. Specifying the Effects of Ethnicity, Gender and Social Ecology. *British Journal of Psychiatry* 174: 31–38.

Jenkins, Janis H., and Martha E. Valiente
1994 Bodily Transactions of the Passions: *El Calor* (The Heat) among Salvadoran Women. In *Embodiment and Experience: The Existential Ground of Culture and Self*. Thomas J. Csordas, ed. Cambridge: Cambridge University Press.

Jones, Nev, J. Harrison, R. Aguiar, and L. Munro
2014 Towards the Future: Transforming Research for Transformative Change in Community Mental Health. In *Community Psychology and Community Mental Health: Towards Transformative Change*. Geoffrey Nelson, Bret Kloos, and Jose Ornelas, eds. Pp. 351–72. London: Oxford University Press.

Jirón, Marcela, Márcio Machado, and Inés Ruiz
2008 Consumo de antidepresivos en Chile entre 1992 y 2004. *Revista Médica de Chile* 136(9): 1147–54.

Jütte, Robert, ed.
2013 *Medical Pluralism: Past—Present—Future*. Stuttgart: Franz Steiner Verlag.

Kagee, Ashraf, and Anthony V. Naidoo
2004 Reconceptualizing the Sequelae of Political Torture: Limitations of a Psychiatric Paradigm. *Transcultural Psychiatry* 41(1): 46–61.

Kane, J., G. Honigfeld, J. Singer, and H. Meltzer
   1988   Clozapine for the Treatment-Resistant Schizophrenic. A Double-Blind
          Comparison with Chlorpromazine. *Archives of General Psychiatry*
          45(9): 789–96.
Kano, Miria, Cathleen E. Willging, and Barbara Rylko-Bauer
   2009   Community Participation in New Mexico's Behavioral Health Care
          Reform. *Medical Anthropology Quarterly* 23(3): 277–97.
Kardiner, Abram
   1941   *The Traumatic Neuroses of War.* Washington, DC: Division of
          Anthropology and Psychology, National Research Council.
Karno, Marvin, and Janis H. Jenkins
   1997   Culture and the Diagnosis of Schizophrenia and Related Disorders
          and Psychotic Disorders Not Otherwise Classified. In *DSM-IV Sour-
          cebook.* Thomas A. Widiger, A. Frances, and H. Pincus, et al., eds.
          Pp. 901–8. Washington, DC: American Psychiatric Association.
Karno, Marvin, Janis H. Jenkins, A. de la Selva, et al.
   1987   Expressed Emotion and Schizophrenic Outcome among Mexican-
          American Families. *Journal of Nervous and Mental Disease* 175(3):
          143–51.
Kaufman, Edward
   1994   *Psychotherapy of Addicted Persons.* New York: Guilford Press.
Keefe, Susan E., and Amado M. Padilla
   1987   *Chicano Ethnicity.* Albuquerque: University of New Mexico Press.
Kelleher, I., H. Keeley, P. Corcoran, H. Ramsay, C. Wasserman, V. Carli, M.
      Sarchiapone, C. Hoven, D. Wasserman, and M. Cannon
   2013   Childhood Trauma and Psychosis in a Prospective Cohort Study:
          Cause, Effect, and Directionality. *American Journal of Psychiatry*
          170(7): 734–41.
Kennedy, John
   1974   Cultural Psychiatry. In *Handbook of Social and Cultural Anthropol-
          ogy.* 2 vols. John Joseph Honigmann, ed. Pp. 1119–98. New York:
          Rand-McNally.
Kieling, Christian, Helen Baker-Henningham, Myron Belfer, et al.
   2011   Child and Adolescent Mental Health Worldwide: Evidence for Action.
          *Lancet* 378(9801): 1515–25.
Kienzler, Hanna
   2008   Debating War-Trauma and Post-Traumatic Stress Disorder (PTSD)
          in an Interdisciplinary Arena. *Social Science & Medicine* 67(2):
          218–27.
Kiev, Ari
   1964   *Magic, Faith, and Healing: Studies in Primitive Psychiatry Today.*
          New York: Free Press.
Kinzie, J.D.
   2007   PTSD among Traumatized Refugees. In *Understanding Trauma: Inte-
          grating Biological, Clinical, and Cultural Perspectives.* L.J. Kirmayer,
          R. Lemelson, and M. Barad, eds. Pp. 194–206. Cambridge: Cam-
          bridge University Press.

Kinzie, J.D., R.H. Fredrickson, R. Ben, J. Fleck, and W. Karls
   1984   Posttraumatic Stress Disorder among Survivors of Cambodian Concentration Camps. *American Journal of Psychiatry* 141(5): 645–50.
Kirmayer, Laurence J.
   1984   Culture, Affect and Somatization. *Transcultural Psychiatry Research Review* 21(3): 159–88.
   1989   Cultural Variations in the Response to Psychiatric Disorders and Emotional Distress. *Social Science and Medicine* 29: 327–39.
   1992   The Body's Insistence on Meaning: Metaphor as Presentation and Representation in Illness Experience. *Medical Anthropology Quarterly* 6(4): 323–46.
Kirmayer, L.J., R. Lemelson, and M. Barad, eds.
   2007   *Understanding Trauma: Integrating Biological, Clinical, and Cultural Perspectives.* Cambridge: Cambridge University Press.
Kirmayer, Laurence J., Joseph P. Gone, and Joshua Moses
   2014   Rethinking Historical Trauma. *Transcultural Psychiatry* 51: 299.
Klein, Naomi
   2007   *The Shock Doctrine: The Rise of Disaster Capitalism.* New York: Metropolitan Books/Henry Holt.
Kleinman, Arthur
   1980   *Patients and Healers in the Context of Culture: An Exploration of the Borderland between Anthropology, Medicine, and Psychiatry.* Berkeley: University of California Press.
   1986   *Social Origins of Distress and Disease: Depression, Neurasthenia, and Pain in Modern China.* New Haven, CT: Yale University Press.
   1988a  *The Illness Narratives: Suffering, Healing, and the Human Condition.* New York: Basic Books.
   1988b  *Rethinking Psychiatry.* New York: Simon and Schuster.
   2007   *What Really Matters: Living a Moral Life amidst Uncertainty and Danger.* New York: Oxford University Press.
   2009   Global Mental Health: A Failure of Humanity. *Lancet* 374(9690): 603–4.
   2012   Caregiving as Moral Experience. *Lancet* 380(9853): 1550–51.
   2014   How We Endure. *Lancet* 383(9912): 119–20.
Kleinman, Arthur, Veena Das, and Margaret M. Lock, eds.
   1997   *Social Suffering.* Berkeley: University of California Press.
Kleinman, Arthur, and Byron J. Good, eds.
   1985   *Culture and Depression: Studies in the Anthropology and Cross-Cultural Psychiatry of Affect and Disorder.* Berkeley: University of California Press.
Kleinman, Arthur, and Joan Kleinman
   1997   The Appeal of Experience, the Dismay of Images: Cultural Appropriations of Suffering in Our Times. In *Social Suffering.* Arthur Kleinman, Veena Das, and Margaret Lock, eds. Pp. 1–24. Berkeley: University of California Press.
Kohrt, B.A., M.J. Jordans, W.A. Tol, R.A. Speckman, S.M. Maharjan, C.M. Worthman, and I.H. Komproe

2008 Comparison of Mental Health between Former Child Soldiers and Children Never Conscripted by Armed Groups in Nepal. *Journal of the American Medical Association* 300(6): 691–702.

Kohrt, Brandon A., and Emily Mendenhall, eds.

2015 *Global Mental Health: Anthropological Perspectives.* Walnut Creek, CA: Left Coast Press.

Korbin, Jill E., and Eileen P. Anderson-Fye

2011 Adolescence Matters: Practice- and Policy-Relevant Research and Engagement in Psychological Anthropology. *Ethos* 39(4): 415–25.

Kornberg, Arthur

1987 The Two Cultures: Chemistry and Biology. *Biochemistry* 26(22): 6888–91.

Korsgaard, Christine M.

1996 The Origin of Value and the Scope of Obligation. In *The Sources of Normativity.* Onora O'Neill, ed. Pp. 131–66. Cambridge: Cambridge University Press.

Kotz, Deborah

2012 Can Analyzing Adam Lanza's DNA Really Provide Answers to Newtown Shooting? *Boston Globe,* December 28.

Koutra, Katerina, Marina Economou, Sofia Triliva, et al.

2014 Cross-Cultural Adaptation and Validation of the Greek Version of the Family Questionnaire for Assessing Expressed Emotion. *Comprehensive Psychiatry.* www.sciencedirect.com/science/article /pii/S0010440X14000455. Accessed March 22, 2014.

Kraepelin, Emil

1919 *Dementia Praecox and Paraphrenia.* Edinburgh: E. & S. Livingstone.

Kring, Ann M., and Marja K. Germans

2004 Subjective Experience of Emotion in Schizophrenia. In *Schizophrenia, Culture, and Subjectivity: The Edge of Experience.* Janis H. Jenkins and Robert J Barrett, eds. Pp. 329–48. New York: Cambridge University Press.

Kring, Ann M., and S.L. Kerr

1993 Flat Affect in Schizophrenia Does Not Reflect Diminished Subjective Experience of Emotion. *Journal of Abnormal Psychology* 102(4): 507–17.

Kristeva, Julia, and Leon S. Roudiez

1982 *Powers of Horror: An Essay on Abjection.* New York: Columbia University Press.

Kuipers, Liz

1979 Expressed Emotion: A Review. *British Journal of Social and Clinical Psychology* 18(2): 237–43.

Kurihara, T., M. Kato, R. Reverger, and G. Yagi

2000 Outcome of Schizophrenia in a Non-Industrialized Society: Comparative Study between Bali and Tokyo. *Acta Psychiatrica Scandinavica* 101(2): 148–52.

Kutsche, Paul, and John R. Van Ness
  1988  *Cañones, Values, Crisis, and Survival in a Northern New Mexico Village*. Salem: Sheffield.
Lakoff, Andrew
  2005  *Pharmaceutical Reason: Knowledge and Value in Global Psychiatry*. Cambridge: Cambridge University Press.
Lambek, Michael
  2003  Introduction: Irony and Illness—Recognition and Refusal. In *Illness and Irony: On the Ambiguity of Suffering in Culture*. Michael Lambek and Paul Antze, eds. Pp. 1–20. New York: Berghahn Books.
Lancet Global Mental Health Group
  2007  Scale Up Services for Mental Disorders: A Call for Action. *Lancet* 370(9594): 1241–52.
Lansen, J.
  1992  A Critical View of the Concept. In *Posttraumatic Stress Disorder*. Loes Van Willigen, ed. Pp. 151–57. The Hague: Ministry of Welfare, Health, and Cultural Affairs
Leff, Julian, and Christine E. Vaughn
  1985  *Expressed Emotion in Families: Its Significance for Mental Illness*. London: Guilford Press.
Leff, Julian, N. N. Wig, A. Ghosh, et al.
  1987  Expressed Emotion and Schizophrenia in North India. III. Influence of Relatives' Expressed Emotion on the Course of Schizophrenia in Chandigarh. *British Journal of Psychiatry* 151: 166–73.
Lende, Daniel H.
  2012  Poverty Poisons the Brain. *Annals of Anthropological Practice* 36(1): 183–201.
Lende, Daniel H., and Greg Downey
  2012  *The Encultured Brain: An Introduction to Neuroanthropology*. Cambridge, MA: MIT Press.
LeVine, Robert A.
  1984  Properties of Culture: An Ethnographic View. In *Culture Theory: Essays on Mind, Self and Emotion*. Richard A. Shweder and Robert A. LeVine, eds. Pp. 67–87. New York: Cambridge University Press.
  1990  Infant Environments in Psychoanalysis: A Cross-Cultural View. In *Cultural Psychology: Essays on Comparative Human Development*. J. W. Stigler, R. A. Shweder, and G. Herdt, eds. Pp. 454–74. New York: Cambridge University Press.
Levinson, David
  1989  *Family Violence in Cross-Cultural Perspective*. Newbury Park, CA: Sage.
Levy, Robert
  1984  Emotion, Knowing, and Culture. In *Culture Theory: Essays on Mind, Self, and Emotion*. Richard A. Shweder and Robert A. LeVine, eds. Pp. 238–56. New York: Cambridge University Press.

Li, Chao-Yin
    2013    Expressed Emotion, Depression, Burden, and Perceived Health in Family Caregivers of Older Adults with Dementia in Taiwan. PhD dissertation, University of Washington. https://digital.lib.washington.edu/researchworks/handle/1773/22783?show=full.

Lichtblau, Leonard
    2011    *Psychopharmacology Demystified*. Clifton Park, NY: Delmar Cengage Learning.

Lieberman, Jeffrey A., and T. Scott Stroup
    2011    The NIMH-CATIE Schizophrenia Study: What Did We Learn? *American Journal of Psychiatry* 168(8): 770–75.

Lin, Tsung-Yi, and Mei-Chen Lin
    1981    Love, Denial and Rejection: Responses of Chinese Families to Mental Illness. In *Normal and Abnormal Behavior in Chinese Culture*. Arthur Kleinman and Tsung-Yi Lin, eds. Pp. 387–401. Amsterdam: Springer.

Longden, Eleanor
    2012    Voice Hearing in a Biographical Context: A Model for Formulating the Relationship between Voices and Life History. *Psychosis* 4(3): 224–34.
    2013    The Voices in My Head. *TED Talks*. www.ted.com/talks/eleanor_longden_the_voices_in_my_head.

López, Steven Regeser, K. A. Nelson, K. S. Snyder, and J. Mintz
    1999    Attributions and Affective Reactions of Family Members and Course of Schizophrenia. *Journal of Abnormal Psychology* 108(2): 307–14.

López, Steven Regeser, Kathleen Nelson Hipke, Antonio J. Polo, Janis H. Jenkins, Marvin Karno, Christine E. Vaughn, and Karen S. Snyder
    2004    Ethnicity, Expressed Emotion, Attributions, and Course of Schizophrenia: Family Warmth Matters. *Journal of Abnormal Psychology* 113(3): 428–39.

Lovell, Anne M.
    1997    "The City Is My Mother": Narratives of Schizophrenia and Homelessness. *American Anthropologist* 99(2): 355–68.
    2012    Tending to the Unseen in Extraordinary Circumstances: Severe Mental Illness and Moral Experience During Hurricane Katrina. Paper presented at 111th Annual Meeting of the American Anthropological Association, San Francisco, CA.
    2013    Tending to the Unseen in Extraordinary Circumstances: On Arendt's Natality and Severe Mental Illness after Hurricane Katrina. *Iride: Filosofia e Discussione Pubblica* 26(20): 563–78.

Low, Setha M.
    1985    Culturally Interpreted Symptoms or Culture-Bound Syndromes: A Cross-Cultural Review of Nerves. *Social Science & Medicine* 21(2): 187–96.
    1994    Protest of the Body. *Medical Anthropology Quarterly* 8(4): 476–78.

Lu, W., K. Mueser, S. Rosenberg, and M. K. Jankowski
    2008    Correlates of Adverse Childhood Experiences among Adults with Severe Mood Disorders. *Psychiatric Services* 59(9): 1018–26.

Luhrmann, T. M.
2000   Of Two Minds: The Growing Disorder in American Psychiatry. New York: Knopf.

Lutz, Catherine
1982   The Domain of Emotion Words on Ifaluk. American Ethnologist 9(1): 113–28.
1988   Unnatural Emotions: Everyday Sentiments on a Micronesian Atoll and Their Challenge to Western Theory. Chicago: University of Chicago Press.
1990   The Erasure of Women's Writing in Sociocultural Anthropology. American Ethnologist 17(4): 611–27.

Lutz, Catherine A., and Lila Abu-Lughod
1990   Affecting Discourse: Language and the Politics of Emotion. Cambridge: Cambridge University Press.

Lyotard, Jean-François
1984   The Postmodern Condition: A Report on Knowledge. Minneapolis: University of Minnesota Press.

Macartney, Suzanne E.
2011   Child Poverty in the United States 2009 and 2010 Selected Race Groups and Hispanic Origin. Washington, DC: U.S. Dept. of Commerce, Economics and Statistics Administration, U.S. Census Bureau.

MacLeish, Kenneth T.
2012   Armor and Anesthesia: Exposure, Feeling, and the Soldier's Body. Medical Anthropology Quarterly 26(1): 49–68.

Magaña, A. B., M. J. Goldstein, M. Karno, D. J. Miklowitz, J. Jenkins, and I. R. Falloon
1986   A Brief Method for Assessing Expressed Emotion in Relatives of Psychiatric Patients. Psychiatry Research 17(3): 203–12.

Malinowski, Bronislaw
1954   Magic, Science and Religion: And Other Essays. Garden City, NY: Doubleday.

Markon, K. E., and R. F. Krueger
2005   Categorical and Continuous Models of Liability to Externalizing Disorders: A Direct Comparison in Nesarc. Archives of General Psychiatry 62(12): 1352–59.

Marsella, Anthony J., Thomas Bornemann, Solvig Ekblad, and John Orley, eds.
1994   Amidst Peril and Pain: The Mental Health and Wellbeing of the World's Refugees. Washington, DC: American Psychological Association.

Marshall, Penny, dir.
1990   Awakenings. Film by Columbia Pictures.

Martin, Emily
1994   Flexible Bodies: Tracking Immunity in American Culture from the Days of Polio to the Age of AIDS. Boston: Beacon Press.
1998   Anthropology and the Cultural Study of Science. Science, Technology & Human Values 23(1): 24–44.

2001 *The Woman in the Body: A Cultural Analysis of Reproduction.* Rev. ed. Boston: Beacon Press.

2007 *Bipolar Expeditions: Mania and Depression in American Culture.* Princeton, NJ: Princeton University Press.

2010 Sleepless in America. In *Pharmaceutical Self: The Global Shaping of Experience in an Age of Psychopharmacology.* Janis H. Jenkins, ed. Pp. 187–207. Santa Fe, NM: School for Advanced Research Press.

Martín-Baró, Ignacio

1988 La violencia política y la guerra como causas del trauma psicosocial en El Salvador. *Revista de Psicología de El Salvador* 31: 5–25.

1989 Political violence and war as causes of psychosocial trauma in El Salvador. *International Journal of Mental Health:* 3–20.

1990 De la guerra sucia a la guerra psicologica. *Revista de Psicología de El Salvador* 35: 109–22.

1996 *Writings for a Liberation Psychology.* Adrianne Aron and Shawn Corne, eds. Cambridge, MA: Harvard University Press.

Mason, P., G. Harrison, C. Glazebrook, I. Medley, and T. Croudace

1996 The Course of Schizophrenia over 13 Years: A Report from the International Study on Schizophrenia (ISoS) Coordinated by the World Health Organization. *British Journal of Psychiatry* 169(5): 580–86.

Massacre in El Salvador during Oscar Romero's Funeral

2008 www.youtube.com/watch?v=EN6LWdqcyuc&feature=youtube_gda ta_player. Accessed March 18, 2014.

Massumi, Brian

2002 *Parables for the Virtual: Movement, Affect, Sensation.* Durham, NC: Duke University Press.

Mattingly, Cheryl

1998 *Healing Dramas and Clinical Plots: The Narrative Structure of Experience.* New York: Cambridge University Press.

2010 *The Paradox of Hope: Journeys through a Clinical Borderland.* Berkeley: University of California Press.

Mauss, Marcel

2007 *A General Theory of Magic.* London: Routledge.

McGruder, Juli H.

2004 Madness in Zanzibar: An Exploration of Lived Experience. In *Schizophrenia, Culture, and Subjectivity: The Edge of Experience.* Janis H. Jenkins and Robert J. Barrett, eds. Pp. 255–81. New York: Cambridge University Press.

McIntosh, John L.

2010 USA State Suicide Rates and Rankings Among the Elderly and Young, 2010. Data from CDC's WISQARS website Fatal Injury Reports, www.cdc.gov/injury/wisqars/index.html. Indiana University South American Association of Suicidology.

McLaughlin, Katie A., E. Jane Costello, William Leblanc, Nancy A. Sampson, and Ronald C. Kessler

2012 Socioeconomic Status and Adolescent Mental Disorders. *American Journal of Public Health* 102(9): 1742–50.

McLaughlin, Katie A., Jennifer Greif Green, Margarita Alegría, et al.
  2012   Food Insecurity and Mental Disorders in a National Sample of U.S.
         Adolescents. *Journal of the American Academy of Child and Adoles-
         cent Psychiatry* 51(12): 1293–1303.
Mead, Margaret
  1928   *Coming of Age in Samoa: A Psychological Study of Primitive Youth
         for Western Civilisation*. New York: William Morrow.
Meltzer, Herbert Y.
  2006   Psychopharmacologic Innovations in the Treatment of Schizophrenia,
         Past and Present: An Expert Interview with Herbert Y. Meltzer,
         MD. January 20. www.medscape.com/viewarticle/519981. Accessed
         October 2, 2013.
Ministerio de Cultura y Comunicaciones
  1985   *Etnografía de El Salvador*. San Salvador, El Salvador: Ministerio de
         Cultura y Comunicaciones, Viceministerio de Cultura.
Mino, Yoshio, Shimpei Inoue, Shuichi Tanaka, and Toshihide Tsuda
  1997   Expressed Emotion among Families and Course of Schizophrenia in
         Japan: A 2-Year Cohort Study. *Schizophrenia Research* 24(3): 333–
         39.
Mino, Yoshio, Shuichi Tanaka, Shimpei Inoue, et al.
  1995   Expressed Emotion Components in Families of Schizophrenic Patients
         in Japan. *International Journal of Mental Health* 24(2): 38–49.
Minuchin, Salvador
  1974   *Families and Family Therapy*. Cambridge, MA: Harvard University
         Press.
Moerman, Daniel E.
  2002   *Meaning, Medicine, and the "Placebo Effect."* Cambridge: Cam-
         bridge University Press.
Mollica, R. F., G. Wyshak, and J. Lavelle
  1987   The Psychosocial Impact of War Trauma and Torture on Southeast
         Asian Refugees. *American Journal of Psychiatry* 144(12): 1567–72.
Morrison, Toni
  2012   *Home*. New York: Knopf.
Murillo, Nathan
  1976   The Mexican-American Family. In *Chicanos: Social and Psychologi-
         cal Perspectives*. C. A. Hernandez, M. J. Haug, and N. Wagner, eds.
         Pp. 15–25. St. Louis: Mosby.
Murphy, Henry Brian Megget
  1982   *Comparative Psychiatry: The International and Intercultural Distri-
         bution of Mental Illness*. New York: Springer.
Murphy, H. B., and A. C. Raman
  1971   The Chronicity of Schizophrenia in Indigenous Tropical Peoples:
         Results of a Twelve-Year Follow-Up Survey in Mauritius. *British
         Journal of Psychiatry* 118(546): 489–97.
Murphy, Jane M.
  1976   Psychiatric Labeling in Cross-Cultural Perspective. *Science* 191(4231):
         1019–28.

Murray, C. J., and A. D. Lopez
   1996   Evidence-Based Health Policy: Lessons from the Global Burden of Disease Study. *Science* 274(5288): 740–43.
Mydans, Seth
   2006   Now Prozac Battles Dark Dreams That Khmer Rouge Left. *New York Times,* February 16.
Myers, Fred R.
   1979   Emotions and the Self: A Theory of Personhood and Political Order among Pintupi Aborigines. *Ethos* 7: 343–70.
Myers, Neely L.
   2010   Culture, Stress and Recovery from Schizophrenia: Lessons from the Field for Global Mental Health. *Culture, Medicine and Psychiatry* 34(3): 500–528.
   2015   *Madness, Moral Agency and Mental Health Care.* Nashville, TN: Vanderbilt University Press.
Nanni, V., R. Uher, and A. Danese
   2012   Childhood Maltreatment Predicts Unfavorable Course of Illness and Treatment Outcome in Depression: A Meta-Analysis. *American Journal of Psychiatry* 169(2): 141–51.
Narváez, Darcia, Jaak Pankseep, Allan N. Schore, and Tracy R. Gleason, eds.
   2012   *Evolution, Early Experience and Human Development: From Research to Practice and Policy.* Oxford: Oxford University Press.
National Commission on Correctional Health Care
   2003   *Correctional Mental Health Care: Standards and Guidelines for Delivering Services.* Chicago: National Commission on Correctional Health Care.
National Institute of Mental Health (NIMH)
   2012   The Numbers Count: Mental Disorders in America. National Institute of Mental Health Publications. www.nimh.nih.gov/health/publications /the-numbers-count-mental-disorders-in-america/index.shtml.
New Mexico Department of Health
   2011   Indicator Report—Drug-Induced Deaths. http://ibis.health.state .nm.us/indicator/view/DrugIndDth.Cnty.Race.html.
Ng, Chee H., Keh-Ming Lin, Bruce S. Singh, and Edmond Y. K. Chiu
   2013   *Ethno-Psychopharmacology: Advances in Current Practice.* Cambridge: Cambridge University Press.
Nietzsche, Friedrich
   1967a   *On the Genealogy of Morals.* Walter Kaufmann, trans. New York: Vintage Books.
   1967b   *The Will to Power.* Walter Kaufmann and R. J. Hollingdale, trans. New York: Random House.
Noh, Samuel
   1987   Living with Psychiatric Patients: Implications for the Mental Health of Family Members. *Social Science & Medicine* 25(3): 263–72.

Nomura, Hiroko, Shimpei Inoue, Naoto Kamimura, et al.
    2005   A Cross-Cultural Study on Expressed Emotion in Careers of People
           with Dementia and Schizophrenia: Japan and England. *Social Psy-
           chiatry and Psychiatric Epidemiology* 40(7): 564–70.
Nordstrom, Carolyn
    2004   *Shadows of War Violence, Power, and International Profiteering in
           the Twenty-First Century.* Berkeley: University of California Press.
Nuechterlein, K. H., and M. E. Dawson
    1984   Information Processing and Attentional Functioning in the Develop-
           mental Course of Schizophrenic Disorders. *Schizophrenia Bulletin*
           10(2): 160–203.
Obeyesekere, Gananath
    1985   Depression, Buddhism, and the Work of Culture in Sri Lanka. In *Cul-
           ture and Depression: Studies in the Anthropology and Cross-Cultural
           Psychiatry of Affect and Disorder.* Arthur Kleinman and Byron J.
           Good, eds. Pp. 134–52. Berkeley: University of California Press.
    1990   *The Work of Culture: Symbolic Transformation in Psychoanalysis
           and Anthropology.* Chicago: University of Chicago Press.
Ochs, Elinor
    1986   Introduction. In *Language Socialization across Cultures.* Pp. 1–16.
           Cambridge: Cambridge University Press.
Ogbolu, R. E., J. D. Adeyemi, and A. R. Erinfolami
    2013   Expressed Emotion among Schizophrenic Patients in Lagos, Nigeria:
           A Pilot Study. *African Journal of Psychiatry* 16(5): 329, 331.
Opakpu, Samuel O.
    2014   *Essentials of Global Mental Health.* Cambridge: Cambridge Univer-
           sity Press.
Orr, Jackie
    2006   *Panic Diaries: A Genealogy of Panic Disorder.* Durham, NC: Duke
           University Press.
Ortner, Sherry B.
    1973   On Key Symbols. *American Anthropologist* 75(5): 1338–46.
Ots, Thomas
    1990   The Angry Liver, the Anxious Heart and the Melancholy Spleen: The
           Phenomenology of Perceptions in Chinese Culture. *Culture, Medicine
           and Psychiatry* 14(1): 21–58.
    1994   The Silenced Body—the Expressive *Leib:* On the Dialectic of Mind
           and Life in Chinese Cathartic Healing. In *Embodiment and Experi-
           ence: The Existential Ground of Culture and Self.* Thomas J. Csordas,
           ed. Pp. 116–36. Cambridge: Cambridge University Press.
Overall, John E., and Donald R. Gorham
    1962   The Brief Psychiatric Rating Scale. *Psychological Reports* 10(3): 799–
           812.
    1988   The Brief Psychiatric Rating Scale (BPRS): Recent Developments in
           Ascertainment and Scaling. *Psychopharmacology Bulletin* 24(1):
           97–99.

Panter-Brick, Catherine, Anna Goodman, Wietse Tol, and Mark Eggerman
  2011  Mental Health and Childhood Adversities: A Longitudinal Study in Kabul, Afghanistan. *Journal of the American Academy of Child and Adolescent Psychiatry* 50(4): 349–63.
Parish, Steven
  2008  *Subjectivity and Suffering in American Culture: Possible Selves.* London: Palgrave Macmillan.
  2014  Between Persons: How Concepts of the Person Make Moral Experience Possible. *Ethos* 42(1): 31–50.
Parker, G., P. Johnston, and L. Hayward
  1988  Parental "Expressed Emotion" as a Predictor of Schizophrenic Relapse. *Archives of General Psychiatry* 45(9): 806–13.
Parsons, Anne
  1969  *Belief, Magic, and Anomie: Essays in Psychosocial Anthropology.* New York: Free Press.
Patel, Vikram
  2000  Culture and the Mental Health Consequences of Trauma. *Indian Journal of Social Work* 61(4): 619.
Patel, Vikram, Arthur Kleinman, and Benedetto Saraceno
  2012  Protecting the Human Rights of People with Mental Illnesses: A Call to Action." In *Mental Health and Human Rights: Vision, Praxis, and Courage.* Michael Dudley, Derrick Silove, and Fran Gale, eds. Pp. 362–75. Oxford: Oxford University Press.
Patterson, Paul
  2013  Attachment, Loss and Expressed Emotion: Developmental Processes in Psychosis. In *Psychosis and Emotion: The Role of Emotions in Understanding Psychosis, Therapy, and Recovery.* Pp. 136–48. London: Routledge.
Payer, Lynn
  1996  *Medicine and Culture: Varieties of Treatment in the United States, England, West Germany, and France.* New York: Henry Holt.
Peacock, James L., and Dorothy C. Holland
  1993  The Narrated Self: Life Stories in Process. *Ethos* 21(4): 367–83.
Pedersen, David
  2013  *American Value: Migrants, Money, and Meaning in El Salvador and the United States.* Chicago: University of Chicago Press.
Petryna, Adriana, Andrew Lakoff, and Arthur Kleinman, eds.
  2007  *Global Pharmaceuticals: Ethics, Markets, Practices.* Durham, NC: Duke University Press.
Phillips, Michael R., Veronica Pearson, Feifei Li, Minjie Xu, and Lawrence Yang
  2002  Stigma and Expressed Emotion: a Study of People with Schizophrenia and Their Family Members in China. *British Journal of Psychiatry* 181: 488–93.
Phillips, Michael R., and Wei Xiong
  1995  Expressed Emotion in Mainland China: Chinese Families with Schizophrenic Patients. *International Journal of Mental Health* 24(3): 54–75.

Pinker, Steven
  2013  Science Is Not Your Enemy. *New Republic,* August 6, pp. 28–34.
Porter, Matthew, and Nick Haslam
  2005  Predisplacement and Postdisplacement Factors Associated with Mental Health of Refugees and Internally Displaced Persons. *Journal of the American Medical Association* 294(5): 602–12.
Porter, Roy
  2002 *Madness: A Brief History.* Oxford: Oxford University Press.
Postero, Nancy
  1992  On Trial in the Promised Land: Seeking Asylum. *Women and Therapy* 13(1–2): 155–72.
Powers, Sally I., Stuart T. Hauser, and Linda A. Kilner
  1989  Adolescent Mental Health. *American Psychologist* 44(2): 200–208.
Pratt, Laura A., Debra J. Brody, and Qiuping Gu
  2011  Antidepressant Use in Persons Aged 12 and Over: United States, 2005–2008. Data Brief, 76. National Health and Nutrition Examination Surveys, 2005–2008. National Center for Health Statistics, Centers for Disease Control and Prevention, Hyattsville, MD.
President's New Freedom Commission on Mental Health
  2003  Report. http://govinfo.library.unt.edu/mentalhealthcommission/reports /reports.htm.
Price, V. B.
  2003 *Albuquerque: A City at the End of the World.* Albuquerque: University of New Mexico Press.
Prince, Martin, Vikram Patel, Shekhar Saxena, et al.
  2007  No Health without Mental Health. *Lancet* 370(9590): 859–77.
Quarantini, Lucas C., Angela Miranda-Scippa, Fabiana Nery-Fernandes, et al.
  2010  The Impact of Comorbid Posttraumatic Stress Disorder on Bipolar Disorder Patients. *Journal of Affective Disorders* 123(1): K71–76.
Quesada, James, Laurie Kain Hart, and Philippe Bourgois
  2011  Structural Vulnerability and Health: Latino Migrant Laborers in the United States. *Medical Anthropology* 30(4): 339–62.
Raballo, A., and J. Krueger
  2011  Phenomenology of the Social Self in the Prodrome of Psychosis: From Perceived Negative Attitude of Others to Heightened Interpersonal Sensitivity. *European Psychiatry* 26(8): 532–33.
Rahimi, Sadeq
  2015 *Madness and Political Subjectivity: A Study of Schizophrenia and Culture in Turkey.* New York: Routledge.
Ran, Mao-Sheng, Julian Leff, Zai-Jin Hou, Meng-Ze Xiang, and Cecilia Lai-Wan Chan
  2003  The Characteristics of Expressed Emotion among Relatives of Patients with Schizophrenia in Chengdu, China. *Culture, Medicine and Psychiatry* 27(1): 95–106.
Rashid, Naheed, Chris Clarke, and Miles Rogish
  2013  Post-Stroke Depression and Expressed Emotion. *Brain Injury* 27(2): 223–38.

Rau, Vinuta, and Michael S. Fanselow
  2007  Neurobiological and Neuroethological Perspectives on Fear and Anxiety. In *Understanding Trauma: Integrating Biological, Clinical, and Cultural Perspectives*. L.J. Kirmayer, R. Lemelson, and M. Barad, eds. Pp. 27–40. Cambridge: Cambridge University Press.
Raune, D., E. Kuipers, and Paul E. Bebbington
  2004  Expressed Emotion at First-Episode Psychosis: Investigating a Carer Appraisal Model. *British Journal of Psychiatry* 184(4): 321–26.
Read, John, Bruce D. Perry, Andrew Moskowitz, and Jan Connolly
  2001  The Contribution of Early Traumatic Events to Schizophrenia in Some Patients: A Traumagenic Neurodevelopmental Model. *Psychiatry* 64(4): 319–45.
Read, J., J.V. Os, A.P. Morrison, and C.A. Ross
  2005  Childhood Trauma, Psychosis and Schizophrenia: A Literature Review with Theoretical and Clinical Implications. *Acta Psychiatrica Scandinavica* 112(5): 330–50.
Read, Ursula
  2012  "I want the one that will heal me completely so it won't come back again": The limits of antipsychotic medication in rural Ghana. *Transcultural Psychiatry* 49(3–4): 438–60.
Read, Ursula, Edward Adiibokah, and Solomon Nyame
  2009  Local Suffering and the Global Discourse of Mental Health and Human Rights: An Ethnographic Study of Responses to Mental Illness in Rural Ghana. *Globalization and Health,* Biomed Central 5:13. www.biomedcentral.com/content/pdf/1744-8603-5-13.pdf.
Regier, Darrel A., William E. Narrow, Diana E. Clarke, et al.
  2013  DSM-5 Field Trials in the United States and Canada, Part II: Test-Retest Reliability of Selected Categorical Diagnoses. *American Journal of Psychiatry* 170(1): 5.
Rhodes, Lorna
  1984  "This Will Clear Your Mind": The Use of Metaphors for Medication in Psychiatric Settings. *Culture, Medicine and Psychiatry* 8(1): 49–70.
  1995  *Emptying Beds: The Work of an Emergency Psychiatric Unit.* Berkeley: University of California Press
  2004  *Total Confinement: Madness and Reason in the Maximum Security Prison.* Berkeley: University of California Press
Rhodes, Rosamond, M. Pabst Battin, and Anita Silvers
  2012  *Medicine and Social Justice: Essays on the Distribution of Health Care.* 2nd ed. New York: Oxford University Press.
Robben, Antonius C.G.M., and Marcelo M. Suárez-Orozco
  2000  *Cultures under Siege: Collective Violence and Trauma.* Cambridge: Cambridge University Press.
Robbins, Joel
  2013  Beyond the Suffering Subject: Toward an Anthropology of the Good. *Journal of the Royal Anthropological Institute* 19(3): 447–62.
Rogler, Lloyd H., and August B. Hollingshead
  1965  *Trapped: Families and Schizophrenia.* New York: Wiley.

Romero, Oscar
  1980 Archbishop Oscar Romero's Letter to President Carter. www1
    .villanova.edu/content/villanova/mission/campusministry/service
    /socialjustice/council/meetings/_jcr_content/pagecontent/download_o
    /file.res/Leadershipactivityandskillset2.10.pdf.
Rosaldo, Michelle
  1984 Toward and Anthropology of Self and Feeling. In *Culture Theory: Essays on Mind, Self, and Emotion*. Richard A. Shweder and Robert A. LeVine, eds. Pp. 137–57. New York: Cambridge University Press.
Rosaldo, Michelle, and Louise Lamphere, eds.
  1974 *Woman, Culture, and Society*. Stanford, CA: Stanford University Press.
Rosaldo, Renato
  1989 *Culture and Truth: The Remaking of Social Analysis*. Boston: Beacon Press.
Roseliza-Murni, Abrahman, Tian P. S. Oei, Yusooff Fatimah, and Desa Asmawati
  2014 Schizophrenia Relapse in Kuala Lumpur, Malaysia: Do Relatives' Expressed Emotion and Personality Traits Matter? *Comprehensive Psychiatry* 55(1): 188–98.
Rousseau, Cécile
  1995 The Mental Health of Refugee Children. *Transcultural Psychiatry* 3 (September 23): 299–331.
Rudnick, Abraham
  2012 *Recovery of People with Mental Illness: Philosophical and Related Perspectives*. Oxford: Oxford University Press.
Ryder, Andrew G., Jiahong Sun, Xiongzhao Zhu, Shuqiao Yao, and Yulia E. Chentsova-Dutton
  2012 Depression in China: Integrating Developmental Psychopathology and Cultural-Clinical Psychology. *Journal of Clinical Child & Adolescent Psychology* 41(5): 682–94.
Sacks, Oliver
  1973 *Awakenings*. New York: Random House.
  1990 *Seeing Voices*. New York: Vintage Books.
Sadowsky, Jonathan H.
  1999 *Imperial Bedlam: Institutions of Madness in Colonial Southwest Nigeria*. Berkeley: University of California Press.
  2004 Symptoms of Colonialism: Content and Context of Delusion in Southwest Nigeria, 1945–1960. In *Schizophrenia, Culture, and Subjectivity: The Edge of Experience*. Janis H. Jenkins and Robert J. Barrett, eds. Pp. 238–52. Cambridge: Cambridge University Press.
Saks, Elyn R.
  2007 *The Center Cannot Hold: My Journey through Madness*. New York: Hyperion.
Sanchez, Armando
  1967 *Placement Services, Procedures, and Results of the Navajo Rehabilitation Project*. Flagstaff: Northern Arizona University.

Sapir, Edward

    1961    *Language: An Introduction to the Study of Speech.* New York: Harcourt, Brace and World.

Sartorius, N., W. Gulbinat, G. Harrison, E. Laska, and C. Siegel

    1996    Long-Term Follow-Up of Schizophrenia in 16 Countries. *Social Psychiatry and Psychiatric Epidemiology* 31(5): 249–58.

Sartorius, N., A. Jablensky, and R. Shapiro

    1977    Two-Year Follow-Up of the Patients Included in the WHO International Pilot Study of Schizophrenia. *Psychological Medicine* 7(3): 529–41.

Satel, Sally L., and Scott O. Lilienfeld

    2013    *Brainwashed: The Seductive Appeal of Mindless Neuroscience.* New York: Basic Books.

Scarry, Elaine

    1985    *The Body in Pain: The Making and Unmaking of the World.* New York: Oxford University Press.

Scheper-Hughes, Nancy

    [1979]

    2001    *Saints, Scholars, and Schizophrenics: Mental Illness in Rural Ireland.* Berkeley: University of California Press.

    1990    Bodies, Death, and the State: Violence and the Taken-for-Granted World. Paper presented at the meetings of the American Ethnological Society.

    1992    *Death without Weeping: The Violence of Everyday Life in Brazil.* Berkeley: University of California Press.

Scheper-Hughes, Nancy, and Philippe I. Bourgois

    2004    *Violence in War and Peace.* Malden, MA: Blackwell.

Schoen, Cathy, Robin Osborn, David Squires, and Michelle M. Doty

    2013    Access, Affordability, and Insurance Complexity Are Often Worse in the United States Compared to Ten Other Countries. *Health Affairs:* 10.1377/hlthaff.2013.0879.

Schore, Allan N.

    2003    *Affect Dysregulation and Disorders of the Self.* New York: Norton.

Scull, Andrew T.

    1984    *Decarceration: Community Treatment and the Deviant: A Radical View.* 2nd rev. ed. New York: Polity Press.

Schütz, Alfred

    1945    On Multiple Realities. *Philosophy and Phenomenological Research* 5(4): 533–76.

Seeman, M. V.

    1995    *Gender and Psychopathology.* Washington, DC: American Psychiatric Press.

Sen, Amarta

    2009    *The Idea of Justice.* Cambridge, MA: Harvard University Press.

Shweder, Richard A.

    1980    Rethinking Culture and Personality Theory. Part III: From Genesis and Typology to Hermeneutics and Dynamics. *Ethos* 8(1): 60–94.

    1990    Cultural Psychology: What Is It? In *Cultural Psychology: Essays on Comparative Human Development.* James W. Stigler, Richard A.

Schweder, and Gilbert Herdt, eds. Pp. 1–46. Cambridge: Cambridge University Press.

Shweder, Richard A., and Edmund J. Bourne
  1982 Does the Concept of the Person Vary Cross-Culturally? In *Cultural Conceptions of Mental Health and Therapy.* Anthony J. Marsella and Geoffrey M. White, eds. Pp. 97–137. Culture, Illness, and Healing. Amsterdam: Springer.

Shweder, Richard A., and Robert A. LeVine, eds.
  1984 *Culture Theory: Essays on Mind, Self and Emotion.* New York: Cambridge University Press.

Siegel, Daniel J.
  2006 An Interpersonal Neurobiology Approach to Psychotherapy. *Psychiatric Annals* 36(4): 248.

Singer, Jerome L.
  1995 *Repression and Dissociation: Implications for Personality Theory, Psychopathology and Health.* Chicago: University of Chicago Press.

Singer, Merrill
  2005 *The Face of Social Suffering: The Life History of a Street Drug Addict.* Long Grove, IL: Waveland Press.

Singer, Merrill, and Hans Baer
  2011 *Introducing Medical Anthropology: A Discipline in Action.* 2nd ed. Lanham, MD: AltaMira.

Sonuga-Barke, Edmund J. S., Kim L. Cartwright, Margaret J. Thompson, et al.
  2013 Family Characteristics, Expressed Emotion, and Attention-Deficit/Hyperactivity Disorder. *Journal of the American Academy of Child and Adolescent Psychiatry* 52(5): 547–48.

Sorel, Eliot
  1978 Schedule for Affective Disorders and Schizophrenia, SADS. New York State Psychiatric Institute, Department of Research Assessment and Training.
  2013 *21st Century Global Mental Health.* Boston: Jones & Bartlett Learning.

Stahl, Stephen M.
  2013 *Stahl's Essential Psychopharmacology: Neuroscientific Basis and Practical Applications.* 4th ed. Cambridge: Cambridge University Press.

Staples, James, and Tom Widger
  2012 Situating Suicide as an Anthropological Problem: Ethnographic Approaches to Understanding Self-Harm and Self-Inflicted Death. *Culture, Medicine and Psychiatry* 36(2): 183–203.

Stewart, Kathleen
  2007 *Ordinary Affects.* Durham, NC: Duke University Press.

Stocking, George W.
  1987 *Malinowski, Rivers, Benedict, and Others: Essays on Culture and Personality.* Madison: University of Wisconsin Press.

Suárez-Orozco, Marcelo M.
  1989 *Central American Refugees and U.S. High Schools: A Psychosocial Study of Motivation and Achievement.* Stanford, CA: Stanford University Press.

1990 Speaking of the Unspeakable: Toward a Psychosocial Understanding of Responses to Terror. *Ethos* 18(3): 353–83.

Substance Abuse Epidemiology Program, Injury and Behavioral Epidemiology Bureau

2011 New Mexico Substance Abuse Epidemiology Profile, 2011. http://nmhealth.org/erd/SubstanceAbuse/2011%20New%20Mexico%20Substance%20Abuse%20Epidemiology%20Profile.pdf.

Sullivan, Harry Stack

1953 *The Interpersonal Theory of Psychiatry.* New York: Norton.

1962 *Schizophrenia as a Human Process.* New York: Norton.

Summerfield, Derek

2000 War and Mental Health: A Brief Overview. *British Medical Journal* 321: 232–35.

Swartz, Leslie

1991 The Politics of Black Patients' Identity: Ward-Rounds on the "Black Side" of a South African Psychiatric Hospital. *Culture, Medicine and Psychiatry* 15(2): 217–44.

Tambiah, Stanley Jeyaraja

1990 *Magic, Science, Religion, and the Scope of Rationality.* New York: Cambridge University Press.

Tamsin, Ford, Robert Goodman, and Howard Meltzer

2003 The British Child and Adolescent Mental Health Survey 1999: The Prevalence of DSM-IV Disorders. *Journal of the American Academy of Child and Adolescent Psychiatry* 42(10): 1203–11.

Tanaka, S., Y. Mino, and S. Inoue

1995 Expressed Emotion and the Course of Schizophrenia in Japan. *British Journal of Psychiatry* 167(6): 794–98.

Tarrier, N., C. Barrowclough, K. Porceddu, and S. Watts

1988 The Assessment of Psychophysiological Reactivity to the Expressed Emotion of Relatives of Schizophrenic Patients. *British Journal of Psychiatry* 152(5): 618–24.

Task Force on DSM-IV

1994 *Diagnostic and Statistical Manual of Mental Disorders: DSM-IV.* Washington, DC: American Psychiatric Association.

Tamsin, Ford, Robert Goodman, and Howard Meltzer

2003 The British Child and Adolescent Mental Health Survey, 1999: The Prevalence of DSM-IV Disorders. *Journal of the American Academy of Child and Adolescent Psychiatry* 42(10): 1203–11.

Taussig, Michael

1987 *Shamanism, Colonialism, and the Wild Man: A Study in Terror and Healing.* Chicago: University of Chicago Press.

Theidon, Kimberly

2012 *Intimate Enemies: Violence and Reconciliation in Peru.* Philadelphia: University of Pennsylvania Press.

Thompson, C. J. S.

1897 *The Mystery and Romance of Alchemy and Pharmacy.* London: Scientific Press.

Throop, C. Jason
 2010    *Suffering and Sentiment: Exploring the Vicissitudes of Experience and Pain in Yap*. Berkeley: University of California Press.
Tol, W. A., I. H. Komproe, M. J. Jordans, A. L. Gross, D. Susanty, R. D. Macy, and J. T. de Jong.
 2010    Mediators and Moderators of a Psychosocial Intervention for Children Affected by Political Violence. *Journal of Consulting and Clinical Psychology* 78(6): 818.
Townsend, John Marshall
 1978    *Cultural Conceptions and Mental Illness: A Comparison of Germany and America*. Chicago: University of Chicago Press.
Treatment Advocacy Center
 2014    The Treatment of Persons with Mental Illness in Prisons and Jails: A State Survey. April 8. TACReports.org/treatment-behind-bars.
Trujillo, Michael L.
 2009    *Land of Disenchantment: Latina/o Identities and Transformations in Northern New Mexico*. Albuquerque: University of New Mexico Press.
United Nations General Assembly
 1948    Universal Declaration of Human Rights. 217A(III). United Nations High Commissioner on Refugees. www.un.org/en/documents/udhr/index.shtml/.
United Nations High Commissioner for Refugees
 2015    Global Report 2015. www.unhcr.org/558/93896.html.
United Nations Office on Drugs and Crime (UNODC)
 2011    *Global Study on Homicide: Trends, Contexts, Data*. Vienna, Austria: United Nations Office on Drugs and Crime.
United Nations Security Council Truth Commission
 1993    From Madness to Hope: The 12-Year War in El Salvador. Report of the Commission on the Truth for El Salvador. United States Institute of Peace. www.usip.org/publications/truth-commission-el-salvador.
U.S. Census Bureau
 2010    U.S. Census. http://2010.census.gov/. Accessed October 10, 2013.
U.S. Committee for Refugees
 1990    *World Refugee Survey: 1989 in Review*. Washington, DC: U.S. Committee for Refugees.
 2012    Health, United States, 2011: With Special Feature on Socioeconomic Status and Health. 2012–1232. Hyattsville, MD: US Department of Health and Human Services, Centers for Disease Control and Prevention, National Center for Health Statistics. www.cdc.gov/nchs/data/hus/hus11.pdf.
Vaillant, George E.
 1986    *Empirical Studies of Ego Mechanisms of Defense*. Washington, DC: American Psychiatric Press.
Van der Kolk, B. A., and O. van der Hart
 1989    Pierre Janet and the Breakdown of Adaptation in Psychological Trauma. *American Journal of Psychiatry* 146(12): 1530–40.

Van Winkel, R., M. Van Nierop, I. Myin-Germeys, and J. Van Os
  2013   Childhood Trauma as a Cause of Psychosis: Linking Genes, Psychology, and Biology. *Canadian Journal of Psychiatry* 58(1): 44–51.
Varma, Saiba
  2012   Where There Are Only Doctors: Counselors as Psychiatrists in Indian-Administered Kashmir. *Ethos* 40(4): 517–35.
Vasconcelos, E. Sa D., Alison Wearden, and Christine Barrowclough
  2013   Expressed Emotion, Types of Behavioural Control and Controllability Attributions in Relatives of People with Recent-Onset Psychosis. *Social Psychiatry and Psychiatric Epidemiology* 48(9): 1377–88.
Vaughn, Christine E.
  1986   Patterns of Emotional Response in the Families of Schizophrenic Patients. In *Treatment of Schizophrenia*. Michael J. Goldstein, Iver Hand, and Phil Habil Kurt Hahlweg, eds. Pp. 97–106. Berlin: Springer Verlag.
  n.d.   Training Manual for Administration of the Camberwell Family Interview and Ratings of Expressed Emotion. (In author's possession.)
Vaughn, Christine E., and Julian Leff
  1976   The Influence of Family and Social Factors on the Course of Psychiatric Illness: A Comparison of Schizophrenic and Depressed Neurotic Patients. *British Journal of Psychiatry* 129: 125–37.
Vaughn, Christine E., K. S. Snyder, S. Jones, W. B. Freeman, and I. R. Falloon
  1984   Family Factors in Schizophrenic Relapse: Replication in California of British Research on Expressed Emotion. *Archives of General Psychiatry* 41(12): 1169–77.
Waldram, James B.
  2004   *Revenge of the Windigo: The Construction of the Mind and Mental Health of North American Aboriginal Peoples.* Toronto: University of Toronto Press.
Wallace, Anthony F. C.
  1961   Chronic Schizophrenia: Explorations in Theory and Treatment. Lawrence Appleby, Jordan M. Scher and John Cumming, eds. *Annals of the American Academy of Political and Social Science* 335(1): 232–33.
Wallis, Claudia, and James Willwerth
  1992   Pills for the Mind: A New Drug Brings Patients Back to Life. *Time*, July 6.
Warner, Richard
  1985   *Recovery from Schizophrenia: Psychiatry and Political Economy.* London: Routledge & Kegan Paul.
Watson, M. K., C. A. Bonham, C. E. Willging, and R. L. Hough
  2011   "An Old Way to Solve an Old Problem": Provider Perspectives on Recovery-Oriented Services and Consumer Capabilities in New Mexico. *Human Organization* 70(2): 107–17.
Watters, Ethan
  2010   *Crazy Like Us: The Globalization of the American Psyche.* New York: Simon and Schuster.

Waxler, Nancy E.

1974  Parent and Child Effects on Cognitive Performance: An Experimental Approach to the Etiological and Responsive Theories of Schizophrenia. *Family Process* 13(1): 1–22.

1977  Is Mental Illness Cured in Traditional Societies? A Theoretical Analysis. *Culture, Medicine and Psychiatry* 1(3): 233–53.

Weisman, A., S.R. López, M. Karno, and Janis H. Jenkins

1993  An Attributional Analysis of Expressed Emotion in Mexican-American Families with Schizophrenia. *Journal of Abnormal Psychology* 102(4): 601–6.

Westermeyer, J.

1988  DSM-III Psychiatric Disorders among Hmong Refugees in the United States: A Point Prevalence Study. *American Journal of Psychiatry* 145(2): 197–202.

Whitaker, Robert

2010  *Anatomy of an Epidemic: Magic Bullets, Psychiatric Drugs, and the Astonishing Rise of Mental Illness in America.* New York: Crown.

White, Geoffrey M.

1982  The Ethnographic Study of Cultural Knowledge of "Mental Disorder." In *Cultural Conceptions of Mental Health and Therapy.* Anthony J. Marsella and Geoffrey M. White, eds. Pp. 69–95. Culture, Illness, and Healing, 4. Amsterdam: Springer.

White, Geoffrey M., and John Kirkpatrick, eds.

1985  *Person, Self, and Experience: Exploring Pacific Ethnopsychologies.* Berkeley: University of California Press.

Whyte, Susan Reynolds

1991  Attitudes toward Mental Health Problems in Tanzania. *Acta Psychiatrica Scandinavica* 83(S364): 59–76.

2009  Health Identities and Subjectivities. *Medical Anthropology Quarterly* 23(1): 6–15.

Whyte, Susan Reynolds, Sjaak Van der Geest, and Anita Hardon

2003  *Social Lives of Medicines.* New York: Cambridge University Press.

Wicks, S., A. Hjern, and C. Dalman

2010  Social Risk or Genetic Liability for Psychosis? A Study of Children Born in Sweden and Reared by Adoptive Parents. *American Journal of Psychiatry* 167(10): 1240–46.

Wig, N.N., D.K. Menon, H. Bedi, A. Ghosh, et al.

1987a  Expressed Emotion and Schizophrenia in North India. I. Cross-cultural Transfer of Ratings of Relatives' Expressed Emotion. *British Journal of Psychiatry* 151: 156–60.

1987b  Expressed Emotion and Schizophrenia in North India. II. Distribution of Expressed Emotion Components among Relatives of Schizophrenic Patients in Aarhus and Chandigarh. *British Journal of Psychiatry* 151: 160–65.

Willen, Sarah
    2012    Migration, "Illegality," and Health: Mapping Embodied Vulnerability and Debating Health-Related Deservingness. *Social Science & Medicine* 74(6): 805–81.
Willging, Cathleen, and Louise Lamphere
    2014    A Dangerous Precedent for Behavioral Health Services under the Affordable Care Act. Scholars Strategy Network, www.scholarsstrategynetwork.org.
Willging, Cathleen E., and Rafael M. Semansky
    2010    State Mental Health Policy: It's Never Too Late to Do It Right: Lessons from Behavioral Health Reform in New Mexico. *Psychiatric Services* 61(7): 646–48.
Willging, Cathleen E., Howard Waitzkin, and Louise Lamphere
    2009    Transforming Administrative and Clinical Practice in a Public Behavioral Health System: An Ethnographic Assessment of the Context of Change. *Journal of Health Care for the Poor and Underserved* 20(3): 866–83.
Willwerth, James
    1992    After the Awakening, the Real Therapy Must Begin. *Time,* July 6.
Wilson, James Q., and Edward C. Banfield
    1971    Political Ethos Revisited. *American Political Science Review* 65(4): 1048–62.
Winerip, Michael
    1992    To Some, Hope Is Just a Drug Too Far Away. *New York Times,* August 9.
Wood, Elisabeth Jean
    2003    *Insurgent Collective Action and Civil War in El Salvador.* New York: Cambridge University Press.
Woolf, Virginia
    2002    *On Being Ill.* Ashfield, MA: Paris Press.
[1930]
World Health Organization (WHO)
    1973    The International Pilot Study of Schizophrenia. Geneva.
    1979    *Schizophrenia: An International Follow-Up Study.* Chichester: Wiley.
    2005    Child and Adolescent Mental Health Policies and Plans. Geneva.
    2008    The Global Burden of Disease, 2004 Update. Geneva.
    2009    Global Health Risks: Mortality and Burden of Disease Attributable to Selected Major Risks. Geneva.
    2013    Mental Health Action Plan 2013–2020. Geneva.
Yang, Lawrence H., Michael R. Phillips, Deborah M. Licht, and Jill M. Hooley
    2004    Causal Attributions about Schizophrenia in Families in China: Expressed Emotion and Patient Relapse. *Journal of Abnormal Psychology* 113(4): 592–602.
Yarris, Kristin
    2011    The Pain of "Thinking Too Much": Dolor de Cerebro and the Embodiment of Social Hardship among Nicaraguan Women. *Ethos* 39(2): 226–48.

Young, A.
  1982  The Anthropologies of Illness and Sickness. *Annual Review of Anthropology* 11(1): 257–85.
  1997  *The Harmony of Illusions: Inventing Post-Traumatic Stress Disorder.* Princeton, NJ: Princeton University Press.
Young, Marta Y.
  2001  Moderators of Stress in Salvadoran Refugees: The Role of Social and Personal Resources. *International Migration Review* 35(3): 840–69.
Zuvekas, S.H.
  2005  Prescription Drugs and the Changing Patterns of Treatment for Mental Disorders, 1996–2001. *Health Affairs* 24(1): 195–205.

# Index

Abilify (aripiprazole), 29, 60
absorption, trauma and, 243
Abu-Lughod, Lila, 143, 168, 275n6
abuse (sexual, physical, and verbal): and adolescent psychiatric inpatients, 225, 230, 232, 233, 234, 235–236, 246; as both physical and psychological trauma, 242; and onset of mental illnesses, 98–99; as related to onset of psychosis, 92, 98; Salvadoran women and sexual abuse, 152. *See also* domestic violence/abuse
Acadia Healthcare, 219–220
Adams, Vincanne, 228
adolescent mental health: and "adolescence" as constructed concept, 217, 277n5; affluent populations and, 216; and continuum of normal/abnormal, 277–278n6; evidence-based and cost-effective treatment as focus in, 217; food insecurity and, 227; as global concern, 216–217; and gun violence, 277n4; prevalence rate of mental illness, 216. *See also* adolescent psychiatric inpatients (New Mexico)
adolescent psychiatric inpatients (New Mexico), 20, 258–259; and anger, 229, 230, 232, 236, 237–238, 279n15; attachment blended with social withdrawal in, 240, 241, 258–259; case studies, 229–239; cultural chemistry and, 258, 259; and depression, 222, 223, 225,

278n14; dynamic phenomenology of, 240–241; and economy of state, 214–215, 277nn2–3; and intergenerational cycles, 235, 239–240, 246–247; managed care and curtailment of services, 217–220, 245, 278n9; methodology of study of, 220–222, 229, 242, 278nn10–12; as multicultural mix of people, 221–222, 226, 239–240, 259; multiple psychiatric diagnoses of, 222, 223, 225, 226–227, 234–235; and practical identity, 221, 246; precarity and, 215–216, 220–221, 222, 237, 239–240, 243, 258; and psychosis, 234–235, 240; PTSD diagnosis/subclinical diagnosis, 225, 231–232, 234, 240, 242; residential instability and, 220–221, 222, 229; and resilience, 236, 237–239, 241; revolving door of discharge and readmission, 219; and self-cutting, 233, 237, 259; and separation anxiety disorder, 226; and sexual, physical, or verbal abuse, 20, 225, 230, 232, 233, 234, 235–236, 246; social abandonment and, 215, 225–226, 233–234, 236, 237, 239, 246, 258, 259; street drugs and, 215; and suicide/suicidality, 222, 223, 234, 237; and trauma as ongoing everyday lifeworld, 20, 221, 222, 226, 227–229, 240–241, 242–243, 258; violence-related problems among, 222, 224